The Lotus Guide to Freelance Graphics for Windows, Release 2.0

Jeff Sutton

BRADY
LOTUS BOOKS

New York   London   Toronto   Sydney   Tokyo   Singapore

Copyright © 1993 by Jeff Sutton

All rights reserved, including the right of reproduction in whole or in part in any form.

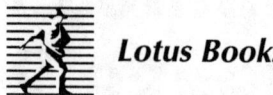 *Lotus Books*

Brady Publishing
A Division of Prentice Hall Computer Publishing
15 Columbus Circle
New York, NY 10023

ISBN: 1-56686-074-1

Library of Congress Catalog No.: 93–16486

Printing Code: The rightmost double-digit number is the year of the book's printing; the rightmost single-digit number is the number of the book's printing. For example, 93-1 shows that the first printing of the book occurred in 1993.

96 95 94 93   4 3 2 1

Manufactured in the United States of America

Limits of Liability and Disclaimer of Warranty: The author and publisher of this book have used their best efforts in preparing this book and the programs contained in it. These efforts include the development, research, and testing of the theories and programs to determine their effectiveness. The author and publisher make no warranty of any kind, expressed or implied, with regard to these programs or the documentation contained in this book. The author and publisher shall not be liable in any event for incidental or consequential damages in connection with, or arising out of, the furnishing, performance, or use of these programs.

Trademarks: Most computer and software brand names have trademarks or registered trademarks. The individual trademarks have not been listed here.

Credits

Publisher
Michael Violano

Managing Editor
Kelly D. Dobbs

Editor
Susan Hunt

Production Editor
Kristin Juba

Copy Editor
Greg Robertson

Editorial Assistant
Lisa Rose

Book Designer
Michele Laseau

Production Team
Dana Bigham
Christine Cook
Lisa Daugherty
Dennis Clay Hager
Joy Dean Lee
Sean Medlock
Roger Morgan
Juli Pavey
Angela M. Pozdol
Linda Quigley
Greg Simsic
John Sleeva
Suzanne Snyder
Alyssa Yesh

Contents

Introduction xxi

Part 1 Getting Started 1

1 Creating Your First Presentation 3

Installing and Starting Freelance Graphics 4
    Try It: Start a New Presentation 4
Creating a Title Page and a Bullet Chart 6
    Try It: Create a Title Page 6
    Adding Another Page and Choosing a Page Layout 8
    Try It: Create a Bulleted List 9
Creating a Data Chart 11
    Try It: Choose a Page Layout and Type a Title 11
    Try It: Choose a Chart Type and Style
        from the Gallery 12
    Try It: Enter Your Data 13
    Tips for Working in the Chart Data
        & Titles Window 14
    Try It: Add an Axis Title 14
    Try It: Preview Your Chart 15
    Switching to a New Chart Type 16
Organizing 17
    Try It: Switch to a New SmartMaster Set 17
    Try It: Move a Page in Page Sorter View 18
    Getting a Textual View in the Outliner 19
    Checking the Flow with Screen Show 20
Printing Your Presentation 20
Getting On-Line Help 22
    Using the Help Icon Bar 22
    Cross-References and Definitions 24
    Adding Bookmarks 24
    Annotating Help Topics 25
    Printing Help Topics 25
Saving the Presentation 25
Closing the File 26
Wrapping Up 26

Part 2 Text Charts 27

2 Bullet Charts and Beyond 29

What Are Text Charts? 29
The Bullet Chart: A True Classic 30
    Creating Bullet Charts with SmartMaster
      Page Layouts 31
    Try It: Create Bullet Charts Fast 31
The Text Chart Variations 32
    Title Pages 33
    Bulleted List 33
    Side-by-Side Bullets 34
    Bullets & Chart 35
    Bullets & Symbol 35
    Paragraph Charts 37
    Novelty Text Charts 38
Rules of Thumb for Bullet Charts 38
    Make Text Legible! 39
    Avoid All Caps 39
    State One Thought per Line 39
    Be Concise! 39
    Observe the Rule of Sevens 40
    Use Parallel Sentence Structure 41
    Use the Active Voice 42
    Write Emphatic Titles 42
A Quick Course in Typography 42
    Typefaces, Fonts, and Families 43
    Measuring the Size of Type 44
    The Best Typefaces for Text Charts 44
    Serif versus Sans Serif 44
    Up-and-Down Style or Lowercase? 44
Wrapping Up 45

3 Creating, Editing, and Formatting Text 47

Text Block: A Definition 48
Creating Text Blocks 48
Using the Text Panel and Text Ruler 49
Editing Text Blocks 50
    Selecting Text 50
    Deleting, Copying, and Pasting Text 52

Changing Character Attributes 53
Editing Multiple Text Blocks 55
Quick Editing with the Right Mouse Button 55
Sizing Text Blocks 56
Sizing with the Mouse 56
Sizing with the Keyboard 57
Understanding Paragraph Styles 57
Starting a New Line without a Bullet 59
Changing Paragraph Style Settings 59
Try It: Change Default Text Attributes 61
Changing Line Spacing and Indents 62
Try It: Make a Numbered List 62
Adding a Border 64
Special Text Effects 64
Rotated Text 65
Curved Text 65
Text with Drop Shadows 68
Use a Symbol as a Bullet 68
Wrapping Up 68

4 Using the Outliner 71

Why Use the Outliner? 71
What the Outliner Shows (and What It Doesn't) 73
Creating Bullet Charts Automatically 73
Bulleted Items in Two Columns 74
Changing Paragraph Styles 76
Selecting, Moving, and Deleting 77
Selecting Lines and Pages 77
Moving Pages 78
Adding a Page 78
Deleting a Page 78
Navigating in the Outliner 79
Moving between the Outliner and Other Views 79
Expanding and Collapsing an Outline 80
Importing and Pasting Text into the Outliner 81
Importing ASCII Text 81
Pasting Text 81
Working Together: Pasting Text
   from an Ami Pro Outline 82
Printing an Outline 82
Wrapping Up 82

	5	**Checking Your Spelling** 83
		Tell Freelance What To Spell Check 83
		Check Spelling in Data Charts, Organization Charts, and Speaker Notes 85
		Create a Custom Spelling Dictionary 87

Part 3 Data Charts 89

	6	**Choosing the Right Chart Type** 91
		What's Your Purpose? 92
		Using the Graph Type Table 92
		Line, Area, or Bar Chart? 93
		Bar Charts 94
		Horizontal or Vertical Bars? 94
		Stacked Bar Charts 95
		Clustered Bar Charts 98
		Three-Dimensional Bar Charts 99
		Line Charts 99
		Area Charts 101
		Pie Charts 103
		Legend vs. Labels 105
		Multiple Pies 105
		Three-Dimensional Pies 105
		High-Low-Open-Close Charts 105
		XY (Scatter) Charts 107
		Radar Charts 107
		Tables 108
		Bar-Line Charts 109
		Wrapping Up 109

	7	**Creating Data Charts** 111
		Chart Terminology 111
		Basic Training: Creating a Chart 112
		Choosing a Page Layout for a Chart 113
		Choosing a Chart Type 114
		Entering Your Data 115
		Entering Legends 119
		Entering Dates Automatically 119

Previewing a Chart 121
Adding Headings, Notes, and Axis Titles 121
Editing Entries in the Chart Data & Titles Window ... 123
Switching Chart Types in Midstream 124
Bar Charts 125
Labeling the Bars with Precise Values 126
Adding Three-Dimensional Effects 126
The 3D (XYZ) Chart 128
Creating a Step Chart by Changing Bar Width 128
Line Charts 129
Bar-Line Charts 130
Area Charts 130
High-Low-Close-Open Charts 131
Pie Charts 133
Tables 134
Creating Table Charts (Number Grids) 134
Changing the Frame 136
The Sum of All Columns 137
Changing the Grid Style 138
Make All Column Widths Equal 138
Placing Several Charts on a Single Page 138
Bulleted List and Chart on One Page 139
Telling a Story with Charts 140
Wrapping Up 141

8 Customizing Data Charts 143

Why Change Chart Components? 143
How To Change Chart Components 144
Use the Chart Menu 145
Double-Click a Chart Component 145
Try It: Change the Color of a Set of Bars 145
Axis Labels and Titles 146
How To Change Axis Labels and Titles 146
What If Your Labels Are Too Long? 148
Hide Axis Labels and Titles 149
Change Text Components Globally 149
On a Scale of 1 to 10 150
Are Charts with a Nonzero Axis Deceptive? 151
Charts with Two Scales 152

Grids and Ticks 153
Add a Frame to Your Chart 155
Legible Legends 155
Headings and Notes 156
Hide Data Sets 157
Add a Number Grid under a Chart 158
Add a Shadowed Background 159
Annotate a Chart 161
    Try It: Make a Custom Text Box 161
Wrapping Up 162

9 Creating Charts from 1-2-3 Worksheets 165

What's the Best Method for You? 165
Importing Data from 1-2-3 Worksheet Files 166
    Try It: Import Data from a Single Worksheet 167
    What's the Difference? File Links
        versus DDE Links 170
    Importing Data from More Than One Worksheet 171
Copying Data from an Open 1-2-3 for Windows
    Worksheet 176
    Try It: Copy Unlinked Data 176
Importing Named Charts 178
    Try It: Import a Named Chart 179
Copying Charts from 1-2-3 for Windows 179
    Copying an Unlinked Chart from
        1-2-3 for Windows 179
    Copying a Linked Chart from 1-2-3 for Windows 180
    Copying a 1-2-3 for Windows Chart
        as a Metafile or Bitmap 181
Editing Links 182
    When Are Linked Graphs Updated? 182
    Editing Links to Worksheets without
        Leaving Freelance Graphics 182
    Deleting Links 184
Wrapping Up 184

Part 4 Organization Charts and Tables 185

10 Organization Charts 187

The Value and Variety of Organization Charts 187
    Try It: Create an Organization Chart 188
Editing Organization Chart Entries 190
    Deleting, Copying, and Pasting Entries 191
    Editing Directly on the Presentation Page 191
    Promoting and Demoting Entries 192
    Collapsing the Entry List 193
    Adding a Staff Position 193
Changing the Look of an Organization Chart 194
    Changing the Format of Lowest-Level Entries 195
    Try It: Change Attributes 196
    Adding Extra Connection Lines 197
    Controlling Text Size 197
Wrapping Up 198

11 Creating Tables 199

When Are Tables Necessary? 199
Creating Tables in Freelance 200
    Try It: Create a Table 200
Changing Table Entries 201
Working with Columns and Rows 202
    Deleting Columns and Rows 202
    Inserting Columns and Rows 202
    Sizing Columns and Rows 203
    Sizing Columns and Rows with the Mouse 204
    Moving Columns and Rows 204
    Try It: Highlight a Single Row 205
How To Change the Look of a Whole Table 206
Using the Mouse in a Table 206
Using the Keyboard in a Table 207
    Selecting with the Keyboard 207
    Navigating a Table with the Keyboard 207
Wrapping Up 208

Part 5 Drawings and Diagrams 209

12 Drawing Objects 211

Try It: Draw Rectangles and Squares 212
Create a Simple Diagram with Rectangles and Text .. 213
Making Rounded Rectangles 215
Drawing Lines and Arrows 217
Try It: Draw a Curve 217
Drawing Circles and Ellipses 218
Drawing Arcs 219
Drawing Polygons 219
Freehand Drawing 220
Changing How the Drawing Tools Work 221
Keep the Drawing Tools Active as You Work 223
Save Drawing Time with SmartIcons 224
Developing an Efficient Working Style 224
Drawing with a Grid 225
Zooming In To Draw 226
Undoing What You Have Done 228
Wrapping Up 228

13 Editing Objects 229

Selecting Objects 229
Select Objects One at a Time 230
Select Several Objects 230
Select All the Objects on the Page at the
   Same Time 230
Deselect Objects 231
Select Additional Objects Based on the
   Currently Selected Object 232
Select Objects by Cycling through Them 233
Changing the Appearance of Objects 233
Change the Attributes of a Single Object 234
Change Attributes with the Right Mouse Button 235
Change the Area Fill of an Object 235
Change the Attributes of Several Objects
   at the Same Time 236

Contents **xiii**

Changing the Size of Objects 237
    Size an Object without Changing Its Dimensions 237
    Sizing Objects with the Keyboard 238
Collecting Individual Objects into a Group 239
Aligning Objects for Precision Drawings 240
Flipping Objects 240
    Create Mirror Images: A Flip Tip 241
Rotating Objects 242
Moving Objects 242
Copying, Pasting, and Deleting Objects 243
    What Is the Clipboard? 243
    Edit Copy and Edit Paste 244
    Copy Objects to or from Other Applications 245
    Copy a Graph from One Page to Another 245
    Try It: Copy and Paste a Graph 245
    Copy and Paste Text 246
    Copy Metafiles and Bitmaps 247
    Duplicate an Object on the Current Page 247
    Delete Objects 248
    Delete Entire Pages 249
Working with Overlapping Objects 249
Wrapping Up 249

14 Transforming Objects **251**

Grouping and Ungrouping Objects 251
    Grouping Several Objects into One 252
    Ungrouping Objects 252
Editing the Points of Objects 253
    Working in Edit Points Mode 253
    Try It: Make a Voice Balloon 255
    Using the Arrow Keys To Move a Point 256
    Try It: Add, Move, and Delete a Point 256
Editing Bezier Curves 257
    Try It: Edit a Bezier Curve 258
Presto! Chango! 259
    Converting Open Objects to Closed Objects 260
    Try It: Change a Line to a Polygon 260
    Converting Closed Objects to Lines 261

Connecting Lines, Arrows, Arcs, and Curves 261
Breaking Up Is Easy To Do 262
    Try It: Break a Circle into Semicircles 263
Wrapping Up 263

15 Creating Business Diagrams 265

Types of Diagrams 265
    Flow Charts 266
    Try It: Create a Flow Chart 266
    Dramatic Drop Shadows 269
    Word Diagrams 270
    Try It: Create a Logo Using Rotated
      and Replicated Text 271
    Procedure Diagrams 272
    Conceptual Diagrams 273
    Maps 274
    Try It: Divide a U.S. Map into Sales Regions 278
The Mechanics of Creating Diagrams 279
    The Arrange Commands 279
    Drawing with a Grid 279
    It's a Snap 280
    Using the Big Crosshair 280
    Working Swiftly with SmartIcons 280
The Principles of Design 281
    Unity 281
    Emphasis 282
    Balance 282
    Proportion 283
    Movement 283
    Simplicity 284
Wrapping Up 284

16 Adding Clip Art 285

Adding Symbols to Your Presentation Page 286
Putting Symbols To Work 287
    Reinforcing Content 287
    Adding Symbols to Graphs 288
    Try It: Create a Pictorial Graph 291
    Adding Symbols to Text Charts 294
    Replacing Bullet Markers with a Symbol 294

Adding Symbols to Diagrams 296
Using a Symbol as a Backdrop 297
Editing a Symbol 298
Creating a Customized Symbol Library 298
Wrapping Up 300

17 Importing and Exporting Graphics 301

Importing Files 301
Try It: Import a Freelance Graphics .DRW File
into a Presentation Page..303
Importing ASCII Files into the Current Page 304
Importing an ASCII File into the Outliner 304
Importing Bitmaps 305
Importing Data Selectively with the
Import Data Window..305
Try It: Import ASCII Text into a Text Block 306
Import a Metafile 308
Exporting Files 308
Copying Text and Graphics via the Clipboard 310
Wrapping Up 310

18 Working with Color 311

The Role of Color in Your Presentation 311
Try It: Change the Color of an Object 312
Color Design Tips 313
Background Colors 313
Text Colors 314
Foreground Colors 314
The Psychology of Color 314
Change the Background Color 315
Limit the Number of Colors 316
When To Use Graduated Fill Patterns 316
Try It: Create a Graduated Fill Background 316
Black-and-White Design Tips 317
Understanding Palettes and the Color Library 319
What Happens When You Choose a
New SmartMaster Set? 320
Creating Your Own Palettes 320
How Freelance Uses Palette Colors 321

Try It: Edit and Save a Palette 323
Change the RGB Value of a Library Color 324
Wrapping Up 325

Part 6 Printing, Screen Shows, and Slides 327

19 Printing a Presentation 329

Choose a Printer 329
Printing Options 330
Choosing a Print Range 330
Choosing a Print Format 331
Adding Headers and Footers 334
Choosing the Page Orientation 336
Try It: Print a Presentation Outside
of Freelance Graphics 337
Printing in Black and White 337
Optimizing Colors for Your Printer 338
Wrapping Up 338

20 Screen Shows 341

Viewing a No-Frills Screen Show 342
Adding Transition Effects 342
Controlling a Screen Show 344
Drawing On-Screen 345
Creating an Interactive Screen Show 346
Adding Multimedia Effects to a Screen Show 349
Using the MultiMedia SmartMaster Sets 349
Creating a Screen Show Button 350
Try It: Add a Ringing Telephone
to a Screen Show 350
Adding Sound That Plays Automatically 352
Try It: The Lion That Roared 352
Launching Another Application from a Screen Show ... 353
Creating Build Slides 354
Automatic Build Slides 354
Data Chart Build Slides 355
Creating a Portable Screen Show 356
Wrapping Up 358

21 Creating 35mm Slides 359

The Process 359
Installing and Setting Up the Autographix Files 360
    Adding Autographix as a Printer Choice 360
    Setting Up the Autographix Driver 361
Preparing Freelance for Slide Output 363
Creating Slide Files 363
Creating a Work Order 364
Wrapping Up 367

Part 7 Presentation Management Tools 369

22 Managing Presentations 371

Views You Can Use 371
    The Three Primary Views 372
    Changing the View of the Current Page 372
    Current Page View 373
    Page Sorter View 373
    Try It: Move a Page in Page Sorter View 375
    Outliner View 375
    View Preferences 376
    Units & Grids 377
    Screen Show View 377
    Moving from View to View 377
Changing the Look 377
Adding Speaker Notes 378
Working with Several Presentations at the
    Same Time 379
    Try It: Copy Pages from One Presentation
        to Another 379
    Activating a Presentation 380
    Rearranging Windows 380
    Tile or Cascade? 382
Wrapping Up 384

23 Using SmartIcons 385
Displaying the Meaning of a SmartIcon 386
Editing the Current SmartIcon Set 386
    Repositioning the SmartIcon Set 387
    Hiding a SmartIcon Set 387
    Changing the Size of SmartIcons 388
Saving a SmartIcon Set 388
Creating Your Own SmartIcons 389
Launching Other Applications 390
Wrapping Up 391

24 Customizing Freelance Graphics 393
About Settings 394
User Setup Options 394
View Preferences 398
Drawing Options 400
    Setting Default Attributes 400
    Setting Up a Drawing Grid 401
Page Settings 401
    Headers and Footers 402
    Page Orientation 402
    Margins 402
Printer Options 403
Setting Up a Default Chart 404
Wrapping Up 404

Part 8 SmartMasters 405

25 Understanding SmartMaster Sets 407
The Structure of SmartMaster Sets 408
    How Page Layouts Work 408
    How Basic Layout Works 412
Placeholders and Prompt Text 413
    SmartMaster Text Blocks 414
    SmartMaster Placement Blocks 414
What Happens When You Switch to a
NewSmartMaster Set? 416

Customizing SmartMaster Sets 417
    Changing Text Attributes 418
    Try It: Change the Colors of Page Titles Globally 418
    Changing Bullet Color 419
    Changing the Spacing in Bulleted Lists 420
    Adding a Logo to Every Page in a Presentation 421
Creating a New Page Layout 421
    Creating a "Click here..." Text Block 422
    Creating a "Click here..." Chart Block 423
    Using the New Page Layout 423
    Copying the New Page Layout to Other
       SmartMaster Sets 424
Wrapping Up 425

26 Creating Your Own SmartMaster Sets 427

The Scenario 427
Start with an Existing SmartMaster Set 428
    Try It: Open Just a SmartMaster Set 428
Create the Design 429
    Use a Palette from an Existing SmartMaster 431
    Change the Background Color 431
    Add a Decorative Rule 431
    Add a Logo 432
    Adjust the Title Block 433
    Create the Title Page Layout 434
    Adjust the Remaining Page Layouts 435
Wrapping Up 437

Introduction

This book is for users of Freelance Graphics for Windows with any level of experience. Novice users learn how to create their first presentation immediately, while experienced users learn tips and techniques that can help them extract the most power from Freelance Graphics for Windows.

Freelance Graphics for Windows Release 2.0

In the space of a year, Freelance Graphics for Windows has rather speedily assumed the mantle of best of breed in the presentation software category. More than anything, it has been the package's unswerving devotion to ease of use that has elicited praise from users and reviewers alike.

Now, with Freelance Graphics for Windows Release 2.0, Lotus has lowered the bar for usability even further. The process of creating a presentation is now even simpler.

The obvious question is this: If it's so easy to create a presentation with Freelance Graphics, why would anyone need this book? The answer is that, while Freelance Graphics for Windows is truly easy to use, this product also has a depth and richness of features that require more in-depth instruction. Release 2.0 adds an abundance of new features, including new tools for creating tables and organization charts, an enhanced outliner with collapsible levels, and new multimedia capabilities that let you add sound and "movies" to your presentations.

In this book, you learn how to tap into these features and get productive as quickly as possible. Whether you need help editing Bezier curves, customizing chart components, or turning your presentation into 35mm slides, you'll find it here.

Finally, throughout this book you discover tips and techniques that can smooth the process of creating presentations, whether it's knowing how many words in a bullet chart are too many or how to choose the best chart type for your data.

How This Book Is Organized

This book has eight parts, each of which contains a set of related chapters. Here's a brief summary of each part.

Part 1, "Getting Started," takes you step-by-step through the creation of your first presentation and introduces many of the basic features of Freelance Graphics.

Part 2, "Text Charts," focuses on what is still the most popular presentation format: text charts. You learn how to create and customize bullet charts, how to use the outliner, and how to check your spelling.

Data charts (such as bar, line, and pie charts) are a staple in most presentations. Part 3, "Data Charts," covers the process of choosing the right chart type for your data, creating and customizing data charts, and importing and linking to data from 1-2-3 worksheets.

In Part 4, "Organization Charts and Tables," you learn the basics as well as the subtleties of creating and customizing organization charts and tables.

Freelance Graphics includes a set of drawing tools that you can use to make simple business diagrams or sophisticated illustrations. In Part 5, "Drawings and Diagrams," you learn how diagrams can illustrate concepts and procedures better than words alone. In the process, you discover new ways to use clip art. You find out how to preserve and share your investment in existing graphics by exporting and importing to and from other graphic formats. Finally, you learn about the structure of color palettes.

Part 6, "Printing, Screen Shows, and Slides," describes how to print your presentation in a variety of formats, including audience handouts and speaker notes. You learn how to create an attention-grabbing screen show with surprising transition effects, create an interactive screen show, and even add multimedia effects. The last chapter of this section describes how you can turn your presentation into crisp, colorful 35mm slides using Freelance's built-in link to a slide service bureau.

Freelance Graphics offers a variety of tools geared to managing your entire presentation, from outline to printed output. In Part 7, "Presentation Management Tools," you find out how to automate tasks with SmartIcons and even create customized SmartIcon palettes. This section also discusses how to customize Freelance to suit your working style.

SmartMasters are at the heart of Freelance Graphics, and the final section of this book—Part 8, "SmartMasters"—explains SmartMasters from the inside out. You learn how to customize existing Smartmasters and create new SmartMaster sets from scratch.

This book makes the entire process of creating presentations with Freelance Graphics a richer, more rewarding experience. Have fun!

Part 1
Getting Started

This part takes you step-by-step through the creation of your first presentation and introduces many of the basic features of Freelance Graphics.
This section includes:

Chapter 1. Creating Your First Presentation

1

Creating Your First Presentation

Most presentations are created under pressure when you don't have time to learn a new software package or relearn the one you haven't touched since last month. You know the story. The presentation is tomorrow, and you are not prepared. Haven't started, in fact. You know what you want to say, but there's that small matter of turning your ideas into a polished presentation.

Here's a chilling statistic. Studies have shown that most people rank giving a presentation as life's number one fear. (Number two is the fear of death.) If you would rather die than give a presentation, Freelance Graphics can help soothe your fears. Stepping in front of an audience when you know you have a sizzling array of professional images to back you up can boost your confidence.

The designers of Freelance Graphics for Windows started with the premise that most presentations are created under the gun, when power, simplicity, and ease of use are the most important features of a presentation software package. They felt that the process of creating presentations was perhaps the most important feature of a presentation software package. Freelance Graphics was their solution to the problem of creating presentations.

In this chapter, you learn how to:

- *Install and start Freelance Graphics for Windows*
- *Create title pages and bulleted lists*
- *Create a bar chart and a pie chart*
- *Move a page in Outliner view*
- *Print your presentation*
- *Get on-line help*
- *Close a presentation file*
- *Leave Freelance Graphics*

Installing and Starting Freelance Graphics

If you haven't installed Freelance Graphics, do so now. The installation routine is self-explanatory after you get started.

Start Windows and go to the Program Manager window. Insert the first diskette into drive A (or in whatever drive you are installing from). Choose File Run and type *a:install* (changing the drive letter as necessary). Click OK or press Enter. Then just follow the on-screen prompts.

The Key to a Professional Presentation

What makes a presentation look professional? The graphics—whether handouts, slides, or overheads—must have an appealing, consistent design. Consistent design produces a unified presentation rather than a clutter of images.

SmartMaster sets are the key to creating consistent presentations with Freelance Graphics. Freelance Graphics comes with 65 SmartMaster sets, designed to give your entire presentation a consistent look by providing the stylistic elements—color scheme, fonts, the placement of graphics, and other design elements—automatically. Each SmartMaster set offers a unique design created by professional artists that includes common design elements such as background color, typeface, bullet style, and other design elements.

Freelance requests you to choose a SmartMaster set whenever you start a new presentation. You can change to a different SmartMaster set at any time without losing content or making design changes.

Freelance Graphics contains a rich array of presentation styles that range from conservative (GRADATE2.MAS, FINANCE.MAS), informal (SKETCH.MAS), industrial (ORNATE2.MAS), flashy (SPOTLITE.MAS), to art deco (DECO.MAS). The choice is yours.

Try It: Start a New Presentation

Each time you start Freelance Graphics, the Welcome to Freelance Graphics dialog box (see fig. 1.1) asks whether you want to create a new presentation or work on an existing one. Click the appropriate radio button to create a new presentation or to work on an existing one.

Creating Your First Presentation 5

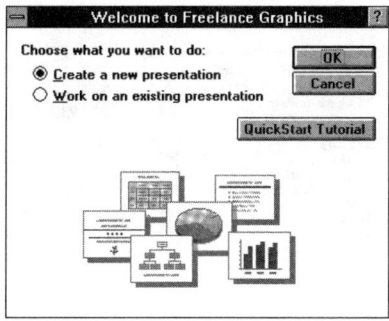

FIGURE 1.1. The Welcome to Freelance Graphics dialog box.

Practice starting a new presentation by doing the following:

1. Click the radio button next to Create a New Presentation and then click OK. The next dialog box encourages you to choose a design template for your presentation by selecting a SmartMaster set (see fig. 1.2). The names of the available SmartMaster sets appear in the list box. When you highlight a name, you see a page layout from the highlighted SmartMaster set. Click the scroll arrow to browse additional SmartMaster sets. To choose the SmartMaster set you want, double-click its name or highlight it and click OK.

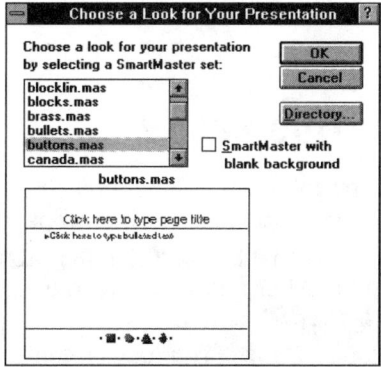

FIGURE 1.2. The Choose a Look for Your Presentation dialog box.

2. Highlight BUTTONS.MAS and then click OK (or just double-click BUTTONS.MAS). Freelance Graphics starts a new presentation using this SmartMaster set. Next, Freelance Graphics asks you to choose the format for the type of page you want to create (see fig. 1.3).

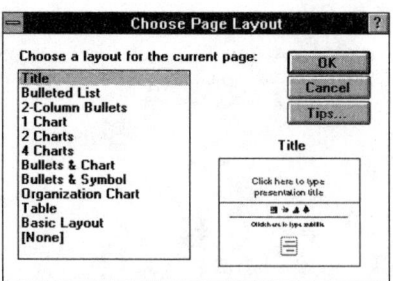

FIGURE 1.3. The Choose Page Layout dialog box.

3. Highlight Title and then click OK. Now you are ready to add text to the title page.

Creating a Title Page and a Bullet Chart

After you have chosen a SmartMaster set, you can add content, which can be either text or graphics. The prompt text (also known as "Click here ..." text), which reads "Click here to type presentation title," tells you precisely what to do. Notice that you see the design of a finished presentation page on the screen, with spaces for a title and subtitle.

Try It: Create a Title Page

Create a title page by following the actions suggested by the prompt text. Figure 1.4 shows the empty title page with prompt text.

1. Click the prompt text that reads "Click here to type presentation title." The prompt text vanishes and you find yourself in a window for entering text (known as *text edit mode*).
2. Type *Flora's Flower Shop*. (You may be tempted to press Enter after you type the title, but this isn't necessary; doing so doesn't hurt anything, but it adds a blank line to the title block.)
3. Click on the prompt text "Click here to type subtitle" or click the down-arrow key to move to the subtitle block.
4. Type *Loan Application*.
5. Now click OK or simply click outside the rectangle around your text to complete the subtitle.

Creating Your First Presentation   7

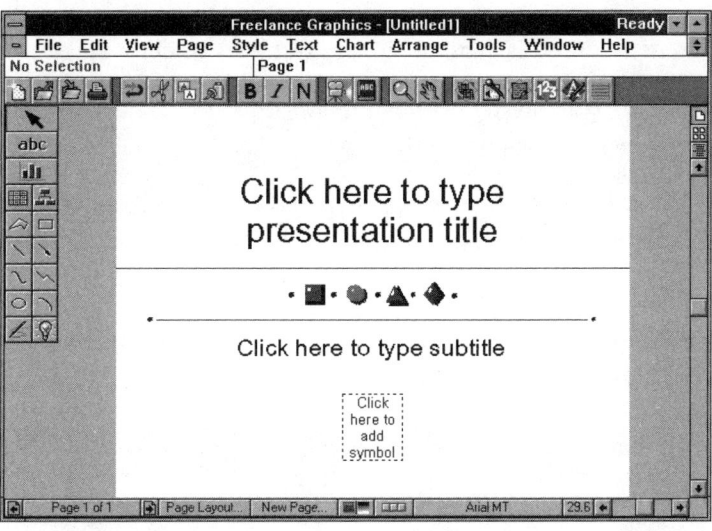

FIGURE 1.4. An empty title page with the prompt text for title, subtitle, and symbol.

You may notice the placement block on the bottom of the page in figure 1.4 that reads "Click here to add symbol." Here, you can add clip art from the symbol library.

Clip art—*symbols* in Freelance Graphics parlance—helps you communicate better by adding visual excitement to a presentation page and by lending visual support to your message. Add a picture of a bouquet on the title page of the presentation to add visual interest and to reinforce the message. Follow these steps:

1. Click the prompt text on the title page that reads "Click here to add symbol." You also can click the light bulb icon in the Toolbox to add symbols to a page. You see the Add Symbol to Page dialog box (see fig. 1.5).

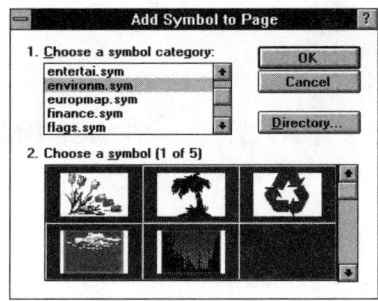

FIGURE 1.5. The Add Symbol to Page dialog box.

2. Highlight ENVIRONM.SYM in the Choose a Symbol list to view the clip art contained in this symbol library. You have to click the down scroll arrow to find this name. (You also can press the letter E, which scrolls to the first name in the list beginning with E.)
3. Double-click the symbol of the flowers. This action closes the dialog box and copies the symbol to the presentation page. Note that the symbol drops automatically into the placement block (the one that contained the prompt text "Click here to add symbol").
4. Click away from the flowers to remove the selection handles from the clip art.

Congratulations! You have just created your first presentation page. Figure 1.6 shows the completed page.

FIGURE 1.6. A completed title page.

Adding Another Page and Choosing a Page Layout

Now you can proceed to create the rest of your presentation. Next, you create a bulleted list, where you can introduce your main topics or list the most important aspects of a specific topic.

To start a new page, you have several choices. Choose Page New or click the New Page button on the bottom border. Either action displays the New Page dialog box (see fig. 1.7).

Creating Your First Presentation 9

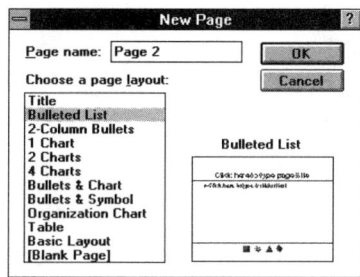

FIGURE 1.7. The New Page dialog box.

When you highlight the name of a page layout, you see an image of it in the area to the right. Click OK to use the selected page layout or simply double-click the name of the page layout.

If you count the names in the Page Layouts list, you will find 11 (12 if you count Blank Page). Every SmartMaster set has these same 11 page layouts. As you learn later (Chapter 25, "Understanding SmartMaster Sets"), this feature enables you to change to a new SmartMaster set without altering the basic design of your presentation.

Each SmartMaster set contains 11 page layouts for the most common presentation formats. Every SmartMaster set, for example, contains a page format for a bulleted list, a title page, and a chart page, as well as various combinations of these such as a format for a bulleted list and a chart on the same page.

A page layout contains special areas, or *placeholders*, to contain the text or graphics you want to add to the page. There are two kinds of placeholders: one for text (SmartMaster text blocks) and one for graphics (placement blocks). You can read more about these in Chapter 25, "Understanding SmartMaster Sets."

Try It: Create a Bulleted List

Start with a bulleted list, that venerable workhorse of presentation page formats. First you start a new page. Then you choose the page layout for a bulleted list. Remember, in Freelance Graphics, a presentation contains multiple pages.

1. Choose Page New or click the New Page button on the bottom border.
2. In the list box, highlight the name of the page layout you want. The sample box on the right shows you how the highlighted page layout looks.

3. Click Bulleted List to choose a format for a bullet chart and then click OK. (You also can double-click the name to accept your selection and close the dialog box in a single step.)
4. Click the prompt text at the top of the page ("Click here to type page title") and then type *Expansion Plans*.
5. Press the down-arrow key. You are now positioned in the text entry area for bullets. Note that the first bullet is already visible, awaiting your text.
6. Type *Open two new shops this summer* and then press Enter. Freelance adds the next bullet automatically.
7. Press Tab to indent the next line and type *East Side (June)*.
8. Press Enter and then type *Green Park (July)*.
9. Press Enter and then press Shift+Tab to move back to the first level. (You also can click the Promote icon: the left-pointing arrow in the text panel.)
10. Type *Offer extended delivery service*.
11. Press Enter and then type *Expand nursery at main location*.
12. Click OK or click outside the text box to complete the bulleted list (see fig. 1.8). You have just created a bullet chart without having to think about format, design, or placement. Chapter 2, "Bullet Charts and Beyond," explains more about the mechanics of creating bullet charts.

What's the Difference between a SmartMaster Set and a Page Layout?

It's essential that you make a clear distinction between SmartMaster sets and page layouts. A SmartMaster set is a design template for your entire presentation. Freelance Graphics has 65 SmartMaster sets, each of which defines the look of a presentation, including typeface, color, and other design elements. Every SmartMaster set has 11 page layouts that provide the format for a particular type of presentation page, such as a bulleted list or a data chart.

Just as you can change to a new SmartMaster set at any time, so you can choose a new page layout for an existing page. To change to a new SmartMaster set, use the command Style Choose SmartMaster Set. To change the page layout for an existing page, use the Page Choose Page Layout command.

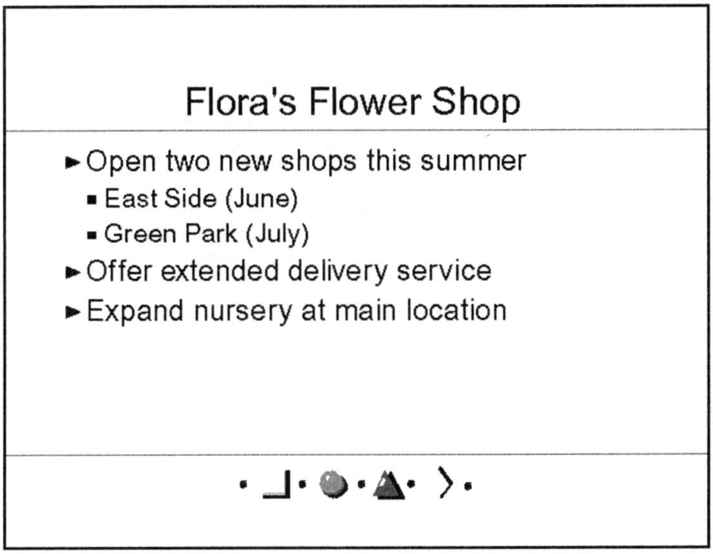

```
                    Flora's Flower Shop
         ▶ Open two new shops this summer
             ■ East Side (June)
             ■ Green Park (July)
         ▶ Offer extended delivery service
         ▶ Expand nursery at main location


                   · ⌐ · ● · ▲ · 〉·
```

FIGURE 1.8. A Bullet chart that uses the Bulleted List page layout from the BUTTONS.MAS SmartMaster set.

Creating a Data Chart

The process of adding graphics to a presentation page is similar to adding text. First you choose a page layout and then you click the prompt text and follow the instructions on screen. Now try creating a data chart.

Try It: Choose a Page Layout and Type a Title

The first step is to start a new page and then to select a page layout for a data chart. Follow these steps:

1. Choose Page New.
2. From the New Page dialog box, highlight 1 Chart and click OK.
3. Click the prompt text "Click here to type page title" and then type *Best-Selling Flowers*.
4. Click the prompt text that reads "Click here to create chart." This action brings up the New Chart Gallery, where you choose a chart type and style (see fig. 1.9).

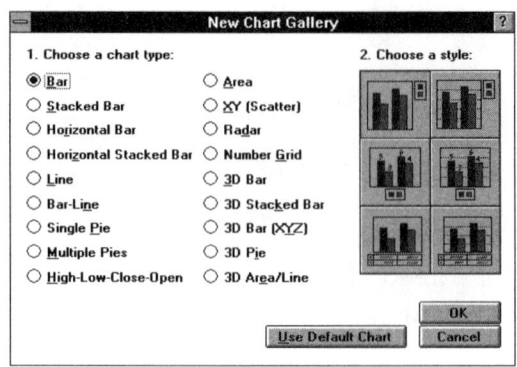

FIGURE 1.9. The New Chart Gallery.

What's Prompt Text?

You encounter the term *prompt text* (or "Click here text...") again and again in this book, so you might as well learn now what it means. Prompt text is a message that appears on page layouts that gives you instructions, such as "Click here to type presentation title" or "Click here to create chart." When you click prompt text, Freelance either displays a text box where you can type your text or launches you into the process of creating a chart or adding a symbol to a page.

Here's another important fact about prompt text. Even though prompt text is visible on screen, it is never printed or visible during screen shows. Its sole purpose is to guide you as you create your presentation.

You can edit prompt text or create your own by working with SmartMaster page layouts in SmartMaster Pages view, but this is an advanced topic. When the time comes, you can read about it in Part 8, "SmartMasters."

Try It: Choose a Chart Type and Style from the Gallery

The Chart Gallery is the place to choose the chart type and style you want to use. (If you need information on selecting the right chart type, refer to Chapter 6, "Choosing the Right Chart Type.") Follow these steps:

1. Click Horizontal Bar. You can choose a chart type from the list of names by clicking a radio button or the name next to it. When you select a name, six styles of that chart type appear in the Choose a Style area.
2. Click the first picture on the bottom row of the Style area and then click OK. (You also can simply double-click this picture.) Now you see the Chart Data & Titles window. You are ready to enter your data.

Try It: Enter Your Data

Entering your chart data is just a matter of typing your text and numbers into a data-entry form. (If your data is in a spreadsheet, you can click the Import button to copy it directly into the data entry area. For more information, read Chapter 9, "Creating Charts from 1-2-3 Worksheets.") Follow these steps:

1. Click the mouse in the first white cell beneath the Axis Labels column.
2. Type *Mixed bouquets*.
3. Press Enter to move down a row and type *Roses*.
4. Enter the rest of your data, as shown in figure 1.10. You can move to any cell by clicking it with the mouse. Complete the data entry in a cell by pressing Enter or by pressing an arrow key to move to the next cell. Here, in the data view, you enter axis labels in the first column and the numbers representing each data symbol in the second column.

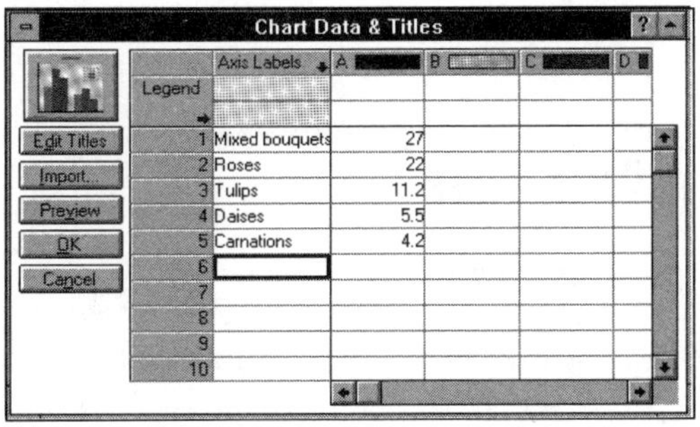

FIGURE 1.10. The Chart Data & Titles window.

5. Click OK to view the completed chart. Freelance closes the Chart Data & Titles window and composes the chart on the page. Notice that Freelance moves the chart into the placement block automatically. Every chart you create by using the 1 Chart page layout is the same size and occupies the same position on the page.

Tips for Working in the Chart Data & Titles Window

For starters, the Chart Data & Titles window is not a spreadsheet, although it looks like one. You cannot enter formulas to sum the numbers in cells, for example, nor can you change the width of cells.

Here is a potential trouble spot. You can enter text or numbers in the Axis Labels column or in the Legend Rows, but you can enter numbers only in the data area of the Chart Data & Titles window. If you attempt to enter (or paste) text in this area, Freelance sounds a tone and discards your entry.

Also note that you cannot enter data in those two gray cells at the top left corner of the Chart Data & Titles window. These two cells are strictly for anchoring the cursor when you are copying or importing data.

Do keep in mind that at any time you can toggle back and forth between the data view and the titles view of the Chart Data & Titles window. Just click the Edit Data or Edit Titles button.

Your data chart looks good now, but you notice that you have neglected to add a title along the horizontal axis (in this case, the scaled axis). You must return to the Chart Data & Titles window to add the title. You can add this title in the following three ways:

- Click the chart to select it and then click the Chart Tool icon in the Toolbox.
- Select the chart and then choose Chart Edit from the menu.
- Double-click an empty area on the chart. If you double-click a chart component, you see a dialog box for that component. Double-clicking a bar, for example, opens the Bar Chart Attributes dialog box.

Try It: Add an Axis Title

The Chart Data & Titles window has two views: the *data* view, where you enter your data, and a *titles* view, where you enter headings, notes, and axis titles. Now, add a title for the scaled axis (the axis that measures your data). In Freelance Graphics, the scaled axis is known as the Y axis even though in this chart the scaled axis is the horizontal axis.

1. Click the Edit Titles button in the Chart Data & Titles window. You see the titles view of the data window (see fig. 1.11). In titles view, you enter headings, notes, and axis titles. Click Edit Data to return to the data view.

2. Click the row for Y axis titles and type *1991 Sales ($000)*. The other areas in the titles view offer places to enter a heading and notes. You already have entered a heading in the page title block, so you can leave the rest of this window blank.

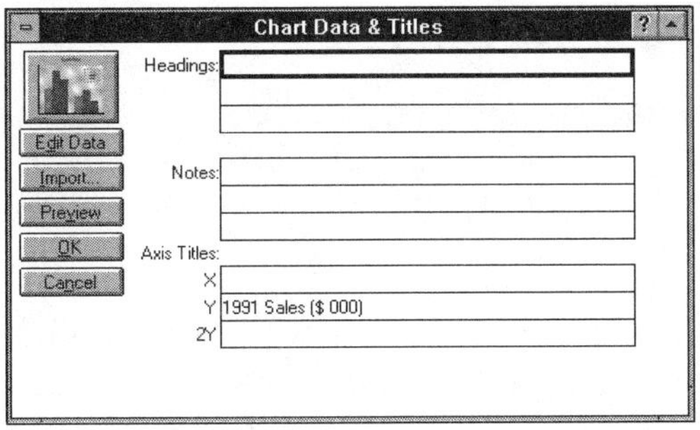

Creating Your First Presentation   15

FIGURE 1.11. The titles view of the Chart Data & Titles window.

Try It: Preview Your Chart

As you create a chart, it's useful to check your progress. Clicking the OK button displays your chart but also closes the Chart Data & Titles window. Click the Preview button to view a chart without leaving the the Chart Data & Titles window. If you click the Preview button once, the data window momentarily vanishes and reveals your chart (see fig. 1.12). If you click and hold the Preview button, you can examine your chart as long as you want. When you release the left mouse button, the data window reappears and you can continue to work.

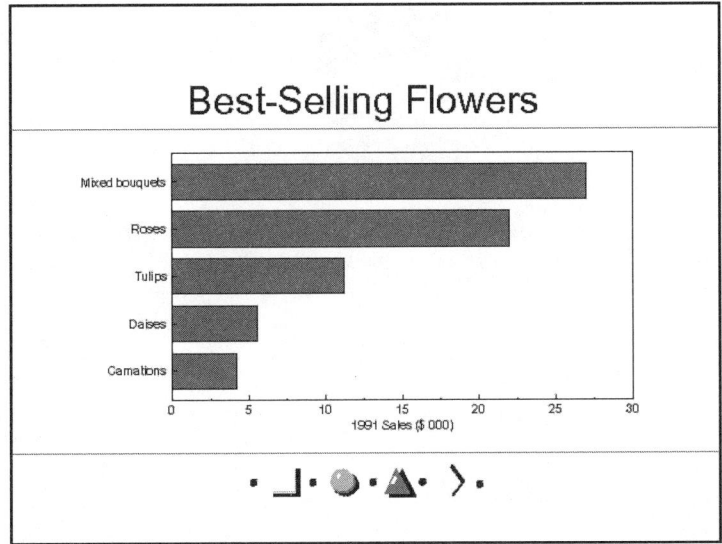

FIGURE 1.12. A preview of the completed chart.

Switching to a New Chart Type

You have successfully created your first chart. The horizontal bar chart looks good, but you decide that a pie chart would better suit your data after all. The pie chart is the best chart type for showing parts of a whole, and your intent is to show the percentage of total sales contributed by each type of flower you sell.

The fastest way to change chart types is to return to the Chart Gallery and select a new type. There are several ways to return to the Chart Gallery. Because you are in the Chart Data & Titles window now, the fastest way to view the Gallery is to click the picture of the chart type (the Chart Sample) in the upper-left corner of the Chart Data & Titles window. This action opens the Chart Gallery. (For other ways to display the Chart Gallery, see Chapter 7, "Creating Data Charts.")

Now click Single Pie and then double-click the first picture in the bottom row as a pie style. Click Preview or OK in the Chart Data & Titles window to see the effects of your change. Freelance recomposes your bar chart on the page as a pie chart (see fig. 1.13). This style automatically explodes the first slice in your data set.

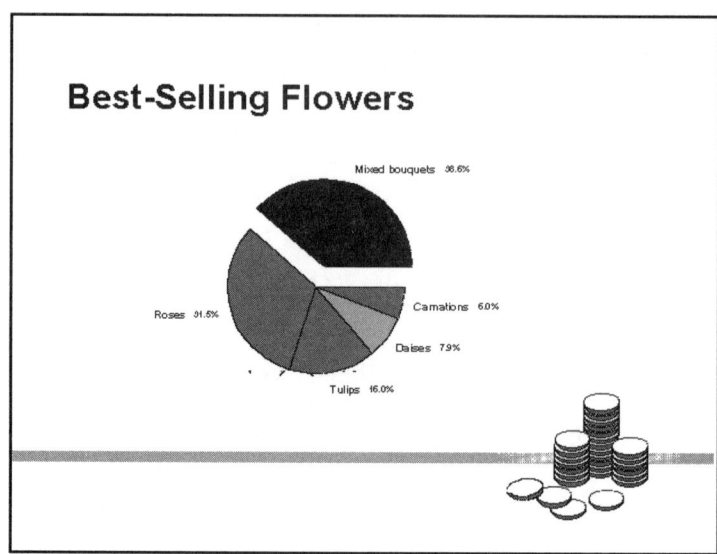

FIGURE 1.13. The result of switching from a horizontal bar chart to a pie chart.

That's the basic procedure for creating graphs. Now you are ready to organize your presentation.

Organizing

Most people find they need to reorganize a presentation as their ideas take form in text charts, graphs, and diagrams. Freelance has a number of tools that can help you organize your presentation.

Try It: Switch to a New SmartMaster Set

After completing the first few presentation pages, you decide the look just isn't quite right. The SmartMaster set you are using, BUTTON.MAS, gives a light, informal look to your data, but, after all, you are applying for a business loan, so maybe you need something more businesslike.

1. Select Style Choose SmartMaster Set from the menu.
2. In the dialog box shown in figure 1.14, highlight the name of a SmartMaster set to view a representative page.

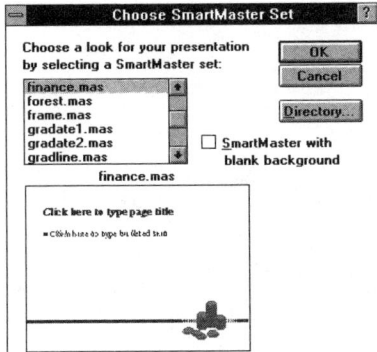

FIGURE 1.14. The Choose SmartMaster Set dialog box.

3. Scroll down and highlight FINANCE.MAS. This design features a stack of coins as part of its design. What could be more businesslike than cold cash?
4. Click OK to choose the highlighted SmartMaster set (or double-click the name). Freelance applies the new SmartMaster set to your presentation (see fig. 1.15).

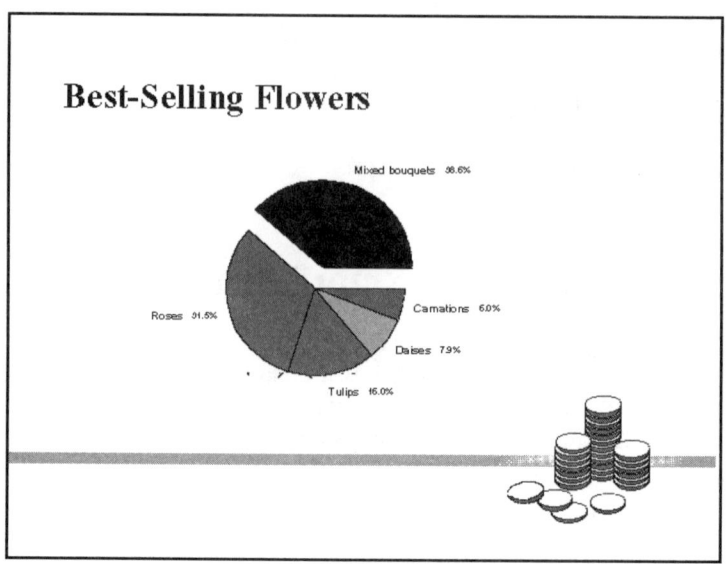

FIGURE 1.15. The pie chart with the new SmartMaster set (FINANCE).

Try It: Move a Page in Page Sorter View

In Page Sorter view, you see your presentation as a series of thumbnail sketches, or miniature presentation pages. The effect is like that of slides on a light table. As on a light table, you can move slides around easily. In Freelance, you just select the page (or pages) you want to move and then drag the selection to a new location. The Page Sorter is a great way to check the sequence of slides in your presentation. Practice by doing the following:

1. Choose View Page Sorter from the menu or click the Page Sorter icon on the right border of the window. You are now in Page Sorter view (see fig. 1.16).
2. Click the third thumbnail (note the heavy border around the page) and drag it to the left.
3. When the wide vertical bar appears to the right of the first thumbnail, release the left mouse button.

Freelance drops the page in its new location and automatically renumbers the page. In this manner, you can reorder an entire presentation in moments. For more information on using the Page Sorter, refer to Chapter 22, "Managing Your Presentations."

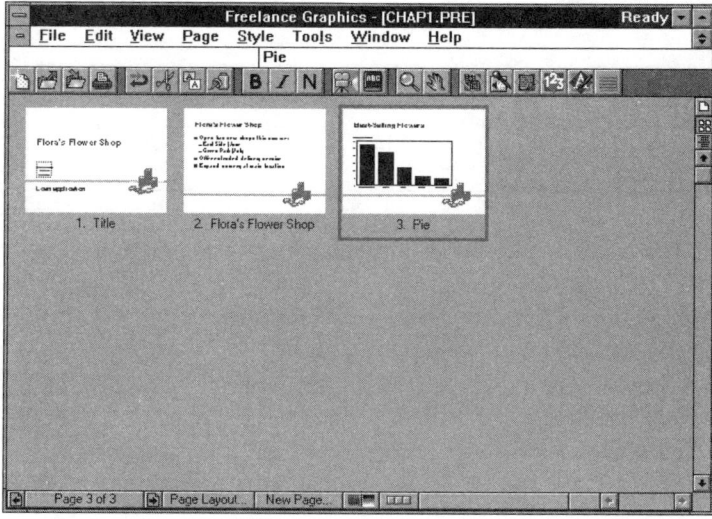

FIGURE 1.16. Page Sorter View.

Getting a Textual View in the Outliner

The Outliner view gives you a textual view of your presentation. To display your presentation in the Outliner, choose View Outliner or click the Outliner icon on the right border.

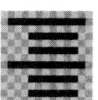

Now you see the text of your presentation pages (see fig. 1.17). Note how your bullet chart is displayed. Notice especially the symbol of the page with the turned-down corner next to the title. This symbol is the Page icon, which marks the start of a new page. If the page contains a data chart, you see a bar chart icon inside the Page icon. When you change the text of your presentation page in Outliner view, the presentation page also is updated. Likewise, the changes you make directly on the presentation page flow automatically to the Outliner view.

You can create bullet charts automatically by typing text in Outliner view. You also can rearrange, move, or delete pages in the Outliner.

To learn more about using the Outliner, read Chapter 4, "Using the Outliner."

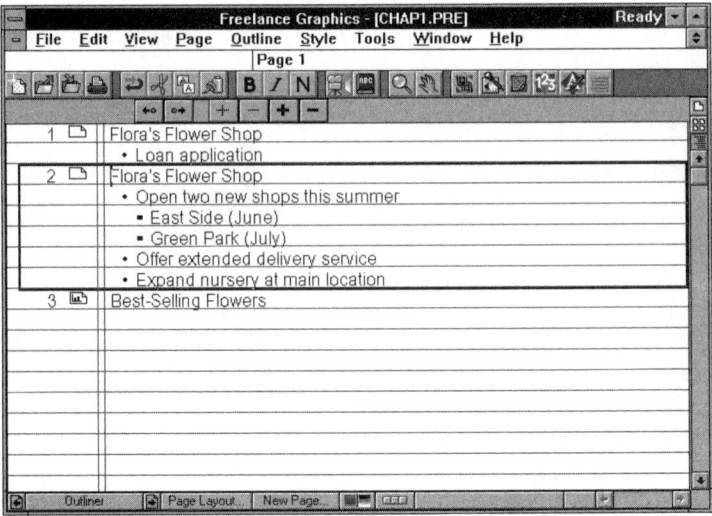

FIGURE 1.17. Outliner view presents you with a textual view of your presentation pages.

Checking the Flow with Screen Show

You can display the pages of your presentation in sequence on your monitor as a *screen show*. Use this feature at any time during the development of your presentation as a way of checking the flow of your presentation. When you display a screen show, you see your images in full-screen form, without the surrounding structure of the Freelance Graphics window.

To start a screen show, choose View Screen Show Run, press Alt+F10, or click the Screen Show SmartIcon.

For more information about screen shows, refer to Chapter 20, "Screen Shows."

Printing Your Presentation

After you have completed your presentation, you may want to print it. If you plan to deliver it as a screen show, this may not be the case. But even then, you may want to create a set of audience handouts.

To print your work, choose File Print or click the Print SmartIcon. Then enter the appropriate printing options in the Print File dialog box (see fig. 1.18). Enter the number of copies you want, select the option to print the current page only, or specify speaker notes, audience notes, or handouts. For fast printing, you can opt to print a presentation without the SmartMaster background.

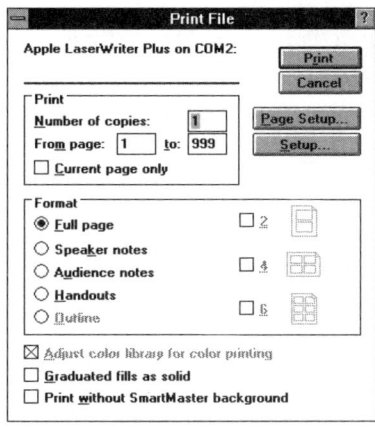

FIGURE 1.18. The Print File dialog box.

For complete information on printing, refer to Chapter 19, "Printing a Presentation."

SmartIcons: Just Click it!

Unless you have changed the program's defaults, you see the row of icons across the top of your screen. These are SmartIcons, with which you can invoke a Freelance command or function with a single mouse click. To print your presentation, for example, click the SmartIcon that looks like a dot-matrix printer. You see the Print File dialog box, where you can choose printing options.

You can add to or subtract from the default SmartIcon set with Tools SmartIcons Customize. Freelance Graphics has more than 100 SmartIcons.

You may not be able to guess what some of the SmartIcons mean. To find out fast, just click and hold a SmartIcon with the right mouse button. You see a brief description of the SmartIcon in the left side of the title bar.

For more about SmartIcons, read Chapter 23, "Using SmartIcons."

Getting On-Line Help

Freelance Graphics has an extensive on-line help system that you can call up anytime during a work session. The help system offers a mix of procedural and reference material. You can use help in the following several ways:

- Press F1 anytime to get help on your current task (context-sensitive help). If you are working in a dialog box, for example, you see information about that dialog box.
- Click the ? in the right corner of any dialog box in Freelance Graphics to open a help screen describing that dialog box.
- Choose Help from the menu (or press Alt+H) to view a list of choices. Select one of these choices to see an index of help topics, a search feature, instructions for using the help system, information about using the keyboard, a list of tasks you can perform in Freelance (How do I?), information for upgraders, an on-line Adobe Type Manager (ATM) reference manual, and an on-line tutorial.

Freelance help observes standard Windows help conventions. If you are familiar with these conventions, you should have no trouble using help. If not, the following sections get you up to speed.

Using the Help Icon Bar

The help icon bar contains six buttons: Contents, Search, Back, History, and the two Browse buttons (see fig. 1.19). Familiarize yourself with these buttons for fast navigation through the help system.

FIGURE 1.19. The help icon bar.

The Contents button displays the major topics in the Freelance Graphics help system.

The Search button displays a list of topics associated with the keyword or phrase you type in the Search box (see fig. 1.20). Use this dialog box to find help topics of interest. Scroll through the list of keywords or just type the first few letters of the keyword. Click the Show Topics button (or double-click the keyword) to view a list of related help topics. Click the Go To button (or double-click the topic) to view the corresponding help screen (see fig. 1.21). Click words underlined with a solid line to view a related help screen. Click a word with a dotted underline to view its definition.

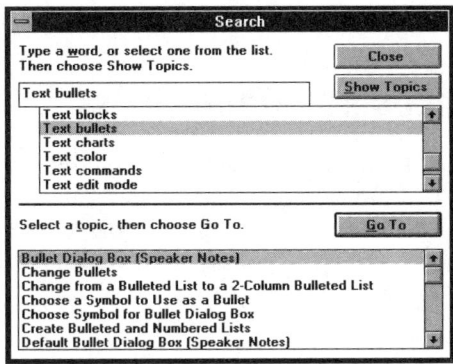

FIGURE 1.20. The Search dialog box.

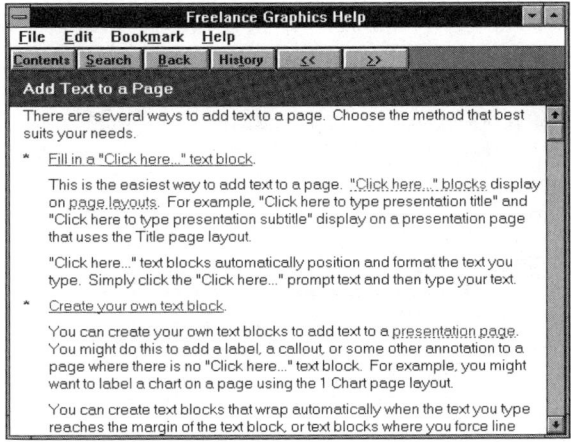

FIGURE 1.21. The help screen for "How Do I Add Text to a Page?"

The Back button takes you back to the preceding help topic you viewed. If you are viewing a series of help screens, Back can return you to your starting point. When you reach the first topic you viewed, the Back button becomes dimmed.

The History button opens a list of the last 40 help topics you viewed. Double-click a topic to see it again.

The Browse << button displays the last-viewed topic in a sequence of related topics. When you reach the first topic in the sequence, the button is dimmed. The Browse >> button displays the next topic in a sequence of related topics. When you display the last topic, the button is dimmed.

Cross-References and Definitions

Pay special attention to the green words in help screens with solid and dotted underlines. You can click the words with solid underlines to view a related help screen (cross-reference) about the underlined topic. Click a word with a dotted underline to open a pop-up box containing information about the underlined word. (Click anywhere in the pop-up box to close it.)

Adding Bookmarks

A bookmark is the electronic equivalent of a paper bookmark. If you find yourself referring to a certain help screen over and over, you can use the bookmark option to access it quickly. Open the help screen for which you want to create the bookmark and then choose Bookmark Define. In the Bookmark Define box, the name of the current help topic appears (see fig. 1.22). Click OK to use this name as a bookmark or type another brief descriptive name, such as *How to import 1-2-3/W graphs*. The next time you choose Bookmark from the Help menu, you see a list of all the bookmarks you have added to the help system. Click the topic you want to view.

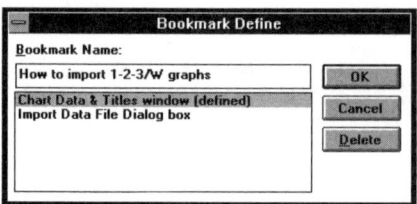

FIGURE 1.22. The Bookmark Define dialog box.

Annotating Help Topics

You can add small explanatory notes to any help topic by choosing Edit Annotate. This action opens a window in which you can type text (see fig. 1.23). As you type, the text wraps automatically. To insert a hard return, press Ctrl+Enter. When you are finished, click OK. Notice the green paper clip icon next to the help topic you just annotated. Click this icon to display your note. Click the Delete button to remove the annotation.

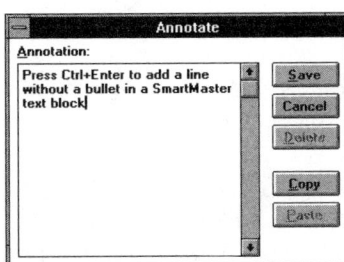

FIGURE 1.23. The Annotate dialog box.

Printing Help Topics

You can print a help topic by using File Print Topic, which prints the entire topic screen. With this option, you can assemble a mini reference manual consisting of help screens that describe commands you use frequently.

Print a help topic by choosing File Print Topic.

Saving the Presentation

As with any program, it's common sense to save your work from time to time. Your power may fail, you may trip over an extension cord, or some other disaster may befall your computer just when you are putting the finishing touches on the presentation that you have been working on for two hours but have not yet saved.

To save your presentation, choose File Save or click the File Save SmartIcon. Freelance also has an autosave option that saves your files automatically at designated intervals. To set up this feature, use the Tools User Setup command. For more information on this and other ways you can change the way the File Save command works, see Chapter 24, "Customizing Freelance Graphics."

Save your presentation by clicking the File Save SmartIcon.

Closing the File

To close your presentation, choose File Close or click the Close a File SmartIcon. If you need to save your presentation before leaving, Freelance Graphics pauses for you to do so. To leave Freelance Graphics, choose File Exit or click the Exit Freelance Graphics SmartIcon.

Wrapping Up

That's it! You have just learned how to create your first presentation. Maybe now giving a presentation has moved a little farther down your list of life's biggest fears.

Armed with the knowledge presented in this chapter, you can now go forth and create your own title charts, bullet charts, or graphs—or even embellish your pages with symbols. Because most presentations consist almost entirely of these three formats, you can get started on your own presentations right away.

Of course, Freelance Graphics has many more features that you can use to create text charts, graphs, and diagrams. In fact, there are enough features to fill an entire book (this one). You can find more in-depth knowledge of any feature of Freelance Graphics in the remaining chapters of this book.

Good luck!

Part 2
Text Charts

This part focuses on what is still the most popular presentation format: text charts. You learn how to create and customize bullet charts, how to use the outliner, and how to check your spelling.
This section includes:

Chapter 2. Bullet Charts and Beyond

Chapter 3. Creating, Editing, and Formatting Text

Chapter 4. Using the Outliner

Chapter 5. Checking Your Spelling

2

Bullet Charts and Beyond

Studies have shown that more than 70 percent of all presentation pages consist of text charts. If anything, this figure is probably low. In fact, most presentations consist of little but bulleted lists.

That's why we start with text charts. If you can create consistent, professional-looking text charts quickly and easily, you can be on the road to presentation success. Add graphs and diagrams if you want, but with a firm foundation of well-crafted text charts that deliver your message emphatically, you're off to a great start.

What makes a text chart a winner? This chapter explores the art of creating effective text charts.

What Are Text Charts?

What exactly is a text chart? Broadly speaking, a *text chart* displays words on a page in various formats, including title pages, bulleted lists, paragraph charts, or just about any page whose primary content is text. But when most people say "text chart," they generally mean bullet chart. This format is without doubt the most common one, and the one this chapter focuses on.

In this chapter, you learn:

- *How to create informative, effective bullet charts*
- *Ways to use the page layouts for bullet charts included with each Freelance Graphics SmartMaster set*
- *The rules of thumb for making your bullet charts attractive and persuasive*
- *Basic typographical terms to help you create effective text charts*

The Bullet Chart: A True Classic

The bullet chart is the most common and useful of all presentation page formats, as well as the classic format for displaying a list of items on a page (see fig. 2.1). It is the workhorse of presentation graphics, and for good reason. Bullet charts are a remarkably effective and economical way of presenting information. The bullet marker—that small round or square symbol that precedes each point—calls attention to each item in a list and draws the eye infallibly to your points.

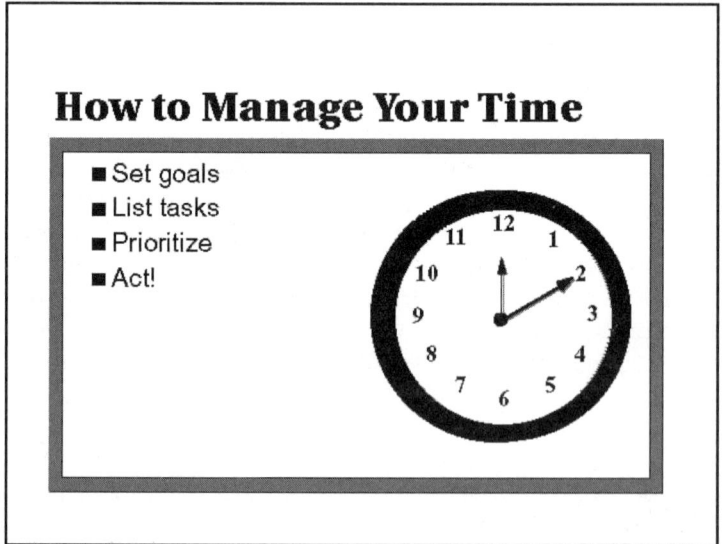

FIGURE 2.1. It's no accident that bullet charts are the number one presentation format. No other format can say so much in so little space.

The two main functions of bullet charts are to list and to summarize. Unlike items in a numbered list, items in a bullet chart have no ranking or sequence. All the items in the list receive equal billing, although a subtle ranking is implied by the order of the items.

Bullet charts dispense with the usual grammatical necessity of including transitions between sentences. You don't need commas or semicolons between bullet points or periods at the end of bullets. They are concise, focused, and direct. In short, bullet charts are the ideal medium for getting your points across in a presentation.

Bullet Charts and Beyond

Bullet charts are signposts to guide both you and your audience through your presentation. They provide the reader with a structure for your ideas, and they provide you with an on-screen cue card to help you remember your points and to keep you on the right road. Like a good highway sign, a bullet chart must be complete enough to be informative but concise enough to be read quickly.

Creating Bullet Charts with SmartMaster Page Layouts

Because bullet charts are the most commonly used presentation page format, you need to be able to create them as quickly and automatically as possible.

Freelance Graphics automates the production of bullet charts. The first step is to choose one of the following bullet page layouts provided with every SmartMaster set:

- Bulleted List
- 2-Column Bullets
- Bullets & Chart
- Bullets & Symbol

Each of these page layouts automatically formats, sizes, and places the text you enter.

Try It: Create Bullet Charts Fast

After you grasp the basics, you can create a series of bullet charts just about as quickly as you can type. Practice by doing the following:

1. After you start Freelance Graphics and select a SmartMaster set, choose Page New to create a new page. You see the New Page dialog box (see fig. 2.2).
2. Choose one of the four bullet page layouts. (Bulleted List is by far the most common.)
3. Click the prompt text that reads "Click here to type page title" and then type your own title. As you type text into a SmartMaster text block (the rectangle that surrounds your text), you see the text panel across the top of the text block.
4. Click the text that reads "Click here to type bulleted text," type the first item, and press Enter.

Freelance Graphics adds the next bullet marker for you.

5. Type the next item and press Enter.
6. Press Tab to type a subpoint or click the right-arrow icon in the text panel. The text you type has a different bullet marker and is indented. Press Tab again to add a third-level bulleted item. To move back a level, press Shift+Tab or click the left-arrow icon in the text panel. For more information about how to change the formats for each level of indentation, refer to Chapter 3, "Creating, Editing, and Formatting Text."
7. Click OK (or click outside the text block) to complete the chart.

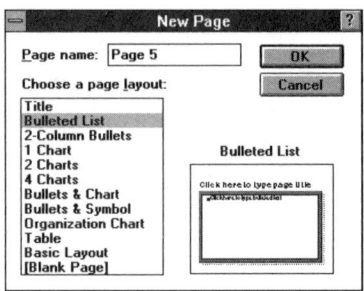

FIGURE 2.2. The New Page dialog box. Choose a page layout for your bullet chart here.

Another way to create a series of bullet charts quickly is to type directly into the Outliner. Refer to Chapter 4, "Using the Outliner," for more information about this technique.

The Text Chart Variations

The standard page layout for bullet charts is the one-column bullet chart, with a title across the top of the page and a list of bulleted items spaced out on the page beneath the title. To create this type of bullet chart in Freelance Graphics, choose the Bulleted List page layout. Although you may use the Bulleted List page layout as your standard format for most of the bullet charts in your presentation, Freelance Graphics has three other bullet chart page layouts: 2-Column Bullets, Bullets & Chart, and Bullets & Symbol.

Most of the time, these formats meet your needs. If you need a custom format, however, you can create your own. Read Chapter 26, "Creating Your Own SmartMaster Sets," for more information.

Title Pages

The title page is the first thing your audience sees, so the title chart must set the tone and style for your entire presentation (see fig. 2.3). Make it informative, lively, and attractive. If your presentation is a high-powered sales pitch, make the language in the title fit the message ("You Can Make $200,000 a Year Selling Yo-Yos!"). If your topic is more serious, use a more formal title ("The Coming Crisis in Housing for the Elderly").

FIGURE 2.3. A title page must make a good first impression. Make it inviting and informative.

Most of the title page layouts in the SmartMaster sets of Freelance Graphics have a placeholder for a symbol. This place is a good location for your corporate logo or another symbol emblematic of your entire presentation.

You also can use the title page format to subdivide the parts of your presentation (coffee and lunch breaks, new themes, and so on).

Bulleted List

As mentioned, this format is the most common page format for bulleted lists and undoubtedly should become your bread-and-butter bullet chart format.

Many presentations consist of page after page of one-column bullet charts (see fig. 2.4). This approach is fine, but you really should consider introducing a bit of variety into your presentation by including some graphs and diagrams as well. Nevertheless, you may find yourself returning to the Bulleted List format again and again.

FIGURE 2.4. The single-column bullet chart is the most popular format for text charts.

Side-by-Side Bullets

Bullet charts with two side-by-side columns typically compare two sets of items (see fig. 2.5). You can use this format to compare or contrast the features of two products or the pros and cons of alternative strategies. You just place parallel items on the left and right sides of the page.

Another good use of the two-column format is to list items in the left column and then expand on them in the right column. The left column might contain product names, for example, and the right column might list the major benefit of that product.

One drawback of this format is that your message is somewhat limited by the width of the columns. If you choose this format, keep your message very short.

Bullet Charts and Beyond 35

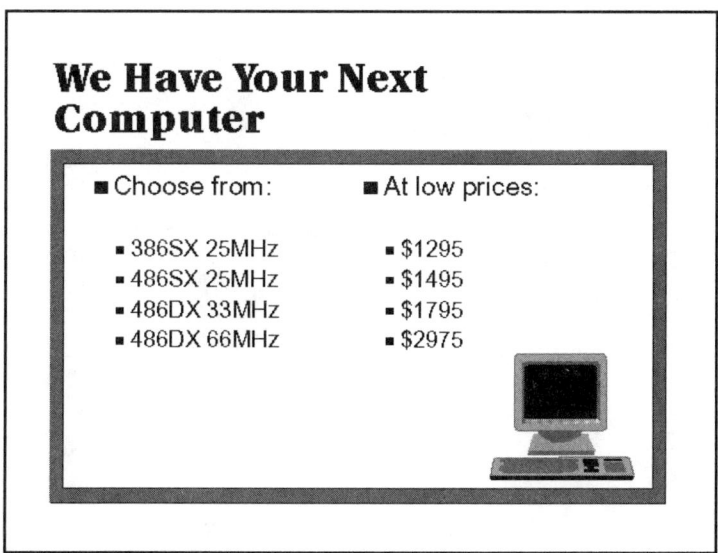

FIGURE 2.5. Use the two-column bullet chart to compare items.

Bullets & Chart

Graphs communicate their message effectively by using symbols that represent numbers. But for all their communicative power, words can help elaborate the message of a graph. That's why placing a bullet chart and a graph side by side is an effective technique (see fig. 2.6). Choose the Bullets & Chart page layout for this purpose.

Bullets & Symbol

Freelance Graphics also has a page layout (Bullets & Symbol) for a side-by-side arrangement of bullet chart and symbol. This page layout has the same format as Bullets & Chart (see fig. 2.7). This format can help break the monotony of a series of one-column bullet charts. Use a symbol that reinforces your point. Obviously, for this format to work, the bulleted list must have rather short lines.

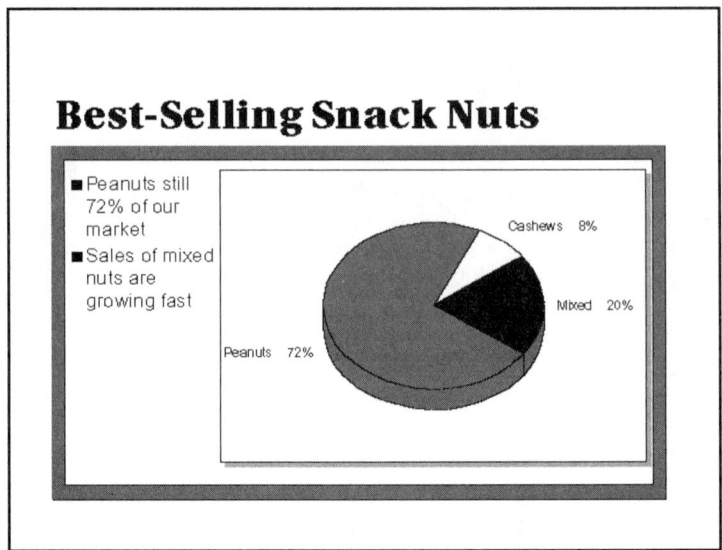

FIGURE 2.6. The bulleted list and the graph complement each other.

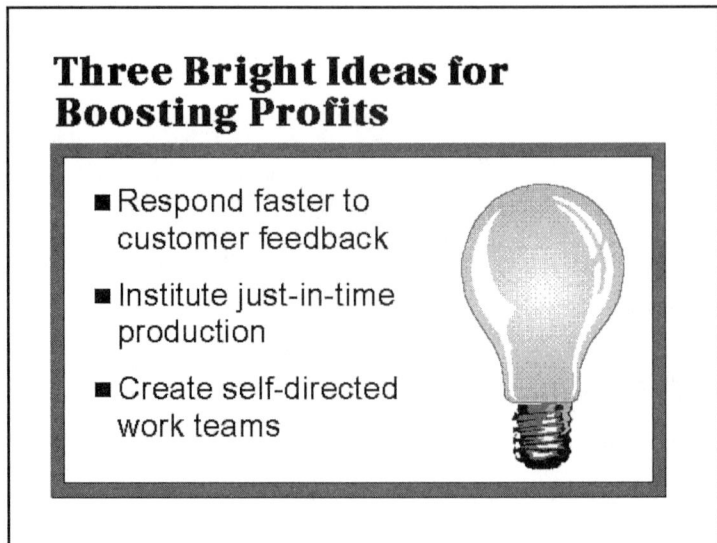

FIGURE 2.7. A symbol reinforces the message in your bullet chart.

Use the graphical placement block on the right as a display area for a symbol that reinforces the text message on the left. If you are talking about factory production on the left, you might place a symbol of a factory on the right. Alternatively, you might place a photograph in the form of a TIFF file in the graphic placement block on the right.

You can browse through the Freelance Graphics symbol library on-screen to find an appropriate symbol. Freelance Graphics sizes and adds the symbol to the placement block automatically, as explained in Chapter 16, "Adding Clip Art."

Paragraph Charts

Paragraph charts display a sentence—often a quotation—in large type on a page (see fig. 2.8). Magazines use this technique when they extract a nugget of prose from an article, pump up the type size, and display it in a box in the middle of an article. It makes the message seem more important and dramatic. You can do the same.

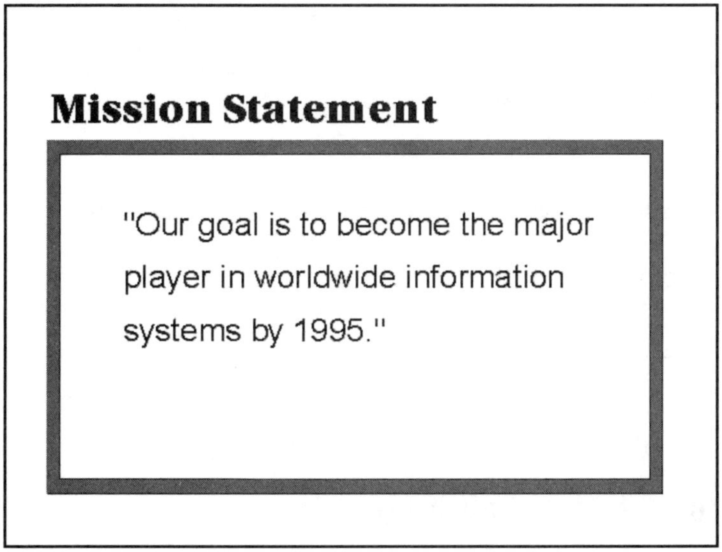

Mission Statement

"Our goal is to become the major player in worldwide information systems by 1995."

FIGURE 2.8. A paragraph chart makes ordinary text seem dramatic and important.

Novelty Text Charts

The standard bullet chart with a title on top and a list of bulleted items below can begin to bore if used too many times in a presentation. You can break up the monotony of a series of identically formatted bullet charts with a few novel styles.

The symbol library of Freelance Graphics has a collection of frames that you can use to create text charts. Because novelty wears off if used too often, exercise restraint and use just a couple of novelty charts in a single presentation (see fig. 2.9).

FIGURE 2.9. Use a symbol as a unique frame for text.

Rules of Thumb for Bullet Charts

The first rule for a good bullet chart is *consistency*. To give your presentation a cohesive look, each bullet chart must have the same typeface, the same color, the same style of bullet markers, consistent spacing between lines, a title in the same typeface and same position from slide to slide, and so on. If you use the page layouts for bullet charts in the Freelance Graphics SmartMaster sets, your bullet charts will have a consistent look automatically.

But the page layouts cannot do the job for you completely. They do a great job of enforcing a consistent layout on your bullet charts. But a clean, direct writing style is also necessary to give your presentation the clarity and cohesiveness that are the hallmarks of a professional presentation.

The rules of thumb in the following sections can help you write effectively and avoid the pitfalls that often trap the unwary writer.

Make Text Legible!

It's remarkable, if inexcusable, how often text charts are simply unreadable. If your audience cannot read or decipher your text charts, you have failed to communicate.

Text charts can be illegible for a variety of reasons. The point size of your typeface may be too small for your audience to read. Perhaps the words blend in with the background color (orange text on a red background is nigh impossible to read). Or maybe you chose some ornate, Gothic font that is difficult to read up close, much less on a screen 30 feet away from your audience.

Avoid All Caps

Don't succumb to the temptation of casting your message in an all caps style. WORDS IN ALL CAPS ARE DIFFICULT TO READ BECAUSE IT IS HARDER TO DISTINGUISH AMONG THE LETTERS. BESIDES, ALL CAPS GIVES THE IMPRESSION THAT YOU ARE SHOUTING.

The all-caps style can work in small doses, especially for very short, declamatory messages or when shouting is appropriate, as in "FIRE!"

State One Thought per Line

Bulleted items lose their value if they are not concise. Limit each item to one thought.

Be Concise!

This rule flows from the last. Just as your viewers cannot digest more than one idea per line, they cannot digest a long line of text in a bulleted list. It is remarkable how often this rule is flaunted in presentations. How many times have you seen a chart similar to that in figure 2.10 in a presentation? Don't let this be your chart.

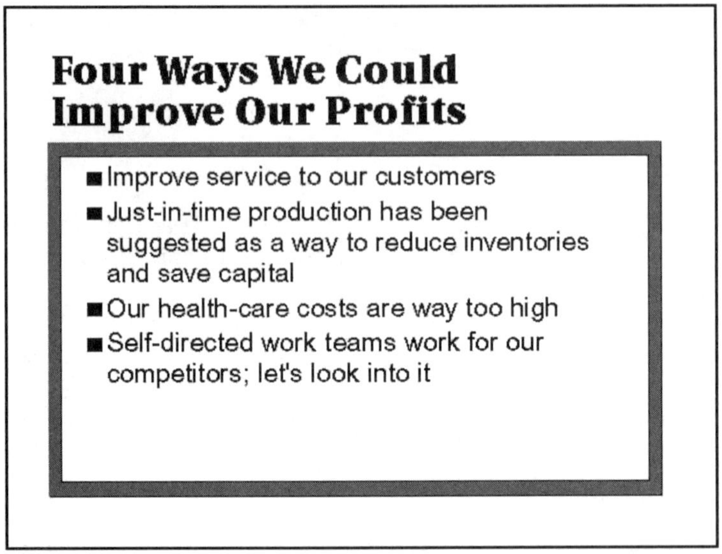

Four Ways We Could Improve Our Profits

- Improve service to our customers
- Just-in-time production has been suggested as a way to reduce inventories and save capital
- Our health-care costs are way too high
- Self-directed work teams work for our competitors; let's look into it

FIGURE 2.10. A long-winded text chart.

Observe the Rule of Sevens

Use seven words per line, seven lines per page. The number seven seems about right for the number of words in a line. Of course, this rule is merely a guideline, not a magic formula. Often ten or even more words per line may be just right. But it's a good rule to remember as a rough guide.

The eye has a difficult time reading a bullet chart with more than seven lines. Note that this number includes main points as well as subpoints. If you cannot say what you want in seven lines, break your chart into two separate text charts.

Compare the long-winded text of figure 2.10 with the more concise version in figure 2.11.

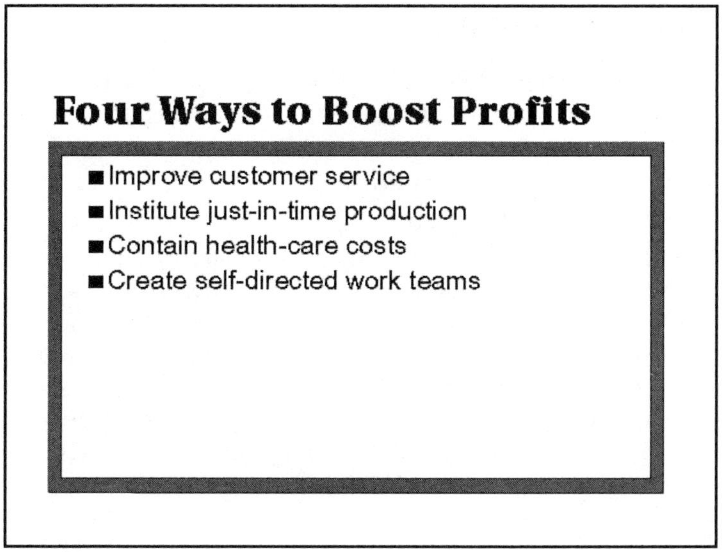

> **Four Ways to Boost Profits**
> - Improve customer service
> - Institute just-in-time production
> - Contain health-care costs
> - Create self-directed work teams

FIGURE 2.11. A more concise version.

Use Parallel Sentence Structure

Keep bulleted items grammatically parallel. In writing, parallelism means that sentences, clauses, or words contain the same grammatical elements. Caesar's "I came, I saw, I conquered" is a classic example of parallel structure. If Caesar had written of his military victory in Zela, "I arrived on the scene, I saw Zela, and then I conquered it," the statement would have been utterly forgettable instead of eminently quotable.

Although bullet lists need not (and probably should not) consist of complete sentences, you nevertheless should make the items grammatically parallel. If you don't, your points seem disjointed and unfocused. Again, compare the two bullet charts in figures 2.10 and 2.11. The second chart packs more punch. Starting each point with a verb is always an effective way of creating bulleted items.

A parallel sentence structure emphasizes your points, conveys a sense of order, and is aesthetically pleasing.

Use the Active Voice

The active voice, which follows subject-verb-noun structure, is more emphatic than the passive voice, in which the subject is acted on by a verb. Compare these two sentences:

> Sales must be increased. (passive)
>
> We must increase sales. (active)

The second sentence is obviously the more emphatic. A passive sentence is inherently weaker than an active sentence. In a passive sentence, the subject is acted on by the verb (e.g., "sales must be increased"). In addition, a passive sentence leaves some doubt as to who is doing the action. Sales must be increased, but by whom? This is why bureaucracies frequently favor the passive construction, especially when the news is bad. In an active sentence, however, the subject acts on the object (e.g., "we must increase sales"). The passive construction has it uses in certain forms of prose, but almost never in bullet charts.

Write Emphatic Titles

In presentation graphics, the title must carry the main burden of the message. Because your reader's eye jumps to the title first, grab this opportunity to state your case powerfully and succinctly.

Here again, favor action words. "Profits Skyrocket in Third Quarter" is better than the neutral statement "Third Quarter Results." Because the second title lacks a verb (and verve), it is unfocused, inert, and dull.

A Quick Course in Typography

The art of typography is complex and arcane (although it is becoming less so with the growth of computers and desktop publishing). Before long, you find yourself mired in an obscure vocabulary that has its roots in the technology of metal or wooden type. You read about ascenders and descenders, x-height, point size, picas, serifs, ligatures, and kerning. Fortunately, you can use type successfully without being steeped in the mysteries of the Gutenberg galaxy. But even the business user can benefit from a basic knowledge of typography.

Typefaces, Fonts, and Families

Beginners often are confused by the terms *typeface* and *font*. Before the era of computer-generated type, typeface and font had distinct meanings.

Strictly speaking, a *typeface* is a set of characters with a particular design, such as Times Roman, Garamond, or Bodoni. A font is a collection of characters (letters, numbers, punctuation, or fractions) in one typeface, size, and weight, such as 12-point Times Roman or 10-point Times Bold.

In the days of wooden or metal type, a skilled craftsman carved or cast each font separately. If you wanted 8-point type, you needed an actual tray of type distinct from 10-point or 12-point type. But, with electronic typefaces, the computer can generate any point size from one basic typeface. As a result, the distinction between typeface and font has blurred, and the terms are now often used interchangeably. In Freelance Graphics, the term *font* is used. But when you are talking about a general style of type (such as Time Roman or Helvetica), *typeface* is the more accurate term.

A family of type is a set of typefaces with the same design that varies in minor ways. Times Roman, Times Bold, and Times Italic, for example, are all members of the Times family of typeface. (Roman type, by the way, is simply regular type without emphasis, such as bold or italic.)

Figure 2.12 illustrates two different fonts.

12-point Utopia Black
abcdefghijklmnopqrstuvwxyz
ABCDEFGHIJKLMNOPQRSTUVWXYZ

14-point Avant Garde
abcdefghijklmnopqrstuvwxyz
ABCDEFGHIJKLMNOPQRSTUVWXYZ

FIGURE 2.12. Two fonts (a font is a collection of characters in one typeface, size, and weight).

Measuring the Size of Type

Typefaces are measured in picas and points. Here's how it works. There are approximately 72 points to an inch. Thus, 12-point type has a height of approximately one-sixth of an inch. As it happens, 12 points equal one pica, another term you may run across.

The typeface and size buttons on the status bar along the bottom border display the typeface and point size of the selected text, or—if no text is selected—the default typeface and size.

The Best Typefaces for Text Charts

Fancy typography has its place in books and print ads, but presentations don't require complex typography. Presentation text must be attractive and legible. A few rules can help you achieve this goal.

Serif versus Sans Serif

Serifs are small strokes that complement the main look of a letter. In printed text, serifs increase the legibility of text by making letters easier to distinguish from each other. The serifs also form a baseline that helps the eye follow a line of text. Serif typefaces help lead the eye through text.

A *sans serif* typeface has no serifs. Typically, sans serif typefaces are used as display type, where the reader has to take in only a few words. A sans serif typeface such as Helvetica or Arial MT (one of the typefaces in Adobe Type Manager, which comes with Freelance Graphics) projects a clean, simple look and is a good choice for display type.

Figure 2.13 illustrates the difference between serif and sans serif fonts.

Up-and-Down Style or Lowercase?

For some reason, people often feel compelled to begin every word in a list of bulleted items in initial caps. The bulleted list then reads "Our Profits Soared in March" instead of "Our profits soared in March." Why do people do this? Partly, it's simply dead tradition. Or perhaps presenters feel that their message seems more important if they use initial caps. This is a mistaken assumption. Reading Studies Have Shown Conclusively That the Up-and-Down Style Is More Difficult to Read Than a Sentence in Lowercase Words. It's not difficult to explain why.

The eye has to take a roller-coaster ride just to get through a sentence riddled with initial caps.

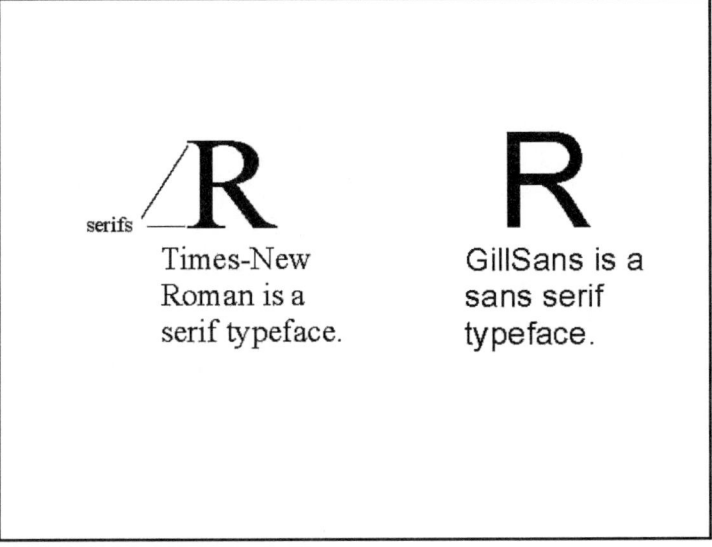

FIGURE 2.13. Serif and sans serif fonts.

Consider two valid uses of the initial capital letter:
- To mark the beginning of a new sentence. For the same reason, it's a good idea to begin each bullet point with a capital letter.
- To denote proper names. But when you start every word with a capital letter (even in a list of bulleted items), you make it difficult for readers to distinguish the proper nouns.

You lose the true utility of initial caps if you use them for every word in your bulleted lists.

Wrapping Up

This chapter has presented you with the basics of understanding and better using that most basic of presentation formats: bulleted lists. You have learned some rules of thumb for creating better bulleted lists. You also have learned a few new ways to present text, including combining words with graphics.

In the next chapter, you get greater detail about the mechanics of creating, formatting, and editing text in Freelance Graphics.

3

Creating, Editing, and Formatting Text

Freelance Graphics has its own word processing environment with many of the features found in standard word processors such as automatic word wrapping, the ability to change text attributes, user-defined margins and indentation, and the usual cut-and-paste operations.

If you use SmartMaster page layouts to create title and bullet charts (as you should), you probably don't need to delve into the more complex text-editing tools of Freelance Graphics. As you have seen, creating a bulleted list or a title page is a simple matter of clicking on the prompt text and typing your message. You don't often need to know how to change paragraph styles, margins, indent levels, or line spacing. The SmartMaster page layouts take care of these details for you. However, you do need to know how to change character attributes within a title or bullet chart so you can, for example, make a word boldface or italic. This chapter shows you how.

Sometimes you may need to go beyond the basics. For example, you may want to create a custom text block or change the typeface or line spacing of all the bullet charts in your presentation. This chapter also shows you how to do more complex editing.

In this chapter, you learn how to:

- *Create, edit, and size text blocks*
- *Change text attributes (such as boldface or color) for selected text*
- *Change default text attributes*
- *Work with paragraph styles*
- *Put a border around a text block*
- *Change margins and indents*
- *Copy, cut, and paste text*
- *Use accelerator keys to select and edit text*
- *Use the mouse to select and edit text*
- *Create special text effects, including rotated and curved text*
- *Use a symbol as a bullet style*

Text Block: A Definition

Text block is a term you encounter many times in this chapter. A text block is an object—with or without a border—that contains words. You can edit the words in a text block just as you can in a word processor. But, in Freelance Graphics, a text block is also an object that you can select, move, delete, copy, or size just as you would any other graphic object.

When you are creating bullet charts using page layouts, you simply fill in the text blocks that Freelance Graphics provides for you. To work on this level, you barely need to know what a text block is. But, when you need to add text to a diagram or annotate a chart, you have to know a little about working with text blocks.

Creating Text Blocks

As you learned in Chapter 2, "Bullet Charts and Beyond," creating a bullet chart is a simple matter of assigning the Bulleted List page layout—or one of the other page layouts for bulleted lists—to a presentation page, clicking the prompt text, and then typing your title and bulleted items. Freelance Graphics places, wraps, and formats the text you type automatically. The result is a well-designed bullet chart that has the same look as the rest of your presentation.

However, from time to time you may need to create your own text blocks for a variety of reasons. One of the most common is to add labels to annotate a chart or diagram.

You can create text blocks that wrap automatically or ones that do not.

- To create a text block, click the Text icon in the Toolbox, drag a rectangle on the page, and then start typing. If you type a long line of text, note that your text automatically wraps when you reach the right side of the text block.

- To create a text block that does not wrap, click the Text tool, click on the page without dragging a rectangle, and then start typing. Nonwrapping text blocks are good for labeling diagrams, charts, or illustrations.

If necessary, you can later change a wrapping to a nonwrapping text block (and vice versa) by marking or unmarking the check box in the Paragraph Styles dialog box.

Using the Text Panel and Text Ruler

As you are typing or revising text, you are working in edit mode. As you type, you see the text panel across the top of the text block. If you wish, you also can display a text ruler. Choose View View Preferences and then mark the Text block ruler check box.

The text panel (fig. 3.1) and ruler (fig. 3.2) contain several icons you can use to change the appearance of a text block.

The text ruler also shows the units of measurements used for measuring the width of the text block (millimeters, centimeters, inches, points, and picas). You can change the units of measurement with the View Units & Grids command.

The text ruler displays the left and right margin icons, as well as an icon for setting the first line indent icon (see fig. 3.2). If you are using SmartMaster page layouts, you can blissfully ignore these for now and still turn out good-looking text charts. When you want to change the left and right margin or the indent for the first line in a text block, read the "Margins" section later in this chapter.

FIGURE 3.1. The text panel contains the indent and outdent icons, a Tips button, and an OK button. Optionally, you can display a text ruler, as shown in figure 3.2.

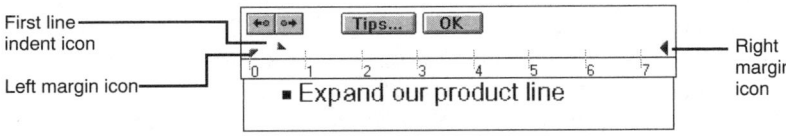

FIGURE 3.2. The text ruler measures the width of the text block. Note the first line indent icon and the margin icons.

When you are done adding text, you can leave text edit mode by clicking the OK button or by clicking outside the rectangle around your text. (If you prefer not to use the mouse, you also can complete the text block by pressing Esc or Shift+Enter.) You now see the completed text block on the page, with the eight selection handles displayed (unless you clicked outside the text block, which clears the selection handles).

Editing Text Blocks

Freelance Graphics offers a range of standard text-editing features. You can edit text—add it, delete it, copy it, or change its attributes—as you type or after you have created a text block. The techniques are the same.

To edit text, you must be in text edit mode. There are several ways to get there:

- Click twice (slowly) on a text block. If you click too quickly (that is, double-click), you open the Paragraph Styles dialog box.
- Click on a text block to select it and then press F2.
- Press F2 with no text block selected (if there is more than one text block on the page, you are placed in the first text block in text edit mode).
- Click the Text icon and then click the text block you want to edit.

All of these methods place you in text edit mode. Note the text panel across the top of the text block. Now you can select text, add new text, delete selected text, or change the attributes of selected text.

Selecting Text

Although you don't often have to change the paragraph styles for the text you add when you use page layouts to create bullet charts, you may want to change text attributes for a word or a line here and there. You can accomplish this without altering the paragraph styles. Read the "Using Accelerator Keys To Change Text Attributes Quickly" section later in this chapter to find out how.

However, before you can perform any action on text (such as changing text attributes or deleting or copying it), you must first select it. Selected text appears in reverse video as shown in figure 3.3.

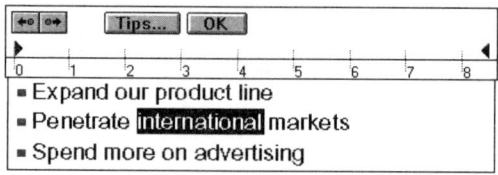

FIGURE 3.3. Selected text appears in reverse video.

The two basic ways of selecting text with the mouse are double-clicking and dragging.

- To select a single word, double-click it.
- To select a text string of any length, position the pointer over the beginning of the text you want to select, press the left mouse button, and then drag the mouse to highlight the text you want. Release the mouse button. This technique is known as *drag-selecting*.

As you type, it is inconvenient to pick up the mouse to select text because you have to lift your hands from their proper position over the keyboard. However, you can select text without removing your hands from the keyboard with various key combinations. Pressing Shift+End, for example, selects text from the insertion point to the end of the line.

Table 3.1 shows how you can use the keyboard to select various portions of text such as one line forward or backward. Table 3.2 shows how you can select text using the mouse.

TABLE 3.1. Selecting Text with the Keyboard

Key Presses	Result
Shift+RightArrow, Shift+LeftArrow	Select one character to the right or left of the insertion point.
Shift+DownArrow, Shift+UpArrow	Select from the insertion point to the next or previous line of text.
Shift+Home, Shift+End	Select from the insertion point to the beginning or end of the line.
Ctrl+Shift+RightArrow, Ctrl+Shift+LeftArrow	Select one word to the right or left of the insertion point.
Ctrl+Shift+DownArrow, Ctrl+Shift+UpArrow	Select from the insertion point to the next or previous period, exclamation point, or question mark.
Ctrl+Shift+Home, Ctrl+Shift+End	Select from the insertion point to the beginning or end of the text block.

TABLE 3.2. Selecting Text with the Mouse

Mouse Action	Result
Click	Moves the insertion point to the I-beam pointer's position.
Drag	Selects text as you drag.
Double-click	Selects the entire word at the position of the I-beam pointer.
Double-click and drag	Selects the entire word the I-beam pointer is on and then selects words and spaces as you drag.

continues

TABLE 3.2. continued

Mouse Action	Result
Shift+click	Selects all text between the I-beam pointer and the insertion point.
Shift+double-click	Selects all text between the I-beam pointer and the insertion point, including the entire word the I-beam pointer is on.
Shift+double-click and drag	Selects all text between the I-beam pointer and the insertion point, including the entire word the I-beam pointer is on, and then continues to select as you drag.

Deleting, Copying, and Pasting Text

You can delete, copy, and paste selected text within a single text block or from one text block to another. Freelance Graphics supports the standard Windows methods for deleting, copying, and pasting text.

- To delete the highlighted word or phrase without copying it to the Clipboard, use Edit Clear, press Del, or click the Edit Clear SmartIcon.

- To remove the highlighted text from your screen and copy it to the Clipboard, choose Edit Cut, press Ctrl+X or Shift+Del, or click the Edit Cut SmartIcon. You can restore objects you cut to the screen with Edit Paste (provided you don't cut any other text in the meantime).

- To copy highlighted text to the Clipboard, choose Edit Copy, press Ctrl+C or Ctrl+Ins, or click the Edit Copy SmartIcon.

- To copy highlighted text from the Clipboard to the text insertion point, choose Edit Paste, press Ctrl+V or Shift+Ins, or click the Edit Paste SmartIcon.

Copying Text between Text Blocks

To copy text from one text block to another, first select the text, and then use Edit Cut or Edit Copy to place the text on the Clipboard. Then select the target text block, press F2 to enter text edit mode, place the insertion point where you want to copy the text, and choose Edit Paste (or click the Edit Paste SmartIcon). If text in the target text block is highlighted when you paste the new text, the new text replaces the highlighted text.

Changing Character Attributes

If you let SmartMasters make your design choices for you (usually a good idea), the only formatting changes you may need to make are to change a word or phrase to boldface type or perhaps to change the color of a line of text. These are known as local changes because they override the settings specified by the paragraph style. You can change text attributes such as typeface, size, color, and appearance (boldface, italics, underscore, and strikeout).

Suppose you want to make a word boldface. First, enter text edit mode. Then use the mouse to select the word. From the Text menu (fig. 3.4), choose Bold. As a shortcut, you can select a word and then press Ctrl+B or click the Bold SmartIcon. This chapter contains tables of shortcuts for selecting and changing text attributes for both the keyboard and the mouse. (You also can use this technique to change all the text in a selected text block at the same time—just select the text block, but don't enter text edit mode. The change you make affects all the text in the block.)

You also can change text attributes for a selected text block. The latter method is good for changing the attributes of all the text blocks on a page at the same time. Suppose that you are creating a diagram with labels and want to make all the labels bold. Press F4 to select all the text blocks on a page and then press Ctrl+B.

The fastest way to change the appearance of selected text is to use the SmartIcons for boldface, italics, underline, and normal.

Edit	F2
Font...	
Bullet...	
✓ Normal	Ctrl+N
Bold	Ctrl+B
Italic	Ctrl+I
Underline	Ctrl+U
Strikeout	
Reset To Style	
Paragraph Styles...	
Frame...	
Curved Text...	

FIGURE 3.4. Use the Text menu to change text attributes locally.

A Design Tip

When you overdo the use of text attributes, your page looks jumbled and disjointed. If you want to use boldface, choose just one or two words to emphasize.

Using Accelerator Keys To Change Text Attributes Quickly

If you are one of those keyboard partisans who shun mice, abhor menus, and generally dislike moving your hands away from the keyboard, Freelance Graphics offers a handful of accelerator keys that enable you change text attributes without taking your hands off the keyboard. For example, press Ctrl+I to turn on italic mode. All the text you now type is displayed in italics. Press Ctrl+I again to turn off italic mode.

All of these keys are toggles; that is, they turn the emphasis mode on if it is off and vice versa. If you press Ctrl+I, everything you type is in italics and remains in italics until you press Ctrl+I again or until you press Ctrl+N, which stands for normal text and removes all emphasis attributes (italic, boldface, underline, and strikeout).

Also note that you can add emphasis modes cumulatively as you type. You can press Ctrl+I to use italics, then press Ctrl+B to use boldface and italics, and so on.

Besides changing text attributes as you type, these keystrokes also change the attributes of selected text. Table 3.3 lists the accelerator keys used for changing text attributes.

TABLE 3.3. Using Accelerator Keys To Change Text Emphasis

Keyboard Accelerator	Result
Ctrl+I	Italic
Ctrl+B	Bold
Ctrl+U	Underline
Ctrl+S	Strikeout
Ctrl+N	Normal: removes italic, bold, underline, and strikeout
Ctrl+C	Color: displays the Text Color dialog box so you can choose a color

Reverting to Paragraph Styles

Suppose you have changed text attributes in a text block and then decide you want to return to the default text attributes as specified in the SmartMaster text block. This is easily done. Just select the text and then choose the command Text Reset To Style.

Editing Multiple Text Blocks

If you are using the 2-Column Bullets page layout, there are three text blocks on a page: one for the title block and two for the side-by-side columns. Suppose you want to move quickly from one to another of these three text blocks. Select the first text block you want to edit and then press F2. Make your edits in text edit mode and then, with the insertion point in the last line of text in the block, press the DownArrow key. This takes you to the next text block and places you in text edit mode. To move to the previous text block, position the insertion point in the first line of text and press the UpArrow key.

Quick Editing with the Right Mouse Button

Release 2.0 of Freelance Graphics for Windows introduces right mouse button support. When you click the right mouse button over an object (including a text block), Freelance displays a pop-up menu (fig. 3.5) of possible actions relating to text. Move the highlight to a choice and release the mouse button to select it. You also can press the first letter of choice to select it. This is often the fastest way to enter text edit mode, change font and bullet styles, edit paragraph styles, and add a border to a text block.

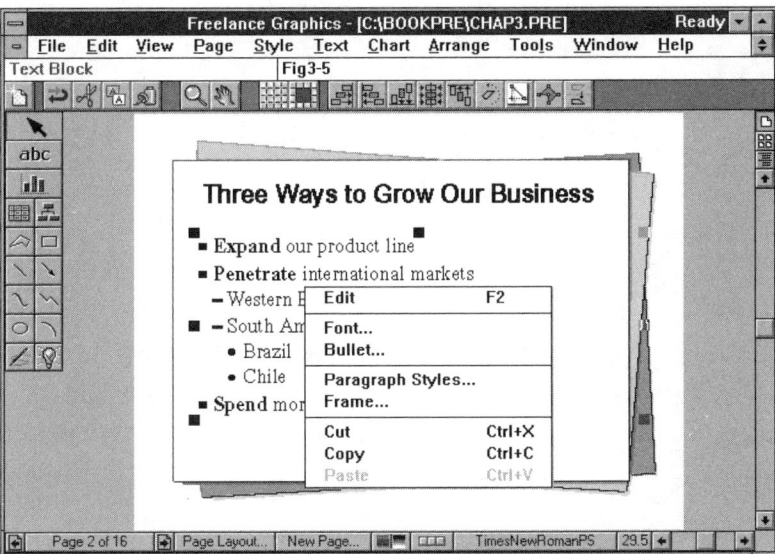

FIGURE 3.5. Pop-up menu of quick text-editing features.

Sizing Text Blocks

You can size text blocks the same way as you do any other graphic object in Freelance Graphics—just drag one of the selection handles in the direction you want. You can use the mouse or the keyboard to change the size and dimensions of a text block.

One limitation of Freelance Graphics for Windows 1.0 was that you could not size or move SmartMaster text blocks on a presentation page. You were forced to make such changes in SmartMaster Pages view. Version 2.0 corrects this problem. Now you can size a SmartMaster text block the same way as any other. If you later want to revert to the size specified by the page layout, you simply choose the page layout again (with the command Page Choose Page Layout).

Sizing with the Mouse

You can change the size of a wrapping text block by clicking a selection handle and dragging it in any direction. The text rewraps to fit within the new text block, but the size of the typeface remains the same (see fig. 3.6).

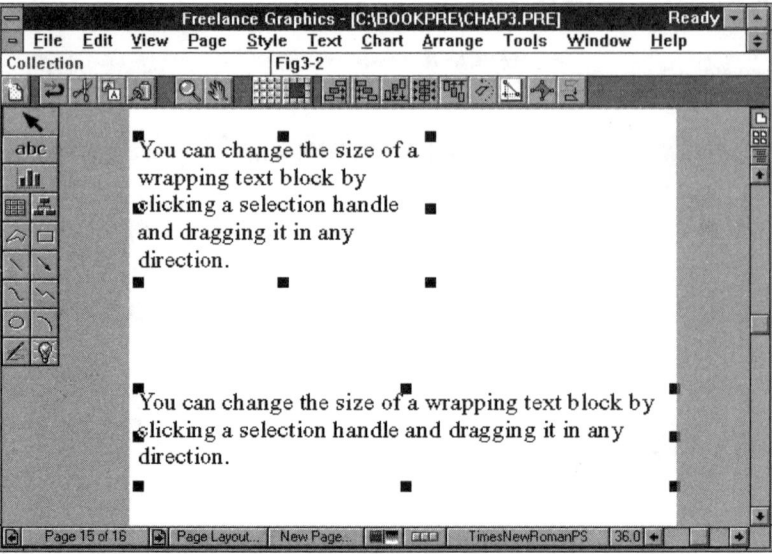

FIGURE 3.6. Drag any one of the eight selection handles to change the size of a text block.

Sizing with the Keyboard

To change the size of a text block with the keyboard, select the text block. Then press the period key to move the cursor to the selection handle from which you want to begin sizing. Each time you press the period key, the cursor moves to the next selection handle. Now press an arrow key to size the block in the direction you want. To size the text block in a different direction, starting from a different selection handle, press Enter and repeat the procedure.

For more information about sizing text and other objects by dragging selection handles, refer to Chapter 13, "Editing Objects."

Changing Font Size by Dragging a Text Block

Here's a quick way to size a text block when you do not require an exact point size. Just select a text block, press Shift, and drag one of the selection handles (or press the arrow keys). As you drag, the text size gets larger or smaller, but the line wrapping remains the same.

Understanding Paragraph Styles

As you create bullet charts using SmartMaster page layouts, you need to understand that Freelance Graphics formats text according to paragraph styles. This understanding is especially helpful if your bullet chart has subpoints, as in figure 3.7, which uses three paragraph styles.

Here's how it works. In the text block that contains the body text of a bulleted list, each bulleted item has a paragraph style assigned to it. Each paragraph style determines the typeface, size, color, bullet style, and indents for all text assigned to that paragraph style. The page layout for Bulleted List, for example, has different settings for each of the three paragraph styles.

Every paragraph in a text block has a paragraph style associated with it. In Freelance Graphics, a paragraph is defined as text separated by a carriage return (which you create by pressing Enter at the end of a line).

If you use page layouts to create bulleted lists, you seldom (if ever) have to change paragraph styles. But, if you do want to change the size of a typeface or the line spacing in your bullet charts at a global level, you can do so by changing the paragraph styles. For more information, read the "Changing Paragraph Style Settings" section later in this chapter.

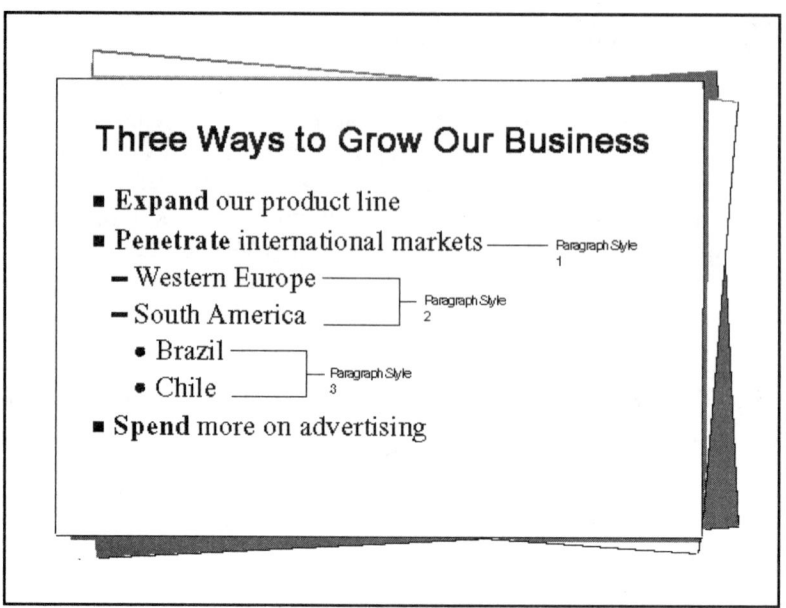

FIGURE 3.7. This bullet chart, which uses the Bulleted List page layout, uses all three paragraph styles.

However, even if you don't need to change paragraph styles, you do need to know how to assign paragraph styles to text. To create a bulleted list with subpoints, for example, you must assign a different style to the subpoints so that they receive the proper formatting. This was covered in Chapter 2, "Bullet Charts and Beyond." To summarize, first position the insertion point (the blinking vertical line that indicates the location of text you type) in the line of text that will be a subpoint. Then do one of the following:

- If you are positioned on the first character of a paragraph, press Tab or click the right-pointing arrow in the text panel to move from style 1 to style 2 or from style 2 to style 3. (If you are not positioned on the first character of a paragraph, Tab works like an ordinary Tab.)
- Press Shift+Tab or click the left-pointing arrow in the text panel to back up one level (from style 3 to style 2 or from style 2 to style 1).

When you change the style of a paragraph, the formatting changes associated with the new style are displayed immediately. (Note that the style assigned to text also is reflected in the Outliner view of your presentation, as described in Chapter 4, "Using the Outliner.")

Starting a New Line without a Bullet

Sometimes you may want to add a new line of text in a bulleted list without starting a new paragraph. Suppose, for example, that you want to add a line or two of text beneath a bullet, but don't want to start a new bullet point or create a subpoint (by pressing Tab to move to the next level).

Each time you press Enter, you begin a new paragraph and, consequently, get a new bullet marker. To avoid this, press Ctrl+Enter at the end of a line. This starts a new line at the same level as the bulleted item, but does not add the bullet (see fig. 3.8).

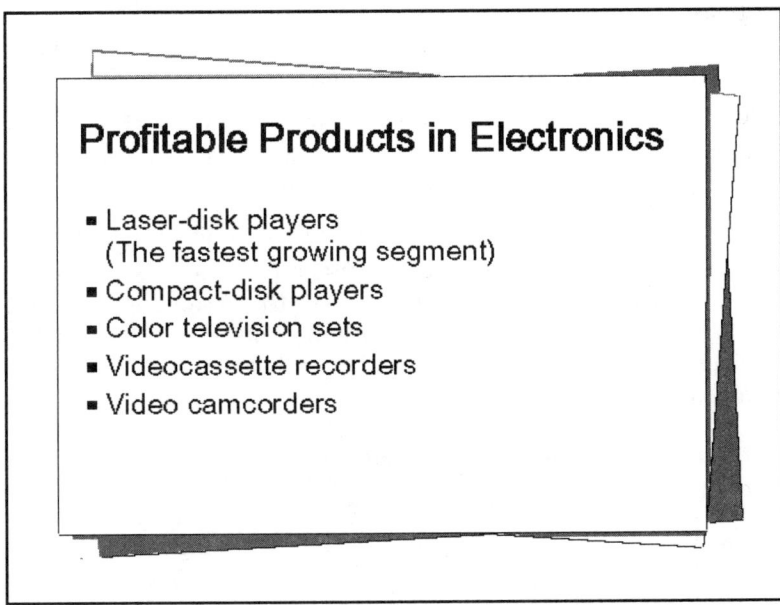

FIGURE 3.8. The line in parentheses after "Laser-disk players" was created by pressing Ctrl+Enter. This line is in the same paragraph and thus has the same paragraph style as the previous line.

Changing Paragraph Style Settings

The appearance of a paragraph in a text block—apart from its content—is determined by the paragraph style that you assign to it. You can assign a first-, second-, or third-level style to any paragraph in a text block. Each style is a collection of settings that specify the precise look of the text, including typeface, size, color, bullet markers, spacing, and indentation levels.

If you create a text block and start typing, the text receives paragraph style 1 formatting until you change it. You can assign a new style to a paragraph by positioning the pointer in a line of text and pressing Tab (or clicking the right-pointing arrow in the text panel) or Shift+Tab (or clicking the left-pointing arrow in the text panel).

When you type a paragraph in a text block (even if it is only one line), you can assign paragraph style 1, 2, or 3 to it. You can assign paragraph styles without regard to hierarchy; that is, the first paragraph in a text block can be style 3 and can be followed by a paragraph style 1 paragraph.

Freelance Graphics uses paragraph styles to set up the formats for SmartMaster text blocks. For more information on page layouts, see Chapter 25, "Understanding SmartMaster Sets."

You can change paragraph styles by changing the settings in the Paragraph Styles dialog box (fig. 3.9). There are three ways to do this:

- Select a text block and then choose Text Paragraph Styles from the menu.
- Double-click the text block (this works whether or not the text block is selected).
- Click the right mouse button over a text block and choose Paragraph Styles.

Now you can make your changes in the Paragraph Styles dialog box. The first step is to choose the scope of your changes. Click the button for 1st, 2nd, or 3rd, or All. If you click 1st, the changes you make apply only to level 1 text. If you click 2nd, the changes apply only to level 2 text. If you click All, the changes you make apply to all paragraph styles.

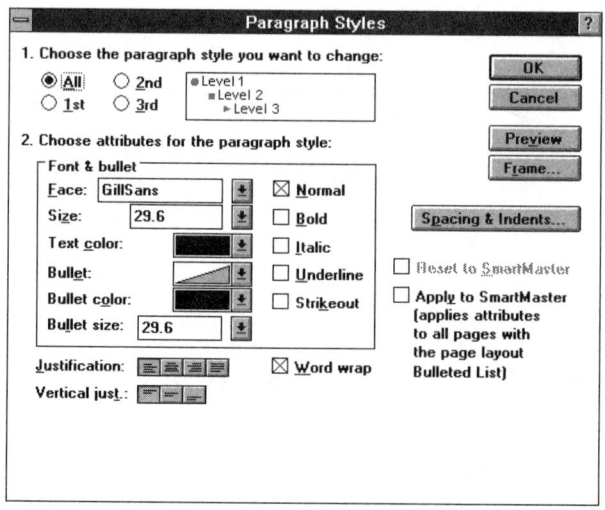

FIGURE 3.9. The Paragraph Styles dialog box.

Note that when you choose All, some attributes boxes may either contain the word "Mixed" or a triangle. Both of these indicate that at least two levels in the text block have different settings for this attribute. For example, if the text color is blue for level 1 and black for level 2, the Text color box contains a triangle. If you change this color to red with All selected, all paragraph styles subsequently have red text. To change the text color for one level only, click the button for 1st, 2nd, or 3rd, then make the color change.

Applying Changes to SmartMaster Page Layouts

What if you make a change to a bulleted list (change the bullet style, for instance) and decide you want to make the same change to all the bulleted lists in your presentation?

In the Paragraph Styles dialog box (fig. 3.9), find the Apply to SmartMaster check box. When you mark this check box, Freelance Graphics applies the attribute changes specified in the Paragraph Styles dialog box to the current page layout. Thus, all pages that use the current page layout also are changed.

For example, double-click the bulleted list on a page that uses the Bulleted List page layout. In the Paragraph Styles dialog box, change the text color to blue. Mark the Apply to SmartMaster text block and then click OK. You have just changed the text color for bulleted lists for the Bulleted List page layout. All presentation pages that use the Bulleted List page layout are changed: In this case, text in bulleted lists is now blue.

Should you want to return to the defaults specified in the original SmartMaster set, use the command Style Choose SmartMaster set to reapply the same SmartMaster set. Click OK in the message box informing you that page layouts have been changed. This will remove the formatting changes you have made.

Try It: Change Default Text Attributes

Suppose you are adding call-outs to a diagram and want to make all the call-outs yellow. The following procedure changes the default text attributes for all new text blocks you add in a presentation (but it doesn't change the default attributes for an existing text block). For more information on changing default Toolbox attributes, see Chapter 24, "Customizing Freelance Graphics."

1. Double-click the Text icon in the Toolbox.
2. Click the 1st button. You may need just the first paragraph style to add call-outs. But, if you want to use two text colors on the page, you could set up different colors for the first and second paragraph styles.

3. Click the arrow in the Text color drop-down box.
4. Click the yellow rectangle in the foreground section of the color palette and then click OK.

Subsequently, each text block you add to the page is yellow. You can use the same basic procedure to change the text attributes for a single text block.

Changing Line Spacing and Indents

If you are using the SmartMaster page layouts provided with each SmartMaster set, you may not need to change the spacing and indents of your text blocks. But, if you create your own text blocks, you may want to change these settings occasionally.

Margins

There are two ways to change margins within a text block. You can use the text ruler or the Spacing & Indents dialog box. Using the text ruler is probably the easiest method if you are changing a margin as you are working in a text block and aren't concerned with a precise margin setting. If you need a margin of precise size, click the Spacing & Indents button in the Paragraph Styles dialog box.

Margin settings are paragraph styles

Note that margin settings are paragraph styles. If you change a margin setting, you change it for every paragraph at the same level. Before you change a margin setting, make sure that the insertion point (the blinking vertical line) is positioned in a paragraph that is assigned to the level you want to change.

Try It: Make a Numbered List

You can easily make a numbered list in Freelance Graphics. You don't have to type the individual numbers. You simply specify a number as the bullet style, and Freelance automatically numbers your paragraphs.

1. Create a text block by clicking the Text tool in the Toolbox and dragging a rectangle on the page.
2. Type the text for the item and press Enter.
3. Type the text for the remaining items and then click OK.
4. Click the right mouse button over the text block and choose Bullet.

5. Click the Style drop-down box, select 1, and then click OK. Each first-level paragraph now has a number in front of it. Freelance automatically takes care of the sequence of numbers. You also can use a letter or a Roman numeral as the bullet style. To create a list with letters or Roman numerals, choose a, A, or I.

Creating an Indented Paragraph

To create a text block in standard paragraph format (see fig. 3.10), with the first line in each paragraph indented several spaces, you can either drag the first line indent icon on the text ruler or type a value in the first line box in the Spacing & Indents dialog box. To view this dialog box, double-click a text block and then click the Spacing & Indents button.

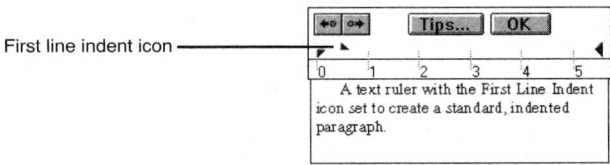

FIGURE 3.10. A text ruler with the first line indent icon set to create a standard, indented paragraph.

Justifying Text

The Paragraph Style dialog box contains settings that affect the text block as a whole, regardless of paragraph styles. These are vertical justification, word wrap, and frame style settings.

Vertical justification controls the vertical position of the text in a text block. Text can be aligned at the top, bottom, or center of a text block.

Word Wrapping

You can turn word wrap on or off for an entire text block. By default, word wrap is turned on, and this is the most useful setting. The only time you might want to turn word wrapping off is to create a label or other short piece of text that you always want to be on a single line (for example, when you are annotating a chart). To create a nonwrapping text block when you create a text block, click the Text tool, click the page, and start typing (don't drag a text block before you start typing). You can change the word wrap setting for an entire text block.

Adding a Border

You can add a border to a text block and fill the area with a color or pattern. Use this feature to add a dramatic effect to a text block or to call attention to it.

The fastest way to add a frame is to click with the right mouse button over a text block and then choose Frame. Next, change the Edge and Area settings in the Text Frame dialog box (fig. 3.11).

You also can open the Text Frame dialog box by double-clicking the text block and then clicking the Frame button or, with a text block selected, choosing Text Frame from the main menu. Figure 3.12 shows a creative use of frames.

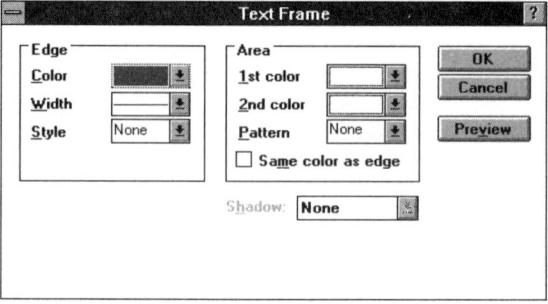

FIGURE 3.11. Use the Text Frame dialog box.

Special Text Effects

The purpose of text is mainly to present a verbal message cleanly and legibly. But, considered as a graphic object, text lends itself to several transformations. You can rotate text, create curved text, or create text with drop shadows.

As with all special effects, exercise good judgment and taste when you choose to transform text. These effects are most useful for creating one-of-a-kind diagrams, flyers, announcements, or title pages.

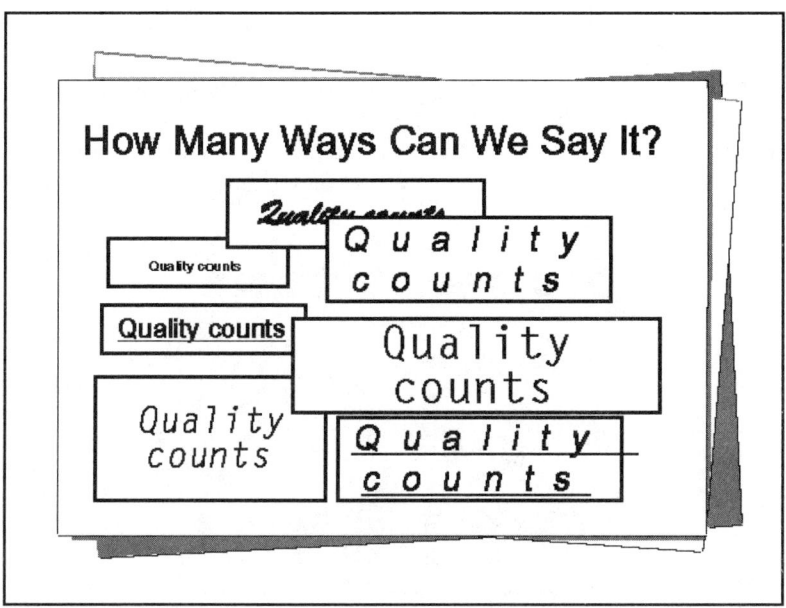

FIGURE 3.12. You can frame text blocks to create a variety of diagrams.

Rotated Text

Especially when you are creating diagrams, rotated text can be an eye-catching effect. To rotate text, select the text block and choose Arrange Rotate or click the Rotate SmartIcon. This feature has one limitation: You cannot rotate a SmartMaster text block on a presentation page.

You can edit rotated text the same way as you do any other text block. When you enter text edit mode, the text appears as a normal, nonrotated text block. When you complete the text block, the text is returned to its rotated form.

Chapter 15, "Creating Business Diagrams," contains a section that shows you how to create a logo using rotated text.

Curved Text

One of the new features of Freelance Graphics 2.0 is the ability to create curved text. Curved text has long been used by skilled graphic artists, but has been beyond the reach of the average user. Now you can create curved text by making choices from a dialog box.

First, type the text that you want to transform. Then, with the text block selected, choose Text Curved Text (fig. 3.13). In the resulting Curved Text dialog box, highlight one of the 29 predefined curved-text styles and then click OK. If you're not sure which style you want, click the Preview button to try out several styles.

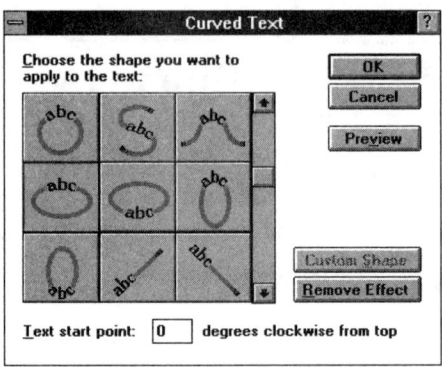

FIGURE 3.13. The Curved Text dialog box.

When you choose an effect that forms a complete circle, the Text Start Point option is available. This option specifies the angle at which the curve starts, as in figure 3.14.

If you select an existing curve and a text block, the Custom Shape button is available: Clicking it uses the selected curve as the shape to apply to the text. Figure 3.15 shows an example of curved text.

Editing Curved Text

After you create a curved text block, you can edit the text the same way as you do normal text. When you select curved text and enter text edit mode, the text block returns to its normal shape so you can make your changes. When you leave text edit mode, the text block returns to its curved shape.

You can size curved text blocks the same way as you do any Freelance object. See Chapter 13, "Editing Objects," for more information about sizing objects. When you drag a selection handle to change the size of a curved text block, the point size of the text also changes.

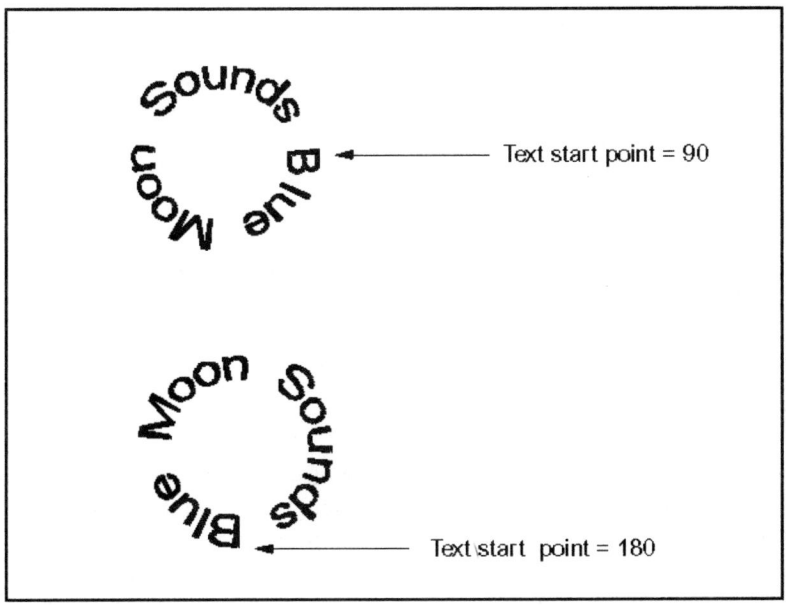

FIGURE 3.14. A text start point value of 0 starts at 12:00 o'clock, 90 at 3:00 o'clock, 180 at 6:00 o'clock, and so on.

FIGURE 3.15. A simple flyer created using one of the curve shapes available in the Curved Text dialog box.

Creating Custom Curves

If none of the shapes available in the Curved Text dialog box is just the shape you want, you can create your own custom shape. You can use lines, polygons, curves, arcs, or lines created with the Freehand tool as the shape for your text. If you want to use a circle as the basis for the curve, you must first use the Arrange Convert command to transform the circle to lines or polygons.

To create a custom shape, select both the line or curve and the text. Then choose Text Curved Text. Click the Custom Shape button in the Curved Text dialog box. Freelance Graphics applies the curve to the selected shape.

Text with Drop Shadows

Text with drop shadows lends depth and drama to ordinary words and is a surefire way to attract the viewer's eye to a page. Unlike rotated and curved text, Freelance Graphics cannot create drop-shadowed text automatically. But the task is nonetheless relatively simple. For step-by-step instructions for creating drop shadows with text, see Chapter 15, "Creating Business Diagrams."

Use a Symbol as a Bullet

For an interesting visual effect, you can use a symbol as a bullet, as in figure 3.16. You can use any symbol in the Freelance Graphics symbol library as a bullet. To set this up, double-click over a bulleted list. In the Paragraph Styles dialog box, choose Symbol from the Bullet drop-down list. This opens the Choose Symbol for Bullet dialog box. Now highlight the symbol you want to use for a bullet style and click OK. Click Preview to see how the new bullet style looks. If the symbol is too small, you can make it larger by choosing a larger value for Bullet Size.

Wrapping Up

This chapter has covered a lot of ground. Because most presentations consist mainly of text, it's important that you learn to use text well. As you've seen, Freelance Graphics has a variety of sophisticated text-handling features.

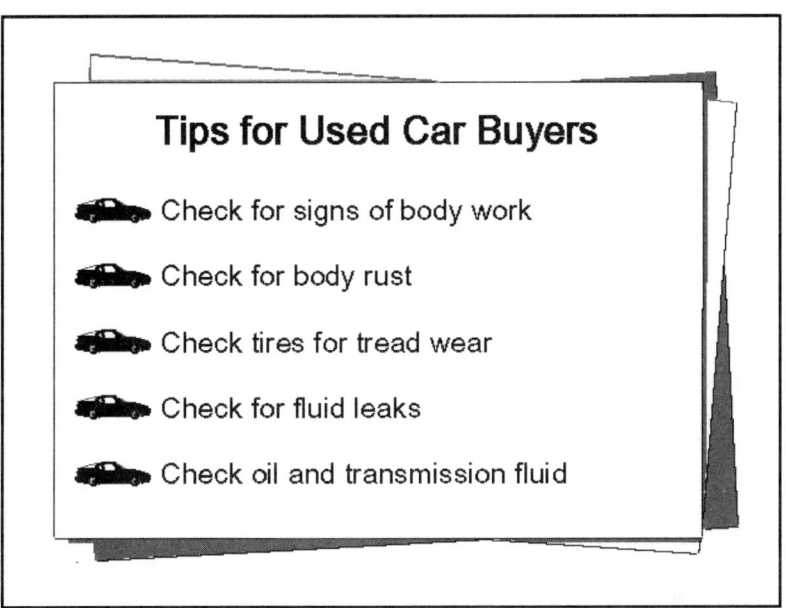

FIGURE 3.16. The car used for bullets is from the TRANSPOR.SYM symbol library. To make the car large enough, a value of 96 was used for Bullet Size in the Paragraph Styles dialog box.

You have learned how to create and edit text. You should now feel comfortable creating and editing your own text blocks, as well as text in SmartMaster text blocks. You can size text blocks or copy text among text blocks. You know how Freelance Graphics uses paragraph styles to control text formatting on page layouts and you should be able to change default text attributes by changing paragraph styles. In addition, you know how to interpret and use the text panel and the text ruler. You also can change margins and indents in text blocks.

You've learned how to use accelerator keys to edit text quickly. If you are a fan of the mouse, you've learned to use the mouse to select and edit text. If you are so inclined, you can now add special text effects such as rotated, curved, and drop-shadowed text.

The next chapter covers the Outliner, which can streamline the process of creating and editing presentations.

4

Using the Outliner

Your sixth grade teacher was right: Creating an outline really is the best way to organize a speech, presentation, or report. An outline provides an instant structure for your thoughts.

The Outliner view in Freelance Graphics is one of the program's three primary views (the other two are Page Sorter view and Current Page view). Besides having many of the features of a standard electronic outliner, the Outliner gives you a high-level view of the text on your presentation pages. Where the Page Sorter view shows the structure of your presentation from a graphical viewpoint, as a series of thumbnails, the Outliner view shows you the structure of your presentation in the form of structured text.

In this chapter, you learn how to:

- *Work in the Outliner view*
- *Create bullet charts automatically by typing text in the Outliner*
- *Change paragraph styles in the Outliner*
- *Add new pages in the Outliner*
- *Move pages in the Outliner*
- *Navigate in the Outliner*
- *Make the Outliner view the default view*
- *Move between the Outliner and other views*
- *Import and paste text into the Outliner*
- *Print an outline*

Why Use the Outliner?

To move to Outliner view, click the Outliner icon on the right border of the Freelance Graphics window or choose View Outliner.

The Outliner view resembles a yellow legal pad. You use it as a starting point to get your ideas down on "paper" (electronic paper), just as you might jot down ideas on a yellow legal pad.

71

> ## Changing the Background Color of the Outliner
>
> By default, Outliner view resembles a yellow legal pad. If you prefer a white background, you can change the view. You make this change in the FLW2.INI file, which you can find in your WINDOWS directory. First, close Freelance Graphics and then open FLW2.INI in any ASCII text editor (the Windows Notepad is fine). Look for the line that reads "White Outliner=0." Change the *0* to *1*. When you restart Freelance, the background of the Outliner will be white.

The Outliner view shows the textual flow of your presentation.

There are several good reasons to use the Outliner. How you use it depends as much on your working style as the job at hand. You can use the Outliner to:

- *Get a feel for the flow of a presentation.* Like the Page Sorter, the Outliner gives you a high-level view of multiple presentation pages at once. However, the Outliner gives you a text-only view. This view is perfect for checking the flow of your ideas. For example, you can examine one bullet chart in the context of adjacent bullet charts; scroll through the text of all your bullet charts to see if your words convey the message you intend; or check the transitions between pages to make sure your ideas are logically connected.

- *Create bullet charts automatically.* If you are the type of person who feels comfortable working with text, and your presentation consists primarily of bullet charts, you can create almost your entire presentation in Outliner view. The text you type becomes bullet charts, as described in the "Creating Bullet Charts Automatically" section.

- *Change text levels.* The text levels in the Outliner correspond to the page title and assigned paragraph styles in bullet charts. The text to the right of a Page icon is the page title. Beneath the page title are bulleted subpoints, corresponding to Paragraph Styles 1, 2, or 3 in bullet charts. You can change text levels in the Outliner (see the "Changing Paragraph Styles" section).

- *Add, move, and delete pages.* Although you cannot add graphics in the Outliner, you can add new pages and then move to Current Page view to add graphics to your text. You can delete any presentation page in the Outliner whether or not it contains graphics. You can also move pages in the Outliner.

- *Assign page layouts.* You can assign new page layouts in the Outliner view. Choose the command Page Choose Page Layout and double-click the name of the page layout you want.

What the Outliner Shows (and What It Doesn't)

You can display any presentation in Outliner view whether you created the presentation in Outliner view or not. The beginning of each new page is denoted by a Page icon and a page number to the left of the icon.

A Page icon denotes the start of each new page.

In the Outliner, the title of a bullet chart (or of any page) appears to the right of the Page icon. The major points in a bullet chart are indented and have bullets. If the bullet chart has subpoints, they are indented further and have a different style of bullet.

What if a presentation contains a graph page? In Outliner view, you see just the title of the page next to the Page icon. However, other symbols inside the Page icon show that the page contains other types of objects, for example, a bullet chart. Figure 4.1 shows the variations of the Page icon.

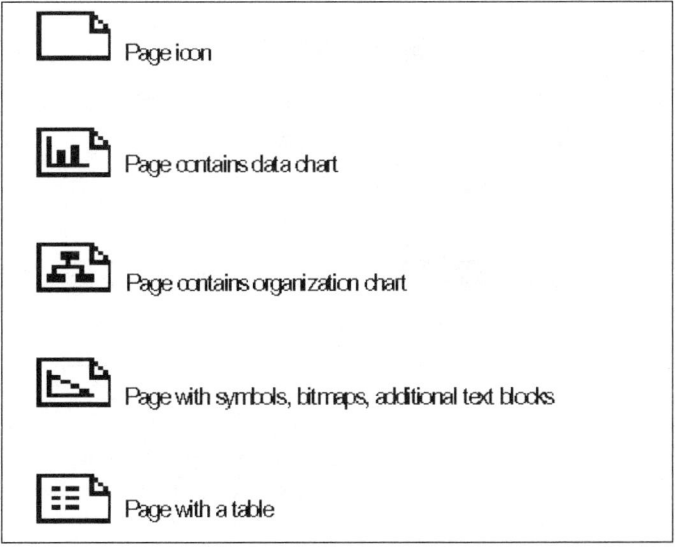

FIGURE 4.1. The Page icon displays different symbols depending on the contents of the presentation page it represents.

Creating Bullet Charts Automatically

Type text in the Outliner to create bullet charts automatically.

If you are verbally oriented, you can create your presentation directly from the Outliner view (see fig. 4.2). This is a very efficient way to create a series of bullet charts. As you type your outline, Freelance Graphics automatically creates a bullet chart for each headline and its subheadings, using the Bulleted List page layout (see fig. 4.3).

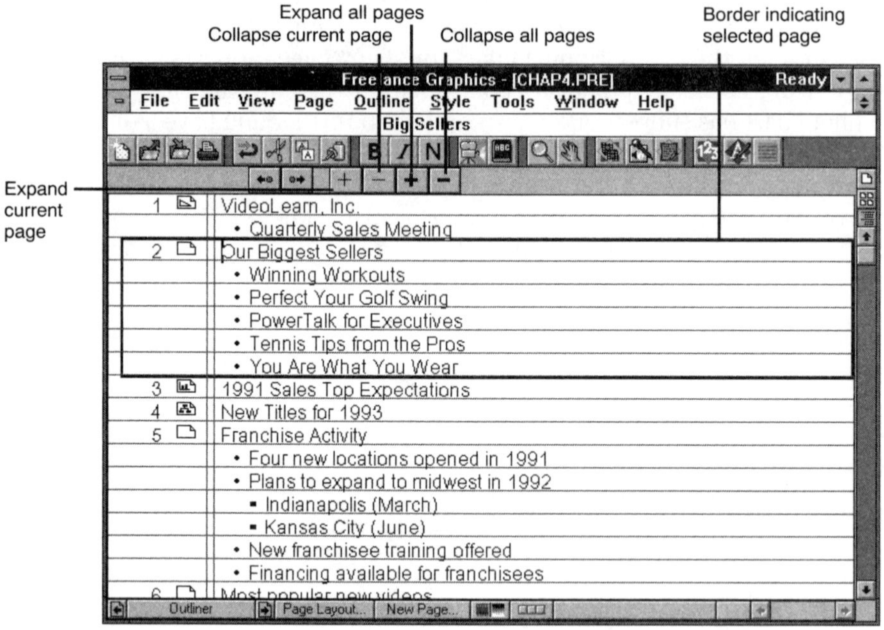

FIGURE 4.2. You can create bullet charts by typing in the Outliner.

As you type in the Outliner, the first line (next to the Page icon) becomes the title of the bullet chart, and subheadings become individual bullet points. You can add up to three levels of subheadings in the Outliner, corresponding to Paragraph Styles 1, 2, or 3.

You also can use the Spell Checker in the Outliner. Choose Tools Spell Check and then select Outliner.

Bulleted Items in Two Columns

In Outliner view, a special symbol marks pages that use the 2-Column Bullets page layout, as shown in figure 4.4. The symbol appears to the left of the line beginning the second column. You can start the second column by clicking in the line in which you want the second column to start and then choosing Outline Make Second Column. This command is not available unless the 2-Column Bullets page layout is assigned to the current page. Figure 4.5 shows a finished two-column bullet chart.

Using the Outliner   75

Our Biggest Sellers

- Winning Workouts
- Perfect Your Golf Swing
- PowerTalk for Executives
- Tennis Tips from the Pros
- You Are What You Wear

FIGURE 4.3. A finished bullet chart.

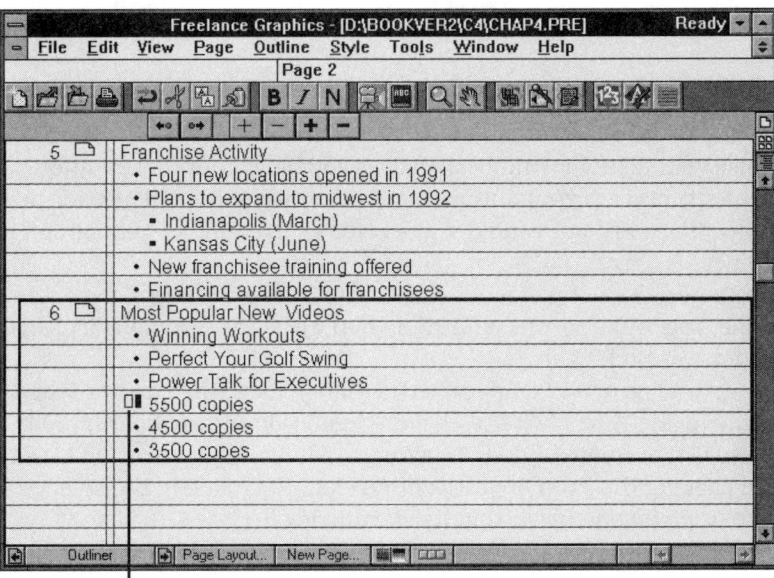

Indicates start of second column

FIGURE 4.4. A page in the Outliner with the two-column page layout assigned.

FIGURE 4.5. A finished two-column bullet chart.

Changing Paragraph Styles

Because your ideas inevitably change as you build your presentation, you can modify the structure of your outline easily by promoting and demoting headlines and subheadings. Promote and demote refer to changing the paragraph style in the Outliner.

To promote a line of text (move it to the left in the Outliner), move the cursor to the line you want to promote and then click the Promote icon. (On the keyboard, press Shift+Tab.)

To demote a line of text (move it to the right), move the cursor to the line you want to move and then click the Demote icon. (On the keyboard, press Tab.)

You also can promote or demote a range of lines by highlighting several lines and then clicking the Promote or Demote icon. Each line in the selected group moves up or down one level from its starting level.

> ### Making Outliner View the Startup View
>
> If you prefer to work in Outliner view, you can set up Freelance Graphics to use Outliner view as the default view whenever you start the program or create a new presentation. Choose Tools User Setup and then click the Outliner button under Startup View. Now, when you start Freelance Graphics, you begin in the Outliner view. For more information on changing the defaults of Freelance Graphics, read Chapter 24, "Customizing Freelance Graphics."

Selecting, Moving, and Deleting

As your presentation evolves and grows, you can change the hierarchy of lines within one page or move entire pages around. Your first task should be to learn how to move entries in the Outliner.

Selecting Lines and Pages

Before you can promote or demote lines or move, delete, or copy lines and pages, you must first select them. There are various ways to select adjacent lines and pages. Try all the methods and then use the method that works best for you.

- Click with the left mouse button over a Page icon to select the first page and then click with the right mouse button to select additional (adjacent) pages. Alternatively, you can click a series of adjacent Page icons with the right mouse button. To select just lines, click on the bullets themselves.
- Drag a box around the pages or lines to be selected. There are two methods you can use to do this. To select pages by dragging, click to the left of the number next to a Page icon and drag a box around the pages you want to select. To select lines by dragging, click to the left of a bullet (outside the double-red lines) and then drag a box around the bulleted items you want to select.
- You also can click to the right of text in the Outliner and then drag to select additional pages or bulleted items.

Moving Pages

To move the position of a page in the Outliner, simply click a Page icon and drag it to a new position. A thick horizontal bar shows you the position of the page.

When you click a Page icon, an outline appears around the entire page, and the triangle-shaped Move Page icon appears. Move the icon above or below another Page icon to move the entire page. You also can move more than one page with this technique. Select several pages and then drag any one page icon to move all the pages.

Adding a Page

There are two ways to add a new page in the Outliner:
- Choose Page New.
- Position the pointer at the end of any line, press Enter, and then press Shift+Tab (or click the Promote icon).

Deleting a Page

Deleting a page in Outliner view removes the page from your presentation. If you delete pages in the Outliner, exercise a bit of caution. Since the Outliner can't display graphics, you can never be sure what you are deleting. If you are uncertain, return to Current Page view before you delete.

To delete a page in the Outliner, first select the entire page by clicking the Page icon. Then press Edit Clear (Del) or Edit Cut (Shift+Del), or click the corresponding SmartIcons. Freelance Graphics asks for your confirmation before deleting the page.

If the cursor is on the last line of a page in the Outliner, pressing Delete removes the page break and merges the next page with the current page. If the cursor is positioned at the beginning of the first line on a page, pressing Backspace removes the page break and merges the line with the previous line on the page above.

Navigating in the Outliner

You can move around the Outliner by pointing and clicking with the mouse or by clicking the scroll bars. However, if you are a keyboard maven, you can zip around quickly with the keystrokes in table 4.1.

TABLE 4.1. Keystroke Navigation in the Outliner

Keystroke	Action
Home, End	Moves to start or end of a line
Ctrl+Home, Ctrl+End	Moves to top or bottom of the outline
PageUp, PageDown	Moves up or down one full screen
Ctrl+PageUp, Ctrl+PageDown	Moves up or down one page (from one Page icon to the next)
UpArrow, DownArrow	Moves up or down one line
Ctrl+Right, Ctrl+Left	Moves right or left one word

Moving between the Outliner and Other Views

As the skeleton of your presentation begins to take shape in the Outliner, you can move to Current Page view at any point to flesh it out with additional text or graphics. Because the Outliner is a two-way outliner, the text you add in Outliner view also updates presentation pages in Current Page view. Also, the changes you make in Current Page view are also reflected in the Outliner view. Such flexibility lets you shuttle between any of the views of Freelance Graphics without losing information or structure.

This freedom to move among views can be useful. For example, as you tinker with the high-level structure of your outline, you may get a brilliant idea for a graphic that you want to add to a particular page right away (before the thought vanishes). There are two ways to move quickly from the Outliner to the current page:

- Choose View Current Page or click the Current Page icon on the right border.
- Double-click a Page icon to move to Current Page view.

Each of these methods displays the Current Page view for the selected page, as determined by the position of the insertion point (the blinking vertical line) in the Outliner. To return to Outliner view, just click the Outliner icon on the right border or choose View Outliner.

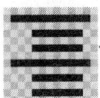

Note that you cannot access Outliner view from Page Layouts view. For more information about Page Layouts view, read Chapter 25, "Understanding SmartMasters."

Expanding and Collapsing an Outline

New with Release 2.0, Freelance Graphics can expand and collapse text in the Outliner. This means that you can view just the title of every page or all of the lower levels of text in each page, as shown in figure 4.6.

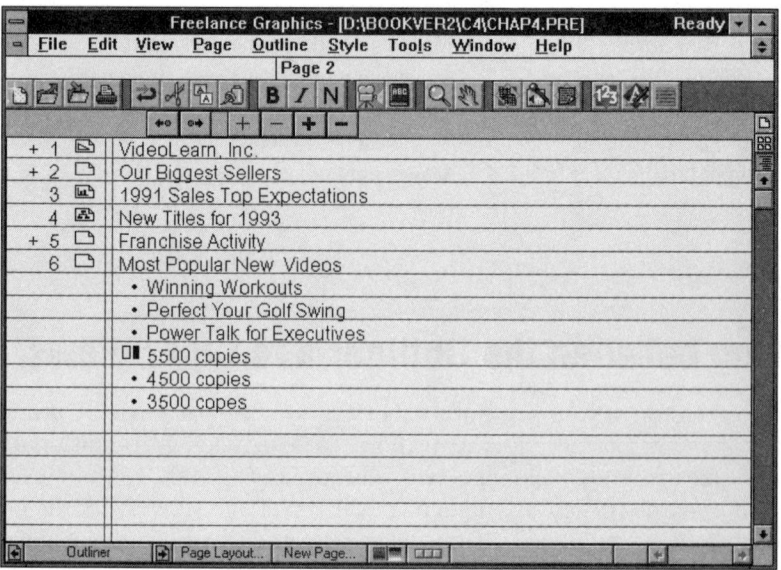

FIGURE 4.6. A partially collapsed outline. The plus sign to the left of a Page icon denotes a collapsed page. Page 6 is fully expanded.

Why display just page titles? In the condensed view, you can get a feel for the flow of the main ideas of your presentation without being distracted by the details of subpoints. The collapsed view also gives you a handy way to rearrange pages. Choose Collapse All, select the page you want to move, and drag it to a new position. This is especially useful with large presentations.

Try It: Expand and Collapse Text

You can expand or collapse text from the menu or by clicking icons:
1. To collapse the text in the Outliner and display page titles only, choose Outline Collapse All (or click the Collapse All icon).
2. To show the page titles and all lower levels of text, choose Outline Expand All (or click the Expand All icon).
3. To collapse or expand the text in a single page, click the Page icon and then choose Outline Expand or Outline Collapse or click the corresponding icons.

Importing and Pasting Text into the Outliner

You can copy text into the Outliner from another part of your presentation, from another presentation, or from another application. You can import text from a file or copy text via the Windows Clipboard.

You can import or paste text directly into the Outliner.

Importing ASCII Text

You can also import ASCII text directly into the Outliner. Choose File Import, type the file name and path for the ASCII file in the File Name text box, and then click OK. Freelance Graphics formats imported ASCII according to the number of leading spaces or tabs in the text. Here's how it works:

- Text with no leading spaces or tabs starts a new page and becomes the page title.
- Text preceded by a single space (or tab) becomes Paragraph Style 1 text.
- Text preceded by two spaces (or tabs) becomes Paragraph Style 2 text.
- Text preceded by three spaces (or tabs) becomes Paragraph Style 3 text.

If you want to selectively import an ASCII text file, press F6 from the Outliner, specify the name of the text file in the Import Data File dialog box, and click OK. Highlight the range of text you want to import and click OK. This copies the text to the Clipboard. Choose Edit Paste to paste the text into the Outliner.

Pasting Text

You can also paste text into the Outliner with Edit Paste (or click the Edit Paste SmartIcon). Here's how it works:

- If text is selected in the Outliner (in reverse video), the new text replaces the highlighted text.
- If no text is selected, the pasted text comes in at the insertion point (as indicated by the blinking vertical line).

Just as when you import text, Freelance Graphics assigns text levels according to the number of spaces or Tabs at the beginning of each line. See the previous "Importing ASCII Text" section.

Working Together: Pasting Text from an Ami Pro Outline

You can create presentations from Ami Pro outlines and transfer the outline structure intact into Freelance Graphics. In Ami Pro, use Edit Copy to copy the text you want to move to Freelance Graphics. In Freelance Graphics, use Edit Paste to copy the text directly to the Outliner.

When you paste text from an Ami Pro outline, outlines levels are translated into Paragraph Styles 1, 2, or 3. If there are more than three levels in the Ami Pro outline, these are pasted as Paragraph Style 3 text in Freelance Graphics.

Copied Ami Pro text with no outline level is not pasted into Freelance Graphics. In Ami Pro, use the Styles Outline Styles command to see which text styles have outline levels.

Printing an Outline

With Freelance Graphics for Windows Release 2.0, you can print your outlines. Choose File Print (or click the Print SmartIcon) and then click the Outline radio button in the Format area of the Print File dialog box.

Wrapping Up

You should now feel at ease working in the Outliner. For roughing out a first draft or for checking the flow of your presentation, Outliner view is perfect. The Outliner is also a great tool for creating bullet charts quickly, rearranging lines and pages, moving and deleting pages, assigning new page layouts, and importing and pasting text.

The next chapter, "Checking Your Spelling," shows you how to banish typos and embarrassing spelling errors from your presentations.

5
Checking Your Spelling

A spelling error in a presentation is embarrassing. There it sits, magnified tenfold by the slide projector, an eyesore. It proclaims loudly, "unprofessional!" Members of your audience may mutter to themselves, "Gee, if this guy can't even take the time to check his spelling, how accurate can the rest of his presentation be?" A small chink in your credibility opens. If you suddenly notice it, your confidence may begin to wilt.

You can avoid your most embarrassing moment in a presentation by using Freelance Graphics's spelling checker to weed out the errors and typos in your presentation. Spell checking is fast and easy.

Spell checkers are similar to backup software packages: People know how to back up their software, but don't want to invest the few moments required to do so. The same is true with a spelling checker. It's easy to use, but worthless unless you use it. So make a habit of using it!

Incidentally, as part of its "Working Together" strategy, Freelance Graphics 2.0 uses the same spell-checking engine as Ami Pro. In fact, if Ami Pro is already installed, the Freelance installation program does not bother to install the spell checker, which saves disk space and makes it easier for users of both products.

In this chapter, you learn how to:

- *Specify the scope of the spell-checking operation (by word or page or for your entire presentation)*
- *Include data charts, organization charts, and speaker notes in the spell check*
- *Add words to your custom dictionary*
- *Add another language dictionary*

Tell Freelance What To Spell Check

You can spell check a word, a page, or an entire presentation. To start the spell-checking process, choose Tools Spell Check or click the Spell Check SmartIcon. A dialog box (see fig. 5.1)

presents you with various choices. The first three items are Selected word(s), Current page, or Entire presentation. Click one of these to set the scope of the spell-checking operation.

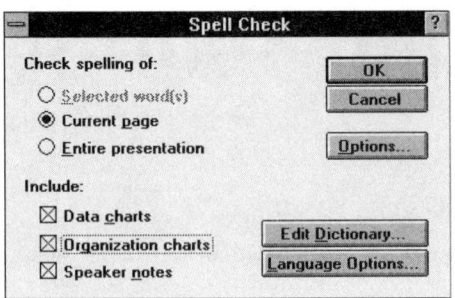

FIGURE 5.1. The Spell Check dialog box.

The next set of choices, in the Include area of the dialog box, enables you to further specify which parts of your presentation you want to check. Freelance can check spelling in data charts, organization charts, and speaker notes. Just mark the check box next to any of these choices. Remember that you can choose only one radio button in a list, but can select multiple check boxes.

Click the Options button to further fine-tune the way Freelance checks the spelling of your work. The dialog box in figure 5.2 appears. You can mark the check boxes to include any of the following options:

- *Check for repeated words*. With this option selected, Freelance will flag repeated words (such as "the the"). Typing double words is a very common typing error that is difficult to spot.
- *Check words with numbers*. If you are writing a technical or marketing document, your work may contain words such as "3rd," "TEST5," or "Part975." If your presentation contains many such words, you may want to exclude them from a spell-checking operation.
- *Check words with initial caps*. This option checks the spelling of words with initial capital letters (Mary, Xylox, Mississippi). You may or may not want this. If your presentation contains many product names, for example, you may prefer not to have the spell checker flag every one. This can slow down a spell-checking session considerably.
- *Include user dictionary alternatives*. If you mark this check box, Freelance lists words that you have added to the custom dictionary in the Alternatives list when it flags a misspelled word. This can be a lifesaver if you, for example, always misspell your boss's name.

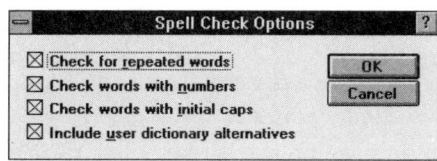

FIGURE 5.2. The Spell Check Options dialog box.

To bypass the Spell Check dialog box, you can check your spelling at any time by pressing Ctrl+F2. This starts the spelling checker and automatically chooses the scope depending on where you are in Freelance.

- If you are in text edit mode, Freelance checks the spelling of the word at the insertion point.
- If you are in Outliner view, Freelance checks the spelling of the word at the insertion point.
- If you are not in text edit mode, Freelance checks the spelling of the current page.
- If you are in Page Sorter view, Freelance checks the entire presentation.

Press Ctrl+F2 to activate the spell checker or click the Spell Check SmartIcon.

Check Spelling in Data Charts, Organization Charts, and Speaker Notes

Although you naturally may be most concerned about checking the spelling in title pages and text charts, spelling errors can also creep into your data charts, organization charts, and speaker notes. And these can be difficult to find, especially in data charts and organization charts, where the text tends to be small.

To have Freelance Graphics check the spelling in data charts, organization charts, or speaker notes, mark the corresponding check box in the Spell Check dialog box. Why wouldn't you always want to check the spelling in your graphs or organization charts? The reason is that checking every part of your presentation can slow down the process. This is especially true of data charts because Freelance checks all the text in a chart, including axis labels.

Incidentally, Freelance examines the words on page layouts as well as presentation pages and allows you to correct the misspelled words in page layouts while you remain in Presentation Pages view.

Try It: Check Your Spelling

You can check the spelling in a presentation page. Make sure there is at least one misspelled word on the page to make the experiment useful.

1. With a presentation page on the screen, click the Spell Check SmartIcon.
2. Choose the options you want in the first Spell Check dialog box (see fig. 5.1) and then click OK.

As shown in figure 5.3, Freelance displays the first misspelled word—it's underlined—in a dialog box along with a few words from the line in which it occurs. At the bottom of this dialog boxes are six buttons. Some of these are obvious, while others require a bit of explanation.

- *Replace All* replaces all instances of the misspelled word in your entire presentation.
- *Replace* replaces the current word only.
- *Skip All* marks the flagged word (and all other instances of this word in your presentation) as correct and makes no changes. Typically, you use this option when the spelling checker flags a product name or proper name.
- *Skip* marks the current word as correct but will flag the next occurrence of the word in the presentation.
- *Add to Dictionary* includes this word in your custom dictionary. Because this dictionary is used for all your presentations, when you add a word to the dictionary, it is included for all future presentations you create or edit.
- *Cancel* halts the spelling check, closes the dialog box, and returns you to the point in the presentation where you initiated the spell-checking operation.

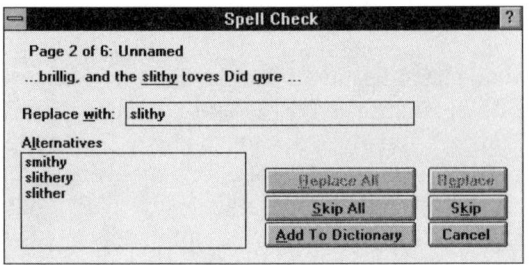

FIGURE 5.3. The Spell Check dialog box.

Create a Custom Spelling Dictionary

You can create your own custom dictionary with this option. The purpose of a custom dictionary is to add words that are unique to your company or group (proper names, jargon, or product names) to a dictionary so Freelance Graphics won't flag them as misspelled whenever they occur. Note that the spell checker already knows many personal names (e.g., Wally, Josh, and Heather) but flags others (e.g., Mehitabel, Frobisher, and Horatio). This can save you the trouble of entering the name of every Tom, Rick, and Mary in your company.

To add a word to the custom dictionary (see fig. 5.4), click the Edit Dictionary button in the Spell Check dialog box. Then type the new word in the New word box and then click Add (simply clicking OK does not add the word). To remove a word, highlight the word in the Current words box and then click Delete. Click OK to save your changes and close the dialog box.

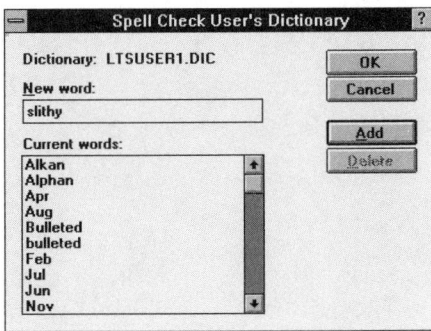

FIGURE 5.4. The Spell Check User's Dictionary dialog box.

Avoid These Traps!

When you add a new word to the dictionary with an initial lowercase letter (foo), Freelance does not flag the word if it occurs with an initial capital letter (Foo). But if you add the new word to the dictionary with a capital letter (Foo), this is the only spelling Freelance accepts.

Here's another caveat. If you enter a misspelled word in the custom dictionary, Freelance Graphics henceforth assumes it is spelled correctly in all future presentations, and you may have sabotaged the effectiveness of the spelling checker. Be careful!

Part 3
Data Charts

Data charts (such as bar, line, and pie charts) are a staple in most presentations. This part covers the process of choosing the right chart type for your data, creating and customizing data charts, and importing and linking to data from 1-2-3 worksheets.

This section includes:

Chapter 6. Choosing the Right Chart Type

Chapter 7. Creating Data Charts

Chapter 8. Customizing Data Charts

Chapter 9. Creating Charts from 1-2-3 Worksheets

6

Choosing the Right Chart Type

After you enter your data into Freelance Graphics—you can type it or import it—Freelance Graphics can crank out over 18 basic chart types. And, for each basic chart type (such as horizontal bar or pie), you can choose numerous variations. You can specify three-dimensional bars, change the position of the legend, customize grid lines and tick marks, change the style of frame around your chart, and so on.

It's exhilarating to have such an abundance of choices, but all the choices in the world don't help you decide which chart type best suits your data. Would a vertical bar chart best show the relationship of your revenues to expenses over the last five years or would a line chart be preferable? How about a pie chart or a hybrid chart type, such as the line-bar chart?

Freelance Graphics can produce well-designed charts for you based on the numbers you give it and the chart type you choose, but it's up to you to choose an appropriate chart type. The purpose of this chapter is to teach you how to choose the right chart type based on your data and the message you want to deliver.

> *In this chapter, you will learn how to:*
>
> - *Determine whether or not a graph is appropriate for your presentation.*
> - *Choose a graph type that fits your data and purpose*
> - *Choose between line, area, and bar graphs*
> - *Determine bar graph options, such as vertical or horizontal bars, stacked bars, 3D bars, and clustered bars.*
> - *Use pie charts effectively.*
> - *Use specialized charts, such as high-low-open-close, XY (scatter), table, and bar-line graphs.*

What's Your Purpose?

Before you embark on the chart-creation process, you should know where your ship is heading. The first question to ask yourself is basic: Do I need a chart at all? Often, the answer is a resounding no! If you only have a few data points to chart, a simple table may be preferable.

If you decide a chart is called for, take a moment to define the purpose of your chart. There are two major categories of charts:

- *Charts that report data.* This type of chart, such as a quarterly report, is the graphical variation of the just-the-facts school of journalism. Charts for reporting purposes don't try to persuade. They merely present the data and let the audience come to its own conclusions.
- *Charts that present data.* This type of chart is the main focus of this book and of Freelance Graphics. Where report charts are neutral, presentation charts strive to persuade an audience. When you create a chart for a presentation, you should already know what you want the chart to convey. And, you must design the chart so that it delivers the message you intend.

You already know that charts deliver your message with more power, persuasiveness, and clarity than words alone. Presumably, that's why you chose a presentation graphics package.

Suppose that you have the numbers you want to use as the basis for creating a chart. So far, so good. But, when faced with the task of creating a chart, you are suddenly confronted with over 18 basic chart types and dozens of variations. How do you choose?

Choosing the right chart type for your data is not always a simple choice; however, it's not brain surgery either. The following sections supply a few simple rules for you to use so that you can create charts with confidence.

Using the Graph Type Table

Table 6.1 provides and easy method of honing in the chart type that's right for you. Use this table as the first step in zeroing in on the appropriate chart type. Check the first column to find out which entry best categorizes your data. The last column lists chart types appropriate for your data. The chart types match those available in Freelance Graphics.

Suppose your data, like most business data, changes with time. According to table 6.1, there are a variety of chart types that are suitable for displaying time-series data. You can choose from line charts, area charts, or several types of bar charts.

To narrow your choice further, turn to the individual sections on these chart types to see which one is best for you. After a while, you may find yourself automatically choosing the right chart type for your data. Sometimes, though, there is no single correct choice for your data. Nevertheless, you can usually narrow your options down to one or two suitable chart types.

TABLE 6.1. Recommended Chart Types

Type of Data	Recommended Chart Types
Data that changes with time	Bar
	3D bar
	Stacked bar
	3D Stacked bar
	3D bar (XYZ)
	Line
	Bar-line
	Area
	3D area/line
Data at a single point in time	Horizontal bar
	Horizontal stacked bar
Parts of the whole	Single pie
	3D pie
	Multiple pies
Stock market data	High-low-close-open
Exact data	Table
	Number grid under chart
	Number grid
Relationships between variables	XY (scatter)
	Radar

Line, Area, or Bar Chart?

If your data varies over time, you are faced with eight chart types from which to choose. The first step in narrowing your choices is to count your data pairs.

For ten or fewer data pairs, choose a bar chart. For more than ten data pairs, choose a line or area chart.

- If the answer is ten or fewer, choose a bar chart to see the exact data.
- If you have more than ten data pairs, choose a line or area chart to see overall trends.

These are rules of thumb only and should not be slavishly followed. However, it's a good place to start.

If you have narrowed your choice to a line or area chart, consult the sections on line and area charts to choose between these chart types.

Bar Charts

Bar charts are certainly the most common—as well as the most versatile—chart type. You can illustrate any number of numeric relationships with bar charts. Bar charts come in a wide variety of flavors including horizontal, vertical, segmented, clustered, and paired.

Bar charts are instantly appealing without much adornment. Whereas lines are sometimes weak, bars are automatically rather majestic looking. Bars rising from the page—like a city skyline—are intrinsically bold and visually gripping.

Moreover, it's easy to interpret bar charts. People easily grasp the significance of bars. They know that the height (or length) of the bar measures a subject (sales, profits, revenues, or inventory). The varying heights of the bars make it easy to make comparative judgments about the relative sizes of bars (and what they represent). You can look at a bar chart and see in an instant which company has the highest profits, which company is number two, and so on.

Horizontal or Vertical Bars?

Use bar charts to measure items in time.

A bar chart is a logical choice for graphing time-series data (fig. 6.1). Each bar in a bar chart displays the data values for an item at regular time intervals (for example, sales data for 1991 by month).

In principle, you can portray the same data with either a horizontal or a vertical bar chart. After all, the only difference is the orientation of the bars and the position of the scaled axis.

In a vertical bar chart—sometimes called a column chart—the items (generally time periods) are displayed along the horizontal (unscaled) axis, and the bars that represent the values for each item are measured against the vertical (scaled) axis.

In a horizontal bar chart, this orientation is reversed. Bars project from the vertical (unscaled axis) and are measured against the horizontal (scaled) axis.

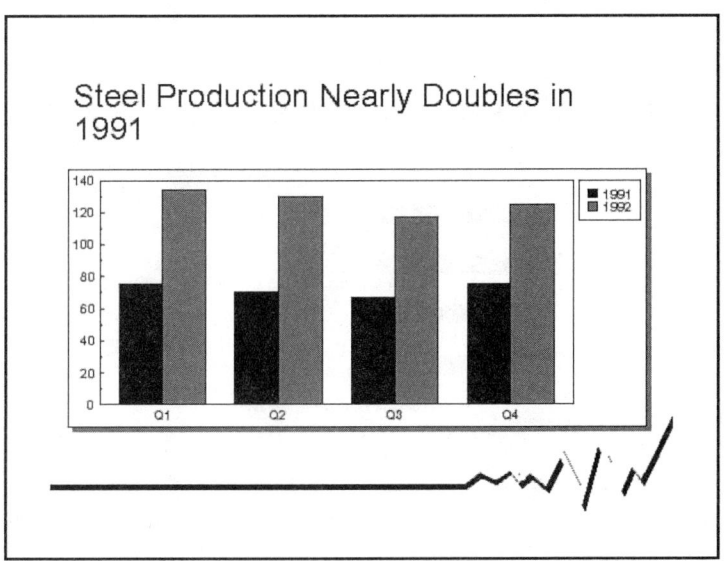

FIGURE 6.1. Vertical bar charts are ideal for showing items that change over time.

In practice, however, vertical and horizontal bar charts serve quite different purposes:

- The vertical bar chart (fig. 6.1), with bars rising from the horizontal axis, is best suited for displaying data that changes over time (profits by quarter, monthly expenditures, and so on). People naturally associate left-to-right movement with the change of time.

- Horizontal bar charts (fig. 6.2), by contrast, are best suited for ranking items at a single point in time (earnings by industry, professions with the highest salary, customer preferences, and so on). Also, horizontal bars accommodate long labels handily.

Stacked Bar Charts

Stacked bar charts display values for multiple sets of related items. Typically, each bar segment in the stack measures a different, but related, item for the same time period. In figure 6.3, the stacked bar chart shows the sales of three products for the same time periods. The primary emphasis is on the total sales of all three products. The secondary emphasis is on the relative sizes of each segment.

Stacked bar charts display values for multiple sets of related items.

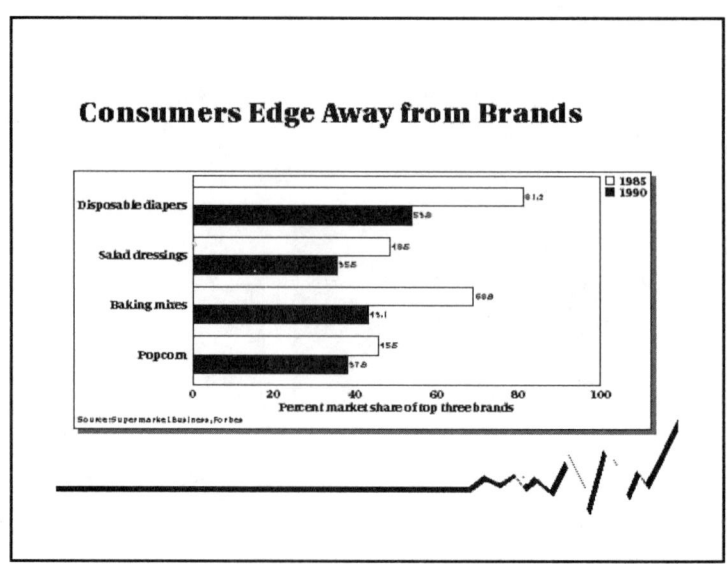

FIGURE 6.2. Horizontal bars are best suited for ranking items at a single point in time.

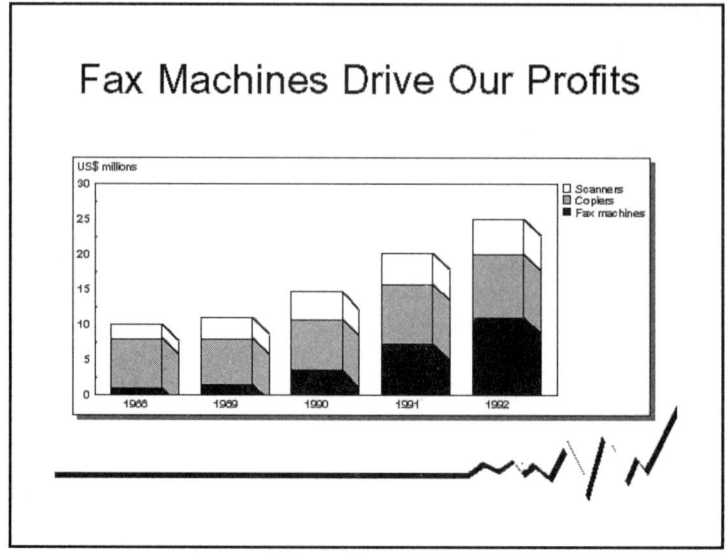

FIGURE 6.3. This stacked bar chart shows the sales of a company's three major products for the same time intervals.

A stacked bar chart depicts two types of information in a single chart. It is really two types of chart in one. The chart in figure 6.3, for example, shows how each product has sold from 1988 to 1992. You can compare the segments in each stack (the sales of fax machines have risen dramatically from 1988 to 1992), or you can measure the total sales of all three items for each year (the sales of all products have increased from 1988 to 1992).

Unfortunately, this dual functionality of the stacked bar chart is also its weakness. Take a look at figure 6.3 again. Are sales of copiers higher in 1990 or 1991? You can't tell by looking at the segments. That's because the segments do not share a common baseline and lack a common reference point. The drawback of a stacked bar chart is the difficulty in comparing the size of bar segments across time.

If you want to emphasize the value of each segment rather than the sum of the segments, use a clustered chart instead. See the "Clustered Bar Charts" section on the next page for more information.

Another way to overcome this limitation is to use the Number Grid Under Chart option. Select the chart, choose Chart from the menu, and then choose Number Grid Under Chart. Now, as in figure 6.4, you can see the exact data for each segment. The table combines a legend and a data table. Note that the axis labels become column headers for the table, and the legend becomes row labels. This overcomes a limitation of segmented bar charts: the difficulty of comparing segments across items.

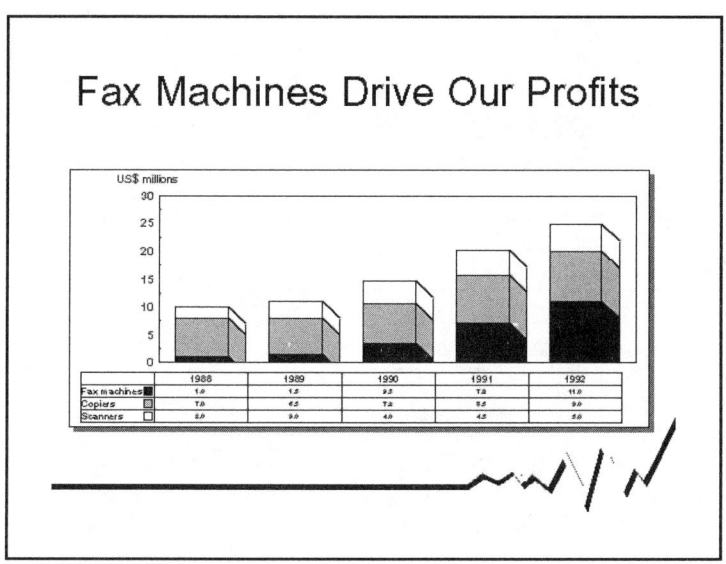

FIGURE 6.4. Place a table beneath a chart automatically with the command Chart Number Grid Under Chart.

Limit bar segments to three or four for optimum readability.

For readability, limit the number of segments. There's no absolute numeric limit here, but two, three, or four segments generally work best. If you do use more than two or three segments, you may want to label each segment on the stack itself, rather than rely on the legend. Readers may have difficulty associating each segment with the legend if there are more than three segments.

Clustered Bar Charts

To make a clustered bar chart, remove each segment from a stacked bar chart and place them side by side along the horizontal axis. *Clustered* refers to the way each set of bars gathers around one label (typically a year, as in fig. 6.5). For every label (say, 1988) there are several bars, each one for a different item.

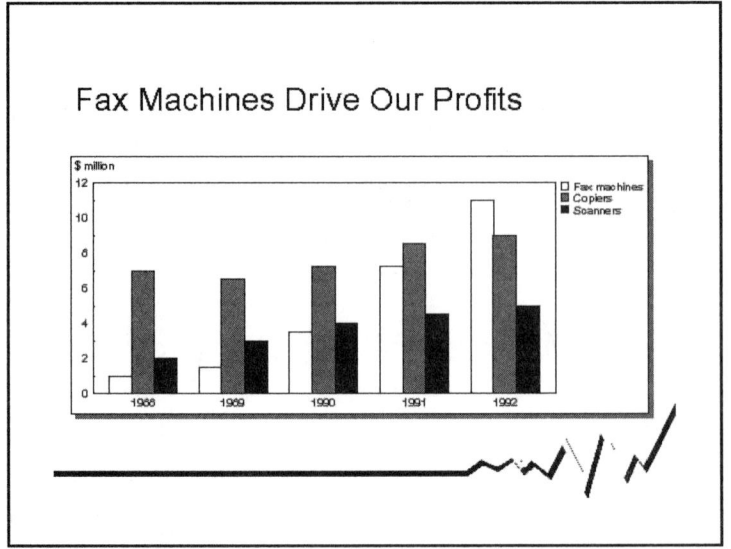

FIGURE 6.5. A clustered bar chart shows the items in a multiple data set side by side.

Clustered bar charts show the same relationship among data sets as a segmented bar chart, but with a subtle difference in emphasis. A clustered bar chart emphasizes the relative size of each bar and ignores the total value of each cluster of bars. The clustered bar chart makes it easy to compare the relative sizes of bars because each bar shares a common baseline.

Three-Dimensional Bar Charts

Freelance Graphics offers two variations of three-dimensional bars:

- The three-dimensional bar chart adds three-dimensional effects to a two-dimensional bar style. (This is sometimes called the two-and-one-half-dimensional bar chart.)
- The 3D Bar (XYZ) chart type has X, Y, and Z axes. This chart type is also known as a three-dimensional perspective chart.

A three-dimensional bar chart is a stylish variation of the basic bar chart. Three-dimensional bar charts present the data symbols in three dimensions. Audiences love them and, consequently, so do presenters. Ironically, three-dimensional bars convey less information than their two-dimensional cousins because it is more difficult to locate the value indicated by a three-dimensional bar than a two-dimensional bar.

Use three-dimensional bar charts for pizzazz, not accuracy.

Another drawback of the 3D XYZ bar chart is that if you are graphing several data sets on a single chart, one set of bars may easily obscure another.

When To Use Three-Dimensional Bar Charts

Use three-dimensional bar charts sparingly and with caution. If your presentation uses numerous bar charts, it's probably best to avoid this chart type altogether. But, if you are using only a few charts and want to make a big splash, the three-dimensional bar is a good choice.

Line Charts

Line charts are sometimes called trend charts, and this latter term is self-defining. Line charts are well-suited for displaying trends, especially long-term trends, with many data points in a time series.

Use line charts to show broad trends.

Both bar and line charts typically show data relationships in a time series. But note the similarities and differences for each chart type. The similarity is that both bar and line charts display time-series data. The difference is that in a bar chart each bar marks a precise measurement at one point in time, whereas in a line chart the line merely connects the data points. Consequently, the emphasis in a line chart is on the general trend as indicated by the upward or downward sloping line.

Here's another difference between bar and line charts. Bar charts are best for displaying data sets with ten or fewer data pairs. Line charts are suited for displaying a greater number of data points. Because the line does not reveal the values for individual data points, it does not matter how many data points are graphed. In fact, the more data points, the clearer the trend.

Another good use for the line chart is to plot two lines, one for actual and one for projected data. Use a dashed line to display the projected data.

Limit the number of lines in a line chart to four or five. More lines make for a very confusing chart, particularly if the lines cross.

As useful as line charts are, they are not as visually interesting as some of the other chart types. Lines can appear thin and weak. One solution to this is to choose the 3D Area/Line style from the Chart Gallery. The result (fig. 6.6) can be visually arresting. The negative aspect of this chart type is that the three-dimensional line does not mark the data points as accurately as an ordinary line.

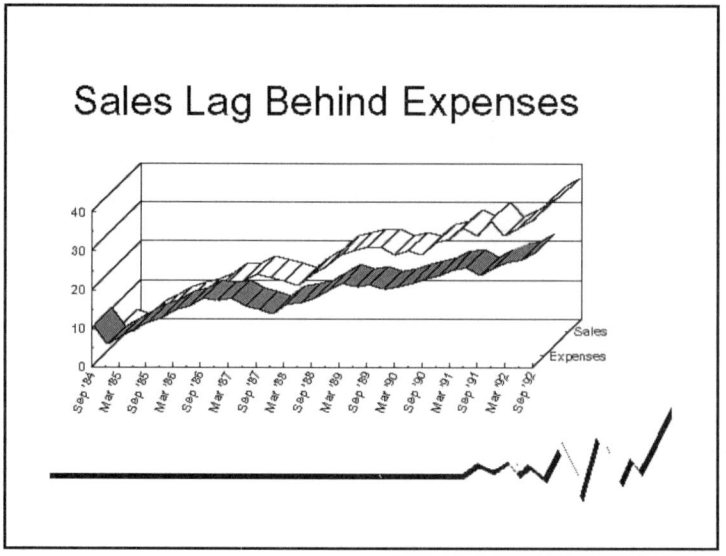

FIGURE 6.6. A three-dimensional line chart, also known as a ribbon chart, turns an ordinary line chart into something more dramatic.

Area Charts

Area charts are closely related to line charts. In both line and area charts, a line passes through each data pair. But in an area chart, the portion of the area beneath the trend line is filled with a color or pattern. This gives the representation of the data a solid, sweeping look and is much bolder than a line chart.

A line chart cuts a trend line with knifelike precision across the surface of the chart, while an area chart paints a broad path with a large brush. Which is best?

Take your pick. But, in general, line charts are more useful than area charts. They are more focused and precise. Reserve area charts for showing the difference in changes in volume over a long time period or to lend solidity to a line chart.

Use area charts to emphasize broad, sweeping trends.

Figure 6.7 illustrates the difference between line and area charts. The line chart (on the left) emphasizes the long-term trend, the peaks and valleys of steel production for each year. The area chart (on the right), with its broad expanses of fill patterns, suggests volume and has a less sharp focus than the line chart. Figure 6.8 shows how a three-dimensional area chart suggests volume even more convincingly than an ordinary area chart.

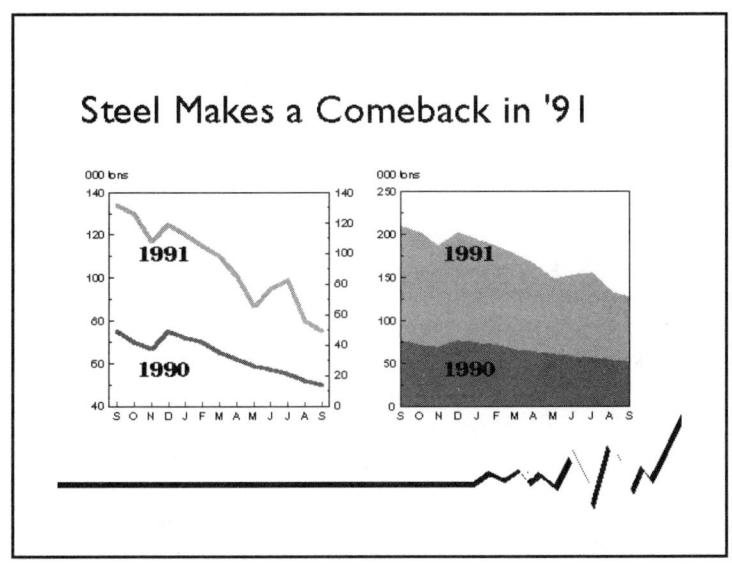

FIGURE 6.7. A line chart and an area chart portraying the same data.

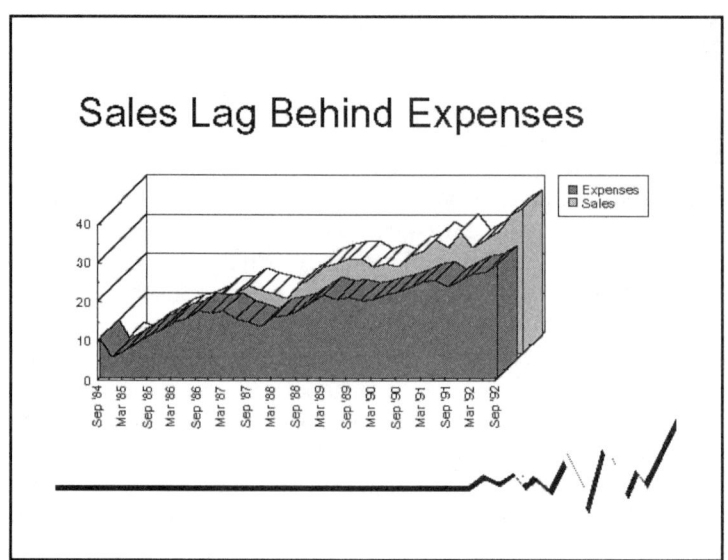

FIGURE 6.8. A three-dimensional area chart.

If you are graphing multiple data sets, area charts pose an additional design problem, described in the upcoming paragraphs.

Furthermore, area charts may be stacked or cumulative, as illustrated in figure 6.9. A stacked area chart plots a line for the first data set and fills in the area beneath it. The second data set is plotted on top of the first data set, much as in a stacked bar chart. The segments in a stacked area chart, like those in a stacked bar chart, lack a common baseline, making it nearly impossible to compare segments with any precision. (However, the stacked area chart is useful for measuring the rise and fall of all the items in the stack.) Because only the area on the bottom of the stack has a straight baseline, it is the only area that you can measure with any accuracy. Consequently, always place the most important segment at the bottom of the stack.

A cumulative area chart plots each data set from the baseline of the chart. This is more often confusing than useful. The overlapping areas, especially for more than two data sets, yield a rather homely chart that forms dark, hard-to-interpret patterns. If you are graphing just two data sets, the cumulative area chart can be a good choice. For example, one standard use of the cumulative area chart is to plot revenues and expenses on the same chart. The overlapping area between the two data sets represents the difference between the two data sets, which in this case equals profits.

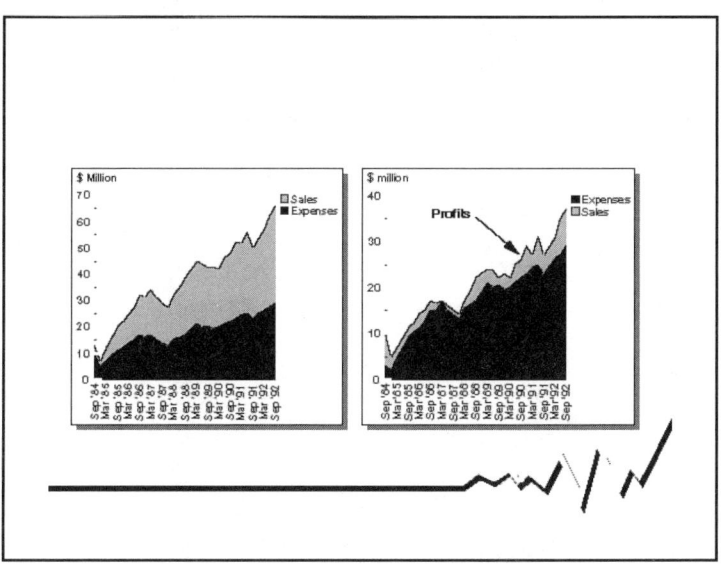

FIGURE 6.9. A stacked area chart (left) and a cumulative area chart (right).

Pie Charts

Pie charts enjoy immense popularity. This is partly because everyone understands a pie chart at first glance. Phrases such as "a piece of the pie" and "how to divide up the pie" are firmly embedded in our language. Even a small child knows the difference between small and large slices of pie.

Another reason for the popularity of pie charts is that much business data is about proportional relationships such as market share, demographic information, responses to questionnaires, budget allocation, product diversification, and the like. For showing parts of a whole in a highly accessible form, a pie chart is a sure thing.

Pie charts show parts of a whole.

If the slices are disproportionate enough, it's easy to grasp the meaning of a pie chart. You can tell at a glance who or what has the largest share.

On the negative side, pie charts are not terribly precise instruments for measuring data. You are hard pressed to tell a difference between a few percentage points in a pie chart, but this doesn't matter. The purpose of a pie chart is to show parts of the whole in a very rough fashion. If you do need to display precise values, you can label each slice with a value (either an absolute value or a percentage).

An exploded slice is a dramatic way of highlighting your company or any slice that you want to emphasize (see fig. 6.10).

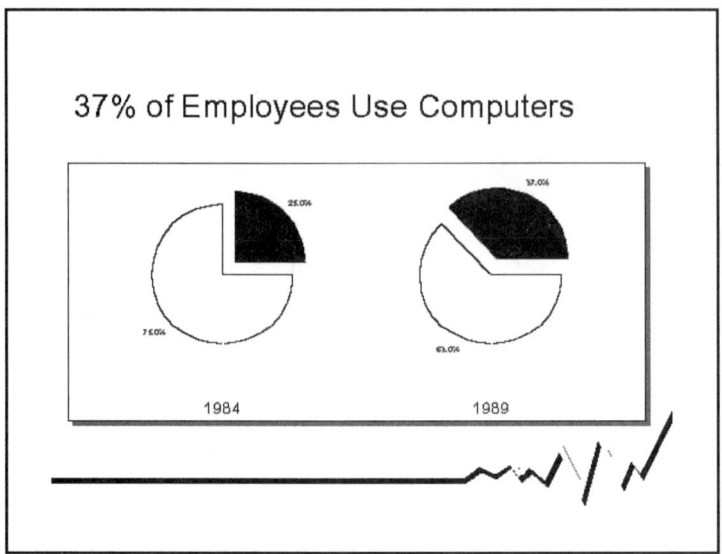

FIGURE 6.10. In this pie chart, the black exploded slices represent the percentage of employees who use computers at work.

Tips for Pie Charts

Place the slice you want to emphasize in the upper right. (Choose Chart Attributes from the menu, select a pie slice, and then change the Start angle.)

For ease of understanding, limit the number of slices to five or six. You can, however, circumvent this rule if you use leader lines and label each slice carefully.

If your pie has too many slices, consider combining the smallest slices into one and giving the slice a label such as "Other" or something more descriptive such as "Sales Less Than $25,000."

Legend vs. Labels

Labels make pie charts easier to read. If a pie chart has a legend, the eye must travel away from the pie to the legend and back again. Labels for each slice eliminate this. However, slice labels are most useful for single pie charts. Legends are preferable for multiple pie charts that show the same items at different points in time. Repeating the same set of slice labels for each pie in a multiple pie chart would create chart clutter.

Place the largest slice at 3:00 o'clock and the rest of the slices in descending order in a counter-clockwise direction. This happens automatically if you enter the label and value for the largest slice first in the Chart Data & Titles window, followed by the next largest, and so on.

Multiple Pies

Multiple pies are excellent devices for showing the different aspects of a related set of items. You can place three or four pies on a single page (use the 4 Charts page layout) and tell a story about your data. The two pie charts in figure 6.10 reveal how computers are used by two segments of the population. The multiple pie chart is a separate type in the Chart Gallery.

Three-Dimensional Pies

In Freelance Graphics, you also can create three-dimensional pies (fig. 6.11). Like three-dimensional bar charts, three-dimensional pies do not communicate any more information than regular two-dimensional pie charts. They just wrap the data in a fancier package. There is something dramatic and appealing about a three-dimensional pie chart. Its abundant dimensions project elegance and authority (not a bad image for your message). Keep in mind that, if you choose a three-dimensional pie, you cannot explode a slice.

High-Low-Open-Close Charts

High-low-open-close charts are almost exclusively used to chart stock market data. This chart type plots the fluctuation of a stock price over time at the time interval determined by your data set. This might be daily, monthly, or quarterly. Figure 6.12 shows a high-low-open-close chart.

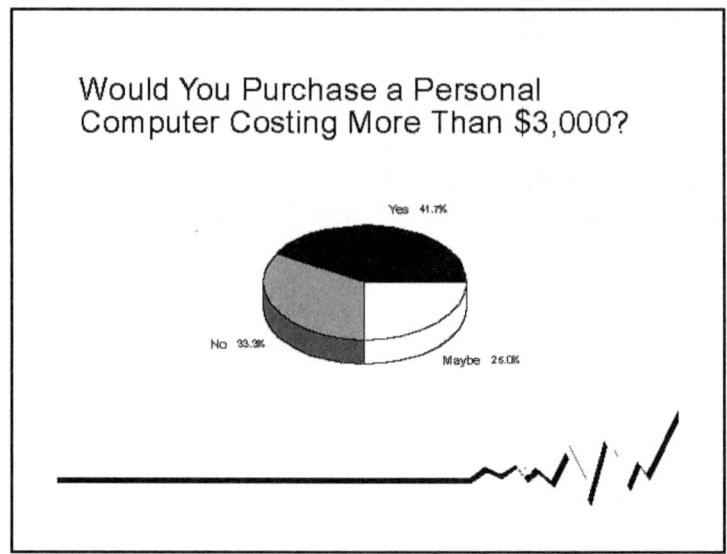

FIGURE 6.11. A three-dimensional pie chart.

If you like, you can add volume bars at the bottom of the chart to show the volume of stocks traded over the time period for which the prices are reported.

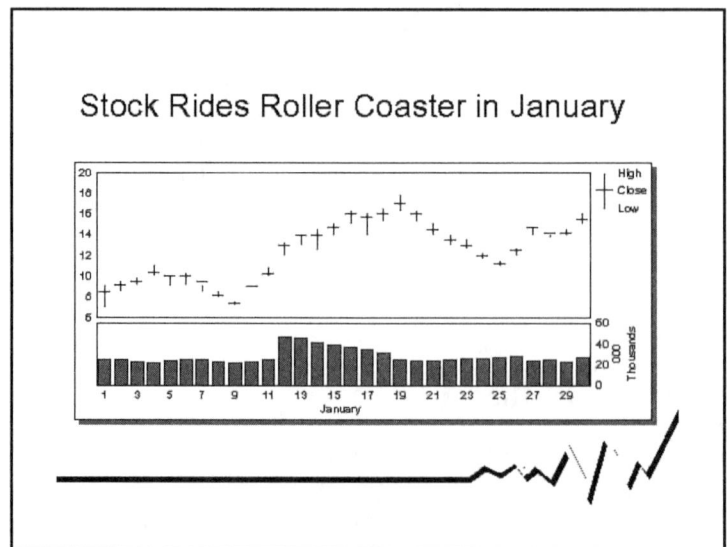

FIGURE 6.12. A high-low-open-close chart.

XY (Scatter) Charts

A scatter chart shows the correlation between two variables. Scatter charts are seldom used in presentations because their focus is on data analysis that requires a bit of statistical knowledge to interpret. However, they are occasionally useful.

Scatter charts are unique among the charts available in Freelance Graphics because they have two scaled axes. Each data point in a scatter chart is a numeric data pair such as (5,150) that defines a unique coordinate on the chart. Figure 6.13 shows a scatter chart.

You can choose either linear or logarithmic axes. If you are plotting data sets with values that vary widely, logarithmic is a good choice.

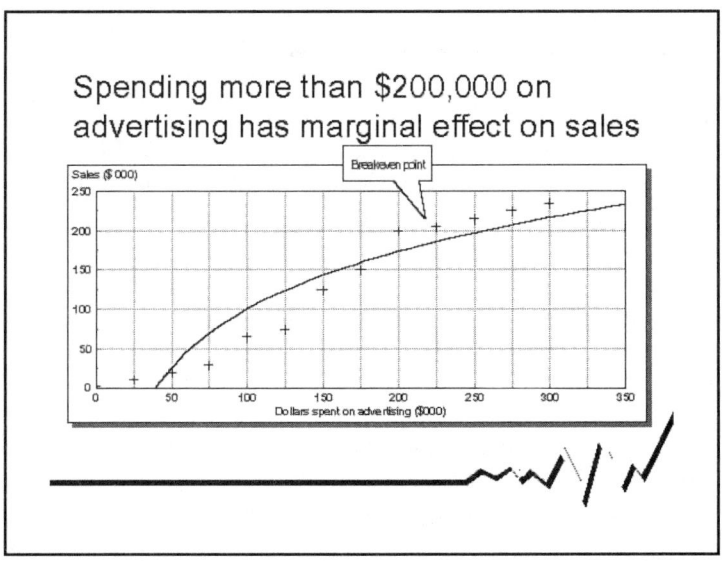

FIGURE 6.13. This scatter chart reveals that at a certain point ($200,000) advertising has a diminishing effect on sales.

Radar Charts

Freelance Graphics for Windows 2.0 introduces the radar chart, which is not a widely known chart type, although it is quite popular in Japan. Radar charts, also known as spider charts (because they resemble spider webs), show the relationship among multiple variables, as in figure 6.14.

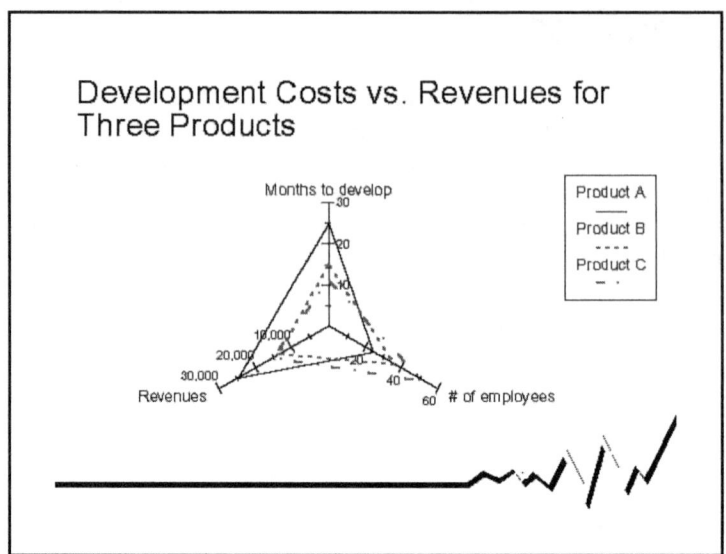

FIGURE 6.14. This radar chart compares development costs (as measured by development time and number of employees) for two products and also depicts the revenues generated by each product.

Tables

Tables, or table charts, display precise data in a column-and-row format. Here are two good reasons to choose a table chart:

- You have a very small amount of data, hardly enough to justify a chart.
- You need to show precise data and are more interested in showing the precise numbers than showing a symbolic relationship between those numbers.

For presentations, a table chart should contain just a few numbers; otherwise, your viewers may not be able to read them. You can, however, use larger tables for printed reports. You might also distribute table charts with handouts.

Freelance Graphics 2.0 introduces the Table tool, which you can use by clicking the Table icon in the Toolbox. For more information, read Chapter 11, "Creating Tables."

Bar-Line Charts

Freelance Graphics has a hybrid chart type, the bar-line chart. This useful chart type displays two or more data sets using a bar for one data set and a line for the other. You can specify which data set is to be displayed in the form of a line or a bar.

This chart type works best with two data sets, one bar and one line. This arrangement gives the chart an interesting visual form: The line provides a nice contrast to the bars and makes the separation of the two data sets easy to see at a glance. Use the line to show the trend, and the bars to show exact values at regular time intervals.

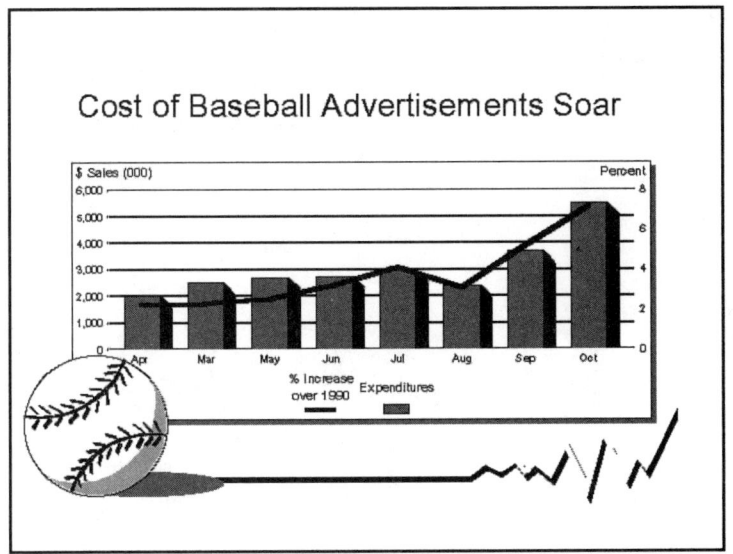

FIGURE 6.15. A bar-line chart.

Wrapping Up

In this chapter, you learned how to approach the task of choosing the right chart type for your data. You should now be able to choose the correct chart type based on your data and the message you want to convey. You also have seen examples of most of the major chart types and should have a sense of the wide variety of chart types available in Freelance Graphics.

In the next chapter, you learn about the nuts and bolts of creating charts in Freelance Graphics.

7

Creating Data Charts

Next to the ubiquitous text chart, the data-driven chart is probably the most common presentation format for displaying information. Charts give shape to numbers—often in dramatic fashion—so you can see trends or compare sets of numbers readily.

Freelance Graphics creates data-driven charts quickly—after you choose a chart type and enter your numbers. You can choose from among all the most common chart types, including line, bar, pie, table, and several types of three-dimensional charts (perennial favorites on the presentation circuit).

This chapter is a nuts-and-bolts guide to creating charts. How to select the correct chart type for your data was discussed in Chapter 6, "Choosing the Right Chart Type."

Chart Terminology

Chart terminology varies wildly from book to book and is a major source of confusion for readers. This section introduces the basic terminology used throughout this book (and within Freelance Graphics) to talk about charts.

What is a chart? Everybody is exposed to charts in textbooks, business magazines, advertisements, and, of course, presentations. But what precisely are they? In a broad sense, a chart tells a story about numbers. That's why charts can be so effective. Plain numbers are dull, dry, and static. But well-made charts are interesting, lively, and dynamic.

In this chapter, you learn how to:

- *Understand basic chart terminology*
- *Create charts from scratch, using the data entry window of Freelance Graphics*
- *Choose a chart type and style*
- *Create bar, line, area, high-low-close-open, pie, and table charts*
- *Add titles, headings, and notes to charts*
- *Preview a chart before leaving the Chart Data & Titles window*
- *Complete the chart and leave the Chart Data & Titles window*
- *Switch chart types*
- *Tell a story with a series of charts*

A chart tells a story about numbers.

More specifically, charts display numbers in symbolic form, on a surface that contains X and Y axes (a pie chart, having no axis, is the exception here). The symbolic forms, known as *data symbols*, are the familiar bars, lines, areas, and marks that measure data and are the defining characteristic of charts.

Data is the information—in the form of text or numbers—that you measure on a chart. This information varies in some way, usually over time.

A *data pair*—generally an item and its associated value—defines a unique location on a chart. In the bar chart in figure 7.1, the label-value combination (Q1, 75) is a single data pair. A data set contains any number of data pairs. A data pair is sometimes referred to as an *observation*, because it represents an observation about the items being measured (for example, that 75 units were produced in the first quarter).

A *data value* is the numeric portion of a data pair. In the data pair (January, 75) 75 is the data value. A data value is sometimes known as the *dependent variable* because it depends on the item with which it is associated.

An *item* is the category you are measuring and constitutes the textual half of a data pair. In the data pair (Q1, 75), Q1 is the label. (Note that an item also can be a number, as in 1991, but here the number is treated as text and has no numeric value in terms of defining a location on a chart.) An item also is called the *independent variable*.

A *data set* is a complete set of data pairs (items and values) in a single chart. A chart may have several data sets, as in a multiple-line chart or segmented bar chart, where each data symbol represents a single data set. Figure 7.1 shows two data sets, one for 1990 and one for 1991.

Time-series data measures data over time. Most charts depict time-series data (sales per month, inventory by quarter, revenues for a 10-year period, and so on).

A *data symbol* is the symbolic representation of a data set as a line, an area, a bar, a pie, or simply a mark at a data point. In figure 7.1, the bars are the data symbols.

Basic Training: Creating a Chart

No matter which chart type you choose to create, the basic procedure is the same. The following sections break this procedure down into easily manageable steps. (Special considerations for creating individual chart types are also covered in this chapter.)

Creating Data Charts 113

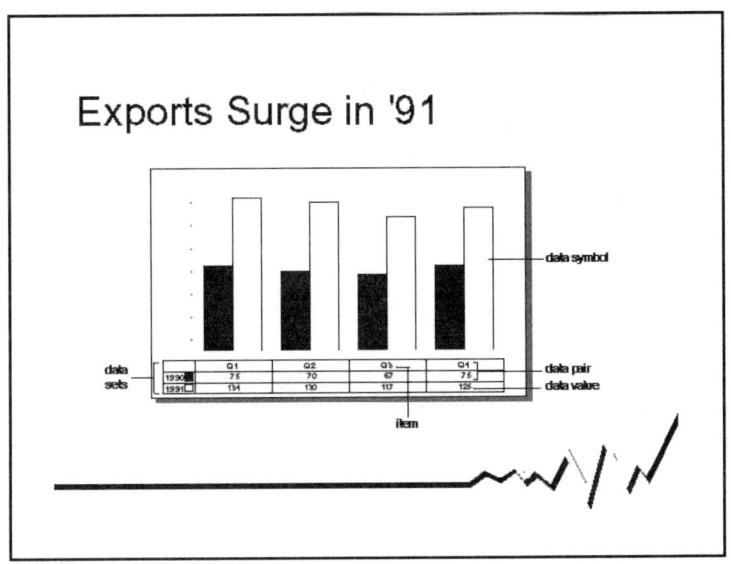

FIGURE 7.1. This bar chart and its accompanying table illustrate the terminology used in this book.

Choosing a Page Layout for a Chart

The first step is to choose a SmartMaster page layout for your chart. Start a new page with Page New command. In the Page New dialog box (fig. 7.2), choose the page layout you want to use: 1 Chart, 2 Charts, 4 Charts, or Bullets & Chart. Choose the appropriate page layout.

First, choose a page layout for your chart.

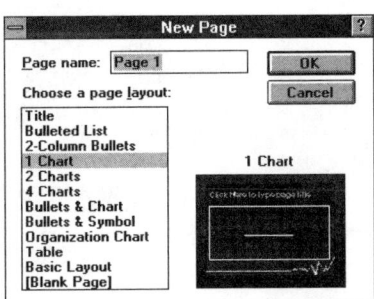

FIGURE 7.2. The Page New dialog box.

Switching Page Layouts

After you create a page with single chart, what if you decide another chart on the same page would present your case with more clarity? You are not committed to your choice of page layout after you create a chart. You can switch to a different page layout at any time with Page Choose Page Layout. For example, to add another chart to a page with a single chart, choose the 2 Charts page layout. When you do this, Freelance Graphics automatically places the single chart in the placement block on the left. You can then add the second chart to the placement block on the right. When you place two or more charts on one page, you may want a separate title for each chart. If so, use the Heading box in the titles view of the Chart Data & Titles window to create a title for each chart separately.

Choosing a Chart Type

Click the prompt text "Click here to create chart." This displays the Chart Gallery (fig. 7.3), from which you can choose a chart type and a chart style. Click the button (or the name next to the button) to choose a chart type. For example, click Stacked Bar.

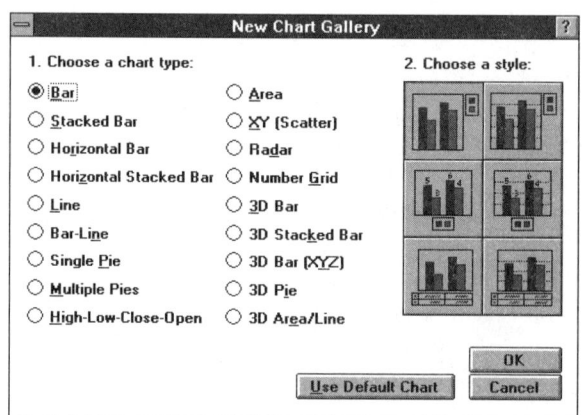

FIGURE 7.3. The New Chart Gallery dialog box.

Now you can choose one of six styles for a stacked bar chart. When you choose a new chart type, the styles change. Just click the picture of the style you like in the Style box and click OK. You also can double-click the picture of a style to select it and close the Gallery in a single step. Now you are ready to enter your data in the Chart Data & Titles window (see figs. 7.4 and 7.5).

Entering Your Data

Take a moment to peruse the Chart Data & Titles window. The miniature picture at the top left of the window represents the chart type you are creating. (You also can click this picture to display the Chart Gallery.) If you change to a line chart from a bar chart, this picture changes to a line chart.

The Chart Data & Titles window has two views, a data view and a titles view (as shown in figs. 7.4 and 7.5):

The Chart Data & Titles window has two views: a data view and a titles view.

- You enter the data for your chart in the data view.
- You enter headings, notes, and axis titles in the titles view.

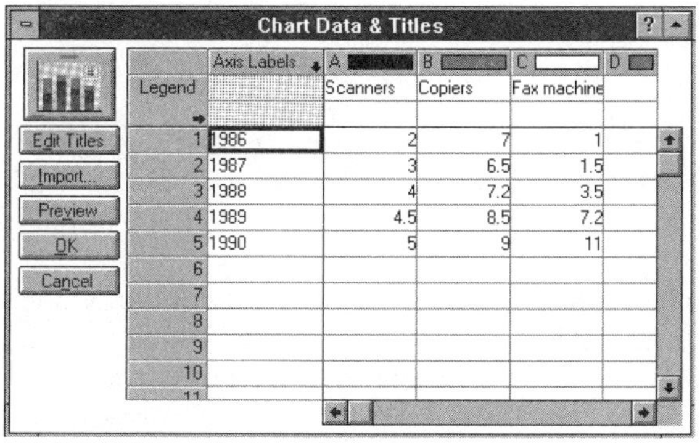

FIGURE 7.4. A data view of the Chart Data & Titles window.

To switch between the two views, click the Edit Data button or the Edit Titles button. Note that both views display the picture of the current chart type, as well as the following three buttons:

- Import lets you import numbers from a variety of sources (see Chapter 9, "Creating Charts from 1-2-3 Worksheets," for more information).
- Preview displays the chart based on the current data in the Chart Data & Titles window. Press and hold the mouse button over Preview to see the chart and then release the button to return to the Chart Data & Titles window.

- OK composes a chart on the page and closes the Chart Data & Titles window. If you are using a SmartMaster page layout for charts (such as the 1 Chart page layout), the chart is automatically placed and sized in the placement block provided.
- Cancel closes the Chart Data & Titles window without keeping any of the changes you made.

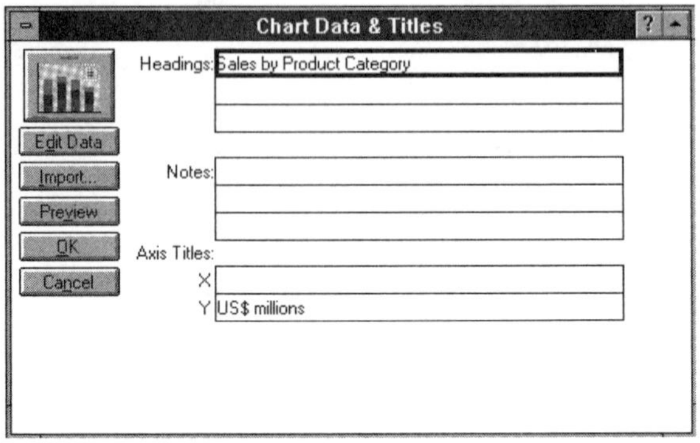

FIGURE 7.5. A titles view of the Chart Data & Titles window.

You enter your chart data in the data view of the Chart Data & Titles window. The data view resembles a spreadsheet, and you enter data in much the same way as you would in a spreadsheet. However, unlike a spreadsheet, you can't enter formulas or perform other calculations.

Note that each row has a number. In the first column with the heading Axis Labels, you enter the axis labels for your chart (for pie charts, this column has the heading Slice Labels). These are the items that you are measuring in the chart. In this example, the years 1986 through 1990 are the axis labels.

In the columns to the right of the axis labels, you type the data values for each data pair. In the example in figure 7.4, there are three data sets. Figure 7.6 shows the chart created using this data.

To enter data, just position the pointer in the appropriate cell and type an entry. To move to another cell, press an arrow key or press Enter.

If you type a text entry in a data cell (that is, anywhere except in the Axis Label rows or Legend columns), Freelance Graphics beeps and does not accept the entry. (The sole exception to this is when you are creating a table chart. See the "Creating Table Charts (Number Grids)" section later in this chapter for more information.)

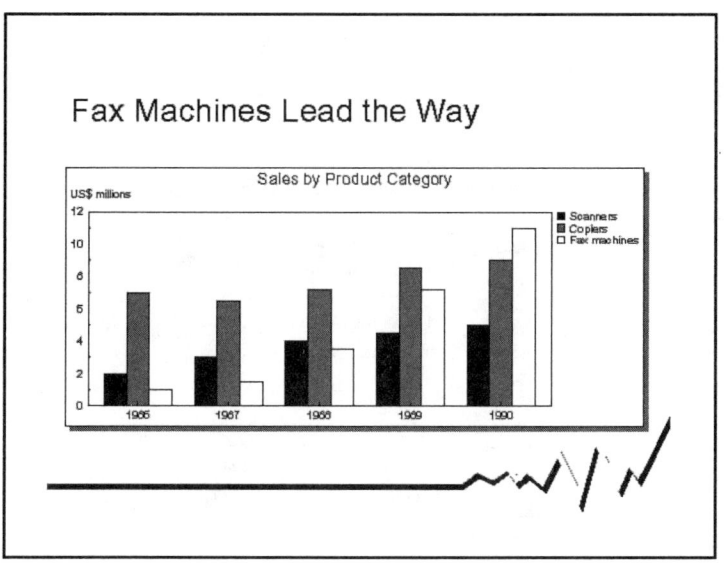

FIGURE 7.6. The finished chart.

Cutting and Copying Data in the Chart Data & Titles Window

You cut and copy labels and data within the Chart Data & Titles window by drag-selecting a contiguous range of cells and then using either the Edit Copy, Edit Cut, and Edit Paste commands or the SmartIcon equivalents for these commands. Note that you can anchor the pointer in either of the gray cells at the top-left corner of the window for cut, copy, and paste operations.

In the Chart Data & Titles window, the column headings above each column are labeled A, B, C, D, and so on. Each letter represents one data set. Our example has three data sets. These columns also reflect the chart type you are using. In this example, the column headings display bar symbols because a bar chart is being created. If you change to a line chart, the column headings display line symbols.

Double-click a data symbol in a column heading to change attributes for that data symbol.

You can double-click the data symbol in the column heading to change attributes for the data symbols (or you can choose Chart Attributes from the menu). In our example, double-clicking one of these column headings displays the Bar Chart Attributes dialog box (fig. 7.7).

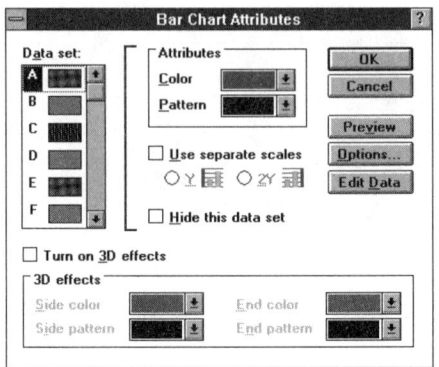

FIGURE 7.7. The Bar Chart Attributes dialog box.

In the Bar Chart Attributes dialog box, you can change the color and pattern of the bars of each data set, including side and end colors for three-dimensional bars. You also can assign a data set to the first or second Y axis scale, hide the display of data symbols for any data set, and turn on three-dimensional bar effects. To change the width of bars and other bar characteristics, click the Options button. To go directly to the Chart Data & Titles window, click the Edit Data button.

After you've entered your data, you are ready to enter headings, notes, and axis titles. If you want to see what your chart will look like based on the data you've entered so far, press and hold the pointer over the Preview button. Then release the mouse button to return to the Chart Data & Titles window.

What about Those Two Gray Cells?

At the top left of the Chart Data & Titles window shown in figure 7.6, note the two gray cells stacked on top of each other. Although you can select these with the pointer, you can't type in them. Why are they there? They exist to give you a cell to anchor the pointer in when you are cutting, copying, or pasting data. See Chapter 9, "Creating Charts from 1-2-3 Worksheets," for more information.

Entering Legends

A chart legend helps the reader connect the data symbols to the data set they represent. Freelance Graphics adds a legend to your chart only if you make an entry in the Legend rows of the Chart Data & Titles window.

The first two rows under each column heading are reserved for legend text. At the far left of these columns, look for the gray square labeled "Legend" and the arrow pointing to the first two rows (fig. 7.8). You can double-click on this gray square to display the Chart Legend dialog box (this is equivalent to choosing the Chart Legend command).

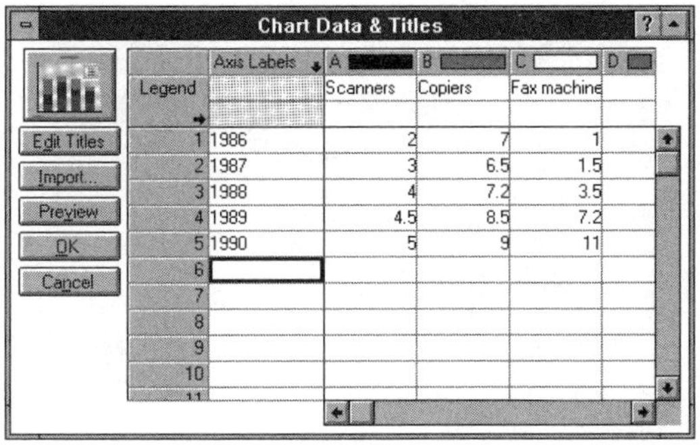

FIGURE 7.8. Add legend text above each column that contains your data values.

Configuring the Enter Key

You can customize the way the Enter key functions in the data view of the Chart Data & Titles window. If you are a 1-2-3 user, you may prefer to have the Enter key not move down a cell when you press it after typing an entry. To set up the Enter key not to move down, choose Chart Options Keyboard and then select the option "Keeps cell pointer at the same place, as in spreadsheets." The other option (and the default) is "Moves cell pointer down a row, as in word processing."

Entering Dates Automatically

Most business charts use time-series data (data that varies over time). More often than not, the unscaled axis of a chart displays days, months, quarters, or years. It can be tedious to type in all those dates. Fortunately, there is a faster way. While you are working in the Chart Data & Titles window, choose Chart Options Date Fill. (If the pointer is not in a Legend row or the Axis Labels column when you choose this command, Freelance Graphics beeps.) The command displays a dialog box (fig. 7.9). Choose a Date style, Start and End dates, and the Interval. Freelance Graphics generates the dates automatically, starting at the cursor location. If your data is based on a fiscal year, you can choose the first month of the fiscal year. Using this option, you can fill the Axis Labels column or Legends row with dates quickly and without worrying about making typing errors (see fig. 7.10). (Incidentally, you also can use this option to fill headings or cells in a number grid.)

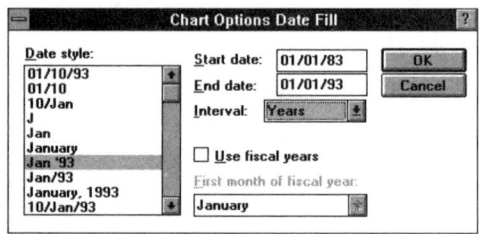

FIGURE 7.9. The Chart Options Date Fill dialog box.

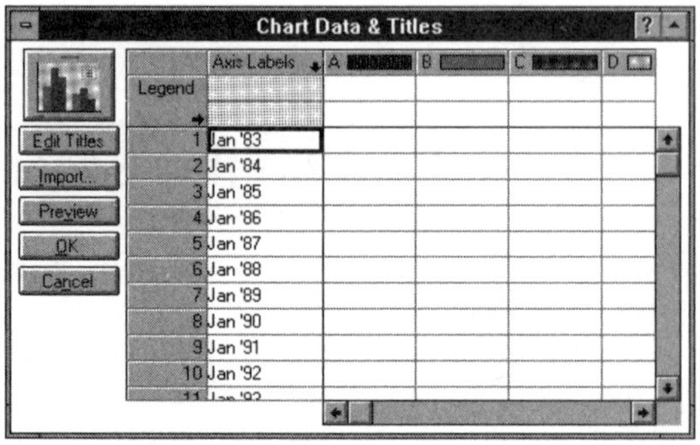

FIGURE 7.10. The Chart Data & Titles window with dates generated automatically with the Date Fill option.

Previewing a Chart

If you want to see how your chart looks based on the current data and titles, but don't want to leave the Chart Data & Titles window, just position the mouse pointer over the Preview button and then press and hold down the left mouse button. Freelance Graphics displays your chart. Release the mouse button to return to the Chart Data & Titles window.

When you are satisfied with the chart, click OK. Freelance Graphics composes your chart and closes the Chart Data & Titles window.

Adding Headings, Notes, and Axis Titles

Bars, lines, areas, and pie slices have little meaning without supporting text. Your audience needs to know what items those bars represent, what the scale on the axis means, what the bars are measuring, and the general intent of the chart. You can convey this information by adding text in the titles view of the Chart Data & Titles window. (If you are not in this view, click the Edit Titles button from the data view.)

To enter text in the rows in this window, just position the pointer in the appropriate row and type an entry. To move to another cell, press an arrow key or Enter.

Headings

Before you add a heading, consider that this is the first element of your chart that your audience sees. Wouldn't it be a good idea to state your message plainly and emphatically in the heading?

In Freelance Graphics, you have two places where you can add headings—in the Headings line of the Chart Data & Titles window or in the Title block in the 1 Chart page layout.

If you are using the 1 Chart page layout as the template for a single chart, the title block (which contains the prompt text, "Click here to type page title") is the best place to put your title. This ensures that all the titles of your presentation pages, whether text or charts, use the same typeface, color, and size, resulting in a consistent presentation.

When should you instead use the Headings box in the Chart Data & Titles window? There are a couple of times when this is a good idea. If you are creating stand-alone charts and are not using a page layout from a SmartMaster set, use the Headings item to display a title for your chart. Freelance Graphics never wraps the title in a single headings line. (On the other hand, a title in the headings line may be truncated if it is too long.) You can change the size of the heading to fit more text by double-clicking the heading and making a choice from the Size drop-down box.

Notes

Use notes to give information that is not central to the meaning of your chart but that is still useful. The source of your data is often given in a note. You also can use notes to display a footnote. You can type up to three lines of notes. Each note appears on a separate line.

Axis Titles

Most data-driven charts have one scaled and one unscaled axis. The scaled axis measures your data. The unscaled axis names the items you are measuring (such as years). Some charts have two scales, in which case you also can add a title for the second (2Y) scaled axis.

Freelance Graphics always refers to the scaled axis as the Y axis and the unscaled axis as the X axis.

- For the Y axis (scaled), type a title for the units of measure for the items you are measuring (e.g., Years or $ Million).
- For the X axis, type a general term for the items you are measuring (e.g., Years, Models, City, Years in Business, etc.).

Just as in the data view of this window, click Preview to check your progress or click OK to draw the chart and leave the Chart Data & Titles window. Figure 7.11 shows a completed chart.

That's all there is to creating basic charts. Now you know enough to create a series of charts for a presentation. Of course, Freelance Graphics gives you the power to customize the look of your charts in numerous ways. These options are discussed in the rest of this chapter and in Chapter 8, "Customizing Data Charts."

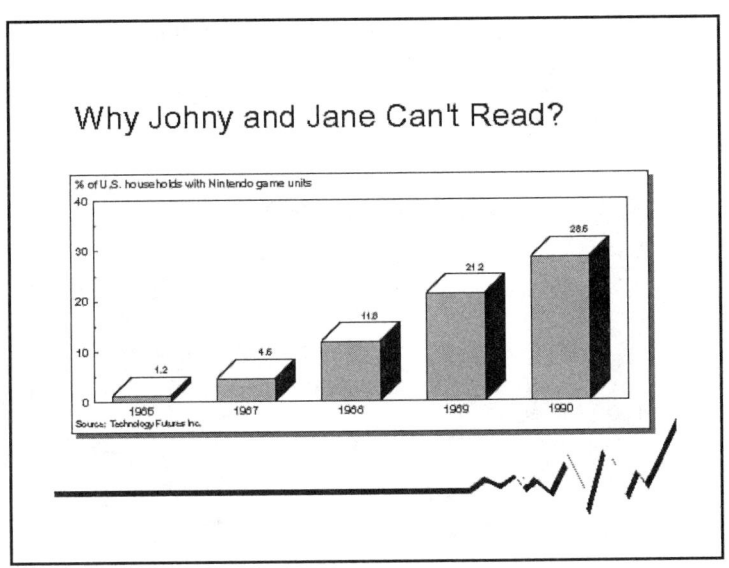

FIGURE 7.11. The Y axis title is most important because it gives meaning to the data symbols. In most time-series data, the X axis title is not necessary.

Editing Entries in the Chart Data & Titles Window

You've added your data and typed helpful headings to elucidate your data. You've clicked the OK button, and Freelance Graphics composed the chart on your page. Now you notice that one bar is about eight times as high as the rest of the bars. You must have typed an incorrect number.

How do you return to the Chart Data & Titles window to edit your data? Freelance Graphics gives you several ways to do this:

- With the chart selected, click the Chart icon in the Toolbox, choose Chart Edit, or click the Edit Chart Data SmartIcon.
- Double-click an empty area in the chart. This can be tricky: If you click in the wrong spot, you are likely to display a dialog box for one of the chart components.

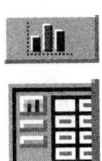

After you are in the Chart Data & Titles window, you can change data in a couple of ways. To replace an entire entry, just select a data cell, type the new entry, and then press Enter or an arrow key. To edit a portion of an existing entry, click the cell that contains the label or number you want to change, and then press F2. This displays the contents of the cell in the edit line (see fig. 7.12). You can edit the cell entry in this line and then click the Confirm button (the check mark) to accept the entry or the Cancel button (X) to restore the original entry.

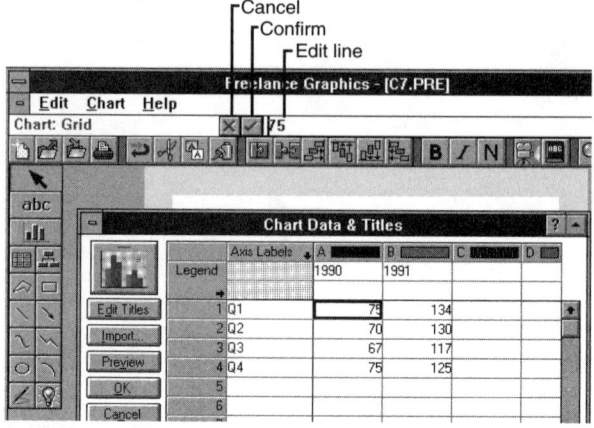

FIGURE 7.12. The edit line in the Chart Data & Titles window.

Switching Chart Types in Midstream

Suppose you create a vertical bar chart and then decide that, because your labels are so long, a horizontal bar chart would look better. You can change to a different chart type quickly, without having to make any formatting changes. Freelance Graphics takes care of the necessary design changes for you automatically. Of course, it's up to you to decide whether the new chart type you choose is appropriate for your data. (Read Chapter 6, "Choosing the Right Chart Type," to make sure.)

There are several ways to change to a new chart type:

- With the chart selected, choose Chart Type and then click the name of the new chart type from the menu.
- With the chart selected, choose Chart Gallery and then click the name of the new chart type from the Gallery. This method also lets you choose a new chart style by clicking a picture in the Gallery.
- From the Chart Data & Titles window, click the picture of the chart in the upper-left corner. This displays the Chart Gallery, from which you can choose a new chart type and style.

- With the chart selected, choose one of the chart type SmartIcons. You have to add these to the current SmartIcon palette with Tools SmartIcons Customize. There is a SmartIcon for every chart type as well as an icon that displays the Chart Gallery.

The latter method is the fastest way to change chart types. Typically, you only use five or six chart types, so adding the chart SmartIcons to the current palette doesn't take up too much space. For more details on SmartIcons in general, see Chapter 23, "Using SmartIcons."

Moving Charts In and Out of Placement Blocks

When you create a chart using a page layout such as the 1 Chart Page layout, the SmartMaster placement block automatically sizes and places the chart in the placement block when you click OK. What if you want to move it?

There are a couple of ways to go about this. You can simply drag it as you would any other object. If you do, the chart moves to wherever you place it. But it is now no longer in the position specified by the page layout. This can be a problem if you move a chart by mistake. What if you want to return the chart to its original position in the placement block? One method is to choose Page Choose Page Layout and reassign the 1 Chart page layout. This automatically repositions the chart in the placement block. Another method is to choose Edit Cut (or click the Edit Cut SmartIcon) to tempo-

rarily erase the chart. This reveals the original placement block. Then, choose Edit Paste (or click the Paste SmartIcon) and drag the chart back into the placement block.

If you want to drag a chart out of a placement block and leave the placement block on the page, press Ctrl as you drag the chart. You see a dashed line around the placement line. When this line disappears, you can release the mouse button: The chart is repositioned where you drag it. Now you can see the placement block and the original prompt text. You can now drag it back into the placement block if you wish. As the pointer crosses the border of the placement block, a dashed line reappears. When you release the mouse button, the chart is again sucked into the placement block.

Bar Charts

To create bar charts, use the same techniques given earlier. However, bar charts also have a few unique characteristics that you need to know about.

Labeling the Bars with Precise Values

Sometimes it is useful to display the precise value for a bar or a line directly on a chart. You see this most often in bar charts. To display value labels, select a chart and then choose Chart Value Labels. In the resulting dialog box (fig. 7.13), mark the Display check box. The data values are displayed at the top or the end of the bars (depending on whether the chart is vertical or horizontal; see fig. 7.14).

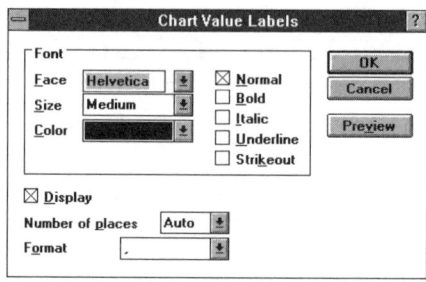

FIGURE 7.13. The Chart Value Labels dialog box.

You also can change the typeface and attributes in the Font box. Combining exact values with the data symbols serves two purposes: The bars show the numbers in symbolic form, and the numbers show the precise values. You also may want to use a data table to show precise values. To do this, use the Chart Number Grid Under Chart command. See Chapter 8, "Customizing Data Charts," for more information.

Adding Three-Dimensional Effects

You can add three-dimensional effects to any bar chart by choosing Chart Attributes and then clicking the check box labeled Turn on 3D effects. This yields the same result as switching to the three-dimensional bar chart type in the Chart Gallery. If you choose to activate three-dimensional effects, you also can change the side color, side pattern, end color, and end pattern of the bars. Choose Chart Attributes and then click the Options button. Figure 7.14 shows the same chart with and without three-dimensional effects.

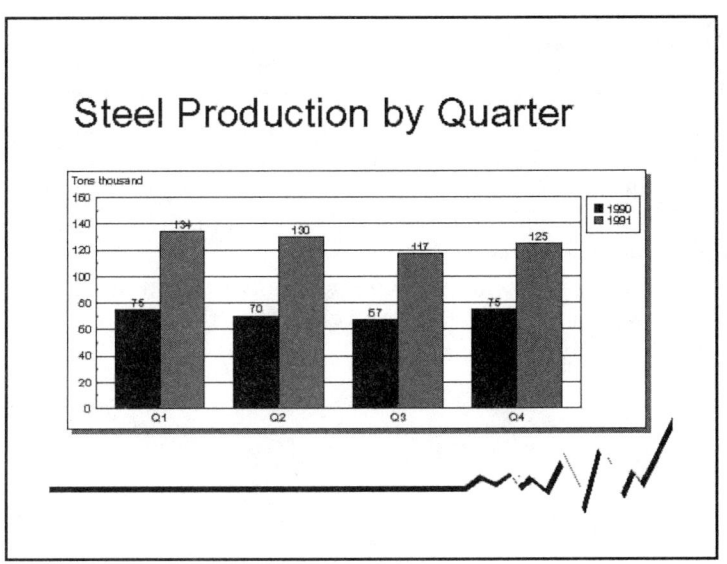

FIGURE 7.14. A bar chart showing the precise values for each bar.

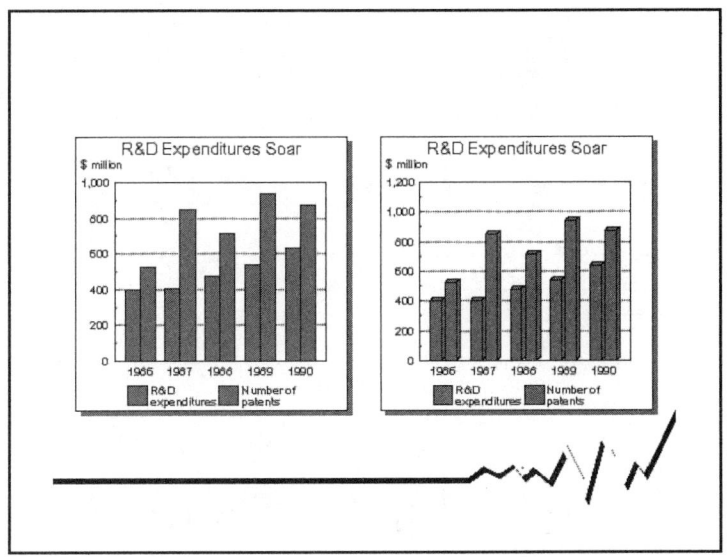

FIGURE 7.15. The same bar chart with (right) and without (left) three-dimensional effects.

The 3D (XYZ) Chart

Freelance Graphics also offers a "true" three-dimensional chart, the 3D (XYZ) chart. This chart type actually has a third axis (the Z axis) so that the entire chart appears in three-dimensional space, not just the bars.

Unfortunately, the 3D (XYZ) chart does not work well with all data, as shown by figure 7.16. Because each data set occupies a row in three-dimensional space, unless the values in each successive data set are larger, the bars in front can obscure the bars in back. Sometimes you can remedy this situation by placing the Z axis in front. Choose Chart Frame and then click the Z in front button under Pivot chart.

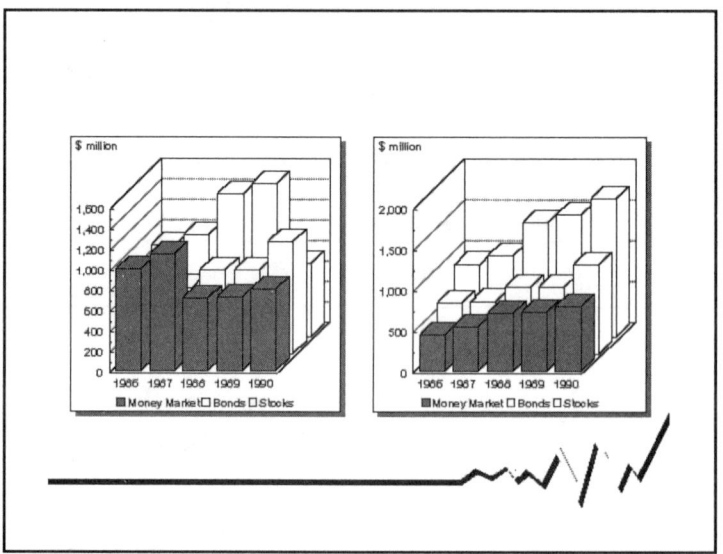

FIGURE 7.16. The three-dimensional (XYZ) chart on the left fails because some of the bars are obscured; the one on the right works because the data values increase with each data set.

Creating a Step Chart by Changing Bar Width

A step chart is simply a bar chart with bars so wide that they bump against each other and form a step pattern (see fig. 7.17). You can turn any non-three-dimensional bar chart into a step chart by choosing Chart Attributes and then clicking the Options button. Change the Bar Width to 100% and click the Contrasting color check box (otherwise, the edges of the bars may not be visible).

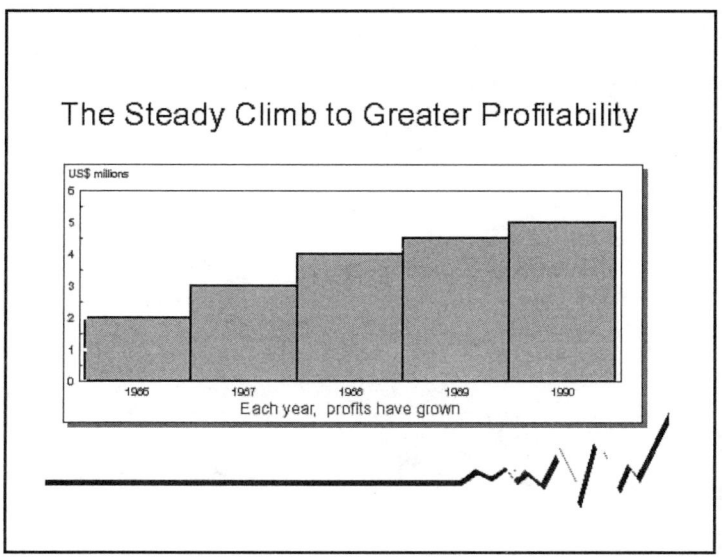

FIGURE 7.17. A step chart.

The step chart has much in common with the area chart: Both chart types emphasize the volume of data. A standard bar chart emphasizes individual bars, whereas a step chart blurs the distinction between each bar and instead creates an effect like the area chart.

Line Charts

You may recall from Chapter 6, "Choosing the Right Chart Type," line charts are best for showing trends in a data set rather than emphasizing data at specific points in time.

You can add markers to data points to emphasize individual values (see fig. 7.18) or even remove the lines altogether. To add markers, choose Chart Attributes, select a data set, and then choose a symbol from the Marker drop-down box. To remove the lines altogether, choose a line style of None in the Attributes box. Wide line widths can help shore up the sometimes weak look of a line chart.

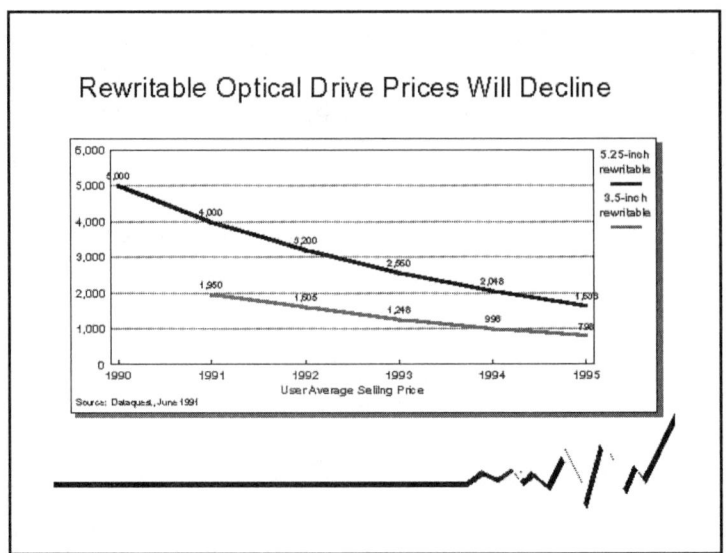

FIGURE 7.18. A line chart with value labels added to emphasize individual data points.

Bar-Line Charts

To create a bar-line chart, choose the Bar-Line chart style and then enter your data in the Chart Data & Titles window. Next, specify which data sets have bars and which have a line to represent the data. In the Chart Data & Titles window, double-click the data symbol just above the Legend rows above each data set. The Bar-Line Chart Attributes dialog appears (fig. 7.19). Select a data set on the left and then click the Bar or Line button in the Type area to specify bars or a line for the selected data set.

Area Charts

To create area charts, use the same procedure for creating other chart types. The main decision to make when you create area charts is whether the data is stacked or cumulative. (See the discussion of area charts in Chapter 6, "Choosing the Right Chart Type," for more information about the difference between these two types of area chart.)

To create a stacked area chart, choose Chart Attributes and then click the Stack data check box (see fig. 7.20).

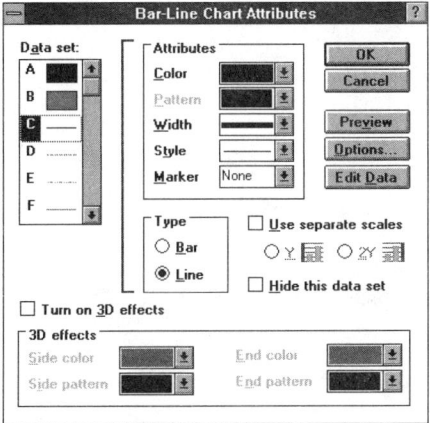

FIGURE 7.19. The Bar-Line Chart Attributes dialog box.

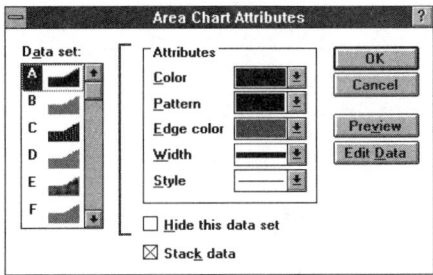

FIGURE 7.20. The Area Chart Attributes dialog box.

High-Low-Close-Open Charts

The steps for creating the high-low-close-open chart are basically the same as for the other chart types. But there are a few special considerations.

The Chart Data & Titles window has four columns with predefined legend labels: High, Low, Close, and Open. You type the corresponding stock prices in each of these columns. Axis labels represent the dates on which the stock price was observed. Don't forget that you can use Chart Options Date Fill to generate date labels automatically (see the "Adding Dates Automatically" section earlier in this chapter for the procedure).

You specify the high-low-close-open chart attributes in the HLCO Chart Attributes dialog box (fig. 7.21). Under Data set, Vert is the vertical line that extends from the low to the high value. A, B, C, and D are the symbols for the high, low, close, and open values, respectively. Click A, B, C, D and then click the drop-down box to change their color or width. E is the symbol for volume bars. You can change the color and pattern of the volume bars. Figure 7.22 shows a completed high-low-close-open chart.

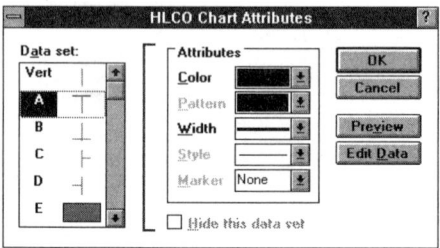

FIGURE 7.21. The HLCO Chart Attributes dialog box.

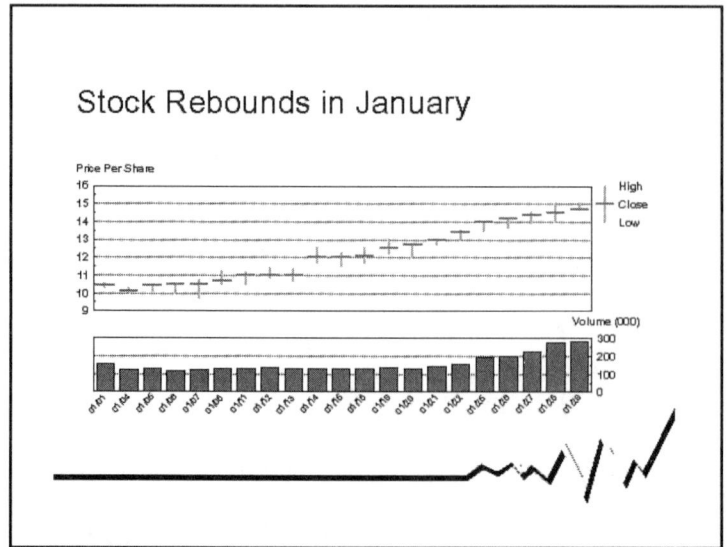

FIGURE 7.22. A completed high-low-close-open chart.

Pie Charts

Pie charts are unique in that they have no axes. Their sole function is to depict parts of the whole, or proportional relationships.

To create a pie chart, choose Single Pie or Multiple Pies as your chart type and then, in the Chart Data & Titles window, enter slice labels and the data values for each pie. If you have chosen multiple pies, there are columns labeled Pie A, Pie B, and so on. Type the numbers for each pie.

By default, when you are using multiple pies, each pie has the same legend and attributes. This make sense because generally a multiple pie chart is used to show the same data for two or more years or products. You might, for example, be comparing the percentage of people who would consider the purchase of a home computer in two different years.

If you want to remove the legend and use separate slice labels for each pie, choose Chart Options Pie and then click the Separate attributes (no legend) button from the dialog box. Now you can return to the Chart Data & Titles window and type separate slice labels for each pie. Using this technique, you can have two pies with a different number of slices. For example (see fig 7.23), in 1990 a company compared the sales of red, blue, and black Mix-O-Matics. The following year they added yellow to their line. To enter the extra slice, it was necessary to enter separate slice labels for each pie.

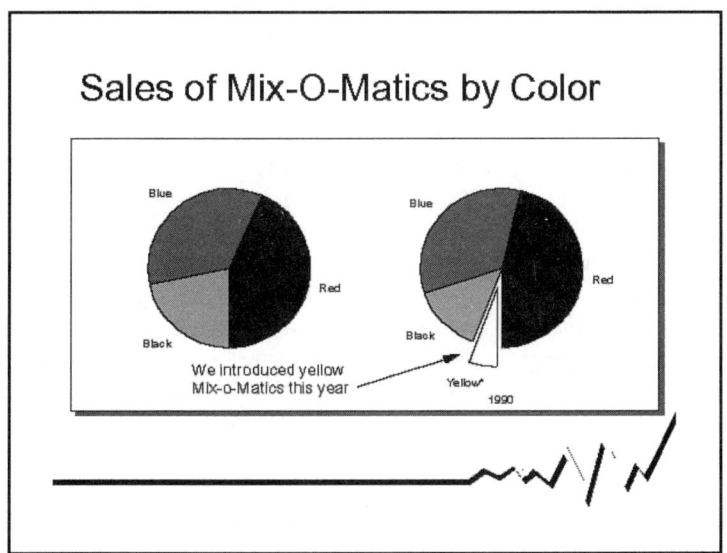

FIGURE 7.23. Two pie charts, without legends and with separate slice labels.

Tables

What kind of data calls for a table chart rather than a chart? Here are three reasons to create a table chart:

- You have a small amount of data that speaks for itself. Numbers alone are sometimes sufficiently dramatic to make a data-driven chart unnecessary.
- You have a large amount of data that you want the reader to be able to consult. This sort of table—the reference table—is suitable for printed reports only. In a presentation, the viewer cannot be expected to pick out a number from a table on a slide or overhead.
- If you can't decide between a table or a data chart, use both! Use the Number Grid Under Chart option to include a table beneath your chart (see Chapter 8, "Customizing Data Charts," for more details).

Creating Table Charts (Number Grids)

Freelance Graphics offers two quite different ways to create tables. The easiest method is to use the Table tool, which you can find in the Toolbox. You choose a table style, specify the number of rows and columns, and then type your entries in the empty table provided. For the procedure for creating tables with the Table tool, read Chapter 11, "Creating Tables."

Freelance Graphics also offers a chart type called number grid, which is also a table chart. Freelance uses this somewhat cumbersome name to distinguish this chart type from the tables created with the Table tool.

What's the difference between a number grid and a table? A number grid creates a table from entries in the Chart Data & Titles window. In most cases, you want to use the Table tool to create tables. It's faster and easier. The main reason to use the number grid is when you want to switch between a table chart and another chart type (such as a bar chart) using the same data. You cannot do this with a table created with the Table tool. Also, the number grid format can calculate and display automatically the total of column entries.

To create a table using the Chart Data & Titles window, enter the Row labels along the left, Column headings along the top (where you would normally type legend labels), and the data for the table in the cells. Figure 7.24 shows the Chart Data & Titles window (although not all the data is visible) for the table chart shown in figure 7.25.

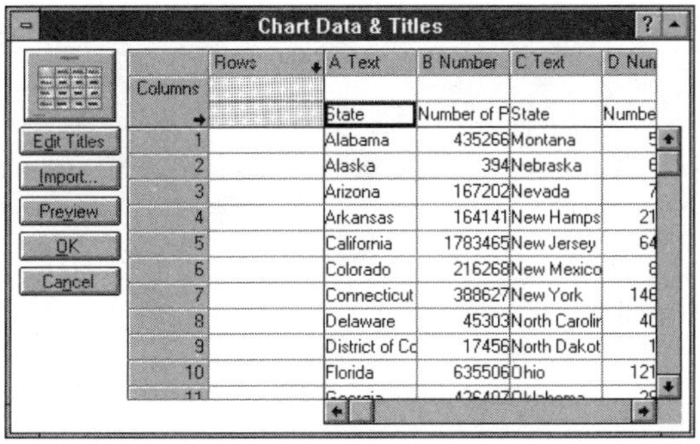

Creating Data Charts   **135**

FIGURE 7.24. The Chart Data & Titles window for a table chart. Note that each column is labeled as either Text or Number.

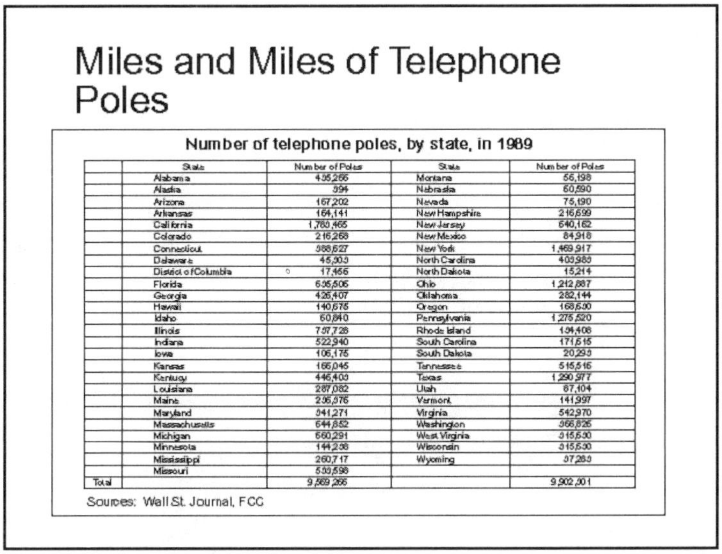

FIGURE 7.25. This table chart is too small to be used in a presentation, but would be fine for a printed report or handout.

You also can specify whether a data set contains text or numbers in the Number Grid Chart Attributes dialog box (fig. 7.26). Highlight the data set (A, B, C, etc.) and then choose Text or Number as the Object type. You also can change the font and other display formats in this dialog box.

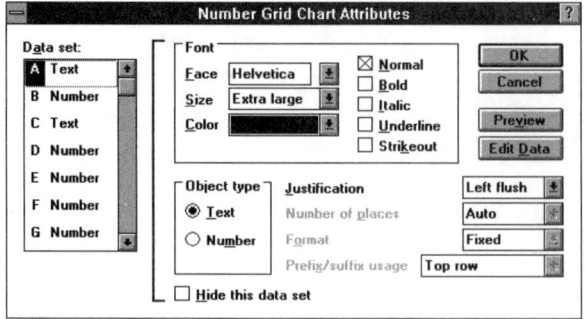

FIGURE 7.26. The Number Grid Chart Attributes dialog box.

Changing the Frame

The frame of a table is the border around it. Choosing the Frame button in the Number Grid Chart dialog box (fig. 7.27), brings up the Number Grid Frame dialog box (fig. 7.28) which enables you to specify frame options. (You can bring up the same dialog box by choosing Chart Frame from the menu.)

In Freelance Graphics, you can place the row and column labels outside the frame, which is sometimes useful (as in the left-hand table in fig. 7.29). In this table, placing the row and column labels outside the frame helps to visually separate the labels from the data.

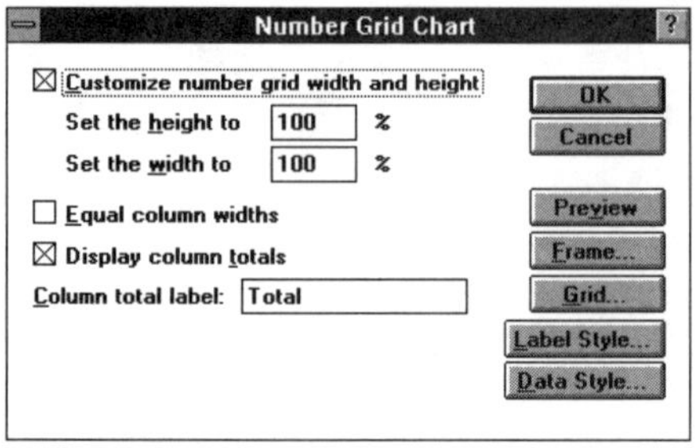

FIGURE 7.27. The Number Grid Chart dialog box.

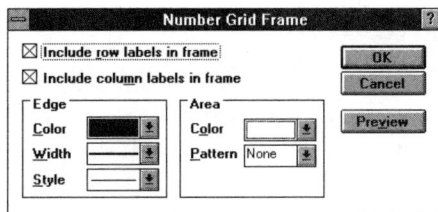

FIGURE 7.28. The Number Grid Frame dialog box.

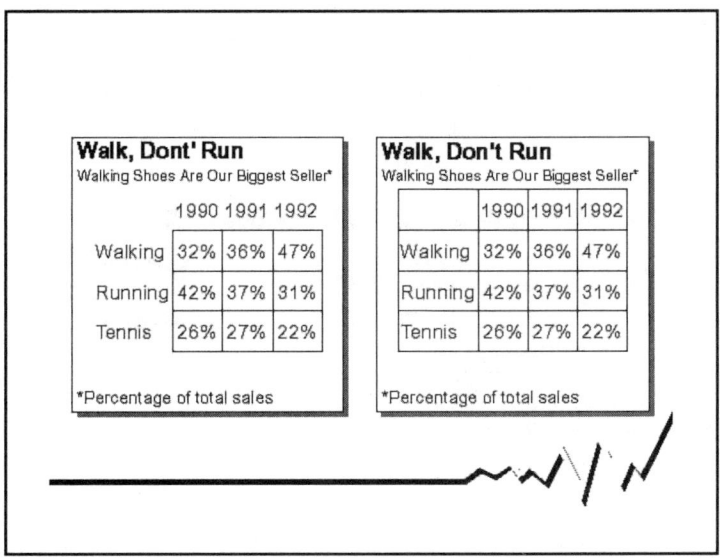

FIGURE 7.29. Row and column labels placed outside the frame (left) and inside the frame (right).

The Sum of All Columns

Tables present statistical observations about various items, and often you want to see the totals of the columns at the bottom of the table. Freelance Graphics can do this for you automatically. Choose Chart Number Grid and then select Display column totals in the Number Grid Chart dialog box (fig. 7.27). You can type a label in the Column Total Label box.

Changing the Grid Style

The grid of a table is the framework of horizontal and vertical lines that surround table entries (like cells in a spreadsheet). A good table chart uses these lines to make the data legible or to highlight the data you want to emphasize. You can choose various combinations of horizontal and vertical lines and specify their color, width, and line style by choosing Chart Number Grid and then clicking the Grid button. This brings up the Number Grid Style dialog box (fig. 7.30). (You can display the same dialog box by choosing Chart Grid from the menu.)

Often, for example, you want the horizontal line between the column headings and the rest of the table to be bolder than the rest of the lines between rows or the vertical line between the first column of data and the rest of the columns of data to be bolder than the rest to set these rows or columns off from the rest of the table. To do this, choose Chart Grid and then make choices from the dialog box.

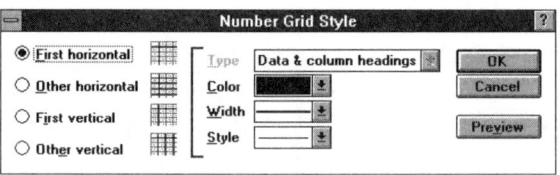

FIGURE 7.30. The Number Grid Style dialog box.

Make All Column Widths Equal

By default, Freelance Graphics Adjusts the column widths to match the width your text or numbers occupy. For a consistent-looking table, however, it is often preferable to make all the column widths equal. This is possible only if all of the columns are nearly equal width to begin with. To make all column widths equal, choose Chart Number Grid and then mark the Equal column widths check box.

Placing Several Charts on a Single Page

Now that you know how to create individual charts, you can expand on this knowledge and think about how you might place two or more charts on a single page.

Why would you want to do this and when? If you are creating a slide presentation or overheads, it is probably best to stick with a single chart per page, although sometimes you can get away with two if the charts are simple.

For printed reports, however, you can use two, three, or even four charts per page.

Each SmartMaster set has four page layouts for charts: 1 Chart, 2 Charts, 4 Charts, and Bullets & Chart. The first three of these are self-evident: They have place holders for 1, 2, or 4 charts per page, respectively. The fourth type, as the name implies, allows you to place a bullet chart and a chart side by side.

Bulleted List and Chart on One Page

If you place a bulleted list and a chart on the same page, they should complement each other (see fig. 7.31). The bulleted items, for example, should clarify or expand on the chart. One consideration for this format is space: The bulleted items must be concise because you have only half a page to work with.

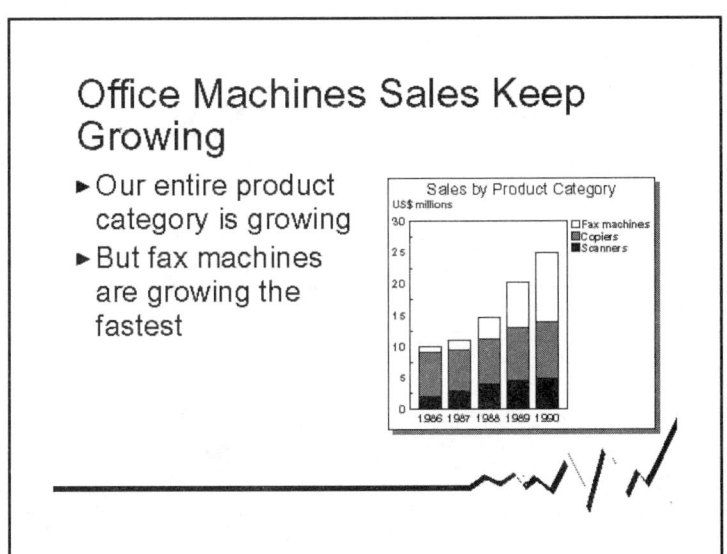

FIGURE 7.31. A bulleted list and a chart on a single page.

Telling a Story with Charts

If you read certain business magazines or newspapers—*The Wall Street Journal*, for example—you may have noticed that several charts are often combined in one frame to tell a story. This is an excellent idea and one that you can emulate easily, as shown in figure 7.32. The three bar charts combine data about vacancy rates, rental prices, and new units built to tell a bleak tale about the construction industry. The last placement block contains a symbol that gives visual support to the theme of the chart.

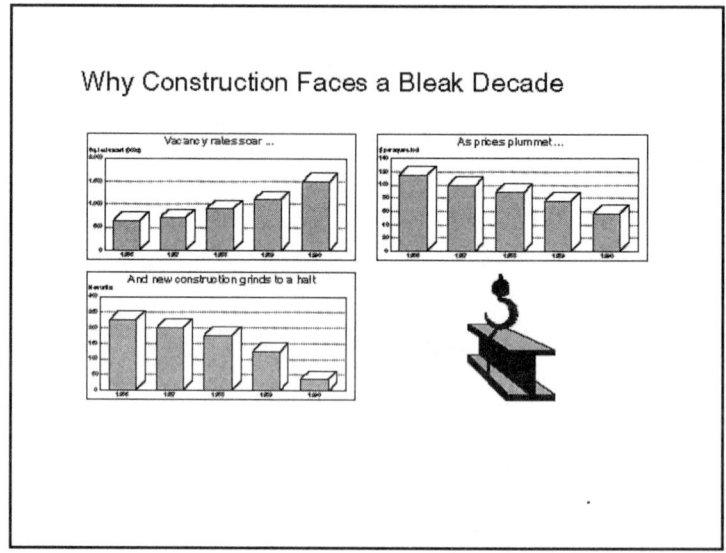

FIGURE 7.32. A presentation page that contains multiple charts.

Start with the 2 Charts or 4 Charts page layout. The 4 Charts page layout obviously lets you tell a longer story. But keep in mind that there is nothing to prevent you from placing three charts in the 4 Chart page layout. Just leave the other one blank. The prompt text does not appear in your printed output or a screen show.

Placing four charts on a page works best for printed reports. It's hard to visually digest that many charts in a slide show or an overhead presentation.

Type a heading for each chart in the titles view of the Chart Data & Titles window. The heading for each individual chart is the story line that makes the transition from chart to chart.

Wrapping Up

In this chapter, after a quick lesson in chart terminology, you learned the general procedure for creating data charts, as well as some techniques for creating specific chart types. You also learned how to add titles and notes to charts.

This lays the groundwork for the next chapter, where you learn how to customize data charts.

8

Customizing Data Charts

After you choose a chart type and enter your data, Freelance Graphics creates well-composed charts for you; that's one of the benefits of a graphics software package. But when you want to give a chart a certain look—perhaps by changing the placement of a legend or the color of a set of bars or by adding annotations or even a symbol to reinforce your point—you have to go beyond the default chart settings and strike out on your own.

With Freelance Graphics, you can change the various components of a chart without disturbing the link between the chart and its data. This flexibility gives you a great deal of freedom to customize charts, but with that freedom comes the need to make sometimes difficult design decisions.

In this chapter, you learn how to:
- *Change the components of a chart*
- *Change axis labels and titles*
- *Change all the text in a chart at once*
- *Specify the chart scale manually*
- *Customize grid and tick marks*
- *Put a frame around your chart*
- *Customize headings and notes*
- *Hide a data set*
- *Place a number grid beneath a chart (instead of a legend)*
- *Add a shadowed background to a chart*
- *Annotate a chart with arrows and text*

Why Change Chart Components?

Many of the chart types in Freelance Graphics have the same components. Most chart types, for example, have grids, frames, axes, and legends. You can change the appearance of these components individually to give a

Before you start changing chart components, consider your purpose. The changes should make your chart more aesthetically pleasing or easier to interpret. Otherwise, stick with the defaults.

chart a different look. You can add grid lines, change their width, place a shadowed frame beneath a chart, change the font for axis titles and labels, and so on.

If you just want to turn out basic, good-looking charts, you can use the basic chart defaults. Changing chart components isn't necessary. Sooner or later, though, you may need to customize a chart component: Perhaps your axis titles are too small; maybe you decide to add grid lines to clarify the interpretation of bar heights; or maybe you need to add a shadowed box to a chart heading.

For whatever reason, when the time comes, you must know how to identify and change the components of a chart. This chapter shows you how to do those things.

How To Change Chart Components

Take a look at the Chart menu in figure 8.1, where most chart components are represented. To change a chart component, you can select the chart and then choose from the Chart menu the component you want to change. If you prefer a more direct approach to changing chart components, you can just double-click the component you want to change. This chapter covers each method.

FIGURE 8.1. The Chart menu.

Use the Chart Menu

To change chart attributes with the Chart menu, the first step is to select the chart, which you can do by clicking once on a chart. The message at the left of the edit line reads "Chart." Now you can choose any item that isn't grayed from the Chart menu. To change the position of a legend, for example, choose Chart Legend and then make the appropriate changes in the Chart Legend dialog box. Choose Grid, for example, to add and customize the appearance of a grid.

Double-Click a Chart Component

A more direct, faster way to change chart components is to double-click the part of the chart you want to change. To display the Chart Legend dialog box, for example, double-click the chart legend. The technique for changing other components is the same. Double-click the axis title, for example, to display the Chart Axis Titles dialog box. You can double-click any chart component.

You can click a chart component to identify it. The message at the left of the edit line tells you which chart component you selected. If you click the axis labels across the bottom of a bar chart, for example, the message in the edit line reads "Chart: x-axis labels." (The word "Chart" always precedes the component you select.) Now you can double-click the same spot to display the Chart Axis Labels dialog box.

Sometimes it can be difficult to click in precisely the right spot to select a particular component. A good trick here is to use the Zoom icon to enlarge the area of the chart that contains the component you want to change. With the component magnified, you should have no trouble double-clicking it.

For greater accuracy, zoom before you click a chart component.

Try It: Change the Color of a Set of Bars

Try changing the color of a set of bars by using the double-click technique. Follow these steps:

1. Position the mouse pointer over the bar representing the set you want to change and double-click. You see the Bar Chart Attributes dialog box (see fig. 8.2).
2. Click the Color list box beneath Attributes.
3. Choose a color from the palette. Click Preview to see the effect of the change without closing the palette. To close the dialog box and make the requested color change, click OK.

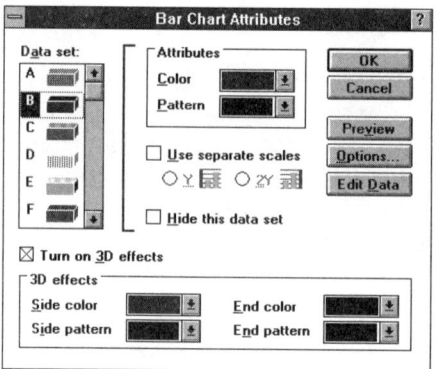

FIGURE 8.2. The Bar Chart Attributes dialog box.

Axis Labels and Titles

Despite the old cliché that pictures are worth a thousand words, the fact is that charts need words to make them comprehensible. Without axis labels, the meaning of the bars in a chart remain a mystery (see fig. 8.3). Without axis titles, who would guess that the numbers on the scaled axis represent values of exports in thousands of dollars?

How To Change Axis Labels and Titles

To edit the attributes of axis titles and axis labels, select the chart and then choose Chart Axis Titles & Labels from the menu bar. Next, choose Titles or Labels. Alternatively, you can double-click the axis titles or labels to display the same dialog boxes (see figs. 8.4 and 8.5).

In the Chart Axis Titles dialog box, click the button for the axis you want to change. Then change the font attributes, rotate the titles horizontally or vertically, or hide the titles altogether. To change the text of the axis titles, click the Edit Text button.

In the Chart Axis Labels dialog box, click the button representing the axis with the labels you want to customize. Then change the font attributes, make adjustments to the way the labels are displayed, set a skip factor, or hide the axis labels. You also can change the display format of numeric labels. To change the text of the axis labels, click the Edit Text button.

Customizing Data Charts   147

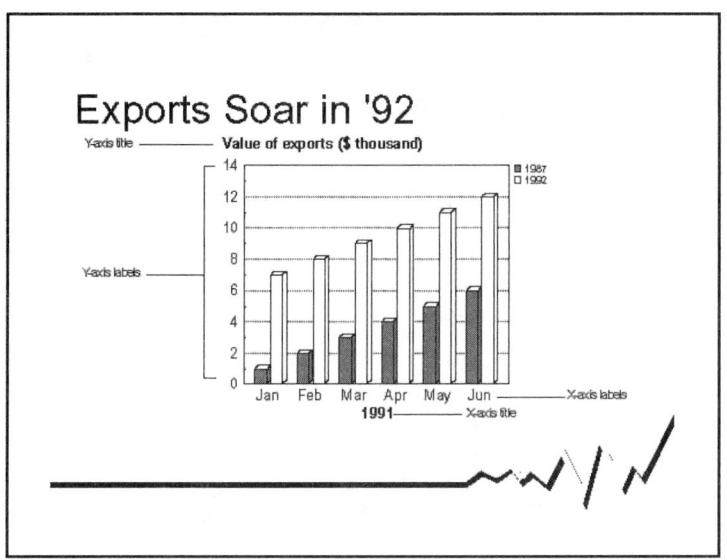

FIGURE 8.3. Axis titles and axis labels help the reader interpret your chart.

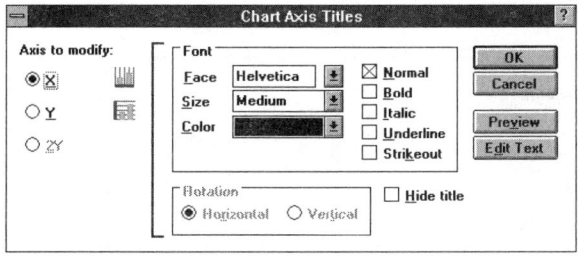

FIGURE 8.4. The Chart Axis Titles dialog box.

It is especially important to give the scaled axis a title so that the viewer will know exactly what is being measured. Without an axis title, the viewer is left wondering, "100 of what?" Typical axis titles are *Units*, *$000*, *$ Thousands*, and *Percent Change*.

A title for the unscaled axis is not as important because the axis labels often reveal the items that are being compared. If the unscaled axis labels are years, for example, axis labels are unnecessary. Sometimes you can use the unscaled axis title to qualify the axis labels. If the axis labels are January, February, and March, for example, the unscaled axis title may be 1993.

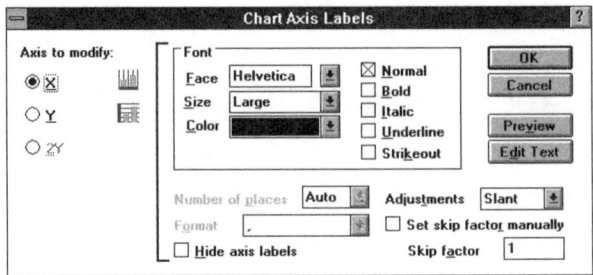

FIGURE 8.5. The Chart Axis Labels dialog box.

What If Your Labels Are Too Long?

If the labels for the unscaled axis are especially long, you can choose the Adjustments option in the Chart Axis Labels dialog box to display them in a different way. The options are Slant, Stagger, and Shrink (see fig. 8.6). You also can set a *skip factor*, which you use to skip labels along the unscaled axis. A skip factor of 2, for example, displays every other label.

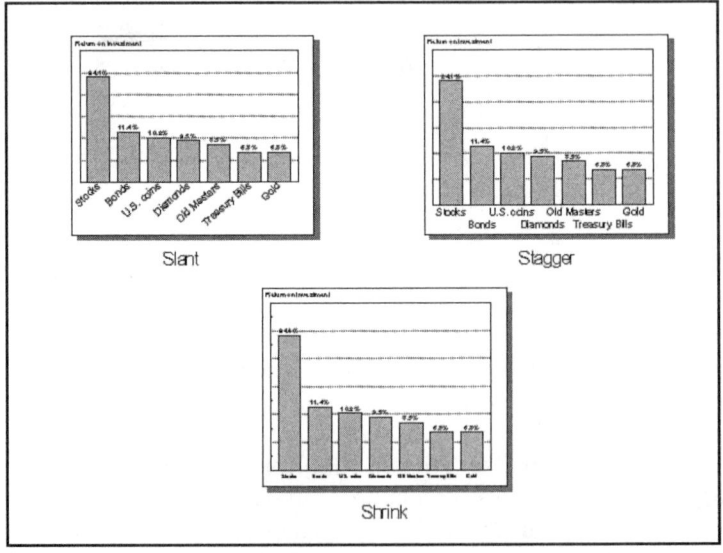

FIGURE 8.6. Three ways to adjust the display of labels: Slant, Stagger, Shrink.

Hide Axis Labels and Titles

Both the Chart Axis Labels and the Chart Axis Titles dialog boxes have a check box that enables you to hide the labels or titles. Checking this box removes the axis labels or titles from your chart. You may not often want to hide your labels, but one reason to do so is to give your chart an uncluttered, abstract look, with all the emphasis on the data symbols rather than the text.

Change Text Components Globally

You can change the typeface and attributes for various chart components such as axis titles, headings, and data values individually, but what if you want to change all the text in your chart at once? You may decide, for example, that for maximum legibility for a screen show, Helvetica should be the font for all text in your chart, including headings, axis titles, axis labels, and legend text. Rather than change each text component individually, you can execute this change globally with the Chart All Chart Text command.

The All Chart Text dialog box has two parts: Text sizes and Font (see fig. 8.7).

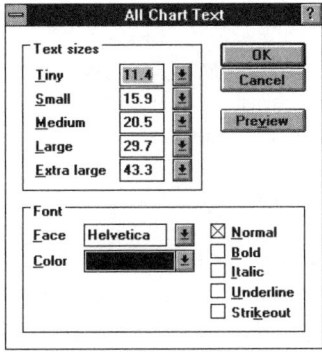

FIGURE 8.7. The All Chart Text dialog box.

Change the Text Sizes settings to establish new defaults for Tiny, Small, Medium, Large, and Extra Large. Freelance Graphics uses these five text sizes to establish the various text components in your chart. When you change the size of axis titles, for example, you do not specify a point size; rather, you choose one of these symbolic names. This approach ensures that your axis titles always are proportionately sized in comparison to the text objects. These values do not represent actual text sizes, but establish relative proportions between all the sizes. Thus, if you specify 10 for Small and 5 for Tiny, Small text always is twice as large as Tiny text, whatever their actual sizes. You can change the values associated with these names in the All Chart Text dialog box. These sizes have been carefully designed to yield an attractive chart, though, so make sure that you have a good reason before you change these numbers.

Change the Font options to change the typeface, color, and emphasis for all text in a chart. Note that the emphasis choices (Normal, Bold, Italic, Underline, and Strikeout) are cumulative; that is, you can choose as many as you like. But for aesthetic reasons, don't check more than two of these boxes at the same time.

On a Scale of 1 to 10

A scale is a measuring device—much like a ruler or yardstick—along which data symbols (bars, lines, and areas) are measured. In a bar chart with a scaled Y axis, for example, the height of a bar represents the data value for that bar.

Most business charts—a pie graph is one exception—have a vertical and a horizontal axis. One axis is scaled and the other is unscaled. The scaled axis measures the data values (dollars, quantity, number, or whatever), and the unscaled axis displays what is being measured or the points in time at which an item is being measured. More often than not, the unscaled axis displays units of time (days, months, quarters, years). But the items on the unscaled axis can be anything at all that can be quantified or measured. A chart showing color preferences for a certain car model, for example, may list Blue, Red, Orange, and Yellow as the items on the unscaled axis, and the scaled axis measures the percentage of users who prefer each color.

The scaled axis can be either the horizontal or the vertical axis (see fig. 8.8). In most time-series charts, the scaled axis is the vertical axis, with the units of time on the horizontal axis. People seem to feel comfortable with the notion of time moving from left to right on a horizontal plane.

Freelance Graphics automatically creates an appropriate scale based on your data. If necessary, however, you easily can change the scale by choosing the Chart Scale command and setting the values manually in the Chart Scale dialog box (see fig. 8.9).

Type new values for Minimum and Maximum to have the chart display the values you want. When you change a Minimum or Maximum value, the check box is selected. Deselect these check boxes to return the chart to automatic scaling. Click Use Separate Scales to set up two different scales. For scaled axis position, choose Left, Right, or Both. Click the Logarithmic button to display plot values against a logarithmic scale.

Customizing Data Charts **151**

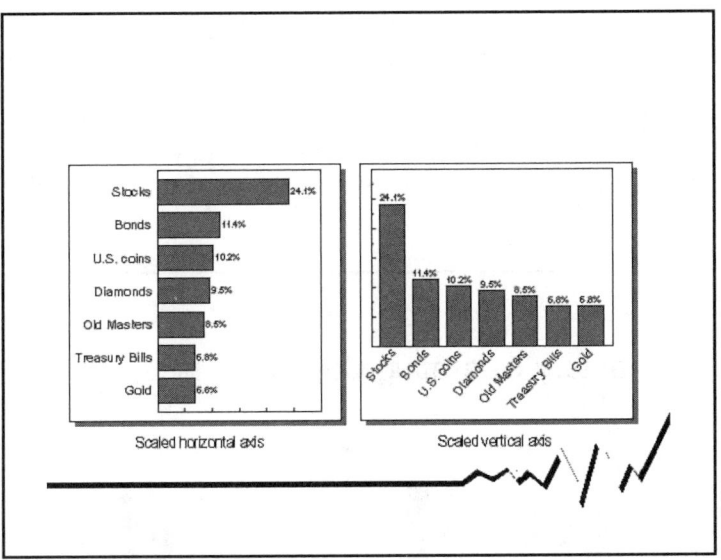

FIGURE 8.8. The scaled axis can be either the vertical or the horizontal axis.

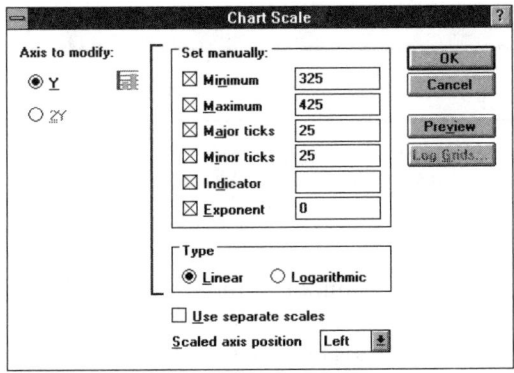

FIGURE 8.9. The Chart Scale dialog box. You also can set the intervals for the major and minor tick marks.

Are Charts with a Nonzero Axis Deceptive?

One reason to change the scale of a chart is to give your data a different slant. Generally, this result is accomplished by starting from a nonzero axis, so that the differences between numbers are magnified (see fig. 8.10). Some people consider this technique unethical because it makes the differences between data symbols seem greater than they are. But nothing is inherently wrong with the technique. If the axes are clearly labeled, no deception is involved. The point is really one of clarity. The fact is that, if you always start with a zero scale, a chart may be difficult to interpret because all the bars look approximately the same height.

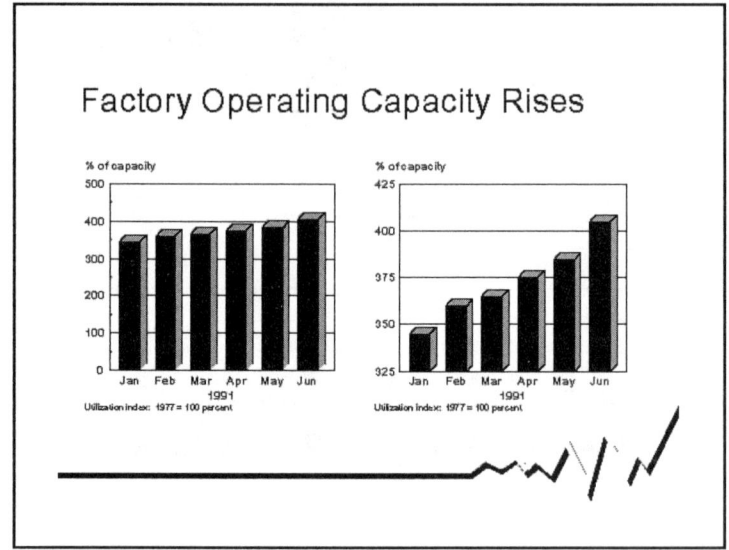

FIGURE 8.10. If variations in a data set are relatively small, but statistically significant, use a nonzero scale, as in the chart on the right.

The point is that sometimes minor differences in values can have a tremendous significance in practical terms. A dollar difference in a stock price can mean millions of dollars of profit or loss for investors. A 2.5 percent dip in sales can mean ruin for a manufacturer. There is no reason not to use a nonzero scale to highlight these not-so-trivial differences. Just make sure that you label the scaled axis clearly so that it is plain that it does not begin with zero.

Charts with Two Scales

If you are displaying data for two or more data sets, you can create a chart with two scales, one on the left and one on the right. This method is useful when you are comparing two data sets that are measured in different units, as in figure 8.11. Here, the bars represent millions of bottles of water purchased (left scale), and the line represents the rising percentage of consumers who are buying bottled water (right scale).

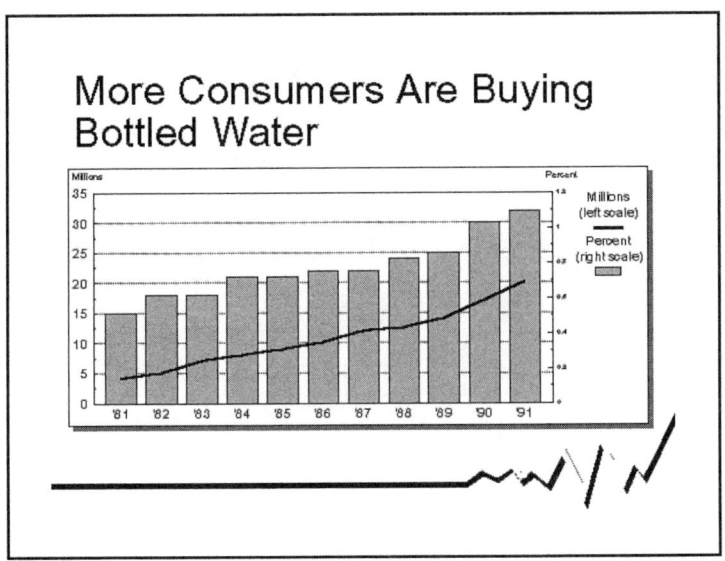

FIGURE 8.11. Charts with two scales are useful for comparing two data sets with widely varying values.

Grids and Ticks

A grid line starts at a value on the scaled axis or at an item on the unscaled axis and proceeds in a horizontal or vertical direction across the width or height of a chart. A tick mark is a short line that marks a data value or label along an axis. A chart may have various combinations of grid lines and ticks, as shown in figure 8.12.

A grid is at once both aesthetic and functional. The grid helps direct the eye to the scale so that you can see what value a data symbol (bar, line, or area) represents. At the same time, a grid adds a nice touch to the look of a chart. Charts with both horizontal and vertical grid lines, for example, have a pronounced financial air about them (check out the charts in *The Wall Street Journal*).

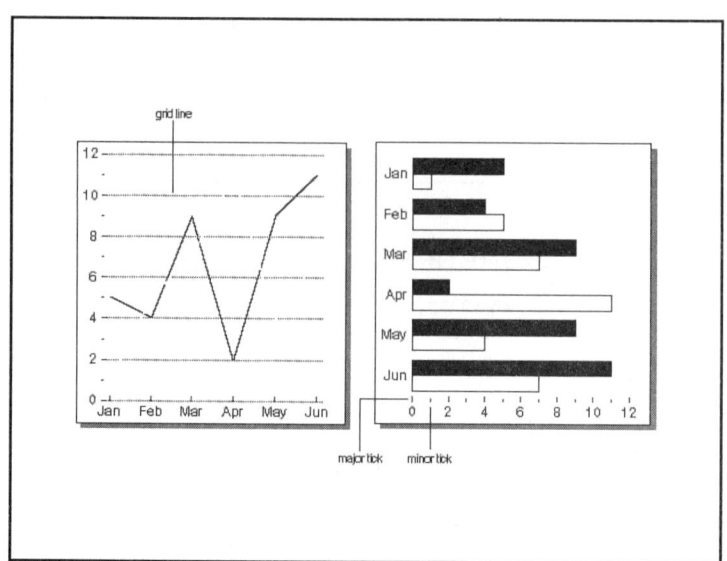

FIGURE 8.12. Grid lines and tick marks.

You can set up vertical or horizontal grids. Generally, you want the grid to emanate from the scaled axis so that you can better measure the values for the data symbols. (In a horizontal bar chart, the Y axis is the scaled axis.)

Tick marks come in two varieties: major and minor. They mark points along the scaled axis exactly like the marks on a yardstick. Major ticks fall whenever a value label appears along the scaled axis. Minor ticks fall between the major ticks and are shorter. You can change the values for which major and minor ticks are displayed in the Chart Scale dialog box. Generally, though, Freelance Graphics places the major and minor ticks intelligently.

Sometimes you may want to turn off the display of major and minor tick marks completely. You can turn them off by deselecting the Display Grid and Display Ticks check boxes in the Chart Grid dialog box.

Why would you want to turn off the tick marks? Generally, for purely aesthetic reasons. A chart without grid or tick marks has a clean, abstract look. This look is useful when you want all eyes on the data symbols without any of the visual clutter of grid lines or tick marks.

You also can display grid and tick marks along the unscaled axis, but doing so generally is not a good idea. Because the unscaled axis does not measure anything, tick marks or grid lines are not necessary to help the viewer comprehend your chart.

Add a Frame to Your Chart

The frame forms a border around the X and Y axes. With the Frame options, you can choose No Frame, an X Frame Only, a Y Frame Only, an X and Y Frame, and Full Frame (see fig. 8.13). The most common choices are Full Frame and X and Y Frame, but for specialized purposes, you can use the other options.

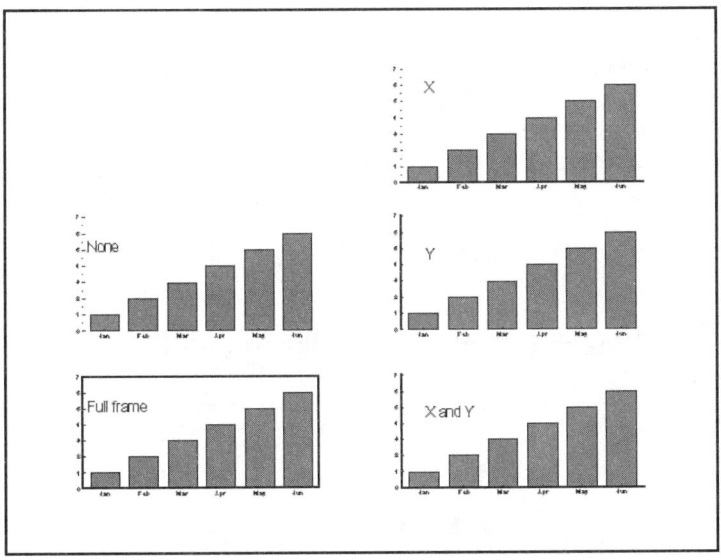

FIGURE 8.13. In Freelance Graphics, you can choose a variety of frame styles to give the chart the look you want.

Legible Legends

The legend on a map describes the meaning of the symbols you see on the map. In some atlases, thick red lines are interstate highways, blue triangles represent rest stops, fir trees stand for state parks, and so on. Similarly, a chart legend shows you what the data symbols on the chart denote. In a bar chart, blue bars might stand for 1987 and red bars for 1992. In a line chart, the thick black line might display profits and the dashed green line might display revenues.

A legend should be plainly visible and easy to interpret but not overly large so as to detract from the main body of the chart.

You can change the position of the legend for most chart types. Select the chart and then choose Chart Legend. You also can double-click the legend. Either method displays the Chart Legend dialog box.

Note that a chart displays no legend at all unless a text entry is in one of the two legend rows above the columns of your data values.

You can hide a legend by checking the Hide Legend check box in the Chart Legend dialog box. Checking this box not only removes the legend from your chart, but also recomposes the chart to make it larger, because it can now fill some of the space taken up by the legend.

Because legends help identify what the data symbols in a chart represent, why would you want to hide them? Suppose that you decided to label the data symbols in a chart. Now the legends are no longer necessary. You also can remove a legend by removing the legend labels in the Chart Data & Titles window, but you may want to keep this information for reference purposes.

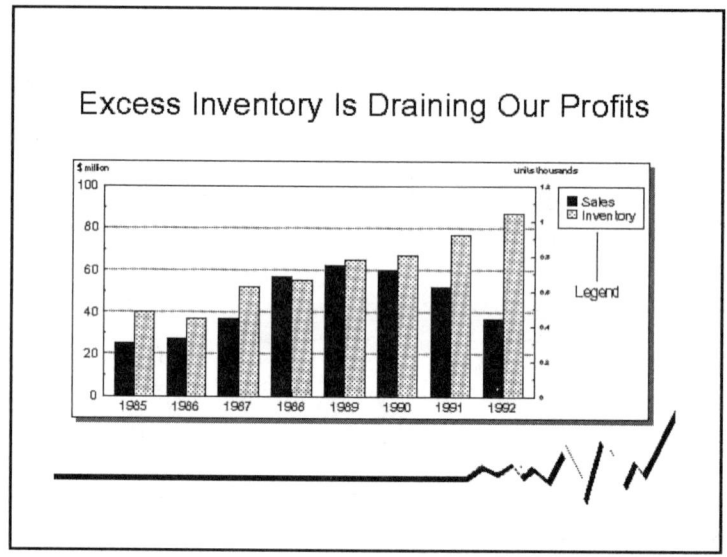

FIGURE 8.14. A legend reveals the meaning of a chart's data symbols.

Headings and Notes

You learned how to add headings and notes to a chart in Chapter 7, "Creating Data Charts." If, after you display or print your chart, you decide the headings or notes aren't large enough—or perhaps they are so large that they obscure your data—you can change their size in the Chart Headings & Notes dialog box (see fig. 8.15). To display this dialog box, select the chart and then choose Chart Headings & Notes, or just double-click any heading or note. You can change the font or attributes of headings and notes in this dialog box. Click the Edit Text button to move quickly to the titles view of the Chart Data & Titles window.

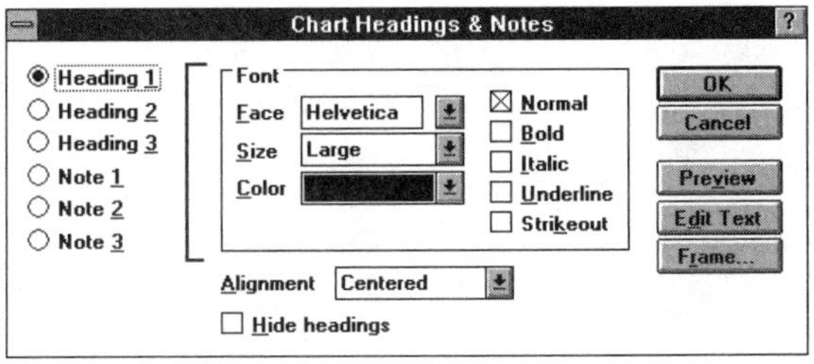

FIGURE 8.15. The Chart Headings & Notes dialog box.

What if you are in the Chart Headings & Notes dialog box and then realize that you want to change the text of a note? To do so quickly, click the Edit Text button to go directly to the Chart Data & Titles window.

You can add a frame around your heading or note to make it stand out. Adding a frame to a heading can make an appealing chart, especially if you choose the shadow option (see fig. 8.16).

Hide Data Sets

Occasionally, you may want to hide some portion of your data in a chart (perhaps the data is not relevant, but you don't want to delete it in case you need to display it later). To hide portions of data, double-click the bar, area, or line representing the data set that you want to hide. In the resulting dialog box, you see a check box labeled Hide This Data Set. When you select this check box, Freelance Graphics recomposes the chart as if this data set did not exist. Where there were four sets of bars, there now are three; where there were three lines, there are two, and so on.

The data hasn't vanished, however. If you return to the Chart Data & Titles window, you can verify that the data remains. Freelance Graphics has just removed that data from the current chart. You can get the data back (and the accompanying data symbols) whenever you want by deselecting the check box. You can hide as many data sets in a chart as you want. Just select another data set you want to hide and select the Hide This Data Set check box.

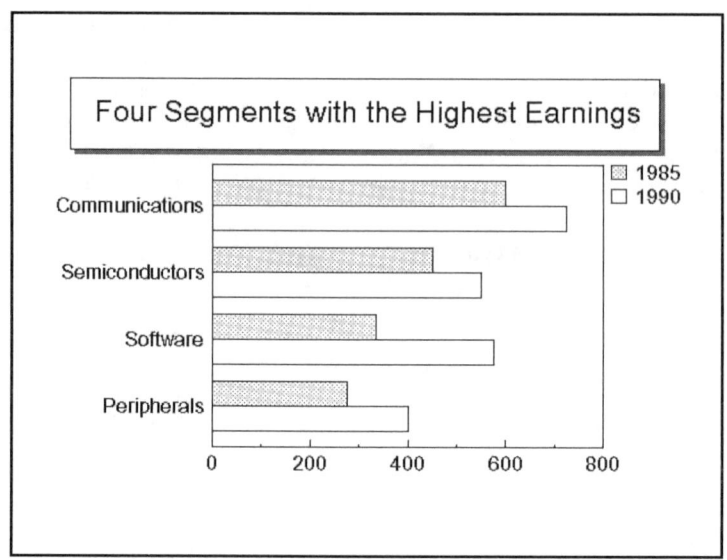

FIGURE 8.16. The shadowed frame emphasizes the heading.

Add a Number Grid under a Chart

A chart with a number grid (table) represents the best of two worlds. It's kind of like hedging your bet. You get the symbolic value of geometric shapes to express data values combined with precise data values in row and column format. Although this book has stressed that charts are powerful communication tools precisely because they display numbers as geometric shapes, there's nothing like hard, actual numbers to convince an audience.

Figure 8.17 shows the Number Grid Under Chart dialog box. The buttons enable you to switch between displaying a legend and displaying a number grid (table) under the chart. To display the total of columns, click the Display Column Totals check box and type a label in the box provided. The Grid, Frame, Label Style, and Data Style buttons lead to other dialog boxes that enable you to customize the look of the number grid.

To display a number grid beneath a chart, choose Chart Number Grid Under Chart and then complete the dialog box. The Use Legend and the Use Number Grid Under Chart options are mutually exclusive. Figure 8.18 shows a bar chart combined with a number grid. Note how the horizontal labels do double-duty as axis labels and column headers for the table.

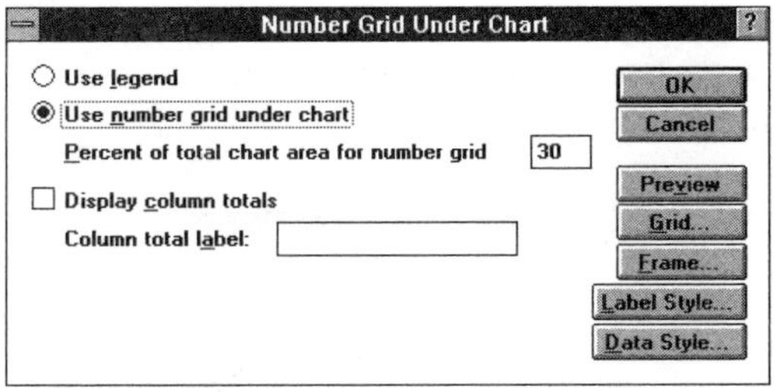

Customizing Data Charts **159**

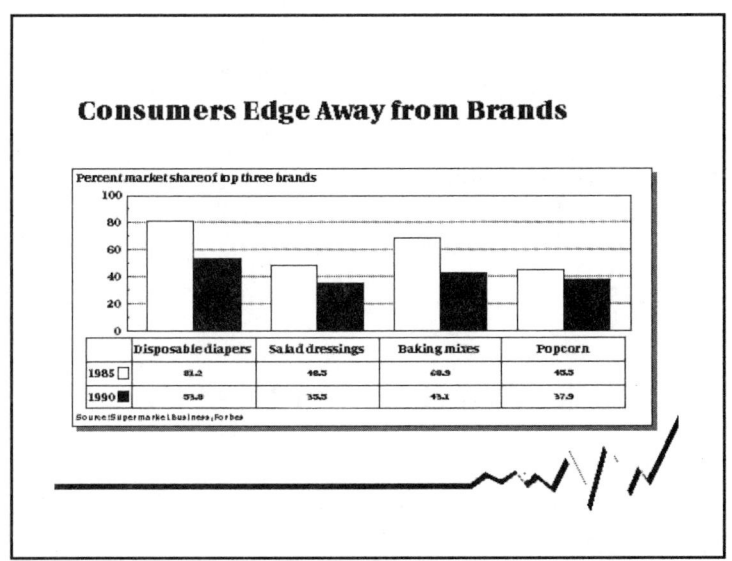

FIGURE 8.17. The Number Grid Under Chart dialog box.

FIGURE 8.18. A bar chart combined with a number grid (table chart).

Add a Shadowed Background

You change the background color of a chart to add visual interest and to make the chart stand out on the page.

To change the background, choose Background from the Chart menu. As you can see in the Chart Background dialog box in figure 8.19, you can change the

Edge Color, Width, and Style as you like and you can add a fill by making selections in the Area box. (For more information on the Area settings, see Chapter 13, "Editing Objects.")

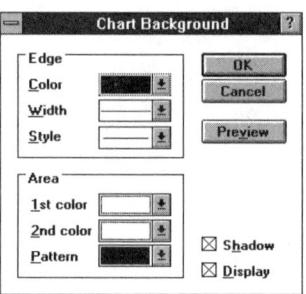

FIGURE 8.19. The Chart Background dialog box.

One of the most attractive options is the shadowed background (see fig. 8.20). To create a shadowed background automatically, click the Shadow and Display check boxes in the Chart Background dialog box.

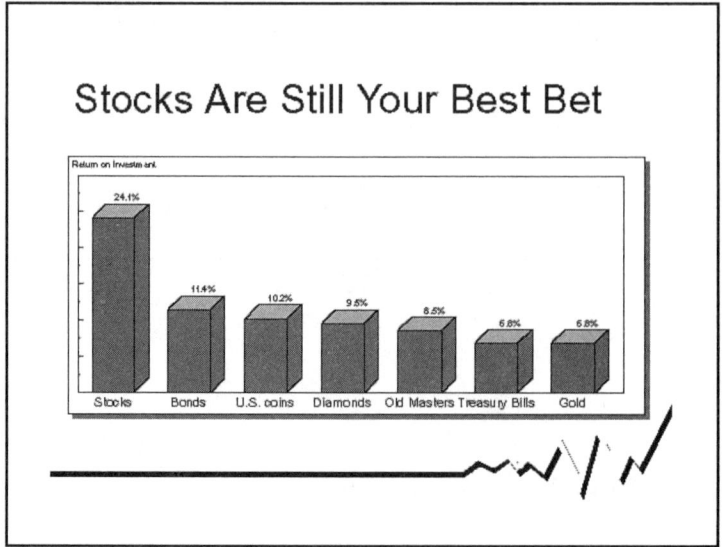

FIGURE 8.20. A chart showing a shadowed background.

Annotate a Chart

Although charts generally convey your message adequately, even charts are subject to individual interpretation. By pointing out a certain area of a chart and stating your conclusion directly, you can make sure that your audience gets the point. An arrow pointing to a single bar in a chart and text that reads "Profits up 50% from 1991" leaves little room for ambiguity or misinterpretation.

Annotations leave no room for ambiguity in a chart.

The simplest form of annotation is to add text and arrows. Click the Arrow icon in the Toolbox and then drag an arrow on the page, pointing toward the data symbol you want to point out. (Press Shift as you drag to draw a perfectly horizontal or vertical arrow.) Next, click the Text icon in the Toolbox, click the page, and then type the text for your annotation. Line up the text and arrow with the Align SmartIcon and you're finished.

Try It: Make a Custom Text Box

Try making a custom text form that you can use to display annotations. After you create this text box once, you can add it to the symbol library to make it available to all other presentations.

1. Choose View Units & Grids and select the Display Grid and Snap to Grid check boxes.
2. Drag a rectangle on the page.
3. With the rectangle selected, choose Arrange Convert To Polygons.
4. Press Shift+F6 to enter points mode or click the Points Mode SmartIcon. (See Chapter 13, "Editing Objects," for more information about working in edit points mode.)
5. Press Ins and note the plus (+) symbol inside the pointer. You are now ready to add a point to an object.
6. Click a grid dot at the bottom of the rectangle to add a point.
7. Repeat steps 5 and 6 to add two more points adjacent to the first.
8. Click the middle point you added and drag it downward and to the right until you see the look you want (see fig. 8.21).

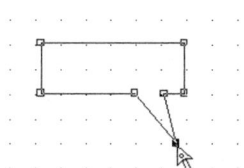

FIGURE 8.21. Dragging a point on a polygon to create a pointer in the text box.

9. Press Shift+F6 to leave edit points mode.
10. Double-click the object and change its attributes so that it has a dark edge and a solid white fill.
11. Select the object you have just created and then choose Tools Add to Symbol Library. You can add it to the CUSTOM.SYM library or to the TEXTBOX.SYM library (which contains other text boxes). Now the symbol is available for any presentation. You can access it as you do any other symbol. Just add a text block over it to display your message.

Figure 8.22 shows a chart with a custom text box added.

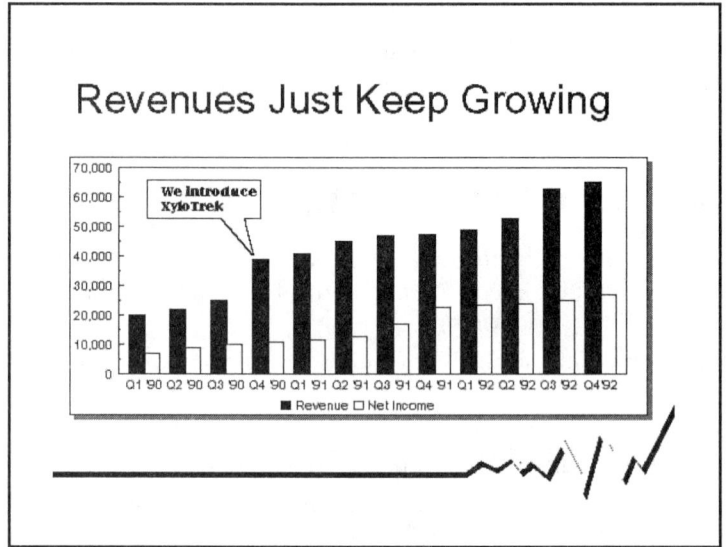

FIGURE 8.22. A chart with a custom text box.

Wrapping Up

In this chapter, you learned how to customize your data charts to help readers understand the charts better and to make them more visually appealing. You learned to use the many options on the Chart menu. You now know how to double-click a chart component to open a dialog box in which you can change that component's appearance. You learned how to add a number grid beneath a chart and how to create a dramatic effect by adding shadowed backgrounds.

Finally, you learned how to make a chart's meaning even more emphatic by adding an annotation.

In the next chapter, you find out how to import 1-2-3 data and charts into Freelance Graphics.

9

Creating Charts from 1-2-3 Worksheets

Getting the raw numbers into the data entry form of your graphics package can be the hardest part of the whole process of creating a chart. And, if the data you need exists on paper only, you have little recourse but to sit down and type the numbers into Freelance Graphics.

But, if your numbers are in a 1-2-3 worksheet, you have a rich source of data at your fingertips that you can copy or import directly into Freelance Graphics without retyping a single number. This chapter shows you how you can save time by importing or copying (via the Clipboard) 1-2-3 data to use as source data for your graphs.

Although this chapter focuses on 1-2-3 data, you also can import data from Lotus Symphony worksheets, Microsoft Excel worksheets, or dBASE, SYLK, or ASCII files. If you are using another open Windows application, such as Microsoft Excel, you also can copy data into Freelance Graphics via the Windows Clipboard.

In this chapter, you learn how to:

- *Import data from 1-2-3 worksheet files to use for Freelance Graphics charts, with or without establishing links*
- *Copy data from an open 1-2-3 for Windows worksheet via the Clipboard and paste it into Freelance Graphics, with or without establishing links*
- *Import 1-2-3 named charts*
- *Copy 1-2-3 for Windows charts to Freelance Graphics in several formats*
- *Edit the links to worksheets without leaving Freelance Graphics*

What's the Best Method for You?

At first glance, your purpose seems plain: You want to use data from a 1-2-3 worksheet to create a Freelance Graphics data chart, or you want to bring a completed 1-2-3 chart directly into Freelance Graphics. In actual practice, though, you have a bewildering number of options available to you to achieve these simple goals. The following are some of the desired ends and the various solutions:

- You want to import data from a 1-2-3 worksheet file (either DOS or Windows) into the Chart Data & Titles window so that you can create a Freelance Graphics chart. As an option, you may want to establish a link to the data in the worksheet so that when the data changes, your graph is updated automatically. Finally, you may have only the 1-2-3 worksheet (whether DOS or Windows) on your system, not 1-2-3 itself. If this describes your situation, read the section "Importing Data from 1-2-3 Worksheet Files."

- You want to import a 1-2-3 named chart (from either a DOS or a Windows worksheet file) directly onto a Freelance Graphics presentation page. For more information on this method, read the section "Importing Named Charts."

- You want to copy the data from an open 1-2-3 for Windows worksheet to the Chart Data & Titles window, with or without establishing a link. For more information, refer to the section "Copying Data from an Open 1-2-3 for Windows Worksheet."

- You want to copy an entire chart from 1-2-3 for Windows to a Freelance Graphics presentation page, with or without establishing a link. See the section "Copying Charts from 1-2-3 for Windows."

Importing Data from 1-2-3 Worksheet Files

If you use 1-2-3, your worksheets represent a mother lode of data. Why bother with the tedious task of entering data for graphs when you easily can tap into this rich source? When you import worksheet data, you can either copy it on a one-time basis or establish a link to the worksheet so that when the data changes, your chart is automatically refreshed with the new data.

If the source application is not open, or if you do not have the source application on your system, click the Import button in the Chart Data & Titles window. When you click the Import button, you choose the worksheet file from which you want to import data, and Freelance Graphics displays its contents on-screen. You can select the ranges you want to import. The primary benefit of this method is that all you need to import from a 1-2-3 worksheet is the worksheet itself. You do not need to have 1-2-3 open or even installed on your computer.

Freelance Graphics enables you to import worksheet data visibly and interactively. This capability means that you actually can view the source data in the worksheet (regardless of whether you have the software for the worksheet) and select the ranges you want to import to Freelance Graphics. The process is relatively straightforward, but the various options can be an obstacle to the novice.

If you decide to import data from a 1-2-3 worksheet, you have two ways to go about it. First, ask yourself, "How is the data I want to import arranged in the worksheet?" Here are two possibilities:

- If each data range is in a single block in a worksheet (for example, in a single row or column), you can import the data in a single pass.
- If the data is scattered about the worksheet (or across several worksheets), you have to import the data in several passes.

This chapter shows you what to do in each of these cases.

Try It: Import Data from a Single Worksheet

First, import a single block of data from a 1-2-3 for Windows worksheet. This technique does not require you to have 1-2-3 for Windows installed on your computer. All you need is the worksheet file itself. You can use the same technique to import data from DOS versions of 1-2-3.

1. Start a new page and choose the 1 Chart page layout.
2. Click the prompt text that reads "Click here to create chart."
3. Choose the chart type and style from the New Chart Gallery dialog box. This example uses a bar chart.
4. Click the Import button in the Chart Data & Title window. The Import Data File dialog box appears (see fig. 9.1). You can select another directory in the Directories box.

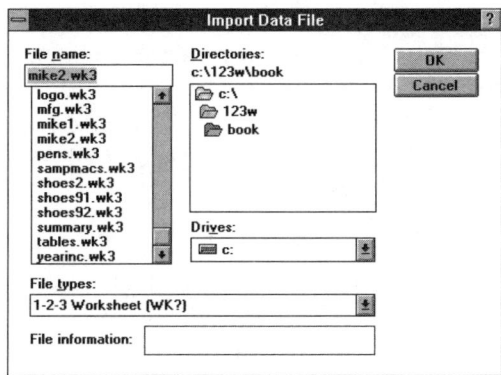

FIGURE 9.1. The Import Data File dialog box.

5. Highlight the name of the worksheet file that contains your data and then click OK or double-click the file you want to import. Freelance Graphics opens the Import Data dialog box (see fig. 9.2). This window is a view of the worksheet you selected (you are not actually in 1-2-3).

The left of the Import Data dialog box has three color-coded options that lead you through the process.

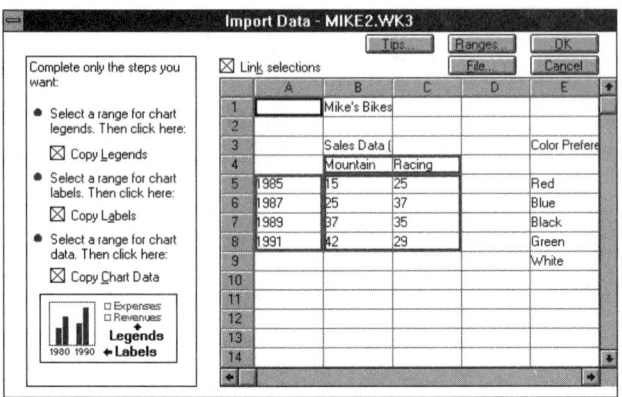

FIGURE 9.2. The Import Data dialog box.

6. The first task is to select the range for your legends. Drag-select the range for your legends and then click the Copy Legends check box. Note that the border around the range you selected is red, to match the red bullet next to the instruction text.

7. Next, drag the mouse to highlight the range for your chart labels. Then click the Copy Labels check box. This range is outlined in green, to match the green bullet in the instruction area.

8. Finally, highlight the range that contains the data. Then click the Copy Chart Data check box. This range turns blue, to match the blue bullet next to the instruction text.

9. Now click the Link Selections check box. This check box sets up a link between the worksheet file and chart. After you import the data, whenever the worksheet file changes, Freelance Graphics is updated automatically.

10. Click OK. Freelance Graphics imports the data into the Chart Data & Titles window. Note that the data is underlined in blue, which means that the data is linked to the source worksheet (see fig. 9.3).

Linked data is underlined in blue in the Chart Data & Titles window.

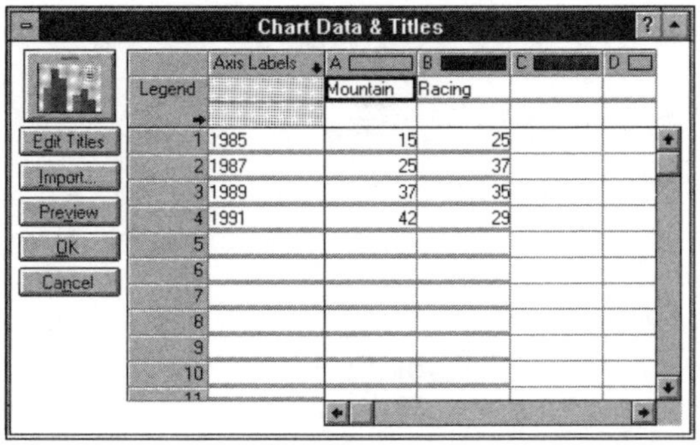

Creating Charts from 1-2-3 Worksheets

FIGURE 9.3. In the Chart Data & Titles window, the data is underlined in blue to indicate that it is linked.

11. Click OK to see the chart on the page. Note that the message in the edit line reads "Linked Chart."
12. Type a title in the text block at the top of the page.

If you want to change the way Freelance Graphics links your data (perhaps you want to expand a range), choose Edit Links. For more details, see the section "Editing Links to Worksheets without Leaving Freelance Graphics."

As shown in figure 9.4, Freelance Graphics composes the chart based on your choices in the Import Data dialog box.

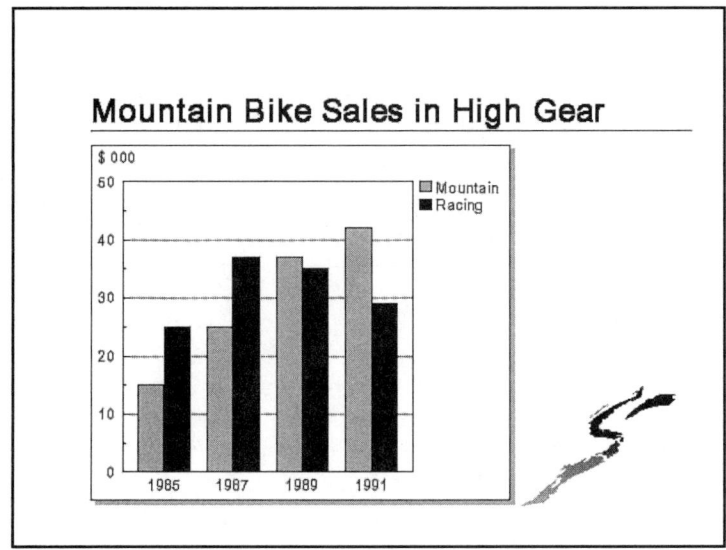

FIGURE 9.4. A chart created from a linked file.

What's the Difference? File Links versus DDE Links

The link between Freelance Graphics and the source data can be either a file link or a DDE (Dynamic Data Exchange) link. A *DDE link* is a link between two open Windows applications (such as Freelance Graphics and 1-2-3 for Windows). A DDE link is updated automatically whenever the data in the source file changes. When you have set up a DDE link between Freelance Graphics and a 1-2-3 for Windows worksheet, as soon as the worksheet data changes, your chart is updated. A DDE link is best if you need to link a chart to a worksheet in real time. This capability can be useful, for example, if you are downloading data from an on-line stock service into a 1-2-3 for Windows worksheet.

A *file link* is a connection to data in a file that is not currently open. A file link is updated only when you retrieve the presentation. As a practical matter, you don't have to worry too much about the distinction between a DDE link and a file link. A file link can become a DDE link (and vice versa), depending on what applications you have open at a given time.

Suppose that you click the Import button in the Chart Data & Titles window to import data from a 1-2-3 for Windows worksheet. Clicking this button establishes a file link between Freelance Graphics and the 1-2-3 for Windows worksheet file. Later, if you open the 1-2-3 for Windows worksheet that is linked to Freelance Graphics (with Freelance Graphics still open), the file link becomes a DDE link. Later, in another work session, if you open only the Freelance Graphics file that contains the link, the link to the source worksheet is now a file link. When you open the presentation file, Freelance Graphics reads the data from the appropriate worksheet file.

To Link or Not To Link?

When you copy data from a worksheet into Freelance Graphics, you choose whether to link the data to its source. When is linking a good idea? Linking has its benefits and drawbacks. If you choose to link the data, the obvious benefit is that whenever the data in the source worksheet changes, your chart is refreshed automatically. This method is especially valuable when you create reports on a regular basis, perhaps quarterly, and want the numbers for each new quarter to be reflected in your graphs automatically.

Then why not always choose the Link option? The main reason is when you know the spreadsheet data never changes. Another reason is when you want to keep an archival record of historical numbers.

Importing Data from More Than One Worksheet

What if the data you need for a single chart is spread out across several worksheets? This situation may occur, for example, if you want to create a chart showing several years' worth of data and the data resides in several worksheets (see fig. 9.5). In this case, you need to use a somewhat different technique for importing and linking worksheet data.

Now try importing data from two worksheets. You can use the same technique if your data is scattered across a single worksheet.

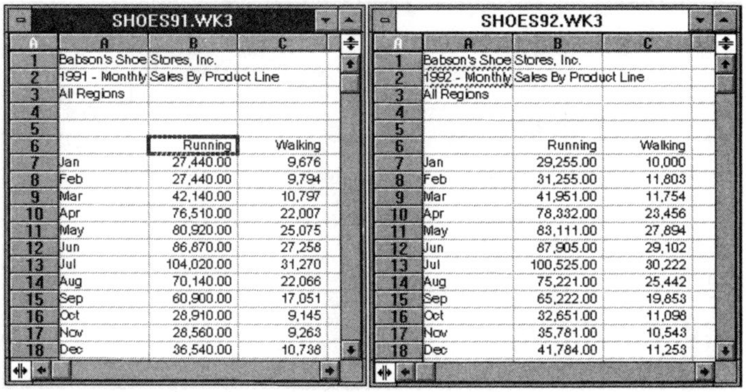

FIGURE 9.5. To create a chart, you may need the data for running shoes for 1991 and 1992.

Import the Axis Labels

The first part of the procedure is to copy the axis labels from the first worksheet. Follow these steps:

1. Create a new page and choose the 1 Chart page layout.
2. Click the "Click here to create chart" prompt text and then choose a chart type and style from the Chart Gallery. This example uses a bar chart.
3. Click the Import button and, in the Import Data File dialog box, highlight the name of the first file and then click OK.
4. Drag to highlight the column of X axis labels (Jan - Dec) and then select the Copy Labels check box. A green border appears around the highlighted range (see fig. 9.6).

5. Mark the Link Selections check box and click OK. The X axis labels are copied to the Chart Data & Titles window. The blue underline denotes the link.

6. Now type the legend labels (*1991*, *1992*) in the Chart Data & Titles window (see fig. 9.7). You *can* import them, but it is easier to type them. You can have a combination of linked and unlinked data in the Chart Data & Titles window. The imported and linked data is underlined in blue. Because 1991 and 1992 are not linked (you typed them), they are not underlined.

FIGURE 9.6. The Import Data dialog box showing X axis labels highlighted.

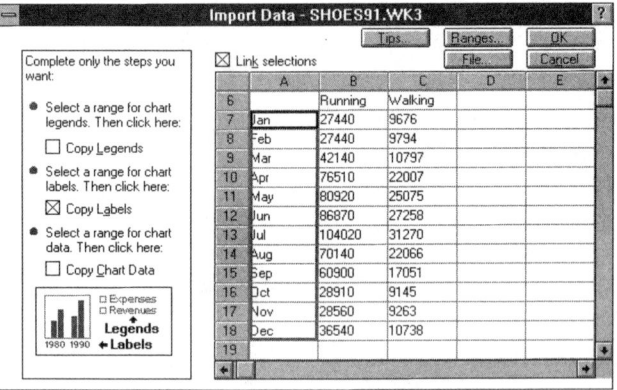

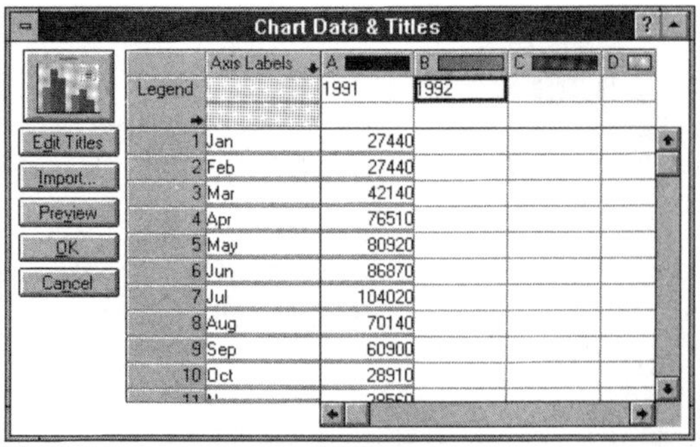

FIGURE 9.7. The Chart Data & Titles window.

Copy the First Data Set

Now you can copy the first data set (the 1991 sales data for running shoes) by doing the following:

1. Click the Import button again and highlight the range for the first data set (the data under the column labeled "Running"). This time, don't use the color-coded check boxes on the left side of the Import Data dialog box. You cannot use this option to import successive data ranges, because the second data set overwrites the first.

2. Click OK (you don't need to mark the Link Selections check box). You see the Information dialog box, which explains that this method uses the Clipboard to copy the selected range of data (see fig. 9.8).

   You see this dialog box when you do not select any of the color-coded check boxes in the Import Data dialog box. Click OK and then use Edit Paste or Edit Paste Special to copy the data to the Chart Data & Titles window.

FIGURE 9.8. The Information dialog box.

3. Click OK to copy the highlighted data to the Clipboard.
4. Choose Edit Paste Special from the Chart Data & Titles window. In the Edit Paste Special dialog box, mark the Link Data check box, highlight Data Set A in the list, and then click OK (see fig. 9.9). The data is copied and underlined in blue to show the link.

   In this dialog box, you choose the destination for the data range you selected. If you are copying a single row or column of data, Part of Chart is selected automatically. Highlight the destination in the list box. To establish a link, mark the Link Data check box.

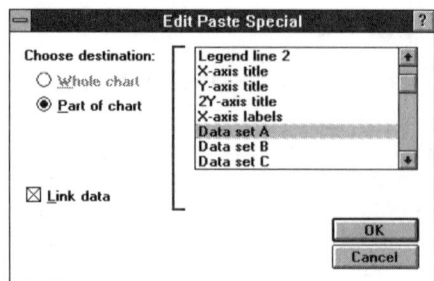

FIGURE 9.9. The Edit Paste Special dialog box.

Copy the Second Data Set

Now you can copy the second data set (the 1992 sales data for running shoes), just as you copied the first. Follow these steps:

1. Click the Import button in the Chart Data & Titles window, click the File button in the Import Data dialog box, and highlight the name of the worksheet file that contains the data for 1992 (SHOES92.WK3).
2. Highlight the column of data for running shoes for 1992. Click OK.
3. Click OK in the Information dialog box to copy the highlighted data to the Clipboard.
4. Choose Edit Paste Special from the Chart Data & Titles window.
5. In the Edit Paste Special dialog box, mark the Link Data check box, highlight Data Set B in the list on the right, and click OK. The data is copied and underlined in blue to show the link.
6. Click OK to view the chart (see fig. 9.10). Then type a title in the title block at the top of the page.

The next time you open this presentation, the chart is updated automatically if the worksheet data has changed. The worksheet file need not be open, but it must be in the same directory as when you created the original link.

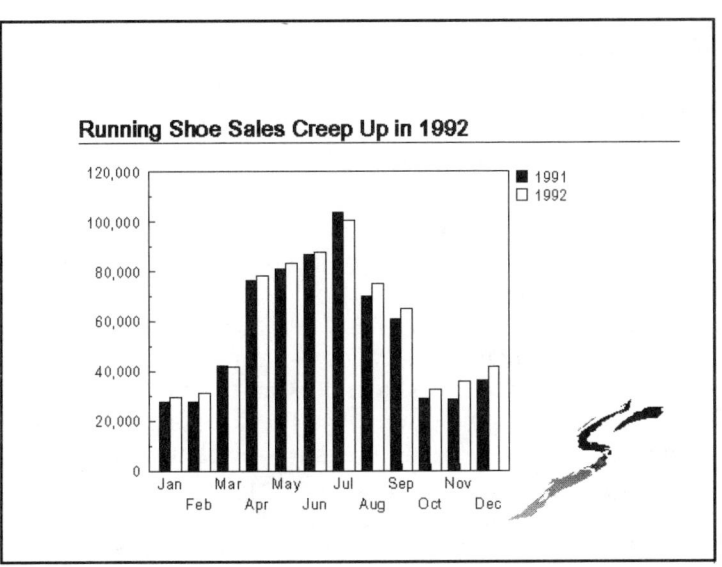

FIGURE 9.10. Type a title in the title placement block to complete the chart.

Double-Clicking a Cell with Linked Data

When you click the Import button in a Chart Data & Titles window that contains linked data (the data is underlined in blue), Freelance Graphics displays an Import Data window that contains the worksheet from the last time you imported data, not the worksheet to which the current chart is linked. To view the worksheet to which the current chart is linked, double-click any linked data cell in the Chart Data & Titles window. This action opens the Import Data window, with the correct worksheet displayed. If you double-clicked an X axis label in the Chart Data & Titles window, the data range for that label is highlighted in the Import Data window, and so on. There is one important exception to this rule: If the linked 1-2-3 for Windows file happens to be open when you double-click a cell, you get an error message stating that the source application does not support OLE. Click the Import button and then click the File button in the Import Data window to view the correct file.

Copying Data from an Open 1-2-3 for Windows Worksheet

If you are working in Freelance Graphics and 1-2-3 for Windows during the same session, you can copy data from an open worksheet and then paste it into Freelance Graphics, with or without establishing a link. This method is often the most convenient way to bring 1-2-3 data into Freelance Graphics, especially if you do not want to establish a link.

In the 1-2-3 for Windows worksheet, just select the range you want to copy to Freelance Graphics and then use Edit Copy to move the data to the Clipboard. Then use Edit Paste to place the data in the Chart Data & Titles window.

If you want to set up a link between the Freelance Graphics chart and the 1-2-3 for Windows worksheet, use Edit Paste Special. If you choose Edit Paste Special, you also must complete the Edit Paste Special dialog box. Because this dialog box can be confusing, this method is not your best option for copying linked data to the Chart Data & Titles window. It's simpler to use the Import button to accomplish this task. (See "Importing Data from 1-2-3 Worksheet Files.")

Try It: Copy Unlinked Data

Now try copying data from an open 1-2-3 for Windows worksheet without establishing a link between the data and the worksheet. Follow these steps:

1. Create a new page and choose the 1 Chart page layout.
2. Click the prompt text, "Click here to create chart," and then choose a chart type and style from the Chart Gallery. This example uses a bar chart.
3. Move to 1-2-3 for Windows and select a range of data in the worksheet that contains the data you want to use (see fig. 9.11).

4. Choose Edit Copy to copy the data to the Clipboard or click the Edit Copy SmartIcon.
5. Move to Freelance Graphics and anchor the pointer in the cell where you want the data to be pasted (see fig. 9.12). Note that you can anchor the pointer in one of the two gray cells in the top left portion of the Chart Data & Titles window if you are pasting axis labels as well as legend labels. Anchor in the first gray cell if the range has two lines of legends; otherwise, use the second gray cell. Note that the data portion of the data entry window accepts numbers only. If you try to paste text into the data portion, you receive an error message.

Creating Charts from 1-2-3 Worksheets   177

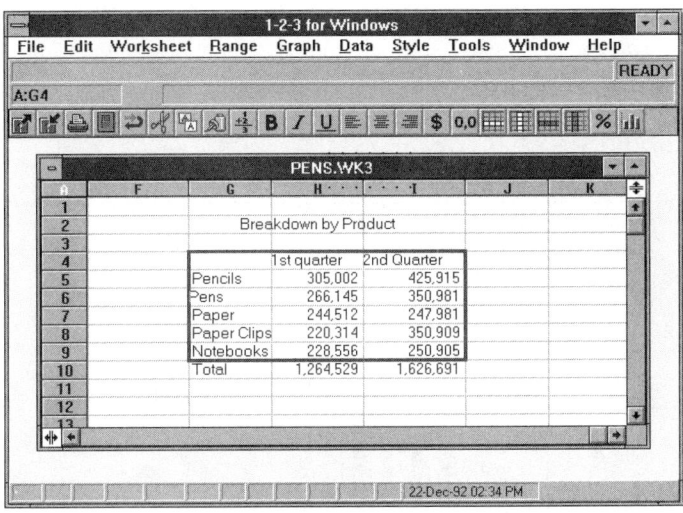

FIGURE 9.11. A worksheet in 1-2-3 for Windows that contains the source data.

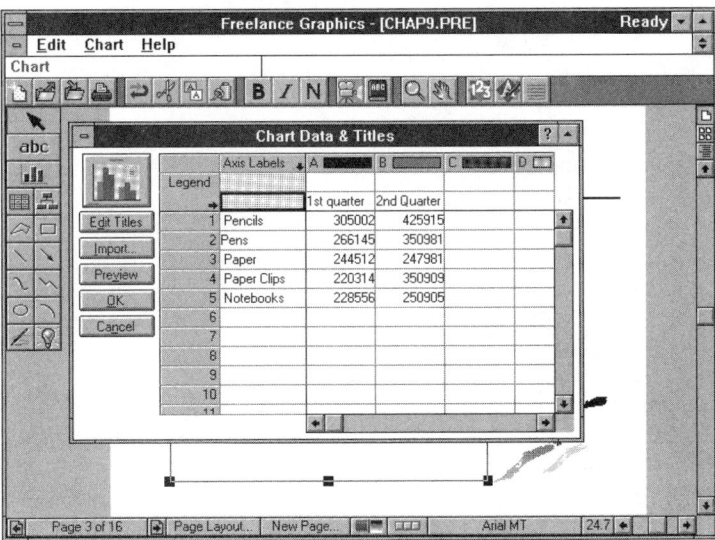

FIGURE 9.12. Anchor the pointer in the Chart Data & Titles window.

6. Choose Edit Paste or click the Edit Paste SmartIcon. This selection copies the data into the Chart Data & Titles window without establishing a link.

7. Click OK to compose the chart and then type the title in the title block (see fig. 9.13).

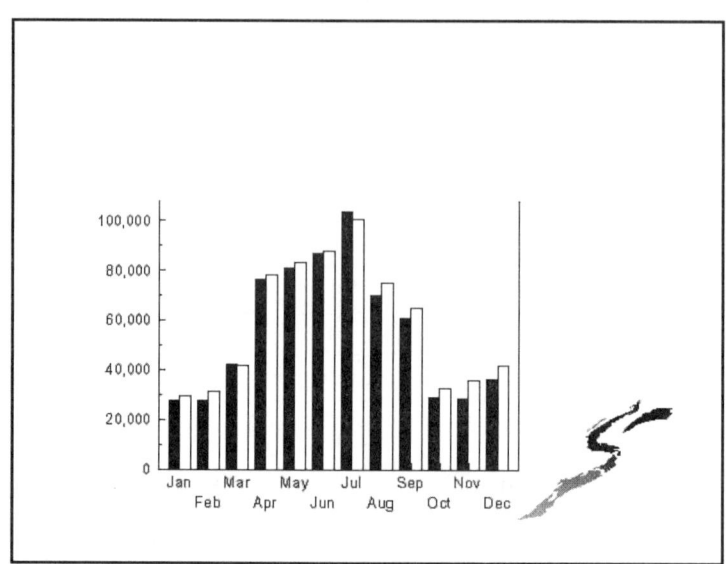

FIGURE 9.13. The completed chart, based on the data in figure 9.12.

Importing Named Charts

If you create charts in 1-2-3, you are probably familiar with the concept of named charts. If your memory needs refreshing, here's a definition: *Named charts* are collections of chart settings that determine the style of a chart in a worksheet. You can have multiple named charts in a single worksheet.

Importing a named chart has the same result as copying a chart from a 1-2-3 for Windows worksheet with Edit Paste. After you import a named chart, you can customize it just as you do any chart in Freelance Graphics. You can change bars, for example, into three-dimensional bars, change chart types, change the scale, and so on.

Try It: Import a Named Chart

Now it's time to try copying a named chart from a 1-2-3 worksheet. Follow these steps:

1. Start a new page and choose the 1 Chart page layout or any page layout for a chart.
2. Choose File Import Chart. (For this procedure, do not click the prompt text "Click here to create chart.")
3. From the File Import Chart dialog box, highlight the name of the worksheet file that contains the named chart you want to import and then click the Named Charts button.
4. In the Import Named Chart dialog box, shown in figure 9.14, highlight a named chart from the list and click OK. Freelance Graphics composes the chart and places it in the placement block.

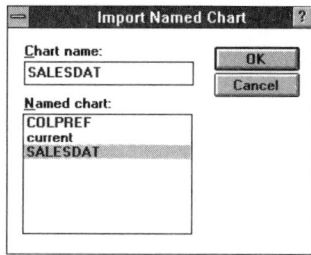

FIGURE 9.14. The Import Named Chart dialog box.

Copying Charts from 1-2-3 for Windows

If the chart you want to use in Freelance Graphics resides in a 1-2-3 for Windows worksheet, you can copy the entire chart directly to Freelance Graphics. Depending on your purpose, you can copy the chart and the data or just the chart. You also can copy the chart with or without establishing links.

Copying an Unlinked Chart from 1-2-3 for Windows

If you are satisfied with a chart that already has been created in 1-2-3 for Windows, you can drop it directly into Freelance Graphics by using Edit Paste.

When you copy a 1-2-3 for Windows chart to Freelance Graphics with the Edit Paste command, you not only copy the chart but the data behind it as well. The benefit of copying a 1-2-3 for Windows chart to Freelance Graphics is that you get an actual Freelance Graphics chart that you can edit. The result of this operation is that you have a chart that you can edit and customize, using all the Freelance Graphics chart options and commands. Use this option when you don't want to create a link to the 1-2-3 for Windows data behind the chart.

To copy a 1-2-3 for Windows chart to Freelance Graphics, first move to the open 1-2-3 for Windows worksheet file that contains the completed chart. Note that the chart may be in the worksheet itself or in a separate window. If the chart is in the worksheet itself, click a single cell occupied by the chart or drag to highlight the entire chart. (If you drag to select just part of the chart, you cannot copy an editable chart to Freelance Graphics). Next, choose Edit Copy or click the Copy SmartIcon.

Next, move to a Freelance Graphics presentation page that uses a chart page layout. (Don't click the prompt text "Click here to create chart.") Finally, choose Edit Paste or click the Paste SmartIcon. Now if you select the chart and click the Chart icon in the Toolbox, you can edit the data behind the chart.

Copying a Linked Chart from 1-2-3 for Windows

When you copy a chart to Freelance Graphics by using Edit Paste Special, you get the Paste Special dialog box, which contains choices that determine the format of the pasted chart (see fig. 9.15). To copy the chart as an editable chart with linked data, choose 1-2-3 Graph and click the Link button.

This method, however, has one limitation. When you first copy the chart, the whole chart is copied, including data, headings, axis titles, and so on. But, if the worksheet chart contains annotations in the form of lines or arrows, these are not copied to Freelance Graphics.

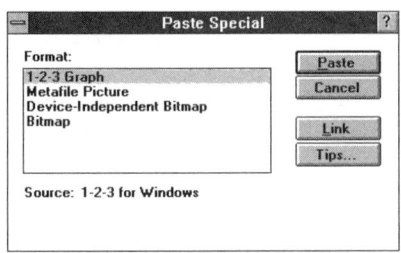

FIGURE 9.15. The Paste Special dialog box.

Now, here's the tricky part. If the chart data, axis labels, or axis titles change in 1-2-3 for Windows, the chart in Freelance Graphics is updated because there exists a DDE link between the source data and Freelance Graphics. The drawback is this: Only the chart data, axis labels, and axis titles are linked to the worksheet. (Note further that only axis titles that are linked to ranges in the 1-2-3 worksheet are linked to Freelance.) If the legend, headings, or notes change in the worksheet, these changes do not flow into Freelance. These chart components are copied to Freelance Graphics only the first time you copy the chart, which is known as a *one-time link*. If, later, the 1-2-3 for Windows chart changes, only the chart data, axis labels, and axis titles are linked. This potential problem is the only drawback of this method of copying 1-2-3 for Windows charts.

Copying a 1-2-3 for Windows Chart as a Metafile or Bitmap

As you now know, copying a linked chart from 1-2-3 for Windows has one limitation: Only certain of the elements from the 1-2-3 chart are linked. If you want to make sure that every part of the original 1-2-3 for Windows chart is linked to Freelance, use the Edit Paste Special command, highlight Metafile Picture, and then click the Link button.

With this technique, the chart is copied as a linked metafile object. When the chart changes in 1-2-3 for Windows, the chart is updated in Freelance Graphics. This update includes any lines or arrows you have added as annotations. The best way to think of it is as follows: Edit Paste Special copies the chart to Freelance Graphics as a picture, not as data that Freelance Graphics uses to generate a chart. When the picture of the chart changes in 1-2-3, the picture also changes in Freelance Graphics.

The drawback is that you cannot edit the chart in Freelance Graphics. Because there is no link to the data, you cannot change the data or add titles or legends in the Chart Data & Titles window. In fact, you cannot even access the Chart Data & Titles window. This kind of link is useful when you are satisfied with the appearance of the 1-2-3 chart and simply want a copy of it in your presentation. The other drawback to this way of linking is that both applications must be open for the link to function. No file link exists in this case.

Editing Links

After you establish links to a worksheet, a few questions remain. When are the links updated? What if you want to extend the ranges of the links? What if you move the file to which the data chart is linked to another directory? And, finally, how can you sever the links to a chart? The following sections take up these questions.

When Are Linked Graphs Updated?

Links are refreshed automatically whenever you open a presentation file.

Freelance Graphics updates the link between a chart and the source data automatically, unless you specifically request a manual update. Generally, an automatic update is precisely what you want. After all, the rationale for having links in the first place is to free you from worrying about whether the source data has changed. With automatic links, you can rest assured that your lined graphs are refreshed automatically with the latest data.

When are links updated? In automatic mode, a link is refreshed whenever you open a presentation file that contains the link or if the source data changes when both the presentation and the application that contain the source data are open (a DDE link).

If Freelance Graphics cannot find the source file, you receive an error message. This situation can occur if the source file has been deleted or moved to a different directory. If you display the Chart Data & Titles dialog box for the chart with the missing link, the data is still underlined in blue (even though the data is not actually linked to a file). If you then click the Import button, you see a list of worksheet files. You can choose another worksheet file to link to, or you can use the Directories option to try to locate the missing worksheet file.

Editing Links to Worksheets without Leaving Freelance Graphics

What happens if you have created a linked chart based on a six-month period and then decide you want to chart the full 12 months of data?

You can use the Import option in the Chart Data & Titles dialog box to change the links or you can use the Edit Links command. The Edit Links command is especially useful for creating or monitoring the links in a single chart that is linked to multiple files. This command enables you to see all the sources at once.

Select a chart and then choose Edit Links from the menu. The link information for the selected chart is displayed in the Links dialog box (see fig. 9.16). Highlight the chart you want to update and then click the Update button. (If you choose Edit Links with no chart selected, the first chart in the Links dialog box is highlighted.) You can highlight as many graphs as you want.

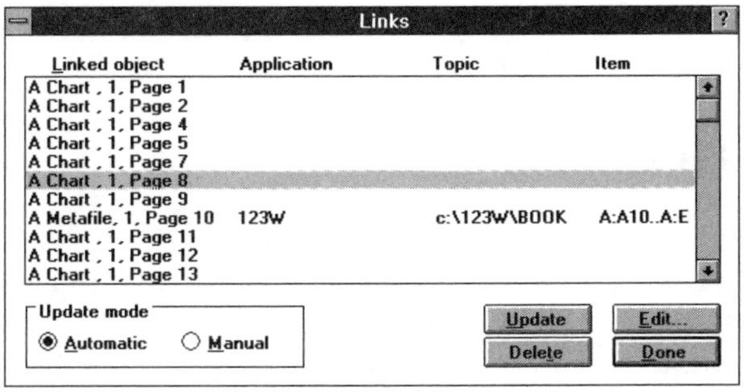

FIGURE 9.16. The Links dialog box.

To change the link status to manual, click the Manual button. The Linked Object column lists the type of object and the presentation page number on which it is found. The Application column gives the source application. The Topic column lists the path and name of the file that contains the source data. The Item column shows the worksheet range that contains the source data (this information also may be a 1-2-3 range name).

To edit the selected links, click the Edit button. (If more than one line is highlighted, the Edit button is dimmed and unavailable.) You see the Edit Links dialog box (see fig. 9.17). Objects are the chart components that have linked data.

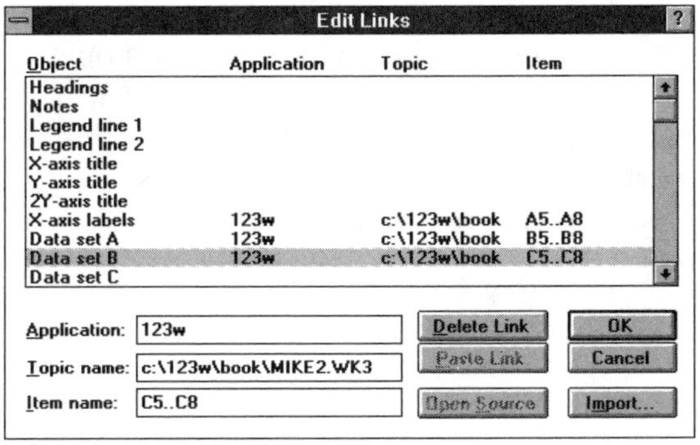

FIGURE 9.17. The Edit Links dialog box.

Select the object for which you want to edit the links (for example, Data Set B) and then click the Import button. In the Import Data window, use the mouse to select a new range for the link and then click OK. Now, back in the Edit Links dialog box, click the Paste Link button to establish the new link. Click OK and then Done to complete the process.

Deleting Links

Suppose that you have linked a chart to a worksheet that is updated on a quarterly basis. Now suppose that you want to preserve the chart that shows the data for the last quarter. If the chart is linked, however, the next time you open the presentation, the chart is updated with the new data. How can you avoid this problem?

The remedy is to delete the links. First, choose Edit Links and then highlight the chart for which you want to delete links. Click the Edit button in the Links dialog box, highlight the link to delete, and click the Delete Link button. Repeat these steps for each link you want to delete. Finally, click OK and then click Done.

Deleting a link does not erase the chart data.

Note that deleting a link does not erase the chart data. But when the worksheet data changes, the data is no longer refreshed. When you delete a link, the blue underlining in the Chart Data & Titles window disappears.

Wrapping Up

In this chapter, you learned about the various ways you can copy 1-2-3 charts or data to Freelance Graphics. You should now be able to import data from DOS or Windows 1-2-3 worksheet files, copy data from an open 1-2-3 for Windows worksheet, import named charts, and copy a chart from 1-2-3 for Windows to Freelance Graphics. You also should be able to establish links between a chart and the source worksheet.

In the next chapter, you learn various tips and techniques to help you organize your presentations.

Part 4
Organization Charts and Tables

In this part, you learn the basics as well as the subtleties of creating and customizing organization charts and tables.

This section includes:

Chapter 10. Organization Charts

Chapter 11. Creating Tables

10

Organization Charts

An organization chart, in ordinary use, reveals the hierarchical structure of a company as a series of boxes connected with lines. Freelance Graphics 2.0 has a dedicated organization chart tool, which is accessible by clicking an icon in the Toolbox. The organization chart tool works on the same principle as chart creation: First you choose a style and then you fill in an entry form with your text. Based on the chosen style and your entries, Freelance composes the organization chart for you automatically.

The Value and Variety of Organization Charts

Although organization charts are not as common as bulleted lists or data charts, you may be called upon to create one at some point. After you create the first one for your company or division, you can update it easily to reflect the constantly evolving hierarchy of the work force.

Organization charts are invaluable reference tools for seeing at a glance who reports to whom in your company. You also may want to keep one handy to remind yourself of your own position and to plot strategies for advancement within the company hierarchy.

Along the way, you may discover that organization charts can serve other purposes beyond illustrating the power structure of a company. An organization chart can depict just about any hierarchical structure. Figure 10.1, for example, uses the organization chart format to illustrate a product line.

> In this chapter, you learn how to:
> - Create organization charts with the Organization chart tool
> - Edit organization chart entries
> - Change the appearance of organization charts
> - Control text sizing in organization charts

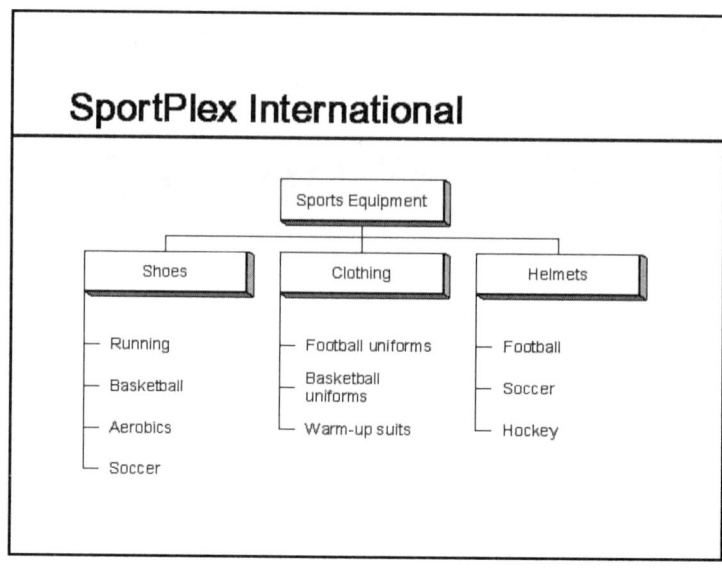

FIGURE 10.1. This organization chart depicts the branches of a product line.

Try It: Create an Organization Chart

Try to create an organization chart by doing the following:

1. Choose Page New, select Organization Chart, and then click OK.
2. Click the prompt "Click here to create organization chart." If you are creating an organization chart on a blank page, you also can click the Organization Chart icon in the Toolbox.
3. Click one of the six style buttons in the Organization Chart Gallery dialog box to choose the look you want (see fig. 10.2). Click a button to choose a style for the lowest level of your organization chart. For most charts, it's best to mark the Automatically Size Entry Text check box.
4. Type your entries in the Organization Chart Entry List (see fig. 10.3). Each entry block has a line for a name, a title, and a comment. Leave the second and third lines blank if you want. Just press Enter to skip over them. After you type the first entry—there can be only one top-level entry—the next entry block is indented to indicate the second level, third level, and so on.

If you have a long entry that you want to break into two lines, press Ctrl+Enter to force the line break. All the entries on the same level appear as a row of boxes in the completed organization chart.

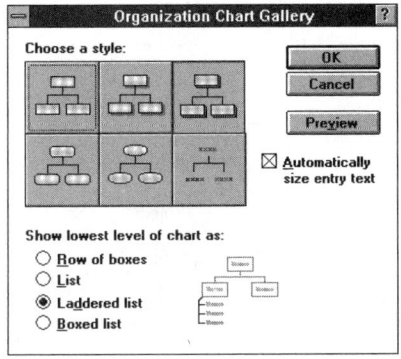

FIGURE 10.2. The Organization Chart Gallery dialog box.

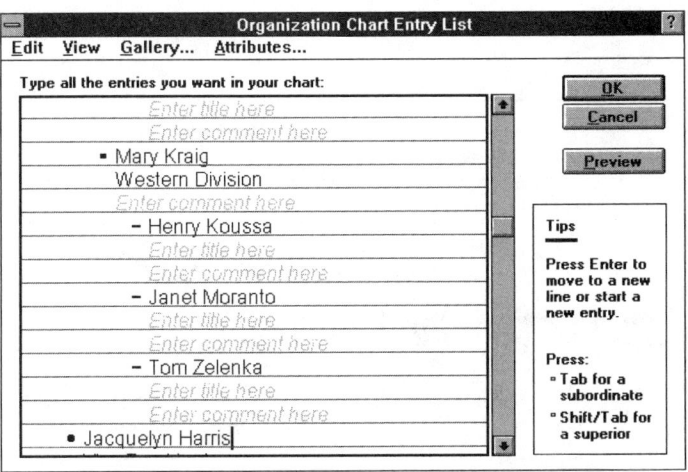

FIGURE 10.3. The Organization Chart Entry List.

5. Press Tab (or choose Edit Demote) to demote an entry to a subordinate level. Press Shift+Tab (or chose Edit Promote) to promote an entry to a superior level.

6. After you type your entries, click OK to view the organization chart. You can press and hold the Preview button as you type entries to check the progress of the organization chart.

Figure 10.4 shows a complete organization chart.

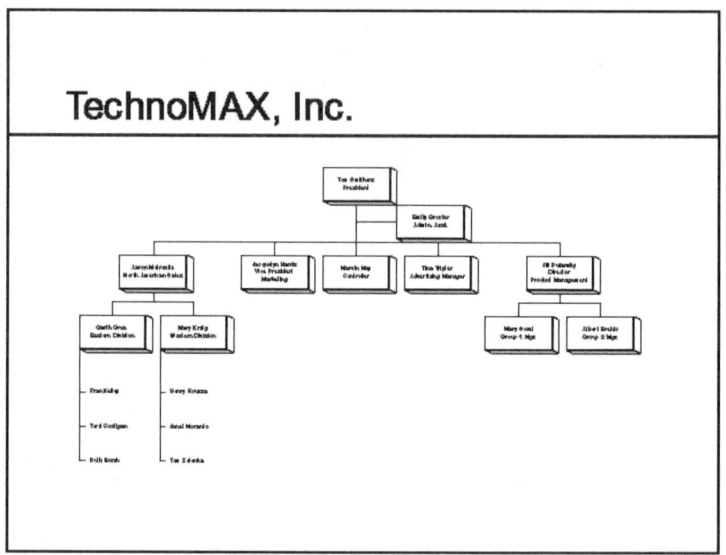

FIGURE 10.4. A completed organization chart.

Editing Organization Chart Entries

After you complete an organization chart, you can edit your entries as you like. To reopen the Organization Chart Entry List for an organization chart, click the chart to select it and then click the Organization Chart icon in the Toolbox or choose Chart Edit. Here's a shortcut: Click the right mouse button over an organization chart and highlight Edit.

All these actions open the Organization Chart Entry List. Note that this window has its own menu, with four choices: Edit, View, Gallery, and Attributes.

After you are in the entry list, position the pointer on the line you want to change and type your changes. To delete individual characters, press the Del or Backspace key. To abandon any changes you have made, press the Cancel button.

From the entry list, you also can copy, cut, and paste entries, promote and demote entries, or add a staff position.

Deleting, Copying, and Pasting Entries

The Edit menu contains choices for cutting and copying entries to the Clipboard, pasting entries from the Clipboard, or zapping entries entirely without copying them to the Clipboard.

To copy or delete an entry, first select it. Highlight one line at a time by dragging the mouse or select all three lines of an entry by clicking the bullet next to the entry: A box appears around the entry. If you select a subordinate level with entries below it, all subordinate entries are selected as well. You can choose the following from the Edit menu:

- Edit Cut removes the selection and copies it to the Clipboard. Note that you cannot delete the top-level entry in a dialog box.
- Edit Copy copies the selection to the Clipboard.
- Edit Paste copies the contents of the Clipboard to the insertion point.
- Edit Clear deletes the selection without copying it to the Clipboard.
- Edit Copy Whole Chart copies all the *text* in the organization chart (with the exception of a staff position) to the Clipboard. Be aware that this command does not copy the organization chart itself, just the text. When you paste the text on a presentation page, the result is not an organization chart, but a text block containing the text of the organization chart. One useful application of this command is to append the entries of one organization chart to another. Position the pointer in an Organization Chart Entry List and choose Edit Paste. The entries are copied at the level indicated by the insertion point. Unfortunately, you cannot use the Edit Copy, Edit Paste, or Edit Cut SmartIcons from the Organization Chart Entry List.

Moving an Entry

To move an entry, click a bullet to the left of an entry. A rectangle appears around the entry to indicate its selection. Now drag the box up or down in the list.

Remember: When you click a bullet, you select an entry as well as any subordinate entries.

Editing Directly on the Presentation Page

Suppose that, after you make the first pass at an organization chart, you want to correct the spelling of a name or change the name of a title. To edit existing entries, it's often quickest to make the change directly on the presentation page, without returning to the entry list.

To edit entries on the presentation page, click twice slowly over a text entry box in the organization chart. A small box pops up to indicate that you are in edit mode. Now you can type new lines or correct errors. Because the text is likely to be small in this view, it's a good idea to zoom in first over the box you want to edit.

If the point size of the text is too small to read at full-page view, click the Zoom icon and then drag a rectangle around the box you want to edit. Click again over the text you want to edit to enter text edit mode and then make your changes.

If the text you enter extends beyond the border of a box, the Automatically Size Entry Text check box in the Organization Chart Gallery dialog box probably is not marked. If this check box is marked, Freelance reduces the point size of the text to make the entry fit within the box. This reduction may not be want you want, however, because the text in every other box also is reduced. If an entry extends beyond the edge of the box, another option is to press Enter to force a line break.

When you make changes directly in an entry box, the changes also are reflected in the Organization Chart Entry List.

Creating an Empty Box

Occasionally, you may want an empty box in your organization chart, perhaps to reserve a place for an as-yet-unfilled position. To create the empty box, just enter a space in the entry list.

Promoting and Demoting Entries

Every entry in an Organization chart has a position in the hierarchy of the chart. All entries at the same level appear in the same row of boxes in the composed organization chart. You can bump entries up and down in the hierarchy with the Edit Promote and Edit Demote commands. Remember, though, that only one top-level entry can be on the chart.

To promote an entry to a superior position, choose Edit Promote or press Shift+Tab. If a promoted entry has subordinate entries, these also are promoted one level.

To demote an entry to a subordinate position, choose Edit Demote or press Tab. If a demoted entry has subordinate entries, these also are demoted one level.

Collapsing the Entry List

In organization charts with many entries, it's easy to lose your place in the list. To find your bearings, you can collapse the view in the Organization Chart Entry List dialog box much as you can in the Outliner. The View menu contains three choices to faciliate this feature:

- Names Only displays just the top-line names in the entry list (see fig. 10.5). Collapsing the list to display just the top-line names makes it much simpler to navigate the list. You can move or delete entries in a collapsed view.
- Names and Titles displays the names and titles in the entry list.
- All shows the complete list: names, titles, and comments.

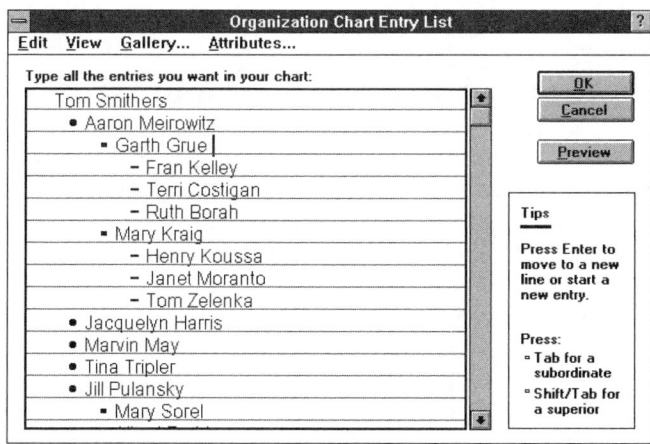

FIGURE 10.5. Use the View menu to collapse or expand the visible entries in the list. Here, Names Only has been selected.

Adding a Staff Position

A staff position reports to the top-level person in a company, but otherwise falls outside of the company hierarchy. No one, for example, reports to the staff person. An administrative assistant is the typical staff position.

To add a staff-level entry, choose Edit Staff and then complete the Organization Chart Staff dialog box (see fig. 10.6). This dialog box contains a space for name, title, and comment. Press Tab to move forward through these items or Shift+Tab to move backward. Caution: Pressing Enter closes this dialog box.

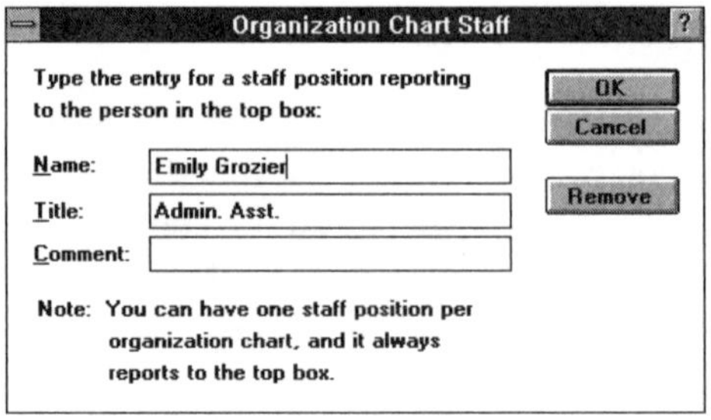

FIGURE 10.6. The Organization Chart Staff dialog box.

Changing the Look of an Organization Chart

The styles in the organization chart gallery generally look good without alteration. To choose a new style for an organization chart, click the right mouse button over the chart, highlight Gallery, and double-click the picture in the gallery that represents the style you want. If you are working in the entry list, choose Gallery to open the Organization Chart Gallery.

One of the more dramatic changes you can make is to use rounded or oval shapes in place of the standard boxes that display the entries in an organization chart. Boxes suggest the rigid and inflexible ("boxed-in") quality of hierarchies. Rounded rectangles or oval shapes somehow give an organization chart a less forbidding look. To see how a new style looks, click the Preview button and hold down the left mouse button. When you release the mouse button, you return to the dialog box, where you can choose a new style or click OK to accept your changes.

Attributes refer to the look of the design elements that make up an organization chart. You can customize the attributes of the organization chart styles offered by Freelance Graphics. By varying text style, the connecting lines between boxes, and the look of the boxes themselves, you can make both aesthetic and functional changes. Suppose that you are depicting a department in your company that consists of both full-time salaried employees and temporary employees. You may differentiate between the two groups by changing the background color of the boxes. You also can show functional grouping within the chart by changing the color or style of connecting lines. Dashed lines may connect all members of the production team, and blue solid lines may connect the members of the marketing team. Use your imagination to think of other innovative ways to use stylistic changes for functional purposes.

The organization chart in figure 10.7 is a customization of figure 10.4. This chart uses a different gallery style, adds a gray background for the frame, and uses wider connecting lines and box edges. The staff position also has a darker background to differentiate it from the rest of the chart. The dashed connection lines between positions in the second level of the chart were added manually with the Line tool.

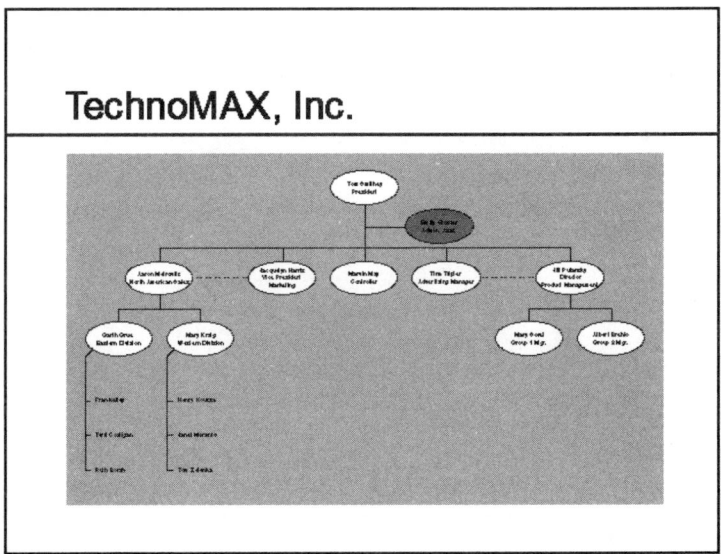

FIGURE 10.7. A customized organization chart.

Changing the Format of Lowest-Level Entries

Organization charts for large companies can be large and unmanageable if they contain dozens of entries. You can conserve space by choosing a more compact style for the lowest level of an organization chart. Assigning a different style to the lowest level also sets up a visual distinction between the higher and the lower levels. Freelance Graphics offers you four choices, as shown in the Organization Chart Gallery.

Try It: Change Attributes

Try changing the attributes of an organization chart by doing the following:

1. First, create an organization chart or display a page containing an existing one.
2. Click the organization chart to select it and then choose Chart Attributes, which displays the Organization Chart Attributes dialog box (see fig. 10.8). For a shortcut, click the organization chart with the right mouse button and then choose Attributes or double-click any box in the organization chart.

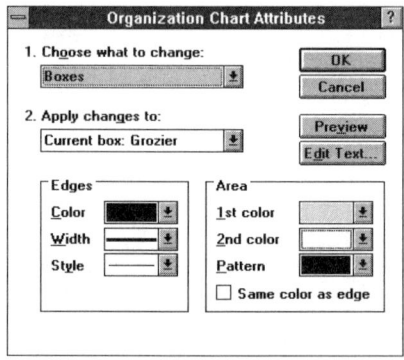

FIGURE 10.8. The Organization Chart Attributes dialog box.

3. Specify your changes in the dialog box. Select the chart element you want to change, choose the scope of your changes from the list box, and then change the attributes in the bottom area of the dialog box.
4. Press and hold the Preview button to see what your changes look like before you commit to them and then click OK to accept the changes.

The following are the elements of an organization chart that you can change:

- Text style. Change the typeface, size, color, emphasis, and justification of the selected text.
- Edges and area of boxes. For example, you can change the color of the current box and the peers—that is, all the boxes on the same level in the hierarchy.
- Color, width, and style of connecting lines. You can change the style of connecting lines for the entire chart only.
- Edge and area style of the frame (the area behind the organization chart).

Adding Extra Connection Lines

Some organization charts have lines connecting boxes at the same level to show communication between equal levels of the hierarchy or other relationships between the people in the organization. Freelance Graphics does not generate such lines automatically, but you easily can add them yourself with the drawing tools. To add a dotted horizontal line to an organization chart as in figure 10.7, for example, click the Line icon in the Toolbox and then draw a line between the two boxes. Double-click the line and choose a dotted line style to indicate that this line is not part of the structural hierarchy of the chart.

Controlling Text Size

A problem you may encounter if you create many organization charts is controlling the text size. How Freelance sizes the text in an organization chart depends on whether the Automatically Size Entry Text check box in the Organization Chart Gallery is marked.

If this check box is selected, Freelance attempts to fit all the text you enter within the boundaries of the boxes. Because Freelance sizes all the text uniformly throughout the organization chart, if one entry is especially long, Freelance uses a small point size for all the text in the organization chart. On-screen, the text may appear *Greeked* (as a series of lines) and unreadable at full page view. To make the text visible, click the Zoom icon and drag a rectangle over the portion of the organization chart you want to view.

If the check box is not marked, Freelance allows entries to spill over the boundaries of the boxes. If you have one especially long entry in an organization chart box, you have a dilemma. If you mark the Automatically Size Entry check box, the result may be miniscule text in all boxes. If you unmark this check box, the text may extend beyond the boundaries of the box. An alternative solution is to add manual line breaks in a long entry. You can split a long line by pressing Ctrl+Enter in the entry list. If you are editing directly in a box on the presentation page, press Enter to add a line break.

Another way of controlling the line lengths in an organization chart is to size the entire organization chart as you would any text block or graphic object. Select the chart and then drag one of the selection handles to make the entire chart smaller or larger. If you drag a chart to make it larger, the point size of the text may grow and the line wrapping within a box may change.

Wrapping Up

In this chapter, you learned how use the Organization Chart tool to create and edit organization charts. You should now be able to create an organization chart rather quickly. If you don't find the style you want in the gallery, you can customize the appearance of an organization chart to suit your taste by changing line, text, and box styles. You also learned how to add annotations or extra connecting lines to an organization chart.

In the next chapter, you learn how to create tables, which is another useful presentation format.

11

Creating Tables

Table charts are the unsung laborers of business graphics. They make up in honest utility what they lack in pizazz. Traditionally found in printed reports, they can be just as useful in a presentation. The main thing to remember is that a presentation table has a different function than a report table. Report tables are reference tools that the reader pores over to pluck out just the fact he or she wants. But tables play a different role in a presentation format. A table in a presentation must contain less information than in its printed counterpart, simply because the viewer cannot be expected to read a dense, detailed table from a distance.

When Are Tables Necessary?

Before you create a table, ponder its purpose. Because Freelance offers such a wealth of chart types, why would you choose a table? The answer is that sometimes numbers speak loudest when presented in an unembellished format. If you have just a few numbers to present, a graphical data chart is unnecessary.

The next question to ask is this: What is the output format of the table? Printed tables can be more detailed and dense than their on-screen counterparts. If you must have a complex table with a lot of entries, you can still use it in your presentation. But, instead of displaying it on screen, print it as an audience handout. This approach enables your readers to peruse the numbers at their leisure and enhances audience involvement. Getting the audience involved in your presentation helps form a bond between you and them.

> *In this chapter, you learn how to:*
> - *Create tables with the Table tool*
> - *Customize tables*
> - *Size, move, insert, and delete rows and columns*
> - *Change table attributes, including text, cell attributes, and border attributes*

When you create a table for your presentation, limit the rows and columns. A matrix of more than 10 rows and 10 columns is likely to overwhelm the viewer. Of course, if you are creating a table to be included in a report, you can pack more information into it.

Creating Tables in Freelance

Freelance Graphics has a Table tool dedicated to the task of creating tables. With the Table tool, you can create a table directly on-screen, not in a form.

Note that you also can create a table by using the Chart tool, but this method usually is your second choice. If you have data that you may want to display either as a table or as a graph, however, click the Chart icon in the Toolbox. Next, choose the Number Grid format from the Chart Gallery. Now you can enter the data for your table in the Chart Data & Titles window. This method enables you to switch back and forth between a table and other chart types. Generally, though, you're better off using the Table tool.

Try It: Create a Table

Try creating a simple table by using the Table icon in the Toolbox. Follow these steps:

1. Choose Page New and then double-click the Table page layout.
2. Click the prompt text "Click here to create table."
3. In the Table Gallery, click one of the six style icons (see fig. 11.1). The different styles vary in the number of horizontal and vertical grid lines used. You also can change these grid lines after you create the table.

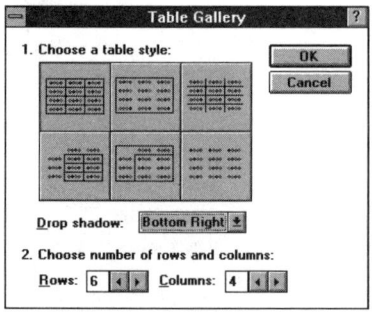

FIGURE 11.1. The Table Gallery.

4. Optionally, choose a drop shadow style from the drop-down list.
5. Type the number of rows and columns you want or click the scroll arrows to advance or decrease these numbers one at a time. Then click OK. Freelance draws a grid of the designated size on the screen. Now just click in the first cell and type your first entry. Click the mouse to move from cell to cell or use the Arrow keys.
6. Click outside the table when you have completed your entries.

Figure 11.2 shows a complete table with six rows, four columns, and a drop shadow. The symbol was added from the TRANSPOR.SYM symbol library.

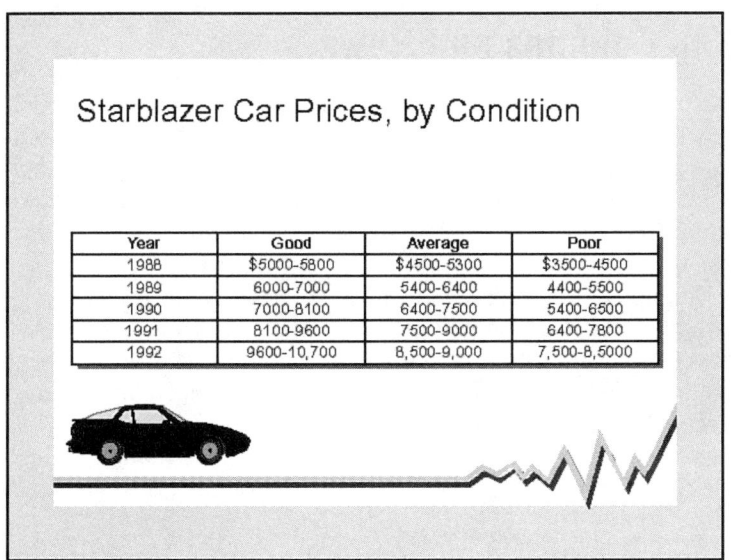

FIGURE 11.2. A complete table.

Changing Table Entries

To change entries in a table, you must be in edit mode. To enter edit mode, click twice (slowly!) within a table. If you click twice too quickly (that is, double-click), you open the Table Attributes dialog box instead. A thick border appears around the table to signify that you are in edit mode. An alternate way to enter edit mode is to click once to select the table and then press F2.

Working with Columns and Rows

A table is simply a matrix of rows and columns, a structure of cells into which you can enter data. In Freelance Graphics, you can perform various actions on columns and rows. You can delete them, size them, or move them.

To select a column or row, first enter edit mode (click twice slowly within the table) and then drag the mouse to highlight the row or column you want to act upon.

Deleting Columns and Rows

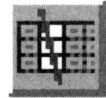

The fastest way to delete columns and rows is with the Delete Column and Delete Row SmartIcons. These icons aren't part of the default palette, so use the Tools SmartIcons command to add them to your icon palette. In edit mode, click the column or row you want to delete and then click the Delete Row or Delete Column SmartIcon. Freelance deletes the row or column without prompting you. To reverse the deletion, choose Edit Undo or click the Undo SmartIcon.

If the Delete Column and Delete Row SmartIcons aren't handy, here's another method you can use. In edit mode, click in the column or row you want to delete (you can select multiple rows or columns) and then click the right mouse button. Choose Delete Column/Row from the list. Click the Column or Row button in the dialog box. Click OK.

To delete just the text in a column or row, drag the mouse to highlight the column or row, choose Edit Clear, press Delete, or click the Cut SmartIcon.

Inserting Columns and Rows

The fastest way to insert a column or row is with the Add Column and Add Row SmartIcons. To add a row, first click twice in a table to enter text edit mode. Then click the pointer in a row or column and click the Add Row SmartIcon. Freelance adds a row after the current row. To insert a column, click the pointer in a column and click the Add Column SmartIcon. Freelance adds the column after the current column.

Another method is to click the pointer in a column or row and then click the right mouse button. From the list, highlight Insert Column/Row. Figure 11.3 shows the Insert Column/Row dialog box, where you click the Column or Row button and then click Before or After to indicate where you want the column or row to be inserted. You can insert multiple rows or columns by entering a value in the Number to add box. Click OK when you're finished.

COLOR FIGURE 1. Clip art from ENVIRON.SYM; text in BrushScript.

COLOR FIGURE 2. Bullets and Symbol page layout; clip art from FRANCE.SYM.

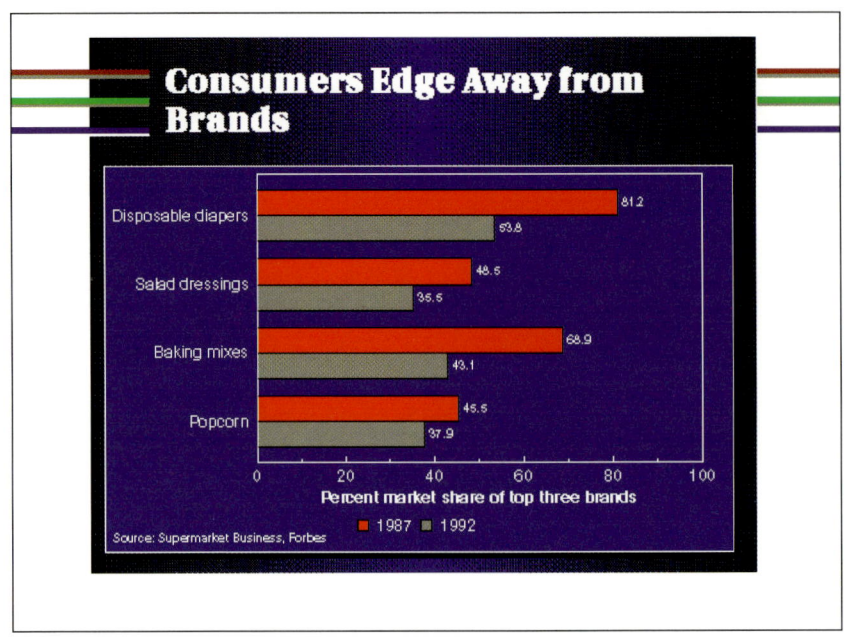

COLOR FIGURE 3. The horizontal bar format permits long axis labels.

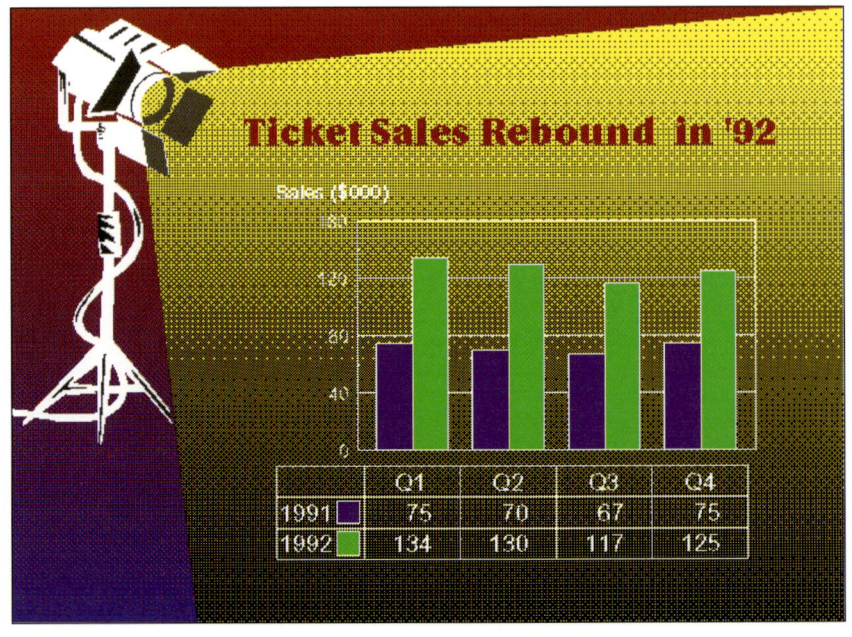

COLOR FIGURE 4. SPOTLIGHT.MAS makes an offbeat background for this bar-table combination.

COLOR FIGURE 5. The satellite dish (COMMUNIC.SYM) reinforces the message.

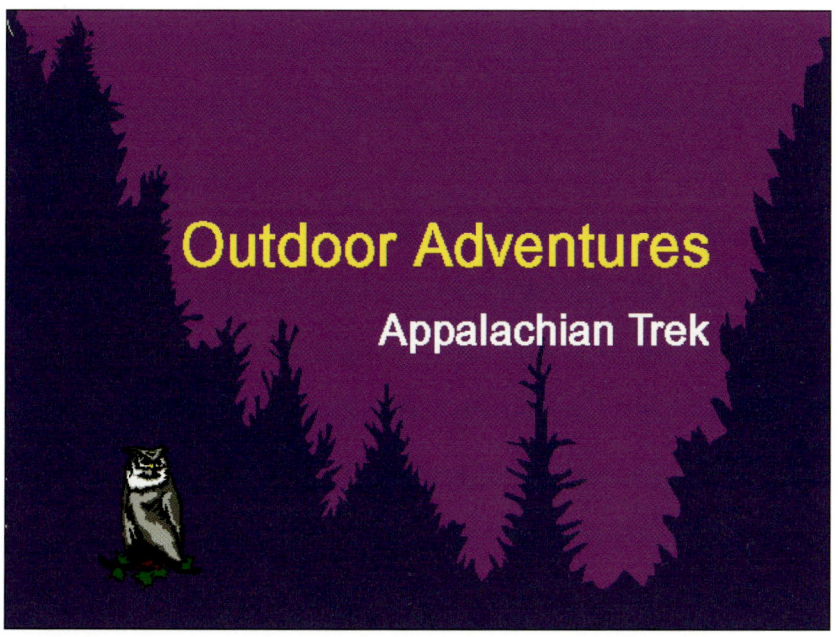

COLOR FIGURE 6. A title page using FOREST.MAS and an owl from ANIMALS.SYM.

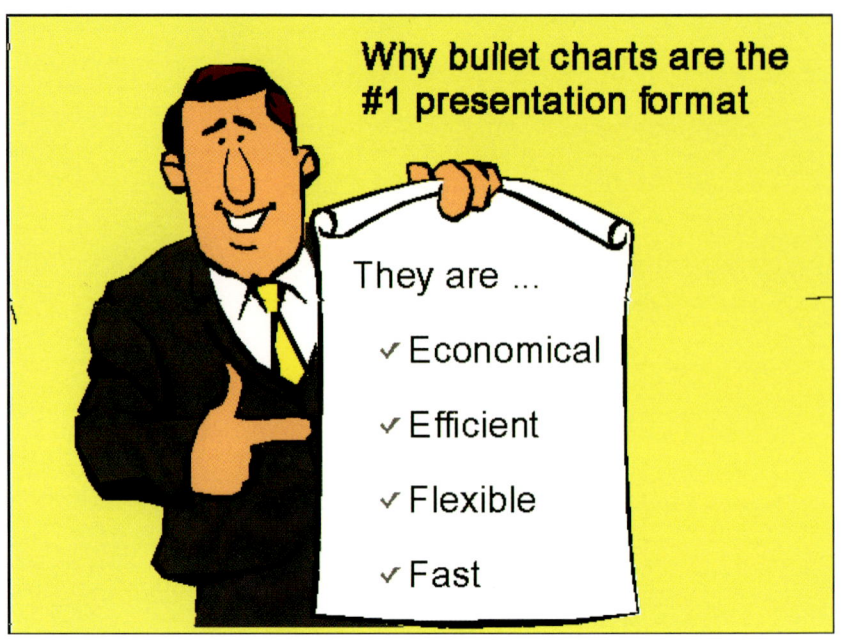

COLOR FIGURE 7. A bullet chart superimposed on clip art from CARTOONS.SYM.

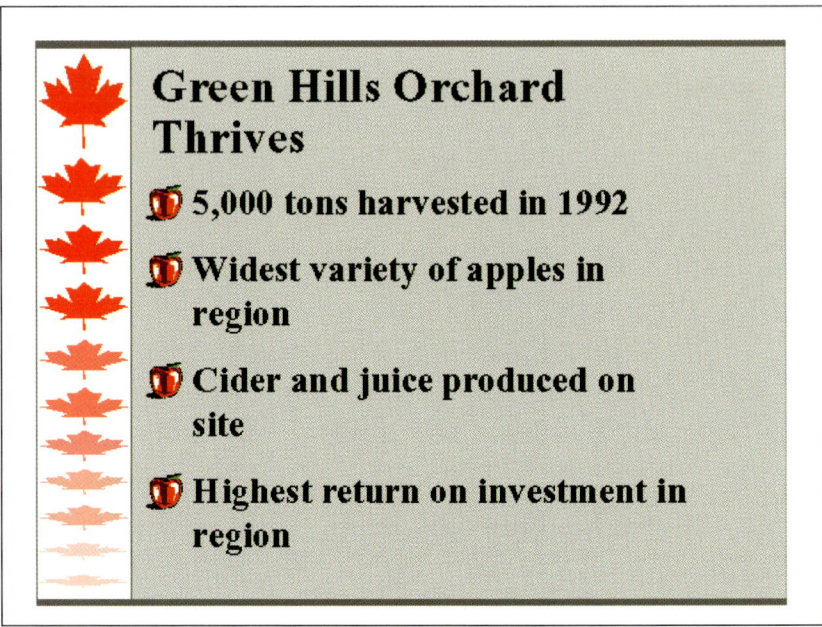

COLOR FIGURE 8. Freelance lets you use any symbol as a bullet marker (the apple is from FOOD.SYM).

COLOR FIGURE 9. WORLD1.MAS makes an appropriate background for this 3D bar chart.

COLOR FIGURE 10. The jet taking off mirrors the title (jet from TRANSPOR.SYM).

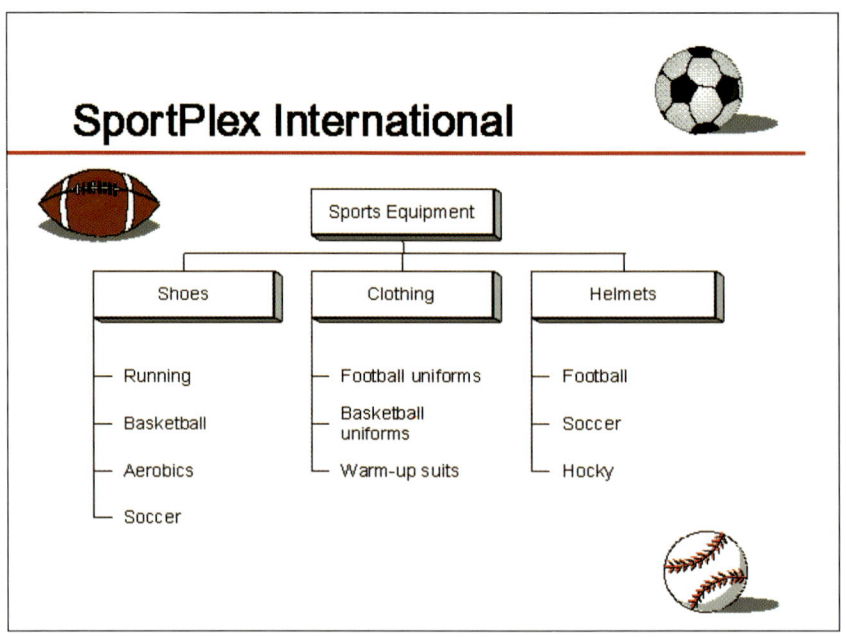

COLOR FIGURE 11. An organization chart created with Freelance's organization tool (symbols from SPORTS.SYM).

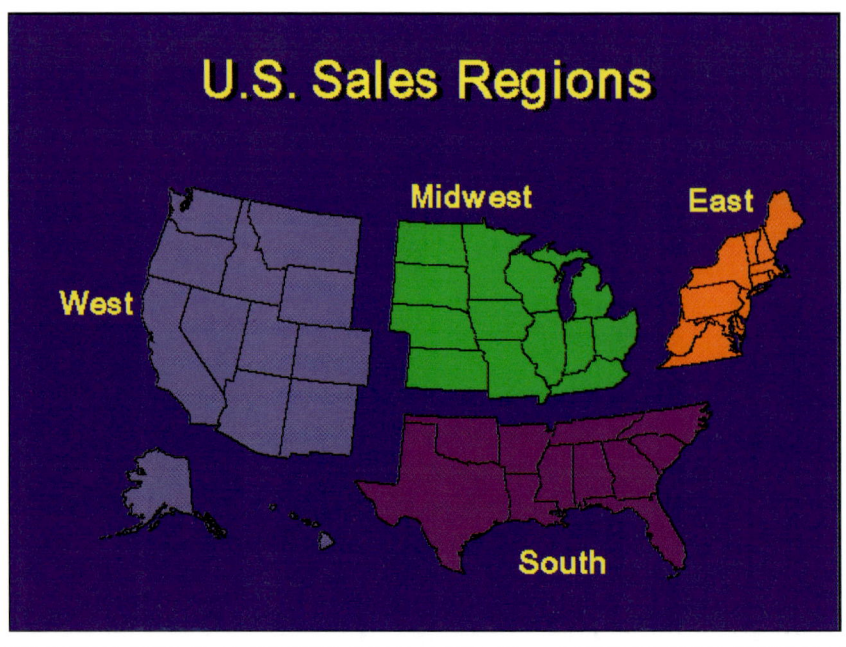

COLOR FIGURE 12. Sales map constructed from USAMAP.SYM.

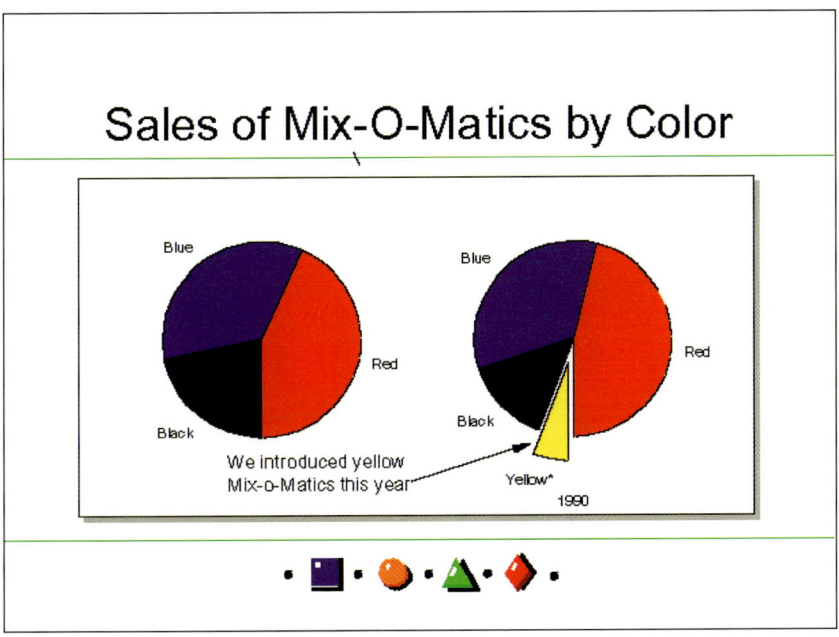

COLOR FIGURE 13. The second pie adds an exploded slice and annotation.

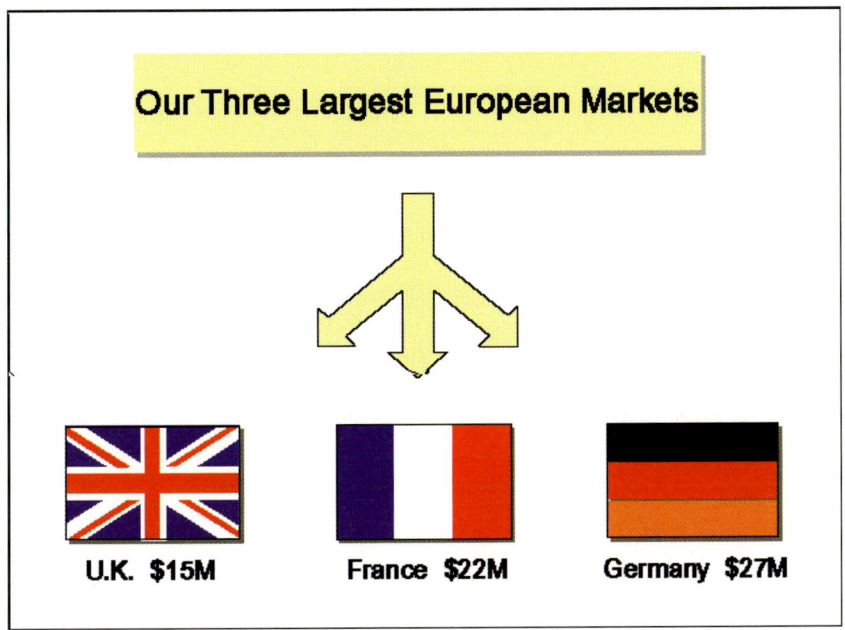

COLOR FIGURE 14. A simple diagram using symbols and text. (Arrows from ARROWS.SYM; flags from FLAG.SYM.)

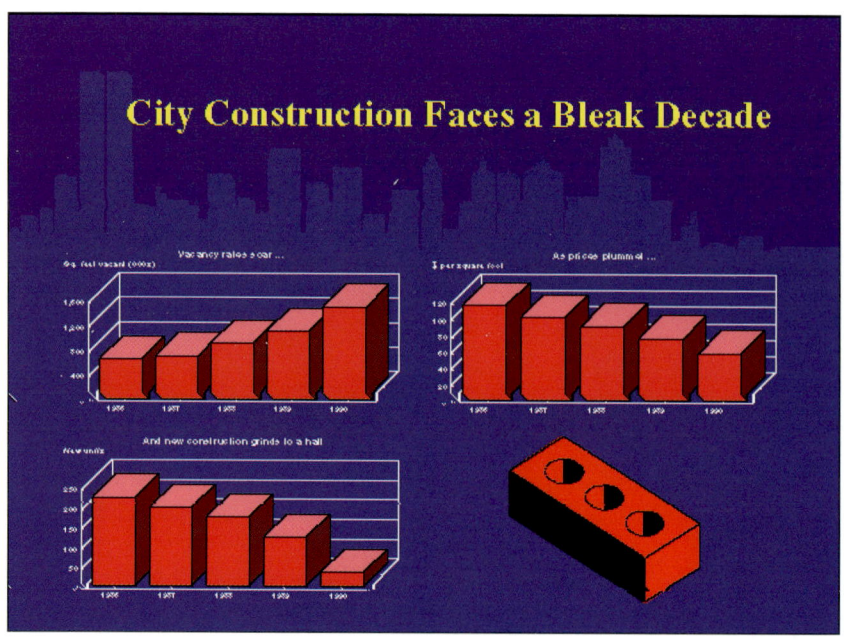

COLOR FIGURE 15. These three charts tell a story (reinforced by clip art from Lotus SmartPics).

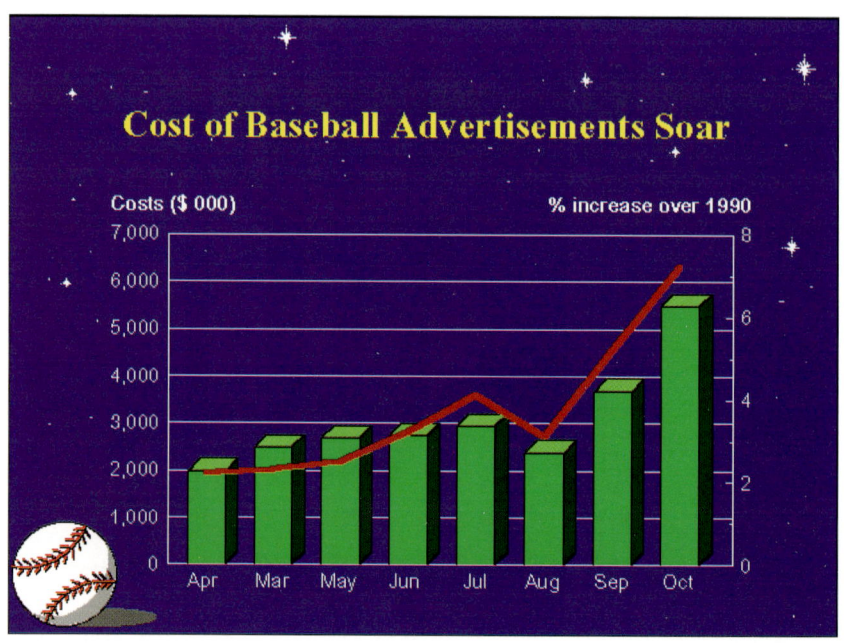

COLOR FIGURE 16. A bar-line graph, using NIGHTSKY.MAS, clip art from SPORTS.SYM.

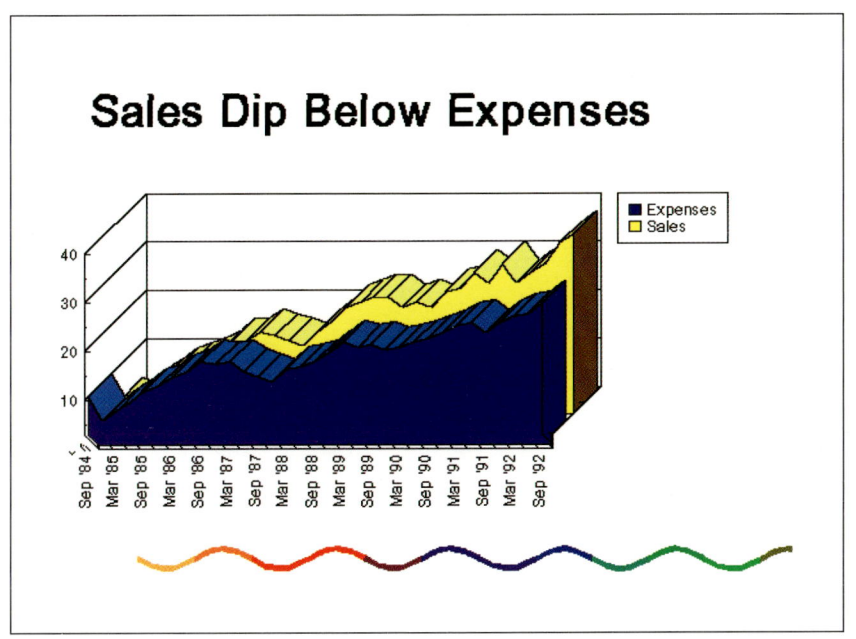

COLOR FIGURE 17. A 3D chart adds drama and a sense of volume (uses WAVE.MAS).

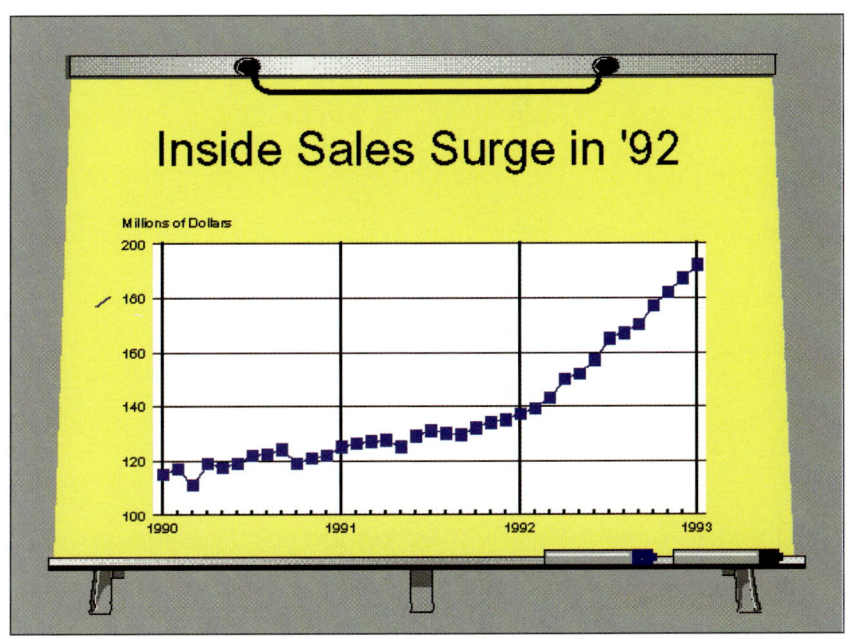

COLOR FIGURE 18. Markers strengthen a line chart. PRESENT.MAS adds an informal look.

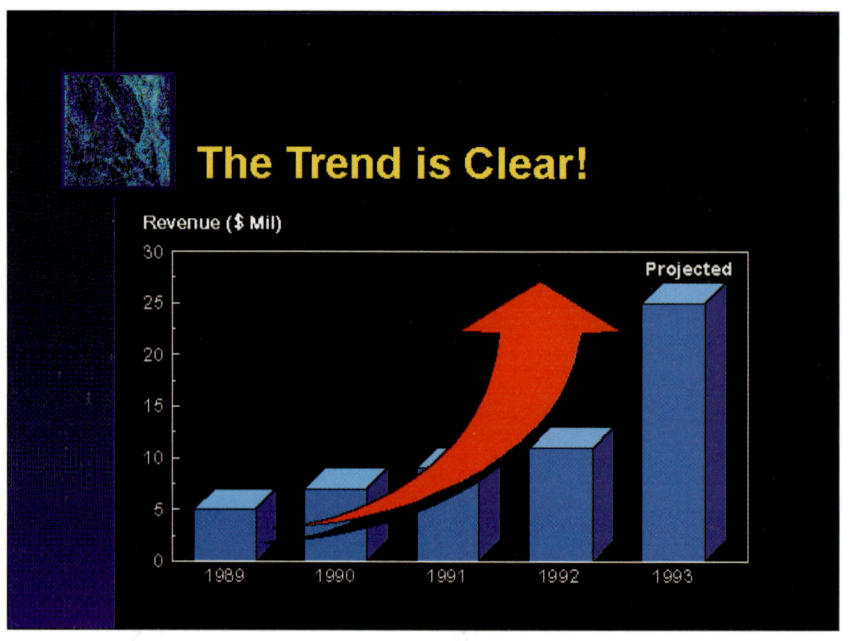

COLOR FIGURE 19. The swooping arrow from Lotus SmartPics reinforces this chart.

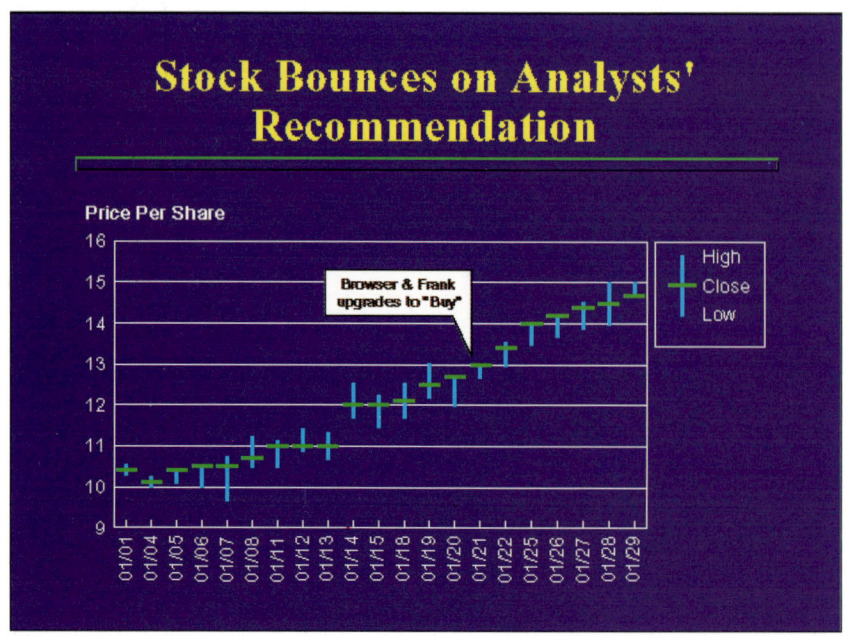

COLOR FIGURE 20. An annotation explains why the stock price rose. (The SmartMaster is BEVRULE.MAS.)

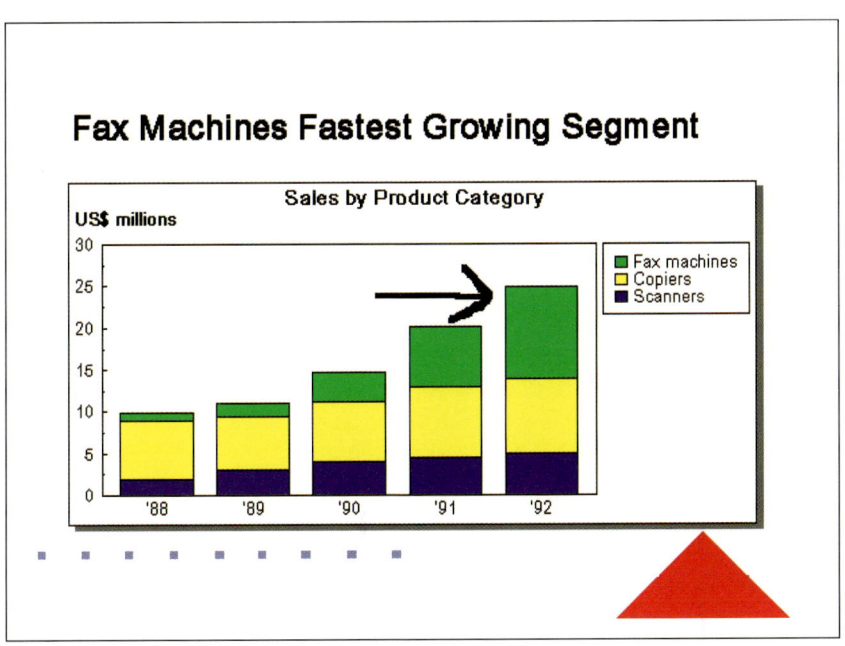

COLOR FIGURE 21. Freelance's "hyperdoodle" feature lets you draw on your monitor during a screen show.

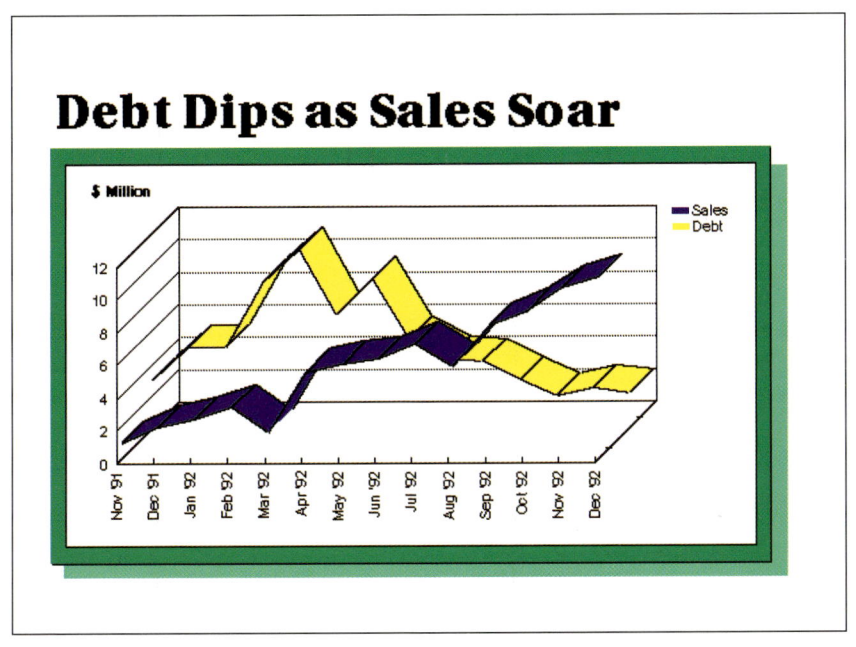

COLOR FIGURE 22. A 3D line chart (ribbon chart) adds visual appeal to an ordinary line chart.

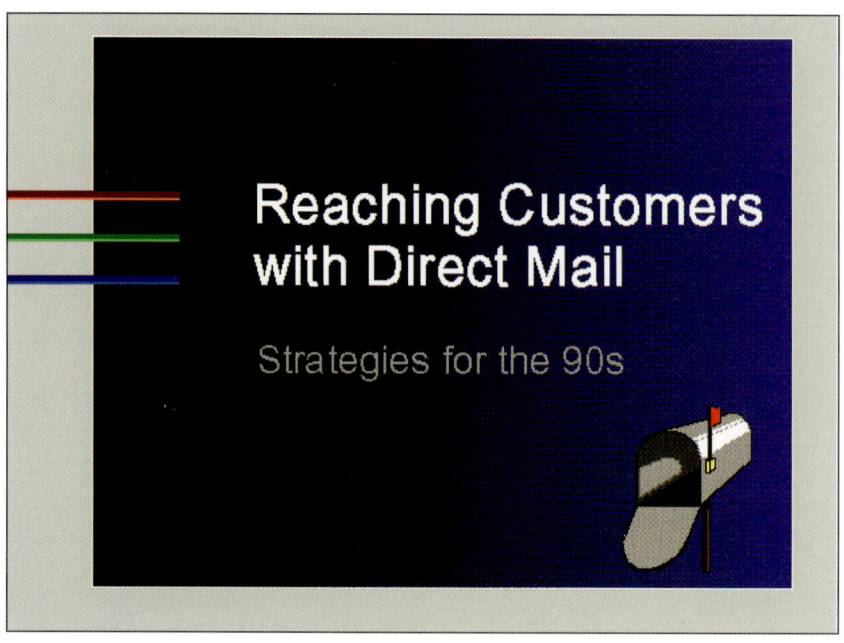

COLOR FIGURE 23. A title page with mailbox added from Lotus SmartPics (uses 3LINE.MAS).

COLOR FIGURE 24. The dinosaur (Lotus SmartPics) strengthens the message with humor.

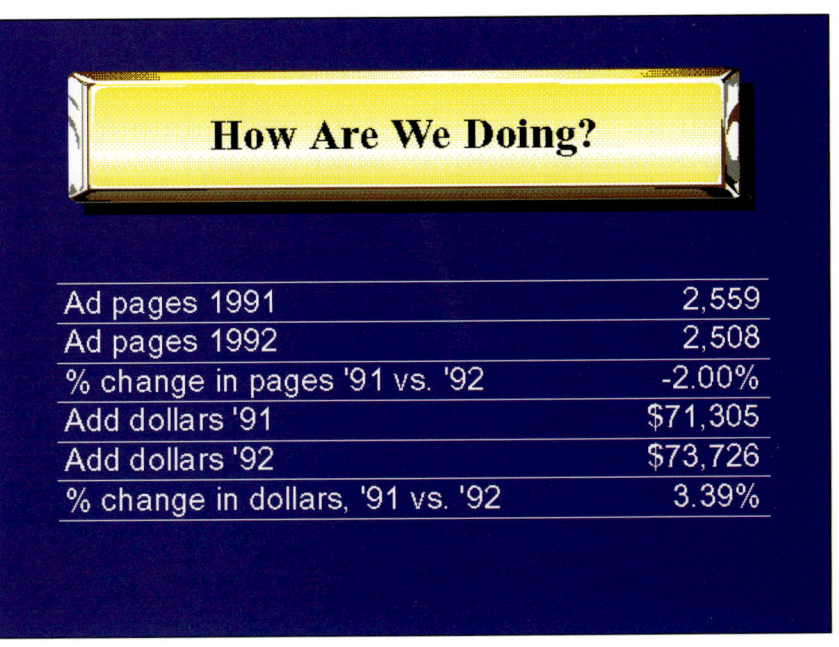

COLOR FIGURE 25. When exact values are important, use the Table tool. (BRASS.MAS adds a boardroom quality.)

COLOR FIGURE 26. Freelance Graphics lets you create curved text automatically.

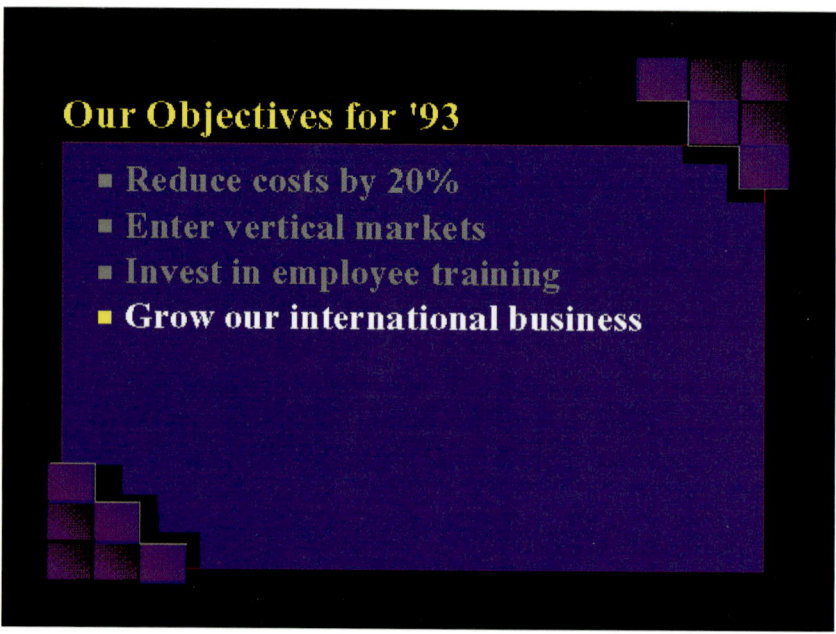

COLOR FIGURE 27. Build charts keep your audience focused on one point at a time. Last chart in a build sequence.

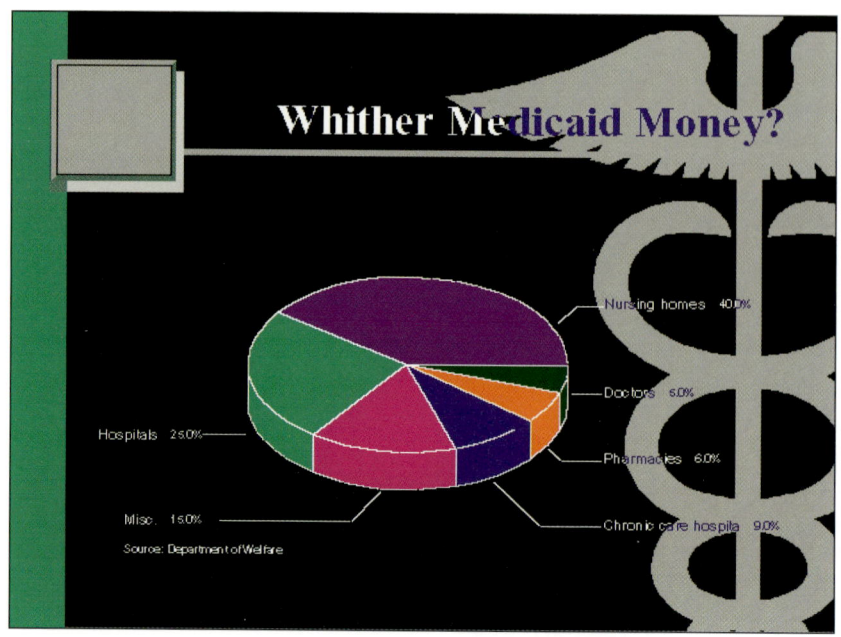

COLOR FIGURE 28. Annotations (created with the Polyline tool) make this 3D pie clearer.

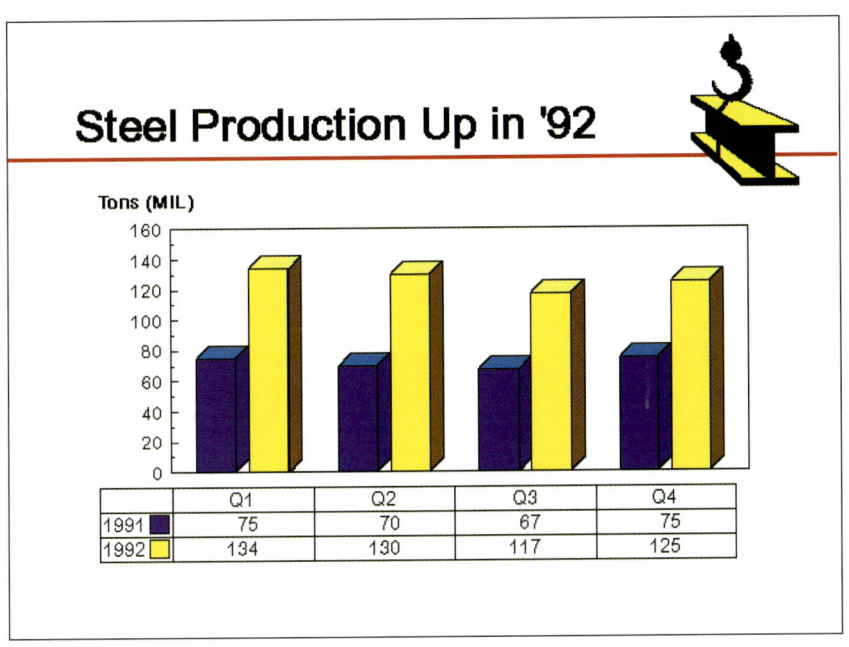

COLOR FIGURE 29. The Number Under Grid option adds a table to this bar chart. (Steel girder from INDUSTRY.SYM.)

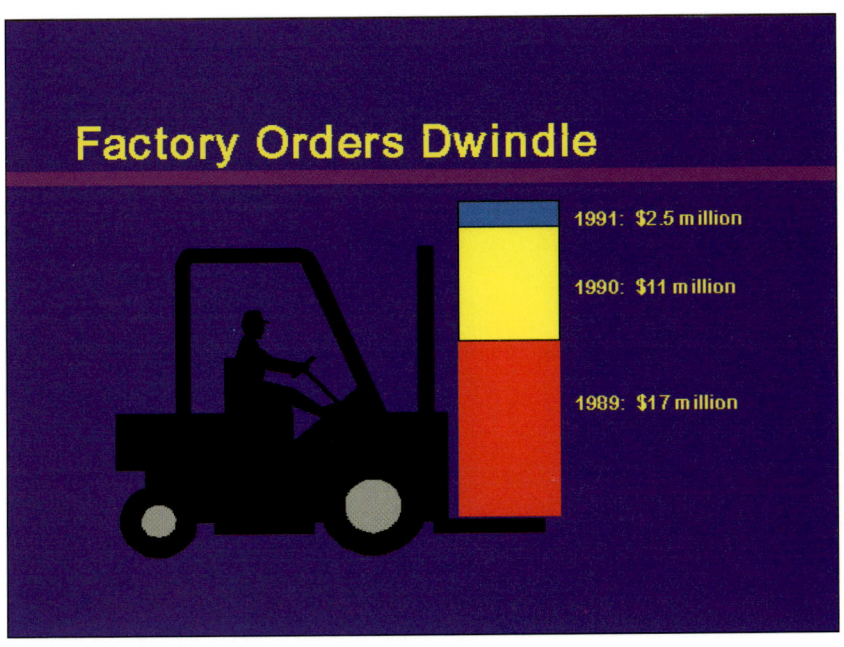

COLOR FIGURE 30. This bar chart was merged with a symbol from INDUSTRY.SYM.

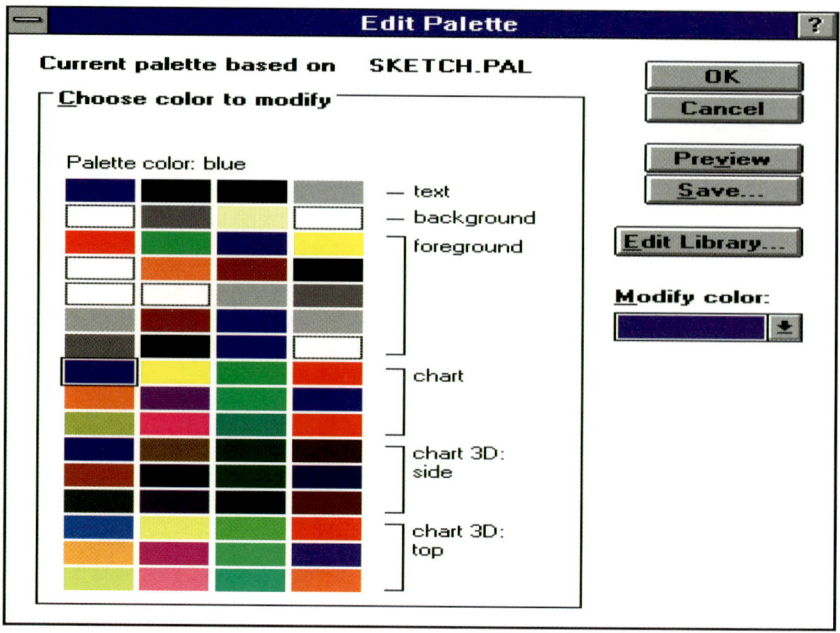

COLOR FIGURE 31. The color palette used to create the page in figure 32.

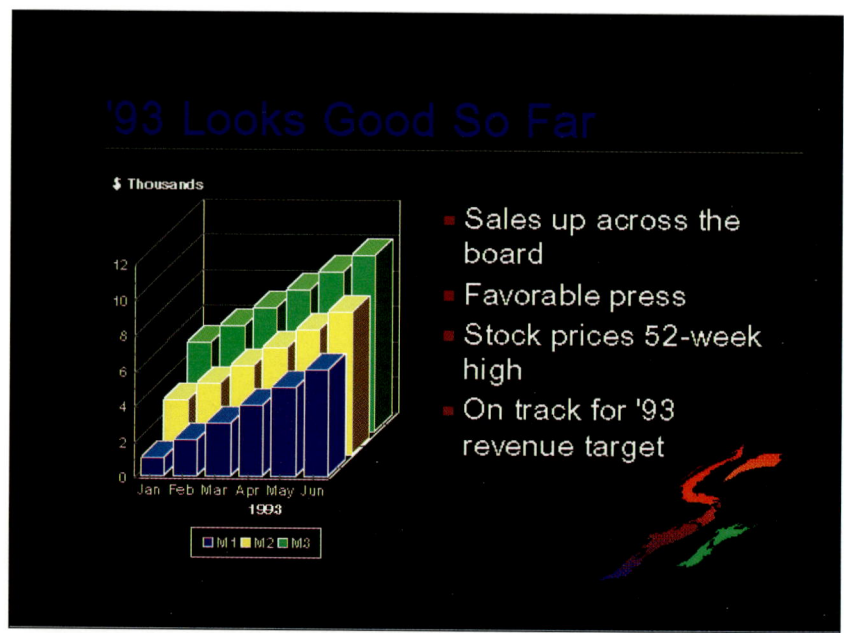

COLOR FIGURE 32. Freelance Graphics uses fixed palette positions to assign colors to titles, bulleted lists, and data charts (see Chapter 18 for more information).

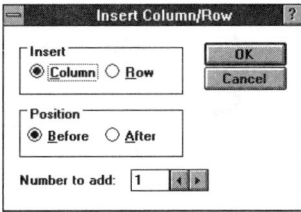

FIGURE 11.3. The Insert Column/Row dialog box.

The Fastest Way To Work with Tables

The fastest way to work with tables is to make sure that all the Table SmartIcons are in your current palette. If you work with tables frequently, it's a good idea to create a special palette designed for working with tables. (For more information about creating custom palettes, see Chapter 23, "Using SmartIcons.")

The right mouse button is the secret to working with tables most effectively. You can select a table and then choose Chart Table to view a cascade menu listing choices, but this method is never the most efficient way of working with tables. It is much easier to click the right mouse button over a selected table: You get the same list of choices.

Sizing Columns and Rows

Tables seldom come out just right when you first create them. After you create a table, you almost certainly want to make a few adjustments. The most common need is to adjust column width. There are several ways to go about adjusting it. You can change the size of all the columns or rows in a table at the same time or you can change the size of selected columns or rows.

To change the size of all the columns or rows in a table at the same time, click the right mouse button over a selected table. Then highlight Size Column/Row, which opens the dialog box shown in figure 11.4. If a check box has a gray fill, it means that the columns or rows in this table have different sizes. The size displayed is the size of the selected column or row or, if no rows or columns are selected, the row indicated by the insertion point.

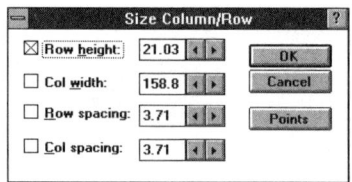

FIGURE 11.4. The Size Column/Row dialog box.

When you click the arrows to choose a new value, this gray fill changes to a check mark. The changes you make now apply to all the selected columns or rows in the table or, if no columns or rows are selected, to the column and row indicated by the insertion point.

Click the bottom button to change the units of measurement. This button is labeled as Points, Picas, Millimeters, Centimeters, or Inches, depending on the current setting.

Sizing Columns and Rows with the Mouse

The quickest and easiest way to size rows and columns is to drag the column or row dividers with the mouse. Enter edit mode and then position the pointer over a column or row divider. The pointer assumes the shape of a double arrow. If you move over a column divider, the double arrow is horizontal; if you move over a row divider, the double arrow is vertical. Drag in the direction of the arrows. Incidentally, the row and column dividers are present even if they are not visible (some table styles don't include border lines between rows and columns). When the pointer changes to the two-headed arrow shape, you know you are in the right place.

One drawback to this method is that it is difficult to ensure that all the columns and rows are the same width or height (if that is your goal). The solution to this problem is to drag one column or row until it looks good to you. Choose the one that looks the best and then change the rest by using the Size Column/Row option.

Moving Columns and Rows

In edit mode, select a row or column to be moved (you can select a range of rows or columns). To move a single row or column, just click the Pointer in a row or column and then click the right mouse button. Highlight Move Column/Row from the list. In the resulting dialog box, click the appropriate button to move the column or row (see fig. 11.5). Then click the appropriate button in the Position area to move a row up or down or a column to the left or right.

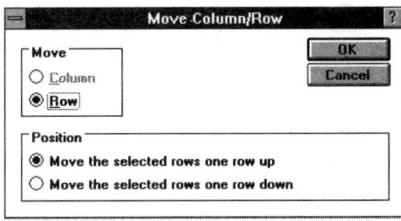

FIGURE 11.5. The Move Column/Row dialog box.

Try It: Highlight a Single Row

Have you ever seen an ad that includes a features table and noticed that the column or row that displayed the data for the advertiser's product was shaded or displayed in a different color? This not-so-subtle technique can be yours when you want to emphasize a row or column in a table chart. Use the following technique to highlight a single row in a table:

1. In edit mode, highlight the row you want to shade with a gray background.
2. Click the right mouse button and choose Attributes.
3. In the Table Attributes dialog box, click the button labeled Background & Border of Selected Cells (see fig. 11.6).

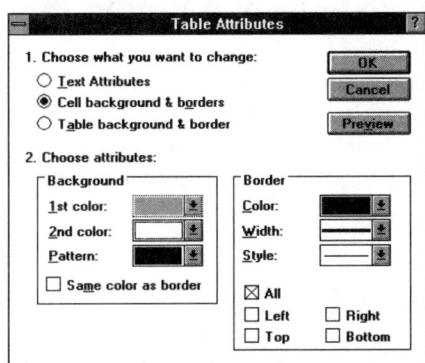

FIGURE 11.6. The Table Attributes dialog box.

4. Click the 1st Color list box. Choose 25% gray (or whatever shade or color you want) from the palette.
5. Click OK and then click outside the table to see your changes.

Figure 11.7 shows the resulting table, with a single row shaded for emphasis.

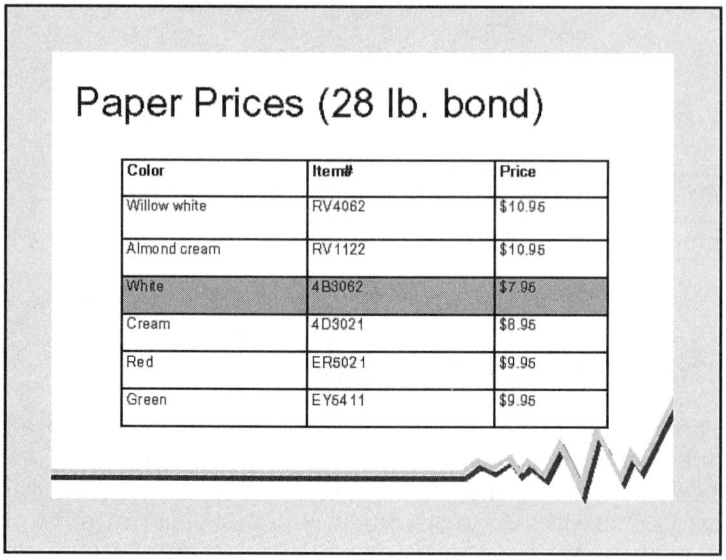

Color	Item#	Price
Willow white	RV4062	$10.95
Almond cream	RV1122	$10.95
White	4B3062	$7.95
Cream	4D3021	$8.95
Red	ER5021	$9.95
Green	EY5411	$9.95

FIGURE 11.7. The resulting table.

How To Change the Look of a Whole Table

You can make global changes to all the text in a table, all the lines in table, or the border of a table. Double-clicking a table opens the Table Attributes dialog box (see fig. 11.6). First, click the button that corresponds to the scope of your change. Then choose the attributes for the selected scope.

Using the Mouse in a Table

You can select data, cells, rows, and columns with the mouse or by using special key combinations. To select a table, click the table. To move around the table or to select characters, you first must enter text edit mode. To enter text edit mode, click a cell twice (slowly). If you click twice too fast, you open the Table Attributes dialog box. You also can enter edit mode by clicking once to select the table and then pressing F2.

To use the mouse to select data in a cell or a range of cells, drag to highlight the data or the range.

To move the insertion point to a cell, just click in that cell.

Using the Keyboard in a Table

You also can move around a table with the keyboard. This method is sometimes more convenient than using a mouse if you are typing a lot of entries.

Selecting with the Keyboard

You can use the following various key combinations to select cells and characters in a table:

- To select characters to the end of a line within a cell, press Shift+End. Press Shift+End again to select the remainder of the cells in a row (moving right). To extend a selection right one column at a time, press Shift+RightArrow.
- To select characters to the beginning of a line, press Shift+Home. Press Shift+Home again to select the remainder of the row (moving left). To extend the selection left one column at a time, press Shift+LeftArrow.
- To extend a selection up one row, press Shift+UpArrow. To extend a selection down one row, press Shift+DownArrow.

Navigating a Table with the Keyboard

To move around in a table with the keyboard, use the following keys:

- To move forward to the next cell in a row, press Tab. To move backward to the preceding cell in a row, press Shift+Tab.
- To move one character at a time, press LeftArrow or RightArrow.
- To move to the end of the preceding cell, press Ctrl+LeftArrow. To move to the beginning of the next cell, press Ctrl+RightArrow.

- To move up one line in a cell, press UpArrow. To move down one line in a cell, press DownArrow. If you are in the first or last line in a cell, pressing these keys moves you to the cell above or below.
- To move to the beginning of the line in the current cell, press Home once. To move to the beginning of the first cell in the row, press Home twice.
- To move to the end of a line, press End once. To move to the end of the last cell in a row, press End twice.
- To move to the first cell in a table, press Ctrl+Home. To move to the end of the last cell in a table, press Ctrl+End.

Wrapping Up

In this chapter, you learned how to use the Table tool to create and edit tables. You learned how to add, delete, and move columns and rows. You learned various keyboard and mouse techniques to make selections and to navigate in a table. You now should be able to change the look of a table by changing its attributes. You also learned a technique for emphasizing a single row or column in a table.

This completes the section on organization charts and tables. In the next section, you move on to the art and practice of creating diagrams.

Part 5
Drawings and Diagrams

Freelance Graphics includes a set of drawing tools that you can use to make simple business diagrams or sophisticated illustrations. In this part you learn how diagrams can illustrate concepts and procedures better than words alone. In the process, you discover new ways to use clip art. You find out how to preserve and share your investment in existing graphics by exporting and importing to and from other graphic formats. Finally, you learn about the structure of color palettes.

This section includes:

Chapter 12. Drawing Objects

Chapter 13. Editing Objects

Chapter 14. Transforming Objects

Chapter 15. Creating Business Diagrams

Chapter 16. Adding Clip Art

Chapter 17. Importing and Exporting Graphics

Chapter 18. Working with Color

12

Drawing Objects

As you have seen, Freelance Graphics provides you with a highly structured environment in which to create presentations. SmartMaster sets provide you with ready-made designs, palettes eliminate the need to create a set of colors that look good together, and symbols give you instant art.

By contrast, the drawing tools give you complete freedom to create your own diagrams and illustrations precisely as you like. You also can use the drawing tools to customize or create new SmartMaster sets.

You don't have to be a skilled illustrator to create effective business diagrams. Most business diagrams consist of words, lines, arrows, and other simple geometric shapes. If you require more sophisticated artwork, you can create it yourself, hire an artist, or choose from the rich source of over 500 professionally drawn images in the Freelance Graphics symbol library. (See Chapter 16, "Adding Clip Art," for more information about symbols.)

Suppose that you have been working on your presentation for a while now and have created a number of bullet charts and graphs. They look good, but now you need to present an idea or concept that doesn't lend itself to words or data-driven graphics. Often, a diagram is just the thing to convey your message.

It's time to pick up the drawing tools. They are in the Toolbox, on the left side of the Freelance Graphics window. Figure 12.1 shows the drawing tools available in the Toolbox. You can use the drawing tools to create the basic geometric shapes you need to create effective business diagrams. Click the appropriate icon to draw lines, arrows, polygons, curves, circles, or arcs. Double-click a drawing icon to set default attributes for the object it creates.

In this chapter, you learn how to:

- *Use the drawing tools in the Toolbox to create lines, arrows, curves, polygons, circles, arcs, and freehand shapes*
- *Customize the drawing tools*
- *Draw with a visible grid*
- *Use Zoom to enlarge a portion of a page*
- *Undo your work*

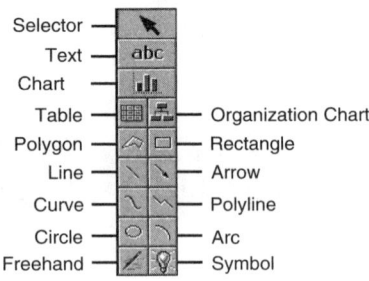

FIGURE 12.1. The Toolbox contains the drawing tools.

Try It: Draw Rectangles and Squares

You find rectangles and squares endlessly useful in creating a variety of business diagrams. A flow chart is the classic example of word-filled rectangles connected by lines. (For the best way to create a flow chart, read Chapter 15, "Creating Business Diagrams.")

Rectangles are easy to draw. If you want to jump right in, just click the Rectangle icon in the Toolbox and then drag the shape of a rectangle on the page. You can drag in any direction to change the size and dimension of the rectangle. Release the mouse button to complete the rectangle. You soon get the hang of it. For a more detailed explanation of what happens when you draw a rectangle, read the following procedure.

1. Click the Rectangle icon. Note that the icon remains in a pushed-in position in the Toolbox (to indicate that it is active) and that the cursor changes to a crosshair.
2. Move the crosshair to the page.
3. Drag the mouse in any direction. As you drag, you see a dashed box on the screen, representing the outline of a rectangle.
4. When the outline is the shape and size you want, release the left mouse button. The dashed rectangle changes to a filled rectangle. Note especially the eight black squares around the border of the rectangle (see fig. 12.2). These squares are *selection handles* that you can use to size objects. If you press Shift as you drag, the shape retains its proportions. (See Chapter 13, "Editing Objects," for information about this feature.) Also note the word "Rectangle" in the edit line at the top of your screen.

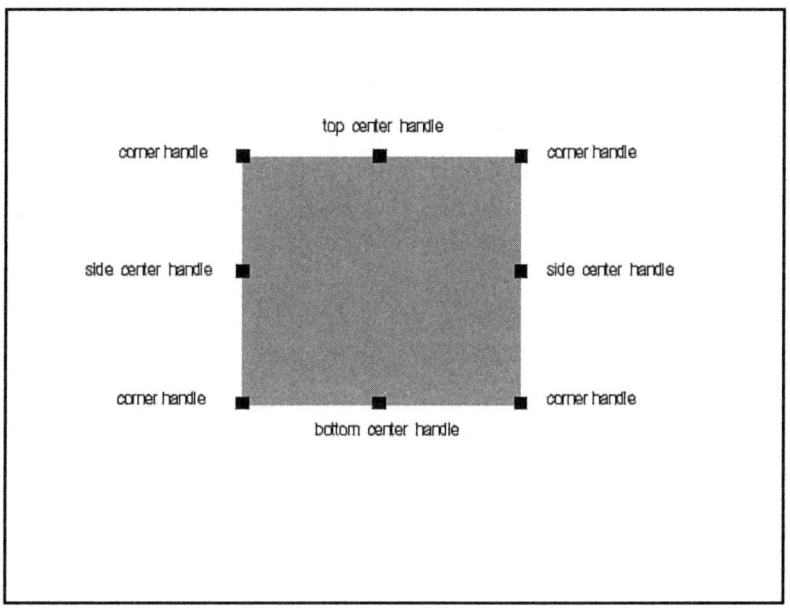

FIGURE 12.2. A selected rectangle with eight selection handles.

5. Now click somewhere outside the boundary of the rectangle. The handles on the rectangle disappear and the edit line now reads "No selection."

6. To create another rectangle, click the Rectangle icon again and repeat steps 1-4. (You can configure the Rectangle tool to make it easier to draw a series of rectangles, without having to click the Rectangle icon each time you create another rectangle. See "Keep the Drawing Tools Active as You Work" later in this chapter.)

To create a square, click the Rectangle icon, press Shift, and drag.

Create a Simple Diagram with Rectangles and Text

You may find many uses for text in boxes. Often you use them simply as borders for explanatory text, as seen in figure 12.3. This diagram consists of nothing but rectangles, arrows, and text.

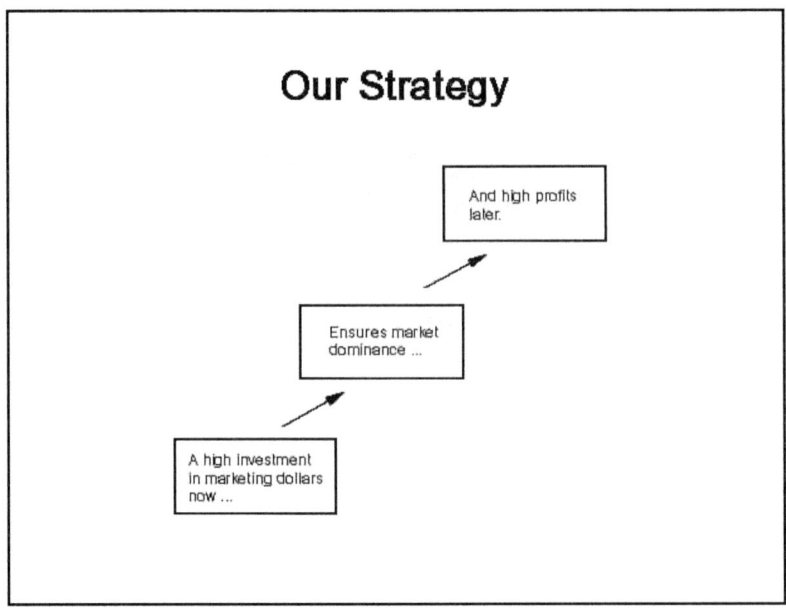

FIGURE 12.3. This simple, yet effective, diagram consists of three rectangles with text in them, two arrows, and a title.

Use the Basic Layout SmartMaster Page as the backdrop for your illustrations.

To create the diagram in figure 12.3, begin by selecting Choose Page Layout and then choose Basic Layout. This page layout gives you a blank page (except for a Title block) to make the page that contains your illustration consistent with the rest of your presentation.

The first step is to create several unfilled rectangles. Double-click the Rectangle icon. You see the Style Default Attributes Rectangle dialog box, which you can use to specify the style of rectangle you want to draw whenever you use the Rectangle icon (see fig. 12.4). Click Color in the Edge box and choose black so that the rectangle has a clearly defined border. In the Area box, click Pattern and choose None, so that the rectangles you create are empty. Click OK. Now, each rectangle you draw (for this presentation only) has a black border and is unfilled. (For more information on setting defaults for the drawing tools, see "Change How the Drawing Tools Work" later in this chapter.)

Now add the text. Click the Text icon in the Toolbox and drag the outline of a rectangle within the rectangle you just created. Type your text and click outside the text block. If necessary, drag the text block to center it within the rectangle.

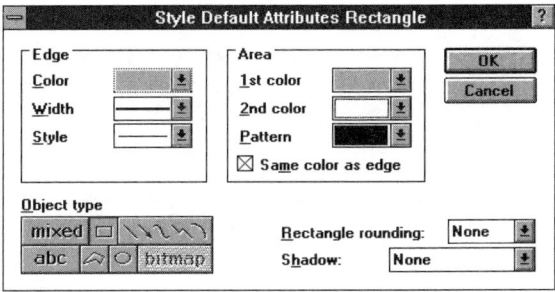

FIGURE 12.4. The Style Attributes Rectangle dialog box.

Use the same technique to create the remaining two text blocks. You also can use the Edit Copy or Edit Replicate commands to copy the first rectangle and text block, and then edit the text. See Chapter 13, "Editing Objects," for more information on Edit Copy and Edit Replicate.

To draw the arrow, click the Arrow icon in the Toolbox and drag the length of the arrow. Repeat, or copy the first arrow and move it to the proper position.

To complete this diagram, type an informative title in the Title block at the top of the page.

That's it. You've produced a striking diagram in about two minutes. It's not a highly complex illustration, but it makes your point.

Notice that you could have used a bullet chart to state the same points. But creating a simple illustration adds visual interest to your presentation and breaks up the monotony of a steady stream of similar-looking bullet charts.

You also could have created figure 12.3 by using text blocks instead of rectangles filled with text, which actually would have been a simpler way to create this diagram. Text blocks can have frames so that they look just like rectangles. For a procedure for creating a diagram using text blocks, refer to Chapter 15, "Creating Business Diagrams." It's good to know both ways of approaching this task. There is one drawback, which is discussed in the next section, to using text blocks instead of rectangles: Text blocks cannot have rounded corners.

Making Rounded Rectangles

A rounded rectangle is a rectangle with rounded corners. You can smooth out the corners of a rectangle by double-clicking the rectangle and choosing one of the four rounding options. Figure 12.5 shows the diagram you just created in figure 12.3 with rounded corners (using the High Rectangle Rounding option). Rounded rectangles give a somewhat softer look to a rectangle and add a nice touch to an otherwise mundane diagram. You also can use ordinary and rounded rectangles in the same diagram to denote different types of information (as in flow charts).

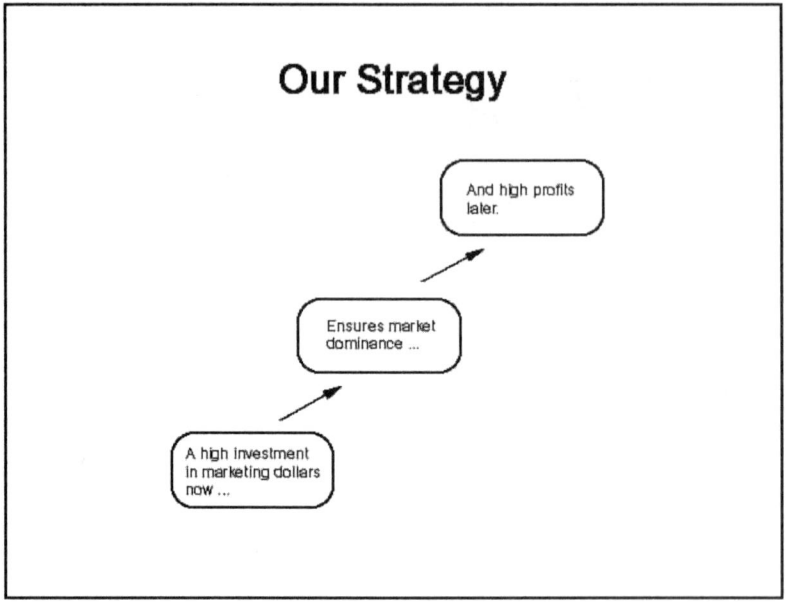

FIGURE 12.5. Rounded corners on these rectangles add a smooth, elegant look to this simple diagram.

How To Draw Squares and Circles

Despite their names, the Rectangle icon also draws squares and the Circle icon draws ellipses.

Click the Rectangle icon and press Shift. Keep the Shift key pressed as you drag the outline of the rectangle. Freelance Graphics constrains the shape of the outline to a perfect square.

If you release the Shift key, you can change the outline to a rectangle. To maintain the square shape, release the mouse button before you release the Shift key.

To draw a circle, click the Circle icon and press Shift. Keep the Shift key pressed as you drag the outline of a circle. Freelance Graphics constrains the shape of the outline to a perfect circle. If you release the Shift key, you can change the outline to an oblong shape, or ellipse. To maintain the circular shape, release the mouse button before you release the Shift key.

Drawing Lines and Arrows

Freelance Graphics has two separate tools for drawing lines, as well as a tool for drawing arrows. The Line icon draws a single line segment, and the Polyline icon draws a line with multiple segments. The procedure for using each of these tools is similar.

To draw a single line segment, click the Line icon and drag a line segment on the page. When you release the mouse button, the line is completed.

To draw a line with multiple segments, click the Polyline icon and drag the line segments on the page. To complete the line, click the Selector icon, double-click, or press Esc.

How To Draw a Straight Line

If you find yourself mumbling that old cliché, "I can't draw a straight line," you may be happy to know that Freelance Graphics eliminates this deficiency. Not only can you draw straight lines, but you can draw lines that are perfectly perpendicular, or connected at a 45-degree angle.

Click the Polyline icon in the Toolbox and then press Shift. As you keep the Shift key pressed, move the crosshair to the page and then drag a series of line segments in different directions. Note that as you draw line segments, Freelance Graphics forces you to draw lines that are vertical, horizontal, or precisely at a 45-degree angle to the previous line segment.

This feature can help you to draw an enormous variety of diagrams. Using the Shift feature as you draw enables you to draw regular geometric illustrations such as floor plans, circuit diagrams, staircases, and virtually any diagram that calls for horizontal, perpendicular, and 45-degree lines.

Try It: Draw a Curve

The Curve tool is the most complicated drawing tool to use, but if you experiment a bit, you soon get the feel for how it works. Freelance creates Bezier curves, which are prized by graphic artists for their power and flexibility in the creation of sophisticated illustrations. If you happen to fall into this category, the Bezier curve adds a powerful tool to your desktop. But even if you don't, you may find this tool quite useful. With it, you can draw perfectly smooth curves easily. After you've drawn a curve, you can edit the individual points of the curve to change the shape of the curve. (See Chapter 14, "Transforming Objects," for details on editing the points of a curve.)

Draw Bezier curves with the Curve icon.

Follow these steps to practice using the Curve tool:

1. Click the Curve icon and move the crosshair to the starting point on the page.
2. Drag and release the mouse button to create each segment of the curve.
3. As you create each segment, try dragging the mouse without releasing the mouse button. This exercise gives you a feel for how you can change the shape of the curve as you are drawing.
4. If you create a segment that is not to your satisfaction, press Backspace to delete it. You can press Backspace repeatedly to remove segments of the curve one by one.
5. Instead of dragging the mouse to create each segment, you also can click points to draw segments or combine the clicking and dragging actions.
6. To complete the curve, double-click the last point or click the Selector tool or press Esc.

Figure 12.6 illustrates how to create curves.

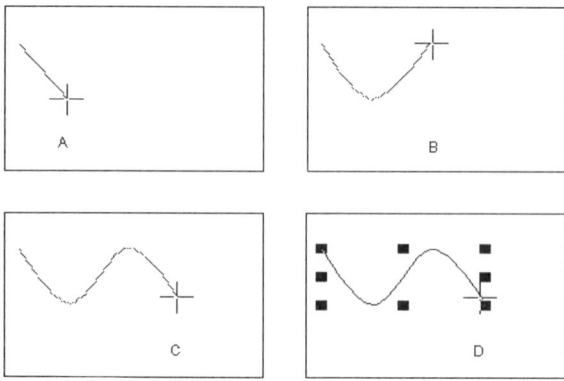

FIGURE 12.6. Creating a curve.

Drawing Circles and Ellipses

To draw a circle or ellipse, click the Circle icon and drag the outline of the circle or ellipse on the page. You can interactively change the outline of the circle until you get just the size and shape you want. Double-click, click the Selector icon, or press Esc to complete the circle.

Drawing Arcs

You can use the Arc tool in two ways.

- Click the Arc icon, drag a line segment on the page, and then click a point outside the line segment. Drag this point to change the curvature of the arc. When you see the outline of the arc you want, release the mouse button. That's it.

- Click three points on the page to define an arc. The first two points define the length of the arc, and the third point determines the curvature of the arc.

Drawing Polygons

The Polygon tool works like the Polyline tool. The difference is that Freelance Graphics fills the polygon after you have completed the outline.

Click the Polygon icon and drag a series of line segments on the page. To complete the Polygon, click the Selector icon or double-click.

For more control over the shape of your polygon, use the View Units & Grid command to display a grid and select the Snap to Grid option. Now you can just click a series of points to draw the polygon you want (you also can use this technique without Snap to Grid enabled). If you make a mistake, press Backspace to retrace your steps and erase one segment at a time. After you have completed the polygon, you can change its shape by moving the points of each segment. See Chapter 14, "Transforming Objects," for more details.

The Polygon tool is useful for drawing a variety of shapes. The star in the logo shown in figure 12.7 was created by clicking the points of a grid to form the star.

Switch Drawing Tools in Midstream

What if you want to create an object that has both straight and curved lines? To do this, you can switch drawing tools as you are drawing an object. You can switch among the Curve, Polyline, and Polygon tools to create such an object with both straight and curved sides. For example, click the Curve icon and draw the first few segments of a curved line. Then click the Polyline tool and draw the straight segments. The object is not completed until you click the Selector icon, double-click, or press the Esc key.

FIGURE 12.7. The Polygon tool was used to create the star in this logo.

Freehand Drawing

Freelance Graphics Release 2.0 adds a Freehand drawing tool. To use it, click the Freehand icon (the pencil) in the Toolbox, move the crosshair pointer to the page, hold down the left mouse button, and draw as you do with a pen or pencil. Release the mouse button when you have drawn the shape you want. Sometimes it's difficult to draw the curve you want the first time. One solution is to choose Arrange Points Mode, select the freehand curve, and then edit the points to smooth out the curve. Deleting individual points generally makes the curve smoother. You also can move individual points to change the shape of the curve. For greater precision, zoom in on the area you want to change. For more information on working in edit points mode, read Chapter 14, "Transforming Objects."

If grid snapping is enabled, you can use the Freehand tool to create perfectly straight lines, from grid dot to grid dot.

The Freehand tool was used to highlight the geographical area shown in figure 12.8. The U.S. map is from the USAMAP.SYM symbol library.

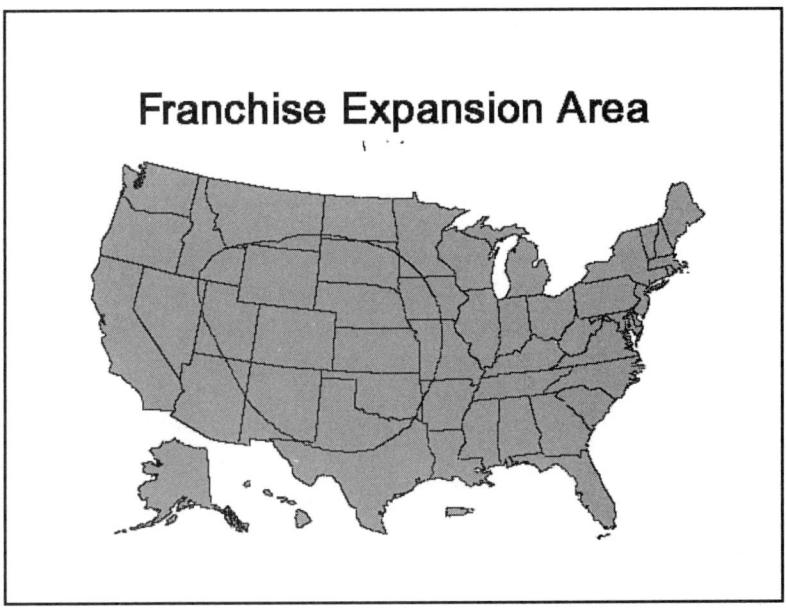

FIGURE 12.8. The Freehand tool was used to highlight an area of this map.

Changing How the Drawing Tools Work

Professional artists generally have a finely tooled working environment with just the right lighting, desk space, and the appropriate set of drawing tools for the job at hand. Similarly, you can set up the drawing tools and environment of Freelance Graphics to work the way you want.

Before you begin work on a drawing, you probably have a pretty good idea of the kinds of graphic elements that you are going to use to create your diagram or illustration. Knowing this, to match your needs, you can change the default attributes that Freelance Graphics uses to draw lines, circles, rectangles, arcs, and curves.

Double-click a drawing icon to change its default attributes.

Suppose that you want all the rectangles in a drawing to be unfilled and to have a wide green border. First, double-click the Rectangle icon. You see the Style Default Attributes Rectangle dialog box (shown earlier in figure 12.3). Consider the major areas of this dialog box.

- The Edge settings change the color, width, and style of the edge of the objects you draw.
- The Area settings change the 1st color, 2nd color, and fill pattern of objects that have fill (rectangles, polygons, circles).
- The Rectangle Rounding list box gives you four degrees of roundness for the edges of rectangles (none, low, medium, high). See figure 12.9 for an illustration of rectangle rounding.

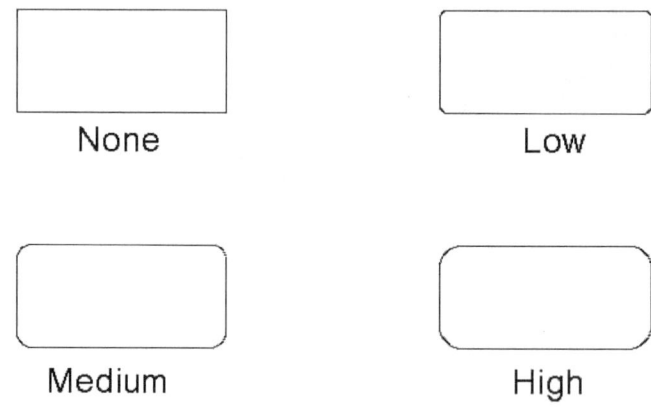

FIGURE 12.9. Examples of rectangle rounding.

Change the settings you want and click OK. The crosshair is now positioned on the page, ready for you to draw the type of object whose default attributes you just changed. Until you change the defaults again, all the rectangles you draw in this presentation have the default settings. (The default attributes for the drawing tools are saved along with each presentation. If you start a new presentation, the system defaults are used. To change the defaults for new presentations, refer to Chapter 24, "Customizing Freelance Graphics.")

Now double-click the Line icon. Freelance Graphics opens a dialog box named Style Default Attributes Line & Curve (see fig. 12.10). This dialog box affects settings for five tools at the same time: the Line, Polyline, Arrow, Curve, and Arc tools. Now take a look at the shaded box, labeled "Object Type," in the bottom left part of this dialog box. One of these boxes contains images of these drawing tools. These images represent all the drawing tools that are changed when you change settings in this dialog box.

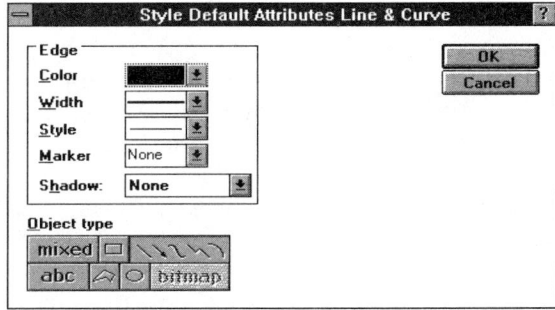

FIGURE 12.10. The Style Default Attributes Line & Curve dialog box.

You can set defaults for the other drawing tools without leaving this dialog box. Just double-click the representation of the tool whose attributes you want to change. Click the representation of the Rectangle icon to change settings for rectangles. (When you change settings, you change the ways objects are drawn from then on; current attributes of drawn objects are not changed.) In a similar fashion, you can change attributes for the Text, Polygon, Circle, and the Arc tools.

One unexplained picture remains: the one labeled "Mixed." The Mixed box enables you to specify default edge and area settings for all the drawing tools at the same time. You can change, for example, the edges of all objects to black and all areas to blue in a single step. Just click the Mixed box and change the settings as you like.

Keep the Drawing Tools Active as You Work

You can set up the drawing tools to function in two ways with Tools User Setup. Suppose that you draw a rectangle. By default, after you draw the rectangle, the crosshair disappears and returns to the shape of the pointer. You now can use the pointer to choose a command, click an icon, or click a drawing icon. But, if you are drawing a series of objects of the same type, it is inconvenient to have to click the Rectangle icon each time you want to draw a new rectangle. Choose Tools User Setup and click the button labeled Keep Tool Active.

Now after you draw a rectangle, the crosshair remains on the page, ready for you to draw another rectangle. Just drag the outline of the next rectangle and click. Again, the crosshair appears and now you can draw another rectangle. When you need to draw multiple objects of the same type, this capability is quite convenient. To draw another object, click another drawing tool. You remain in drawing mode until you click the Selector icon.

You also can choose commands or click icons in this mode. When you move the crosshair off the drawing page, the selector returns to the Pointer shape and you can choose a command or click an icon. But, if you want to move an object or double-click an object to change its attributes, you first must click the Selector icon in the Toolbox.

Save Drawing Time with SmartIcons

Nowhere in Freelance Graphics do SmartIcons save you more time or make more sense than in the drawing environment. By way of illustration, consider how much faster it is to align objects with the Align SmartIcons than choosing the Menu commands to accomplish the same task. Suppose that you want to align four text-filled boxes along the left side in a vertical column. Click each box with the right mouse button and then just click the Align Left SmartIcon. Contrast this procedure with choosing Arrange Align from the menu bar and then clicking the left button in the Arrange Align dialog box. Moreover, you can quickly test the alignment of objects with SmartIcons. Click the Align Left SmartIcon to see how the boxes look lined up on their left sides. Then click the Align Right SmartIcon to see whether they look better lined up along their right sides. You can use this same technique with the Align Top and Align Bottom SmartIcons.

Developing an Efficient Working Style

As you become more comfortable with the drawing tools, you may find yourself repeating the same actions again and again, and you may be surprised how quickly you can create simple drawings.

Here's a useful sequence of commands. Press F4 to select all the objects on the page. Click the Group SmartIcon so that you can treat all these objects as a single entity. Now move or size the group as you like. Finally, click the Ungroup SmartIcon so that you can work on each individual object again. Similarly, you may find yourself automatically using the Align commands to line up boxes or other shapes in conceptual diagrams. As these actions become second nature, you soon can create basic diagrams very quickly. All it takes is practice.

Drawing with a Grid

Effective illustrations require balance and proportion. The graphic elements on a page must maintain the proper proportions to each other as well as to the size of the page itself. One of the best ways to create drawings with balance and proportion is to use a grid to lay out the various elements of an illustration (see fig. 12.11). Using grids is a time-honored method of graphic artists, sometimes known as the grid system.

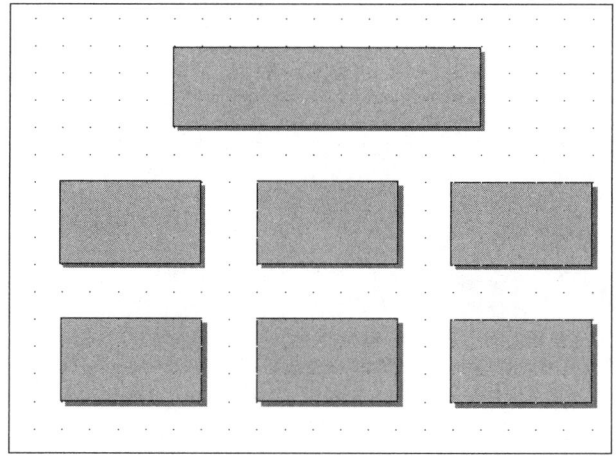

FIGURE 12.11. Using a grid makes it much easier to create illustrations with balance and proportion.

You can display a grid of whatever size you want in Freelance Graphics and use it to lay out the elements of your diagrams. Use the Units & Grids dialog box to choose the units the grids are measured in (see fig. 12.12). If you choose, you also can turn on the snap feature, which causes objects that you create, move, or size to automatically lock into the nearest fixed increments on the grid in this dialog box.

Shift+F7 turns the snap feature on and off.

The grid is especially useful when you are creating organization charts, which rely on rectangles spaced out in a regular pattern on the page. (See Chapter 10, "Organization Charts," for a procedure for creating organization charts.)

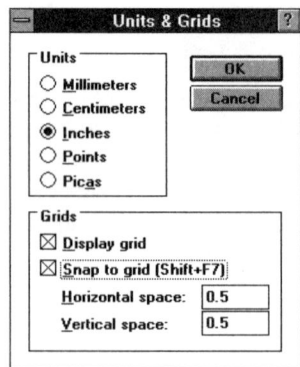

FIGURE 12.12. The Units & Grids dialog box.

Zooming In To Draw

Not to be overlooked is the Zoom SmartIcon, in the shape of a magnifying glass. This most utilitarian tool can help you draw more precisely. Its primary use is to hone in on a small detail of a drawing so that you can add a delicate detail. But you also can use it to zoom out of the page. Some users find it convenient to use the area outside the printable margin (the gray area) as a graphical scratch pad or as a holding area for shapes to be used again.

The great benefit of working in a zoomed-in portion of a drawing is that when you zoom back to a normal perspective, any minor errors of precision in the drawing are rendered invisible.

The Zoom tool is right for a number of tasks, including lining up an arrow at exactly the right point, adding the small finishing touch to a diagram, or placing a very small object within another.

You can use the following three methods to zoom in on an area of a drawing:

- Click directly over the portion of the drawing you want to view at a larger size. Freelance Graphics enlarges the area by a fixed amount. Each time you click, the area is enlarged by the same fixed amount.
- Click the Zoom icon and then drag a rectangle around the area of the drawing you want to zoom in on (see figs. 12.13 and 12.14).
- Choose View In from the menu.

Drawing Objects **227**

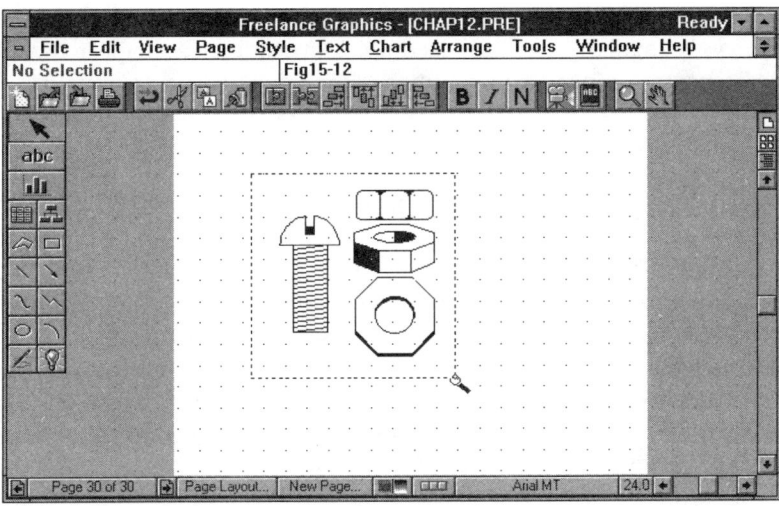

FIGURE 12.13. One method of zooming: Click the Zoom tool and drag a box around the area to be enlarged.

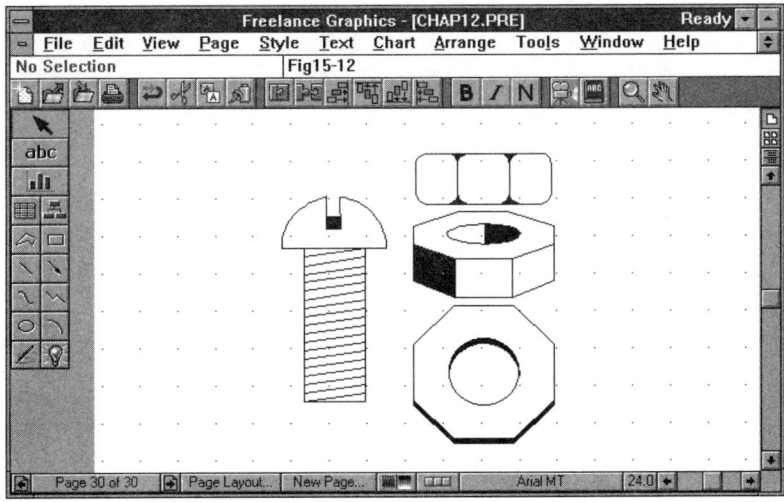

FIGURE 12.14. The enlarged area from figure 12.13.

To zoom out again, choose View Out from the menu or press Shift as you click the Zoom icon. You also can return to a full-screen view in a single step by choosing View Full Page.

You can use the Zoom tool in conjunction with the Edit Select Cycle command to select a very small object within a complex drawing. See Chapter 13, "Editing Objects," for more information about the Edit Select Cycle command.

Undoing What You Have Done

In life, people don't have the luxury of being able to undo their mistakes. In Freelance Graphics, though, you can reverse your last ten actions with the Edit Undo command. If you draw five objects, for example, you can undo these actions by choosing Edit Undo five times. This command is quite useful if you are working on a complex diagram and you make a mistake. Edit Undo restores the drawing to its state before you made an error. Instead of choosing Edit Undo, you can press Ctrl+Z or click the Edit Undo SmartIcon.

Wrapping Up

In this chapter, you learned how to draw those objects you need to create business diagrams: lines, arrows, curves, polygons, circles, and arcs. You also learned how to customize the drawing tools, draw with a grid, zoom in on an area of your drawing, and "undo" mistakes you have made.

In the next chapter, you learn how to edit the basic shapes you have just learned to create.

13

Editing Objects

As you are working on a presentation, you can alter the appearance or position of text or graphic objects in many ways. Freelance Graphics has a wide variety of commands and features that enable you to edit and manipulate the objects you have created. This chapter focuses on the basic editing commands that you use again and again in the course of your work. Because many of these commands are used frequently—such as Edit Copy and Edit Paste—they may become second nature. Others—such as Arrange Rotate—may be used less frequently but are nevertheless powerful tools that should be part of your skill set.

After you learn the basics, you are ready to begin creating original diagrams and illustrations. You can refer to Chapter 15, "Creating Business Diagrams," for design tips and techniques to help you along the way. To learn more sophisticated ways of working with graphic objects, read Chapter 14, "Transforming Objects."

Selecting Objects

You can perform a number of actions on the graphic objects you create. You can size them or move them, change their borders or fill, alter their shape, copy them, delete them, or—for a stack of overlapping objects—specify which object covers another object (object priority). As you produce diagrams, you use all these features again and again, so it pays to learn them well.

In this chapter, you learn how to:

- *Select and deselect objects*
- *Change the attributes of objects*
- *Change the size of objects*
- *Collect objects into a group*
- *Align, flip, and rotate objects*
- *Move, copy, duplicate, paste, and delete objects*
- *Understand the concept of object priority*

Before you can do anything at all to objects, you first must select them. This section tells you all you need to know about selecting objects. To make this lesson a true learning experience, fill a blank page with five or six objects of different types (lines, arrows, arcs, circles, rectangles, and polygons) before you read on.

Select Objects One at a Time

The easiest way to select a single object is to click it. Try it now. The selection handles appear on the object you clicked, and the type of object you selected is displayed in the edit line.

Now click another object. The new object is selected, and the first object is deselected. The selection handles are now displayed on the second object, and the edit line shows its type. Each time you click a new object, the previous object is deselected.

Select Several Objects

If you want to perform an action on several objects (such as grouping or aligning), you have to select them first. After you select the first object, you can select additional objects by holding down the Shift key as you click. Try it. Note that each time you click an object with Shift+click, the previously selected objects remain selected, as you can see by the selection handles. Now look at the edit line. The message in blue is "Collection" (see fig. 13.1). In Freelance Graphics, a *collection* is a group of selected objects. Deselect objects from a collection by Shift+clicking the objects.

Press F4 to select all the objects on a page or click the Select All SmartIcon.

Select All the Objects on the Page at the Same Time

Sometimes you need to select all the objects on a page. Perhaps you want to group them so that you can resize everything proportionately at the same time. Perhaps you want to group all the objects so that you can delete them or move them. Whatever the reason, all you have to do is press F4. Pressing F4 selects all objects, regardless of whether they were selected before. You also can click the Select All SmartIcon.

Editing Objects **231**

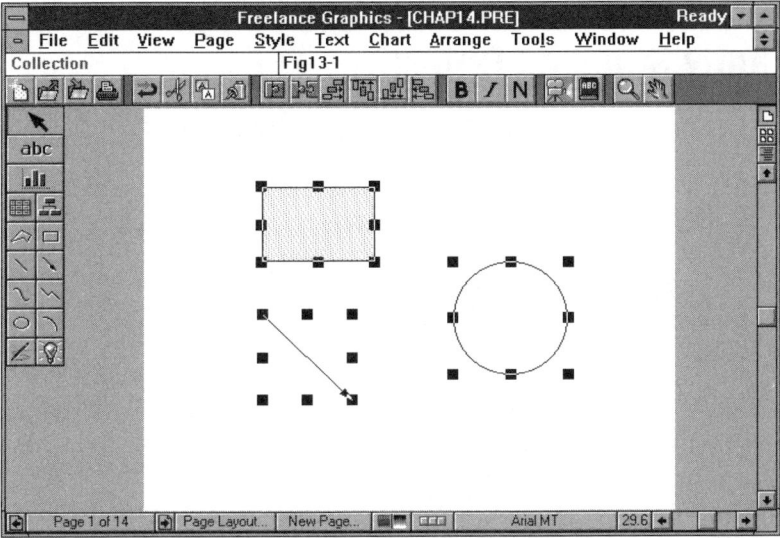

FIGURE 13.1. Several objects selected at the same time.

Deselect Objects

Selection handles enable you to size objects interactively; when you want a clear vision of your drawing, however, selection handles make the page look cluttered. You can deselect objects in the following several ways:

- To deselect one or more objects, select a new object by clicking the left mouse button. This method deselects all objects except the one you just selected.
- To deselect all the selected objects on a page, click with the left mouse button anywhere on the page except on an object.
- To deselect objects from a collection of objects one at a time, Shift+click each object you want to deselect.

Select Additional Objects Based on the Currently Selected Object

You can select additional objects based on the attributes of the currently selected object. This feature may sound obscure, like something only a power user would dream of doing, but actually it can be quite useful in everyday situations. This feature enables you, for example, to select all red rectangles on a page. You can select all green lines with a certain line width, all blue circles with a red edge, or all black Times Roman text.

You also can select objects by their type only. In other words, you can select all rectangles, text, circles, polygons, curves, arcs, or lines, without regard to their attributes.

Suppose that you are creating a diagram that contains many rectangles, perhaps filled with text (as in a flow chart). You decide that the rectangles would look bolder and more convincing if their edges were thicker.

Instead of changing them one by one, you first select any one of them and then choose Edit Select Like. Now, in the Select Like Objects dialog box, choose the attributes that you want to use as the basis for matching other rectangles (see fig. 13.2). If you want to select all rectangles without regard to their attributes, mark the Object Type box and remove all other marks. This selection means that you don't care about the color, edge width, or fill of the rectangle. If it's a colored rectangle, you want to select the Color box. Freelance Graphics selects all rectangles that are of the same color as the selected rectangle. By selectively marking the check boxes for the attributes you want to match, you can effectively filter selections based on any combination of matching attributes you choose.

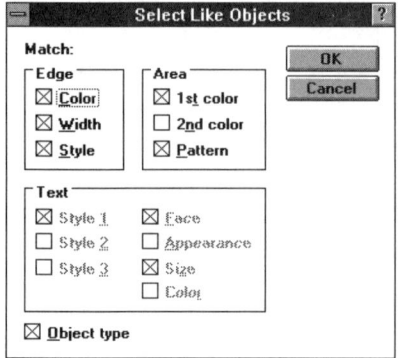

FIGURE 13.2. The Select Like Objects dialog box.

Select Objects by Cycling through Them

In some diagrams, particularly a complex diagram that has several objects very close to or even on top of each other, you may have difficulty selecting the object you want. When you try to click the object you want, you keep selecting another object. If this happens to you, try the Edit Select Cycle command, which enables you to select each object visible in the current view one at a time.

Try it to see how it works. First choose Edit Select Cycle. Then select the object you want by using the Cycle Selection dialog box (see fig. 13.3). Use this dialog box to cycle through each object on a page. Choosing Next puts a dashed box around an object. Click Select to select the indicated object. Click Previous to put a dashed box around the previous object.

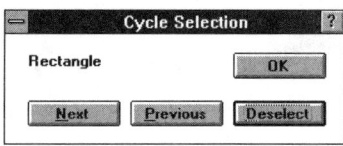

FIGURE 13.3. The Cycle Selection dialog box.

If a complex drawing is built from numerous small objects, an effective technique is to zoom in on the area that contains the object you want to select and then use the Edit Select Cycle command. The Edit Select Cycle command cycles through objects in the visible drawing area only, so zooming in limits the number of objects to be selected. Objects are selected in the order of *drawing priority* (the order in which objects are drawn on the page).

Changing the Appearance of Objects

You can change graphic or text objects in Freelance Graphics. Graphic objects can be lines, curves, rectangles, circles, polygons, arcs, or combinations of these (known as shapes).

Besides having a certain shape, an object also has attributes that define its appearance. You can change an object's attributes without changing the shape of the object. A line, for example, may be thick or thin, solid or dashed; a circle or polygon may be filled or unfilled; the edge of a rectangle may be thick or thin; any object may be blue, green, or any other color you want. Figure 13.4 illustrates this feature by using stars.

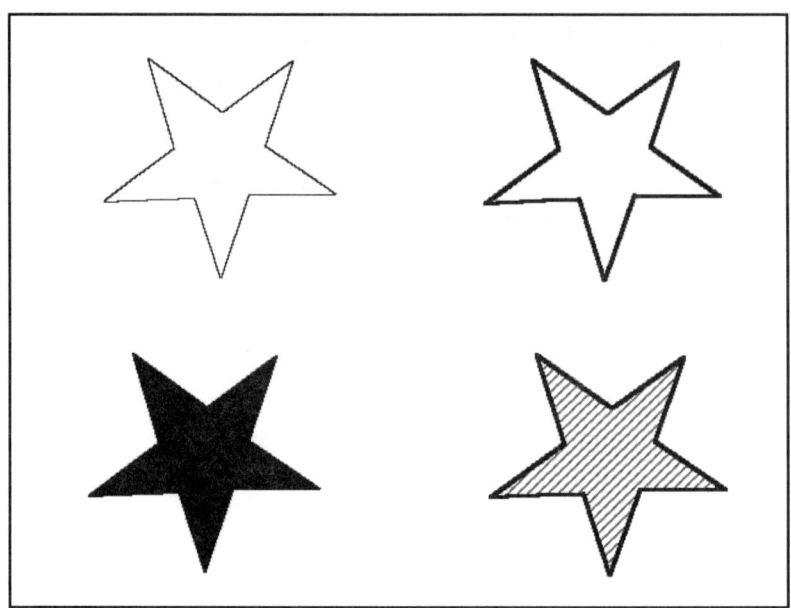

FIGURE 13.4. These four stars have the same shape but varying edge widths and fill attributes.

After you create an object or a complete diagram, you can change the attributes of objects without affecting the basic look of the diagram. Changing attributes is another kind of fine-tuning that you use to complete a finished diagram.

Change the Attributes of a Single Object

To change an object's attributes, double-click the object or click the right mouse button.

The easiest way to change an object's attributes is to double-click the object, which displays a dialog box you can use to change attributes selectively. Figure 13.5 shows the Style Attributes Polygon & Shape dialog box. You see this dialog box when you double-click a polygon. As you can see, you can change attributes for the edge of the box (color, line width, and line style) as well as attributes for the area, or fill, of the polygon (1st color, 2nd color, and pattern). If you mark the check box labeled Same Color as Edge, the edge color and area color change in tandem; that is, if you change one, you change the other.

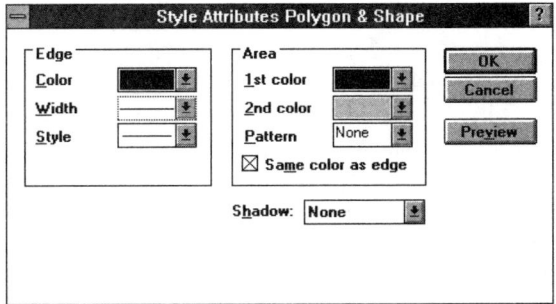

FIGURE 13.5. The Style Attributes Polygon & Shape dialog box.

Change Attributes with the Right Mouse Button

When you want to do more than change an object's attributes, you can click an object with the right mouse button. You see a floating menu that lists the available actions you can take for the selected object (see fig. 13.6). If you're not sure which commands work with a certain type of object, clicking the object with the right mouse button is a good idea. The menu varies according to the object type. You see a different menu, for example, if you click a text block and then click a rectangle.

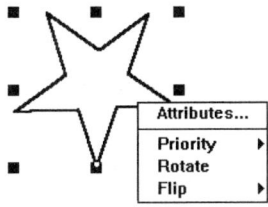

FIGURE 13.6. Click an object with the right mouse button to open a menu with options relating to the object.

Change the Area Fill of an Object

You can change both the color and the pattern for the fill of an object. If you choose the solid (all black) pattern for an object, Freelance uses the 1st color for the fill and ignores the 2nd color. If you choose None, Freelance ignores both 1st and 2nd color.

If you choose any other pattern, Freelance uses both 1st and 2nd color to create the fill. Here's how it works. Note that the patterns in the Pattern list box are in black and white. The black portions of the patterns use 1st color, and the white areas use 2nd color.

You also can use the Area options to create a graduated fill, which is a gradual blending of two colors over a pattern.

Several of the Freelance SmartMaster sets use graduated fills for the page background (for example, GRADATE1.MAS, GRADATE2.MAS, and GRADATE3.MAS). Graduated fills look best with slides and certain color output devices, such as color PostScript printers. For black-and-white output devices, they are not the best choice. To create a graduated fill, you make choices from the 1st color, 2nd color, and Pattern list boxes.

Change the Attributes of Several Objects at the Same Time

You also can change the attributes of several objects at the same time, regardless of whether they are of the same type. If you are creating a diagram that contains circles, rectangles, and polygons, for example, you may conclude that your diagram would be more effective if you changed the line width for all these objects.

To make these changes, first select all the objects to be changed. Then choose Style Attributes or double-click any of the selected objects. You see the dialog box shown in figure 13.7. If you have selected objects of different types—say, a rectangle, a polygon, and a circle—these objects may have different edge widths or have a different fill color or pattern.

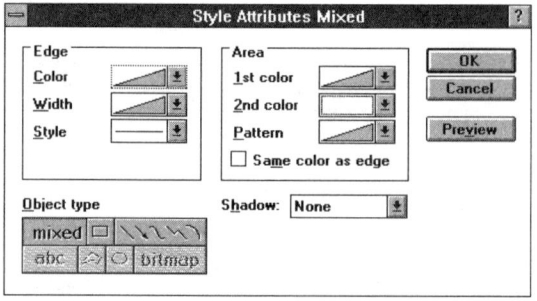

FIGURE 13.7. The Style Attributes Polygon & Shape dialog box after selecting objects of different types.

Suppose that the selected objects have different line widths. You see a triangle in the Edge Width box (instead of the chosen line width) to signify that the line widths of the objects you selected are different. But, if you change the attribute in this box, you change the attributes for all the selected objects at once.

In addition, note the Object Type icons at the bottom of the dialog box. These icons enable you to change attributes for selected object types only. To change attributes for rectangles only, for example, click the Rectangle icon.

You also can change the attributes of objects that you have combined with the Group command, as well as symbols (which are simple grouped objects).

Changing the Size of Objects

When you are creating a diagram or illustration, you frequently need to change the size of objects. You may need to size one object to make it fit within another object, size all the objects at the same time to make them fit within the page boundaries, or size a line to make it longer.

To size an object, you drag one of an object's eight selection handles.

When you change the size of an object, you also can change its dimensions. You can size a rectangle in one direction only, for example, making it longer but not higher. If you size a circle in the horizontal direction only, you end up with an ellipse.

The objects shown on the right in figure 13.8 were sized by dragging the center right selection handle. This action sizes an object in the horizontal direction only. Drag a top or bottom center handle to size an object in the vertical direction only. Drag a corner handle to size an object in both directions at the same time.

Size an Object without Changing Its Dimensions

Press Shift as you drag a corner handle to size an object proportionately.

Often you want to retain an object's proportions when you size it. This is almost always true when you are sizing a symbol. To size an object proportionately, click a corner handle and press Shift simultaneously. Then drag the outline to the size you want. Make sure that you release the mouse button before you release the Shift key; otherwise, you lose the proportionate sizing.

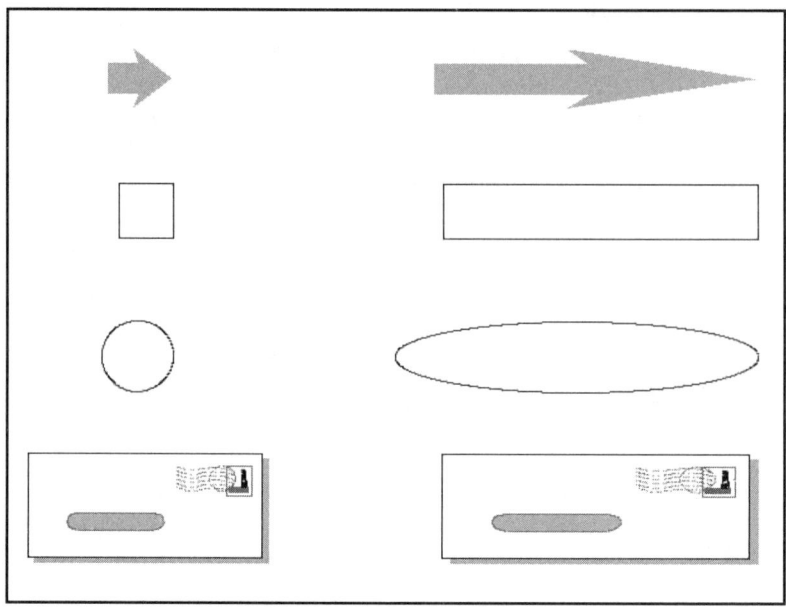

FIGURE 13.8. Examples of sizing figures.

Sizing Objects with the Keyboard

You also can size objects with the arrow keys when you need to be precise. Select an object and then press the Period key to display the sizing crosshair on the upper left selection handle. Press the Period key repeatedly to move to the next selection handle around the perimeter of the object. When the sizing crosshair is positioned on the selection handle you want, press an arrow key in the direction you want to size the object. Each time you click an arrow key, the object becomes smaller or larger by one pixel.

If grid snap is enabled (choose View Units & Grids and then select Display Grid and Snap to Grid), the object is sized one grid unit each time you press an arrow key.

Collecting Individual Objects into a Group

The reason to group objects—that is, turn multiple objects into a single object—is to enable you to manipulate several objects as if they were a single object. You may want to size several objects at the same time while maintaining the relative sizes of the objects, for example, or you may want to save a drawing as a symbol so that you can use it in other presentations.

Another reason for grouping objects is so that you can place a group of objects into a placement block. Grouping is necessary because a placement block can contain only one object.

Often you may need to group objects for a brief time only. As an example, suppose that you need to center the illustration you have been creating. Just press F4 to select all the objects, choose Arrange Group or click the Group SmartIcon, and then center the grouped object on the page. To continue working on the illustration, choose Arrange Ungroup or click the Ungroup SmartIcon.

You can build complex objects by combining single objects. Then you can manipulate the grouped object as if it were a single object. This technique is a good one to use whenever you have created a complex object and want to manipulate it as a single object. (This is how the symbols of Freelance Graphics are structured, incidentally, and this is how you can create your own symbols and add them to your custom symbol library. See Chapter 16, "Adding Clip Art," for more information.)

To group several objects, just select them and then use the Arrange Group command or click the Group SmartIcon.

After you group them, each object loses its individual selection handles and the group now has one set of selection handles. The message in the edit line now reads "Group."

Suppose that you are working on a diagram and all the objects in your diagram seem too large. You want to size all the objects at the same time but retain the original proportions among all the objects.

Select the objects to create a collection and then use Arrange Group. Click a corner selection handle, press Shift, and drag to make the collection smaller or larger. All the objects are sized at the same time but retain their original proportions and their size in relation to the other objects. To work on individual objects once more, select the collection and then choose Arrange Ungroup.

Aligning Objects for Precision Drawings

As you work on a diagram, perhaps no command is more useful than Arrange Align. For good reason, this command is a favorite of most users. A successful design for a diagram must be well ordered and symmetrical. One surefire way of making a drawing balanced and symmetrical is to line up objects.

Instead of attempting to line up objects by sight, the Align command precisely lines up selected objects on a designated boundary (right, left, top, or bottom). The stars, lines, and text in the diagram shown in figure 13.9 were lined up by using the Align SmartIcons.

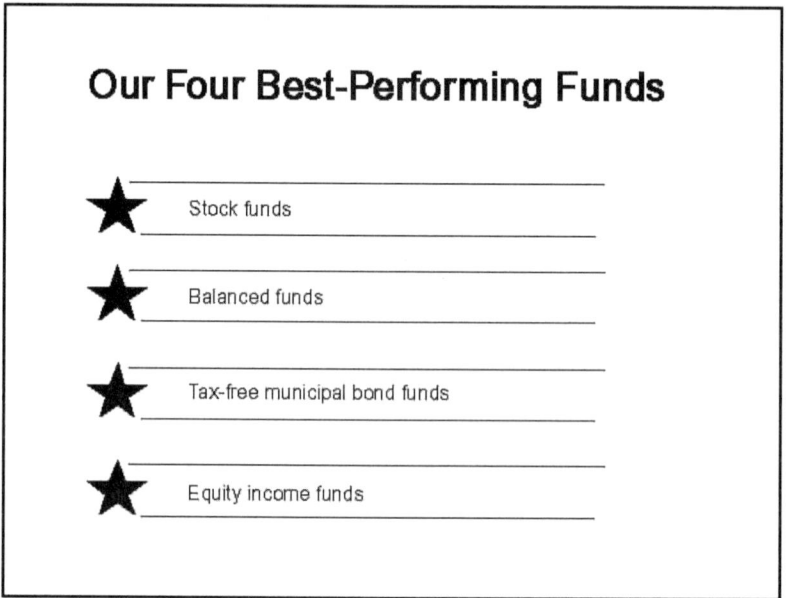

FIGURE 13.9. Use the Align command to create clean, well-structured diagrams.

Flipping Objects

Sometimes you draw an object (perhaps an arrow) that is pointing in the wrong direction. For a special effect, however, you may want to create a duplicate of an object pointing in the opposite direction.

You can use the Arrange Flip command in both these instances. You can flip an object horizontally or vertically with the Arrange Flip Left to Right or Arrange Flip Top to Bottom commands, respectively. As shortcuts, click the Flip Left to Right or Flip Top to Bottom SmartIcons. Note that you cannot flip text or graphs.

Create Mirror Images: A Flip Tip

To create mirror images of objects easily, first create the original object. If you are working with several objects, first combine them with Arrange Group. Then select the object and choose Edit Copy. Next, choose Edit Paste. Then move the pasted objects to where you want the mirrored objects to be. Choose an Arrange Flip command to create the mirror image.

The arrow in figure 13.10 came from the ARROWS symbol library. The arrow was replicated and then flipped with Arrange Flip Left to Right.

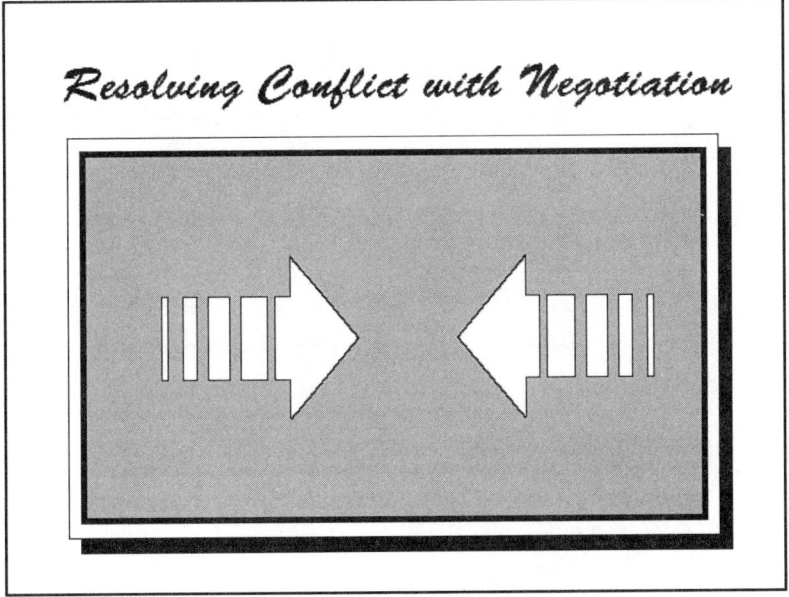

FIGURE 13.10. Arrows created by using the Arrange Flip Left to Right command.

Rotating Objects

You can rotate objects about their axes by using the Arrange Rotate command. For a shortcut, click the Rotate SmartIcon.

To rotate an object, first select it. Then choose Arrange Rotate (or click the Rotate SmartIcon). You see the Rotation pointer. Drag the mouse to rotate the object as much as you want. The edit line displays a readout of the angle of rotation, so you can rotate an object by an exact angle.

Figure 13.11 shows a presentation page with a rotated object.

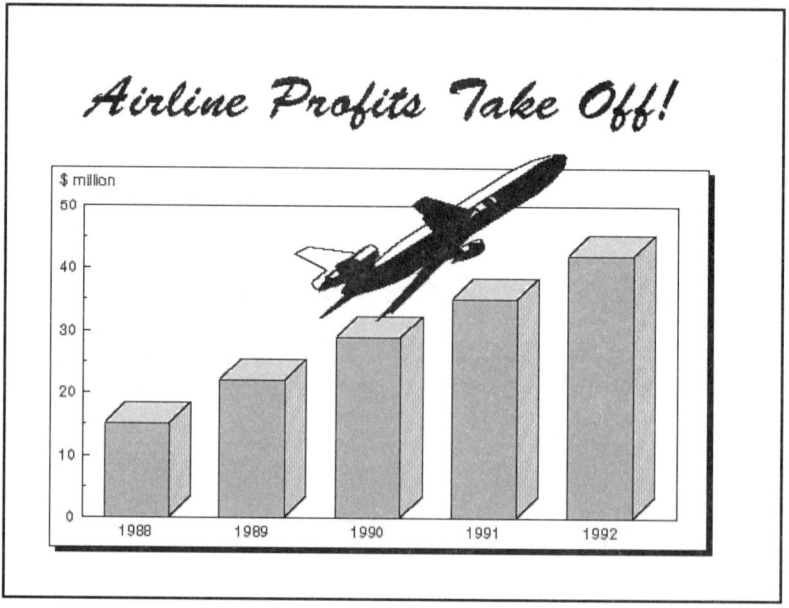

FIGURE 13.11. The airplane symbol was rotated to better reflect the message of the headline.

Moving Objects

The simplest way to move an object on a single presentation page is to drag it with the mouse. Just click the mouse within the boundaries of an object, hold down the mouse button, and drag the object to a new location. Note that, if an object is unfilled, you must drag the edge of an object; dragging within the borders of an unfilled object has no effect.

To move several selected objects at the same time, drag any single object in the selection group.

If an object is selected, make sure that you don't drag a selection handle. Doing so sizes the object.

You also can move objects with the keyboard, which is very useful for precision drawing. Select the object (or objects) you want to move and then press the arrow keys to move the selection in the desired direction. Each time you click the arrow key, you move an outline of the section one pixel in the specified direction. To move the selection rapidly, hold down the arrow key. If the snap-to-grid feature is turned on, pressing an arrow key moves the selection one grid dot at a time.

Copying, Pasting, and Deleting Objects

Copying objects is a basic function that you use over and over as you create your presentations. You can copy objects (whether text or graphics) from one page to another, from one presentation to another, or even from one application to another.

To copy pages from one presentation to another, you use the Page Sorter, as described in Chapter 22, "Managing Your Presentations."

To understand the Edit Copy command (and its counterpart, Edit Paste), you need to know a little about the Windows Clipboard.

What Is the Clipboard?

The Windows Clipboard is a temporary holding place for text and graphics. When you use the Edit Copy or Edit Cut commands, Freelance places a copy of the selected object on the Clipboard. You can subsequently use the Edit Paste command to place a copy of the Clipboard contents on another page, another presentation, or even another application.

The Clipboard stores only the object or objects from the most recent Edit Copy or Edit Cut command. This fact is important to keep in mind as you are working on a presentation. If you use Edit Cut to delete an object from a page, with the intent of copying it to another page, make sure that you use Edit Paste before you use another Edit Cut. Each time you cut or copy to the Clipboard, the previous contents of the Clipboard are discarded. See "Delete Objects" later in this chapter for more information about using Edit Cut.

Also note that using Edit Paste does not clear the Clipboard, which means that you can paste multiple copies of the Clipboard contents on one page, on different pages, or on pages in several different presentations. Data copied to the Clipboard may be in various formats, including text, Freelance objects, bitmaps, or metafiles.

You can view the contents of the Clipboard by clicking the Clipboard icon in the Windows Program Manager.

Clipboard Keystrokes

If you are keyboard partisan, you should learn the following keyboard accelerators to cut, copy, and paste information to and from the Clipboard:

Ctrl+X	Cuts a selection from Freelance Graphics to the Clipboard
Ctrl+C	Copies a selection from Freelance Graphics to the Clipboard
Ctrl+V	Pastes a selection from the Clipboard to Freelance Graphics

Edit Copy and Edit Paste

Edit Copy and Edit Paste go hand in hand. Edit Copy copies the selected object (or objects) to the Clipboard. Edit Paste copies the object to another page, another presentation, or even another Windows Application.

To copy an object from one presentation page to another, first select the object and then use Edit Copy (to leave the original object intact) or Edit Cut (to remove the object from its original location). Move to another presentation page and issue the Edit Paste command, press Ctrl+V, or click the Edit Paste SmartIcon.

When you paste an object onto another page, it is pasted in the same location as it was on the original page.

Remember that the Edit Copy command alone has no effect on the presentation page. The command merely copies the selected object (or objects) to the Clipboard. If you select an object, use Edit Copy and then use Edit Paste on the same page, the copy of the object is placed directly on top of the original object. You cannot see that you have copied the object until you move the copied object out of the way. If you want to make duplicates of objects on the same presentation page, the Edit Replicate command is a better choice (see the section "Duplicate an Object on the Current Page" later in this chapter).

Copy Objects to or from Other Applications

You can copy objects from other applications directly to your presentation page via the Clipboard. Freelance Graphics can receive data from the Clipboard in the form of a Windows metafile, a bitmap, or as text.

To copy data from another application, first start the application that contains the data you want to copy to Freelance Graphics, move to the page where you want to copy the data, and then choose Edit Paste (or press Ctrl+V or click the Edit Paste SmartIcon).

Copy a Graph from One Page to Another

You can copy a graph from one presentation page to another within the same presentation or from another presentation to the current page of the presentation you are working on. The process is the same as for copying any object.

Try It: Copy and Paste a Graph

Try copying a graph from one presentation page to another by doing the following:

1. Click the graph to select it and then choose Edit Copy (or press Ctrl+C or click the Edit Copy SmartIcon).
2. If you want to delete the graph from its original location as you copy it to the Clipboard, use Edit Cut instead.
3. Move to the page where you want to paste the graph and choose Edit Paste (or click the Paste SmartIcon or press Ctrl+V).

If the page contains a placement block for the graph, you have to drag the graph into the placement block.

Copy and Paste Text

You can paste ASCII text that you have copied from another presentation (or from any other Windows package) directly to a presentation page or into Outliner view. If you want to create text charts from the text you paste automatically, you should be in the Outliner view. But, if you just want to paste a text block onto a presentation page, you should be in Current Page view.

Paste Text to a Presentation Page

You can paste text to a presentation page either in or out of text edit mode.

If you paste text in text edit mode, Freelance Graphics adds the text at the insertion point (denoted by the blinking vertical line). The pasted text takes on the paragraph settings in effect at the insertion point. If the source of the pasted text was Freelance Graphics, any character attributes are preserved when you paste the text. If you have text selected when you use the Paste command, the new text replaces the existing text.

If you paste text and are not in text edit mode, Freelance Graphics creates a new text block at the top left portion of the page and uses level 1 settings to format the text. (For more information on paragraph styles, read Chapter 3, "Creating, Editing, and Formatting Text.")

Paste Text Directly into Outliner View

If you have text from another source, you can paste it directly into the Outliner view of Freelance Graphics and, if the text is formatted properly, create bullet charts automatically.

As in text edit mode, if text is selected, the new text replaces the selected text. If no text is selected, the text is pasted at the insertion point.

You also can import ASCII files directly into Outliner view or paste an Ami Pro outline into the Outliner.

Refer to Chapter 4, "Using the Outliner," for more information about importing and pasting text into the Outliner.

Copy Metafiles and Bitmaps

Bitmaps and metafiles are standard graphics file formats that you can copy to the Clipboard and paste into any application that supports these formats. Freelance Graphics for Windows supports both bitmaps and metafiles. You can paste either of these onto a presentation page. These file formats are commonly used by many graphics packages and desktop publishing packages.

Duplicate an Object on the Current Page

If you want to make one or more copies of an object on the current page (without removing the original), use the Edit Replicate command. Edit Replicate makes a duplicate of a selected object on the current presentation page without copying the object to the Clipboard. Another difference between Edit Copy and Edit Replicate is that when you use Edit Copy, you do not see the copy of the object unless you use Edit Paste. But when you select an object and use Edit Replicate, you get a copy of the selected object immediately, offset from the original object. (You can configure Edit Replicate so that it does not offset the replicated object. Use Tools User Setup, as described in Chapter 24, "Customizing Freelance Graphics.")

Edit Replicate has additional features that make it suitable for creating special effects. After you select an object and use Edit Replicate to duplicate it, the new object is selected. Now you can move, rotate, or size this new object. When you Choose Edit Replicate again (without any intervening commands), Freelance replicates the object and repeats the move, rotation, or sizing operation for the new object it creates.

Figure 13.12 shows two examples using Edit Replicate. On the left, a rectangle was replicated several times. To create a similar illustration, just draw a rectangle and then choose Edit Replicate multiple times or, easier, press Ctrl+F3 as many times as necessary. Each time, the original object is offset slightly to the right and down from the preceding object, creating a stacked look.

On the right is a more sophisticated use of Edit Replicate. Draw an ellipse on the page. Then choose Edit Replicate. Now, with the replicated ellipse still selected, choose Arrange Rotate and rotate the ellipse a few degrees in a counterclockwise direction. Then press Ctrl+F3 repeatedly to create the flower-shaped object.

Chapter 15, "Creating Business Diagrams," has a section on creating a logo from text, using Edit Replicate in conjunction with Arrange Rotate.

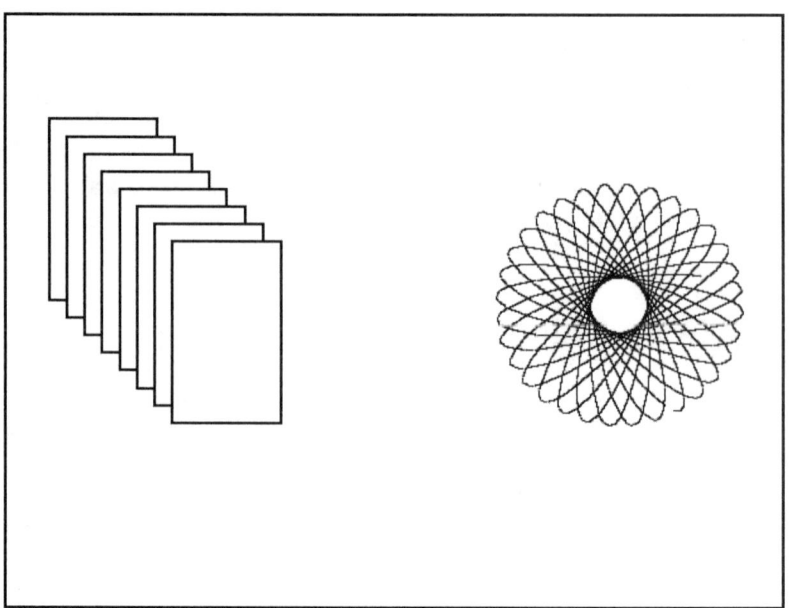

FIGURE 13.12. A rectangle that was replicated several times (left) and a more sophisticated use of Edit Replicate (right).

Delete Objects

Deleting objects is another basic task that you have to do frequently. Freelance has two commands that remove selected objects: Edit Cut and Edit Clear. The difference between the two is important, as follows:

- Edit Cut removes the selected object and copies it to the Clipboard. The keyboard accelerator for Edit Cut is Shift+Del.
- Edit Clear removes the selected object but does not place it on the Clipboard. Edit Clear has no effect on the Clipboard at all. Thus, Edit Clear is most useful if you want to delete an object from the page yet preserve the contents of the Clipboard for a subsequent Edit Paste operation. The keyboard accelerator for Edit Clear is Del.

Delete Entire Pages

To remove all the objects on a page, press F4 and then Del. This action deletes every object on the page, but leaves the page itself. To remove an entire page, choose Page Remove. In Page Sorter view, you can delete multiple pages by selecting as many pages as you want and then choosing Edit Cut or Edit Clear or pressing the Del key.

Working with Overlapping Objects

Priority is the order in which objects are drawn on the page. When you draw an illustration using traditional mechanical methods such as pen or pencil, you can, of course, draw objects on top of one another. In fact, this is often necessary to get the effect you want. But after you draw something on top of something else, you have committed yourself and you cannot change it without erasing or starting over.

With the electronic drawing tools of Freelance Graphics, however, you quickly can change the drawing priority of objects. If you draw overlapping objects, one on top of the other, you can reverse their drawing priority and quickly place the other object on top.

Many of the Freelance Graphics symbols contain complex, overlapping objects. Keep in mind that these symbols may not output well on plotters, because plotters are really just mechanical pens. If you overlap a blue block and a red block on a plotter, the result is a rather muddy-looking color.

A knowledge of drawing priority is helpful for creating a variety of special effects. One of the most popular of these effects is the drop shadow, which you can use to give a text block a dramatic effect. Chapter 15, "Creating Business Diagrams," contains a procedure for creating drop shadows.

If you are creating a drawing with many overlapping objects, you can use the priority SmartIcons to good advantage. To bring an object to the top of a stack of objects, click Bring to Front. To send an object to the bottom of a stack of objects, use Send to Back. You also can step objects forward or backward one level at a time with the Forward One and Back One SmartIcons. These four SmartIcons correspond to the Arrange Priority commands.

Wrapping Up

This chapter taught you the basics of working with graphic objects. You learned how to select, size, move, and copy objects. You now know how to align a series of objects and how to flip or rotate objects. You also learned how to change the order in which overlapping objects are stacked (priority).

In the next chapter, you learn more sophisticated ways to change the appearance of objects.

14

Transforming Objects

As discussed in Chapter 12, "Drawing Objects," you can use the Toolbox icons to create circles, lines, arrows, curves, arcs, rectangles, polygons, and shapes (a combination of a polygon and a curve). As you learn in this chapter, you can further manipulate these objects in various ways. You can group several objects into one, break an object apart, reshape an object entirely by dragging the points that define its shape, and even transform one object type into another.

The commands that perform these transformations may not be in your everyday tool set, but at times you may find them useful.

Grouping and Ungrouping Objects

Working with one object is simpler than working with many distinct objects. After you have created an illustration (or part of an illustration) from several objects, it is most efficient to combine them into a single object. Then you can select it with a single mouse click or move, size, copy, or delete it in a single step. In addition, placement blocks can only hold one object, which is another excellent reason for grouping objects.

In the course of creating a drawing, you often find the need to group and ungroup objects again and again. You group objects when you want to move, size, or copy them as a whole. But when you need to change the shape or size of one of the constituent elements of a grouped object, you have to ungroup the object so that you can work with the original components. A final reason to group

> In this chapter, you learn how to:
> - Group and ungroup objects
> - Add, delete, and move the points of objects
> - Work with Bezier curves
> - Change an object to another type of object
> - Connect lines, arrows, arcs, and curves
> - Break apart objects

objects is so that you can add them to the Custom symbol library (as described in Chapter 16, "Adding Clip Art").

Grouping Several Objects into One

To group several objects into one, first select the objects and then choose Arrange Group or click the Group SmartIcon.

When you select several objects, the message in the edit line is "Collection." When you group these selected objects into one, the message changes to "Group."

When you group several objects into one, the resulting group has only one set of selection handles (see fig. 14.1).

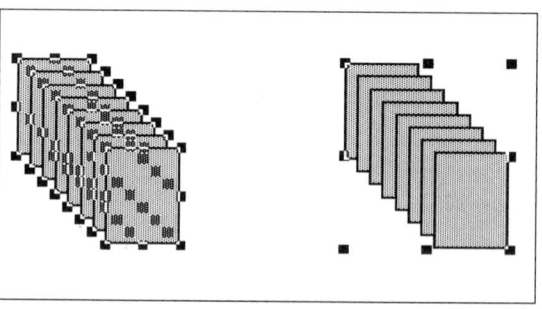

FIGURE 14.1. Selected objects before they are grouped (left) and the resulting group (right).

Ungrouping Objects

To ungroup previously grouped objects, first select the object and then choose Arrange Ungroup or click the Ungroup SmartIcon.

The Group and Ungroup SmartIcons are among the most useful and easy-to-use SmartIcons. Keep them right next to each other in the SmartIcon palette (as they are by default). As you work on a drawing, you can group and ungroup objects quickly with a single click.

You also can combine groups of grouped objects. This feature is often useful as you build a complex illustration or symbol. If you are drawing a truck, for example, you might create a wheel out of several objects and then group the wheel into a single object. The cab might be formed from several objects as well. When the truck is complete, you group all the objects into a single truck. If you subsequently had to make a change to the wheel, you would have to ungroup the truck again. In fact, you would have to use the Ungroup command several times to reverse the grouping process.

How can you tell when an object is completely ungrouped? For one thing, when you select the object, the message in the edit line reads "Collection" rather than "Group." In addition, the Arrange Ungroup command is dimmed when you have completely ungrouped an object.

Ungrouping a Graph or a Metafile

You can ungroup a graph or a linked metafile, but if you do, the link between the graph or metafile and its source is severed, and the graph or metafile is broken up into its original objects. When you are editing a graph, this capability can be useful when you want to customize the graph in a way not possible by using the standard graph options and commands. But be careful! After you ungroup a graph, you lose the data and cannot recompose the graph. It's a good idea to keep a copy of the original linked graph or metafile somewhere (perhaps outside the page border) in case you have to return to it. Also note that an ungrouped graph looks the same when ungrouped, but a metafile may look a bit different because it is transformed into Freelance objects.

Editing the Points of Objects

Objects are composed of points. Four points make a square or a rectangle, for example, but any number of points may define the shape of a polygon. Freelance Graphics enables you to change the shape of an object by moving the individual points of an object, deleting them, or adding new ones. This feature is convenient when the shape of an object is almost right but needs just a little tweaking.

Working in Edit Points Mode

Before you can manipulate the individual points of an object, you must enter edit points mode. Choose Arrange Points Mode, press Shift+F6, or click the Edit Points SmartIcon.

Notice what happens to the on-screen display of the object before and after entering edit points mode. Normally, an object has eight selection handles. When you enter edit points mode, the following several changes occur on your screen to indicate that you are in a different mode:

- The selection handles disappear and are replaced by the individual points that determine the line segments of which the object is composed (see fig. 14.2).
- The message "Edit Pts" appears at the left of the Freelance Graphics title bar.
- The Selector tool has a small circle within the point.
- Points Mode on the Arrange menu has a check mark next to it.

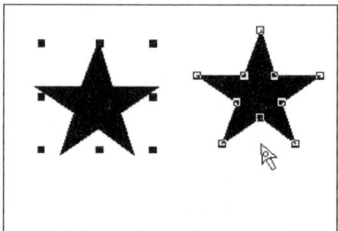

FIGURE 14.2. A star shape with selection handles (left) and the same star shape in edit points mode (right).

Add a Point

You can add points to any object type except circles and rectangles. You must convert the latter to polygons or lines first. Why add a point to an object? This capability is useful when you want to add detail to an object. Perhaps you want to add another side to a polygon or another bend to a line. First you can add the point and then drag it to make the desired shape.

Delete a Point

You can delete points from lines, curves, or polygons. (If you want to delete points from a rectangle or circle, first convert the rectangle or circle into a polygon with the Arrange Convert to Polygon command.)

To delete a point, first enter edit points mode, click the point you want to delete, and then press Del or choose Edit Clear. Freelance Graphics redraws the object, based on the remaining points.

Note that Edit Cut deletes entire objects in edit points mode.

Move a Point

To move a point, first enter edit points mode, click to select one point, and then drag the point to a new location. Freelance Graphics redraws the object, based on the new arrangement of points. You also can move several points at the same time by using the same method.

Try It: Make a Voice Balloon

Working in edit points mode, you can make a "voice balloon" of the sort you see in comic strips to display dialog. Follow these steps:

1. Create an ellipse.
2. Choose Arrange Convert to Polygons.
3. Press Shift+F6 to enter edit points mode or click the Edit Points SmartIcon.
4. Press the Ins key to add a point. Click the perimeter of the ellipse where you want to add the point.
5. Repeat step 4 to add two more points (see fig. 14.3).

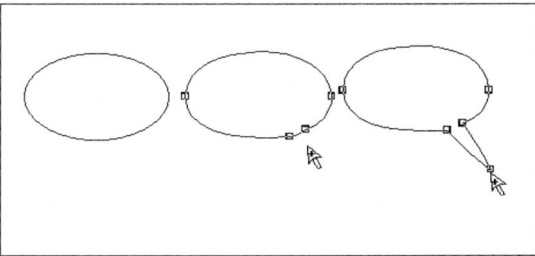

FIGURE 14.3. Create an ellipse (left), add three points (middle), and drag the middle point (right).

6. Click the middle point you added and drag it down to create the tail of the balloon.

To complete the cartoon, add text and a symbol from the MEN.SYM symbol library (see fig. 14.4).

FIGURE 14.4. The completed cartoon.

Using the Arrow Keys To Move a Point

If you need to move objects with a high degree of precision (perhaps you need to place the point of one object on top of a point in another object), you can use the four arrow keys to move the point of an object. First select the point you want to move and then press the arrow key for the direction in which you want to move (up, down, right, or left). Each time you press the arrow key, the object moves precisely one pixel in the specified direction. Click the mouse or press Enter to end this operation.

Try It: Add, Move, and Delete a Point

Try adding, moving, and deleting a point. In this exercise, you change a pentagon into a six-sided figure. The first step is to add a point to the original polygon. The following procedure works best if you are working with a grid and have enabled the snap feature. Follow these steps:

1. Choose View Units & Grids and select the Display grid options.
2. Draw a five-sided figure by using the Polygon tool.
3. Choose Arrange Points Mode, press Shift+F6, or click the Edit Points SmartIcon.
4. Press the Ins key. Note that the pointer now has a plus sign in it, which means you now can add a point.
5. Position the pointer on the edge of the object where you want to add the new point and click. The new point appears.
6. Drag the new point to a new location to create the six-sided figure (see fig. 14.5).

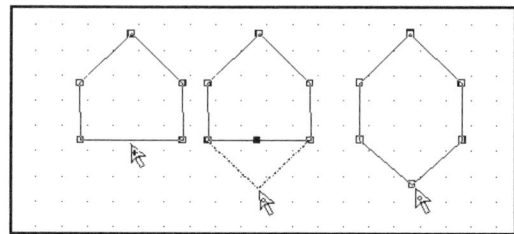

FIGURE 14.5. To add a point (left), drag the point to a new location (middle), and release the mouse button to create the six-sided figure (right).

7. To return the six-sided figure to its original shape, just select the point you added and press the Del key.

Editing Bezier Curves

Bezier curves permit a fine degree of control over the shape of curves. Graphic artists who work on computers use Bezier curves to create complex shapes in illustrations. But you may find them equally useful in reshaping curves and curved objects as you create basic diagrams.

Although seemingly complex, and certainly cumbersome to describe in words, working with Bezier curves is not all that difficult. The best way to learn is to experiment. You soon learn how to manipulate Bezier curves to get just the shape you want.

Try It: Edit a Bezier Curve

A Bezier curve has a vertex and two control points.

Edit a Bezier curve by dragging the vertex and control points. Follow these steps:

1. Select the curve you want to edit.
2. Enter edit points mode. (Choose Arrange Points Mode, press Shift+F6, or click the Edit Points SmartIcon.) This action displays each vertex on the selected curve.
3. Click a vertex on the curve. A vertex is any point on the curve except the start and end points. A curve may have one or more vertices. You see two control points connected by a line that passes through the vertex. You can drag the vertex or either of the two control points to change the shape of the curve.
4. Drag a control point to see its effect on the shape of the curve. A dashed line shows you the shape of the curve as you drag the control point. When you see the shape you want, release the mouse button (see fig. 14.6).

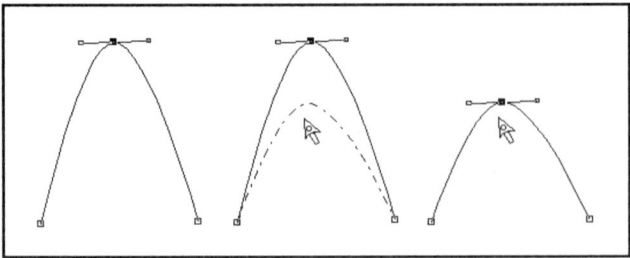

FIGURE 14.6. Vertex and control points in edit points mode (left), dragging the vertex (middle), and the resulting object (right).

Note the following points about editing Bezier curves:

- The control point opposite the one you are dragging moves in line with the one you are moving (they are connected with a fixed line).
- To move only the selected control point, press Ctrl as you drag the control point. The other control point now remains fixed in place. Use this technique to create a cusp—a sharp point, as in a crescent moon—in the curve (see fig. 14.7).
- You can create a loop by dragging one control point to the original position of the opposite control point.

- If you press Shift as you drag a control point, the other control point maintains the same distance from the vertex as the one you are dragging. Use this technique to create smoother curves.

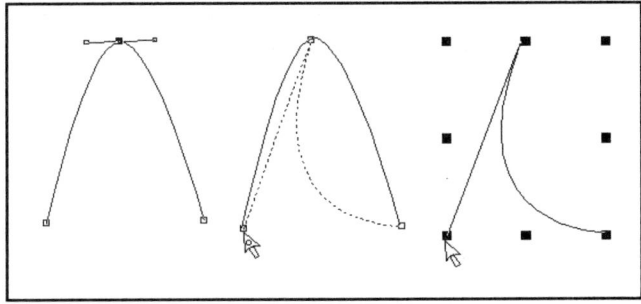

FIGURE 14.7. Select a control point (left), drag the control point to create the cusp (middle), and release to complete the operation (right).

Presto! Chango!

Freelance Graphics enables you to transform, or convert, one type of object into another. You can convert lines to polygons, curves to shapes, polygons and shapes to lines and curves, and rectangles to lines.

You may want to convert one object type to another for several reasons. You may have created the outline of an object with a line or a curve, for example, and now you want to change it to a polygon so that you can fill it with a pattern or a color.

Another reason to convert an object is so that you can edit its points. You cannot edit the points of a circle or a rectangle, for example, without first changing them to lines or polygons (use the Arrange Convert to Lines or Arrange Convert to Polygons commands for this action).

The easiest way to understand this concept is to categorize objects as either open or closed, as follows:

- Lines, curves, and arcs are open objects because their start and end points are not connected. You can convert open objects to polygons or shapes (a shape is a combination of lines and curves).
- Polygons, shapes, rectangles, and circles are closed objects because their start and end points are connected. You can fill a closed object with a color or pattern. You can convert all closed objects to lines or curves.

Converting Open Objects to Closed Objects

You can convert lines, rectangles, curves, circles, and arcs to polygons or shapes. First select the object and then choose Arrange Convert to Polygons. The resulting object depends on what object type you started with, as follows:

- A line or rectangle becomes a polygon.
- A curve (or an object composed of lines and curves) becomes a shape.
- An arc or a circle becomes a shape.

Try It: Change a Line to a Polygon

Follow these steps to practice changing a line to a polygon:

1. Select the line you want to change to a polygon. For this procedure to work, the line must have at least two segments.
2. Choose Arrange Convert.
3. Choose To Polygons. When you convert a line to a polygon, Freelance Graphics connects the start and end points of the object and then fills the resulting object.

Figure 14.8 shows how you might use the Convert to Polygons command.

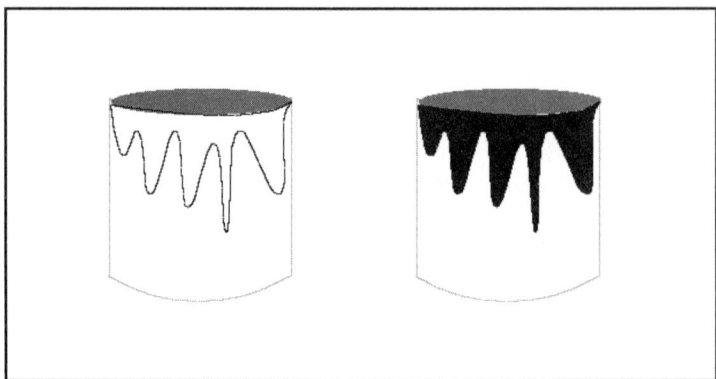

FIGURE 14.8. The outline of the dripping paint is a curve (left). Converting it to a polygon fills the resulting shape (right).

Converting Closed Objects to Lines

You can convert closed objects, such as polygons, shapes, rectangles, and circles, to lines. You can convert a rectangle or a circle to either a polygon or a line. If you want the resulting object to be filled, choose polygon; if unfilled, choose line.

Connecting Lines, Arrows, Arcs, and Curves

You can connect lines, arcs, arrows, or curves with the Arrange Connect Lines command. You can use this command to create a single object from two or more lines. When you issue the Arrange Connect Lines command, Freelance adds a connecting segment between the selected lines, arcs, arrows, or curves (see fig. 14.9).

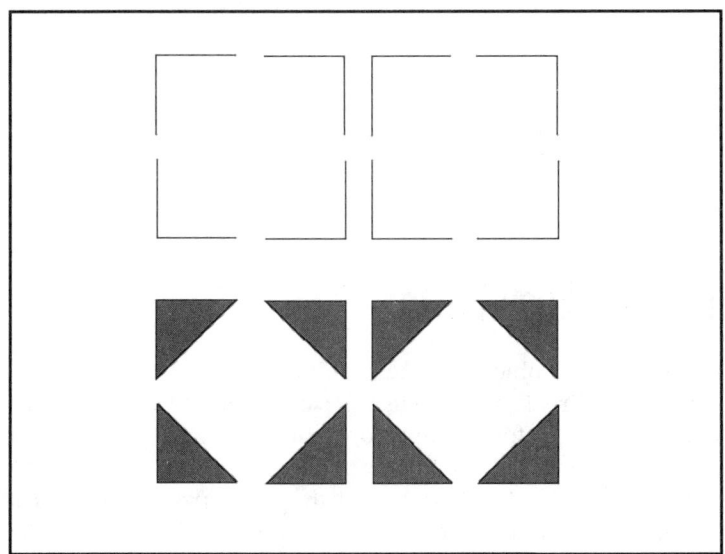

FIGURE 14.9. Eight lines (top) converted to polygons (bottom).

How does this feature work? Freelance locates the start and end points of the selected lines or curves that are nearest and connects them by drawing a straight line segment. If more than two objects are selected, Freelance connects the first two objects and then repeats the process until all selected lines or curves are connected. If you connect two arrows, only one end of the resulting object receives the arrowhead (see fig. 14.10). To connect two or more lines, arrows, curves, or arcs, first select them and then choose Arrange Connect Lines. The message in the edit line now reads "Line/Curve."

You can choose Edit Undo or click the Undo SmartIcon to undo this action.

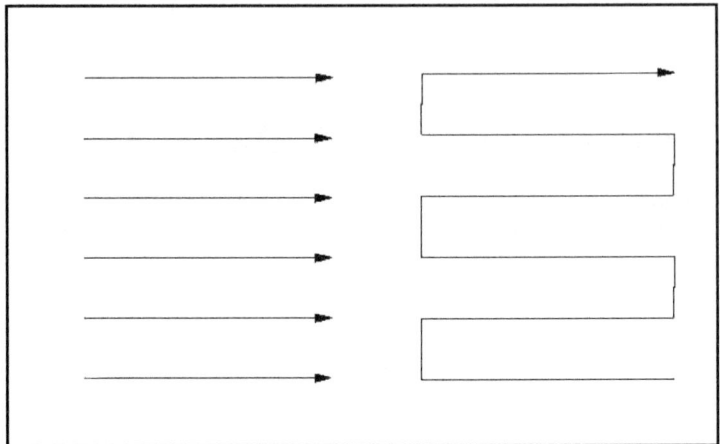

FIGURE 14.10. Six arrows (left) connected with Arrange Connect Lines (right).

Breaking Up Is Easy To Do

You can break apart objects along specified points by using the command Arrange Edit Points Break. You can use this command to chop a single line into any number of segments, for example, or to break a circle into two semicircles.

Again, the concept of closed and open objects is necessary to understand how this command works. When you break apart an open object, you get two or more open objects. To break apart a circle or a rectangle, you first must convert these objects to a polygon or a line.

Try It: Break a Circle into Semicircles

Try breaking a circle into semicircles by doing the following:

1. Select a circle and then choose Arrange Points Mode, press Shift+F6, or click the Edit Points SmartIcon.
2. Choose Arrange Convert to Polygons.
3. Select the object and then select both points on the polygon (which still looks like a circle) where you want to split the object.
4. Choose Arrange Edit Points Break. Although the circle does not look any different, it has been broken into halves.
5. To verify the two halves, press Shift+F6 to leave edit points mode, click one half of the circle, and drag it out of the way (see fig. 14.11).

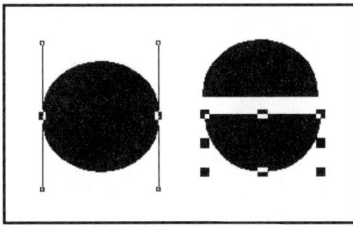

FIGURE 14.11. Select both points on the circle and choose Arrange Edit Points Break (left). Drag one half of the circle away to see the resulting two objects (right).

Wrapping Up

In this chapter, you learned about object alchemy: how to perform feats such as changing the shape of objects by editing their points, how to work with Bezier curves, how to turn a line into a polygon, how to connect objects with lines, and even how to split an object into pieces.

In the next chapter, you use what you have learned in the last several chapters to create effective business diagrams.

15

Creating Business Diagrams

Text charts and data charts make up the bulk of most presentations, but don't overlook the value of diagrams and illustrations. Well-designed diagrams break up the visual monotony of a series of text charts and data charts, but that's only one reason you should consider adding them to your repertoire. Diagrams help you communicate better, and that's the sole purpose of a presentation, isn't it?

Besides being sure-fire attention-getters, diagrams can help people comprehend difficult information in a way that words cannot.

Many presenters shy away from creating diagrams because they feel they lack the artistic skills required to create anything but the crudest diagram. But that's not true. Although you may not have the skills of a talented illustrator, there's no reason you cannot learn to create effective business diagrams.

Just as Freelance Graphics has features to help automate the process of creating text charts and graphs, it also has features to help you create simple (or complex) diagrams.

This chapter discusses the various types of business diagrams and shows you how to start creating diagrams by using Freelance Graphics.

> *In this chapter, you learn:*
> - About the types of diagrams you can create
> - How to create a flow chart
> - How to harness the features of Freelance Graphics to ease the drawing process
> - How to use principles of good design

Types of Diagrams

Just as there are bar charts, pie charts, text charts, and so on, so there are also many types of diagrams. You can create organization charts to show the hierarchical structure of a company, diagrams that illustrate concepts, and diagrams that include maps, to name just a few. This section discusses the types of diagrams that should prove most useful to you.

Flow Charts

Flow charts typically are built from boxes, text, and lines. A flow chart can illustrate a process, show the movement of goods and services from one place to another, or depict the flow of control in a computer program.

You have two major ways of creating a flow chart. You can use either rectangles or text blocks for the boxes in the chart. If you use rectangles, you have to superimpose a text block over the rectangle. Often, a better way is to use framed text blocks for the boxes in the organization chart. This technique enables you to center the text in each box automatically.

Try It: Create a Flow Chart

Create a flow chart made from framed text blocks. The first step is to set the default attributes of the Text tool so that every text block you create has a border and the text is centered within the frame. Follow these steps:

1. Start with a new page without a page layout assigned to it.
2. Double-click the Text tool. You see the Default Paragraph Styles dialog box (see fig. 15.1). Here, you choose default attributes for text you add with the Text tool.
3. To center text within the block (both horizontally and vertically), click the centering icons for Justification and Vertical Justification. Also, choose 14-point Arial MT for the default text style.
4. Click the Frame button to add a border to the text block. This action displays the Default Text Frame dialog box (see fig. 15.2). The text frames you are going to create feature centered text in a white frame, with a black border and a drop shadow.
5. In the Edge box, choose black for Color and, in the Style list, choose the line style you want for the border. (The default is normally None, which creates a text block without a frame.) In the Area box for 1st color, choose White and, in the Pattern list box, choose Black. Finally, in the Shadow drop-down box, choose Bottom Right. This choice creates a drop shadow for all the text boxes you create.
6. Click OK until you return to the drawing page.
7. Click the Text icon, drag a text block on the page, and type *Define Problem*.

Creating Business Diagrams 267

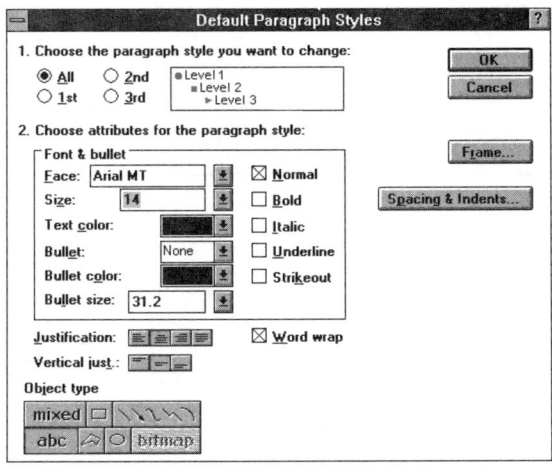

FIGURE 15.1. The Default Paragraph Styles dialog box.

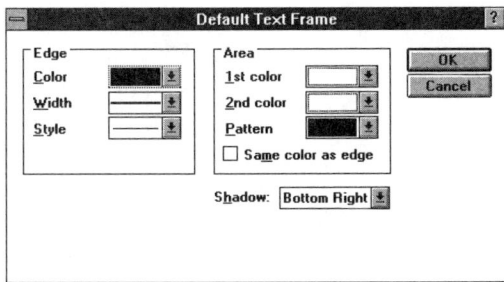

FIGURE 15.2. The Default Text Frame dialog box.

8. When you click OK, you see the text you typed framed and centered in a box with a drop shadow.
9. Use Edit Replicate (or click the Replicate SmartIcon) to make five more copies of this text block.
10. Drag these boxes into the positions you see in the final flow chart, as shown in figure 15.3.
11. When they are approximately in the right position, select all the text boxes in the middle row and then choose Arrange Space. In the resulting dialog box, mark the Space Horizontally check box. This choice spaces the text boxes evenly in a row. With the text boxes still selected, click the Align Top SmartIcon to line up the text boxes along their top borders.

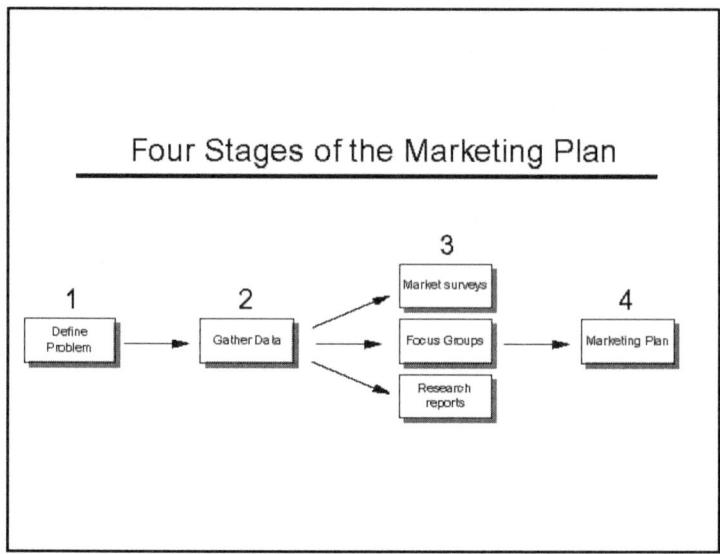

FIGURE 15.3. The completed flow chart.

12. Now select the three text boxes that are stacked in the final diagram and choose Arrange Space. In the resulting dialog box, mark the Space Vertically check box and click OK. You also may have to align these boxes along their left edges with the Align Left SmartIcon.

13. Now you can edit the text in the blocks. Select a text block, press F2, highlight all the text, and then type the new text. Click OK to complete the text block.

14. Click the Arrow tool in the Toolbox, hold down the Shift key, and draw a horizontal line between the first and second text blocks. Pressing Shift as you drag the arrow constrains the line to a horizontal, vertical, or 45-degree angle.

15. Select the arrow and choose Edit Replicate (or click the Replicate SmartIcon) to create two duplicates of the arrow.

16. Add the two angled arrows between the second and third text blocks. Pressing Shift as you drag the lines enables you to constrain the line to a 45-degree angle. After you draw the first arrow, use Edit Replicate to make a copy of it. Then choose Arrange Flip Top to Bottom. This action makes a mirror-image copy of the arrow. Drag these two arrows into place (as shown in fig. 15.3) and, with both arrows selected, click the Align Left SmartIcon to line them up properly.

17. Click the Text tool and add the numbers 1-4 above each stage of the process (figure 15.3 uses 32-point Arial MT for the numbers).

18. Type the title at the top of the page, using 36-point Arial MT.
19. To add the line beneath the title, click the Line icon in the Toolbox, hold down the Shift key, and drag the line beneath the title. Double-click the line and choose the next-to-the-last line width in the Width list box. Then click OK.

Your diagram should now look pretty much like figure 15.3.

Dramatic Drop Shadows

Drop shadows add depth and drama to rectangles, circles, or any shape, as well as text. Moreover, Freelance adds these shadows automatically to any text frame or rectangle you create.

To create the title block in figure 15.4, just drag a rectangle on the page and type the text (pressing Enter after *Add*). Then click the OK button. Now double-click the text block and click the centered icons for Justification and Vertical justification. Click the Frame button and, in the Text Frame dialog box, choose a black Edge Color and a solid Edge Style. In the Area box, choose white for 1st color and black for the pattern. Click the Shadow list box and choose Bottom Right. Click OK to return to the drawing page. If you need to adjust the size of the framed text block, just drag a selection handle. The text remains centered in the frame.

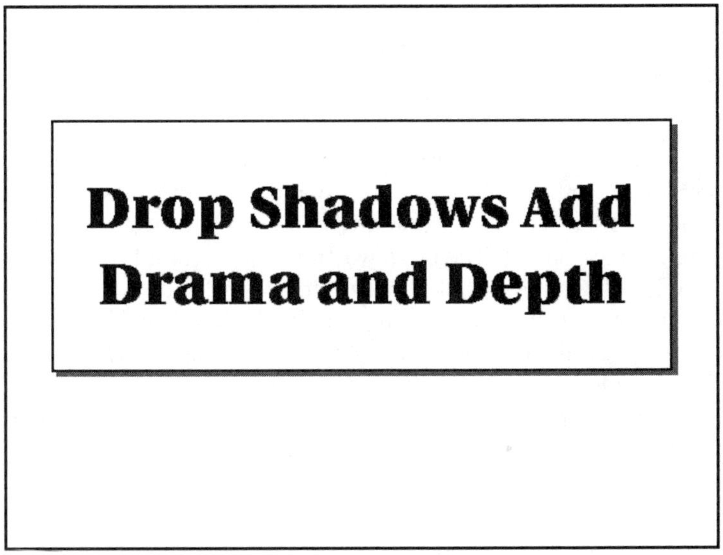

FIGURE 15.4. Drop shadows add depth and drama to text or rectangles.

Word Diagrams

Word diagrams are text charts that use graphical frames instead of bullet markers to itemize points in a list (see fig. 15.5). The DIAGRAM and TEXTBOX symbol libraries of Freelance Graphics contain a collection of frames that you can fill with text.

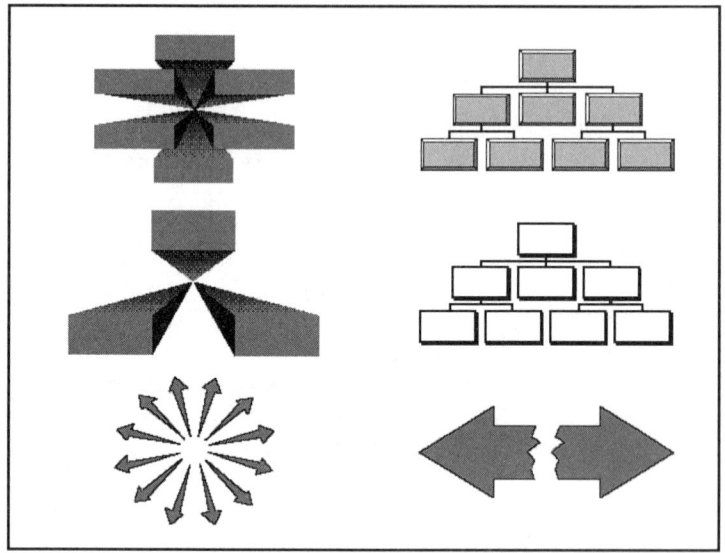

FIGURE 15.5. Several diagram templates in the DIAGRAM.SYM and TEXTBOX.SYM.

Figure 15.6 uses one of the pyramid-shaped text frames in the symbol library DIAGRAM.SYM. To create this diagram, first add the pyramid symbol to the page. Next, double-click the symbol to change the fill to a lighter gray so that the text can be more legible. Change the edge width of the pyramid to a thicker line for a bolder graphic statement. Click the Text icon to add the four text blocks and then size and position them as shown in figure 15.6. After you have added the text, select the pyramid and the text and click the Group SmartIcon to combine the individual components into one object. Then choose the 1 Chart page layout and drag the object into the placement block. Type a title at the top of the page and you're finished.

Creating Business Diagrams   271

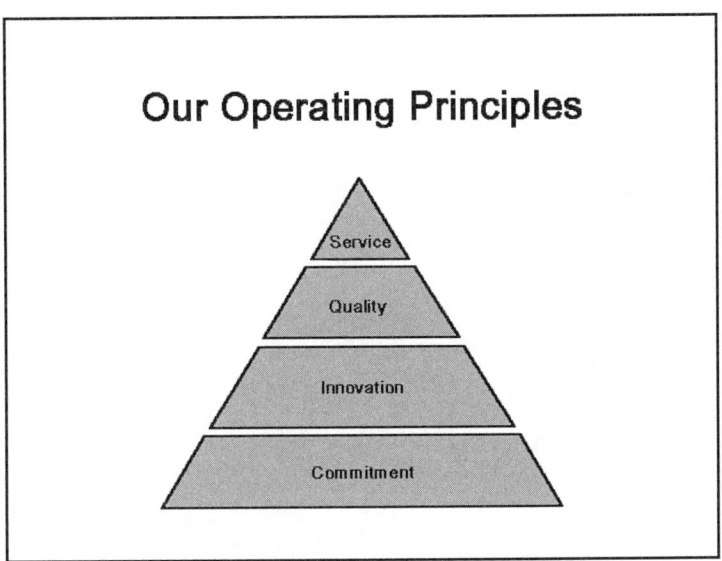

FIGURE 15.6. This word diagram was created by using a symbol from the DIAGRAM.SYM symbol library.

Try It: Create a Logo Using Rotated and Replicated Text

Try creating a logo for a copying business by rotating and replicating a text string. Follow these steps:

1. Create a new page without a page layout (choose Blank Page from the page layout list).
2. Click the Text icon, position the cursor on the page, and then type *Copy Shop*.
3. Choose Arrange Rotate or click the Rotate SmartIcon.
4. Move the mouse in a counterclockwise direction until the object is rotated about 25 degrees (you can see the angle of rotation in the right half of the edit line).
5. Press Ctrl+F3 four times. Each time you press Ctrl+F3, the object is copied and rotated by the same amount as the last rotation.
6. Select all but the original text string and change their attributes to gray.

7. Press F4 to select all the text on the page and then click the Group SmartIcon.
8. Add the text at the bottom of the page and draw a rectangle around the drawing. Assign the gray-filled rectangle bottom priority and choose a Bottom Right drop shadow.
9. Press F4 to select everything on the page and then again click the Group SmartIcon. You now have a logo that you can add to your custom symbol library (see fig. 15.7).

FIGURE 15.7. The complete logo.

Procedure Diagrams

The next time you're in an airplane, take a look at the card in your seat pocket that contains a diagram telling you what to do in the unlikely event of an emergency. Or, in a restaurant, note the sign next to the kitchen that describes the Heimlich maneuver in pictures. Whenever clear and rapid communication is required, people rely on diagrams. That's testimony to their effectiveness.

The step-by-step diagram can assume a variety of forms and can explain a variety of tasks or actions. You may create a diagram to explain how to connect a printer to a network, for example, or the steps to follow in a typical sales call.

Figure 15.8 shows that a very simple diagram can be very effective. The picture of the fax machine comes from the symbol library named COMPUTER.SYM. The circled numbers that correspond to the steps were created by adding a circle and then using the Text tool to create a number that was centered within the circle. The leader lines were created with the Line icon in the Toolbox.

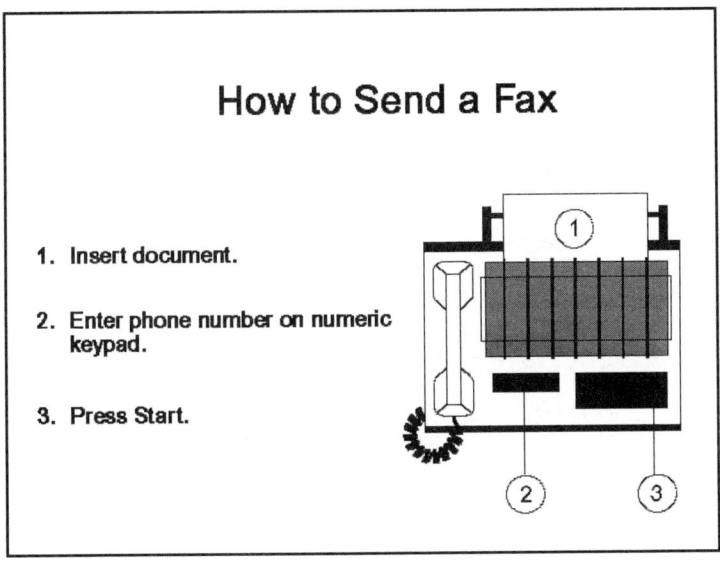

FIGURE 15.8. A procedure diagram.

Conceptual Diagrams

Conceptual diagrams can throw light on abstract ideas that are difficult to explain in words. You can use conceptual diagrams to elucidate scientific theories, economic models, problem-solving approaches, and other types of abstract information. The danger in conceptual diagrams is that you can end up creating a meaningless diagram. Just putting words in circles or boxes and adding a few connecting arrows doesn't guarantee that you have communicated anything. All too often, such diagrams leave readers baffled.

Even when you are illustrating abstract ideas, try to make your conceptual diagrams as concrete as possible. The conceptual diagram shown in figure 15.9 typifies the pitfalls of trying to express abstract concepts with a diagram. The result is an incomprehensible message. Compare this with figure 15.3, a better model.

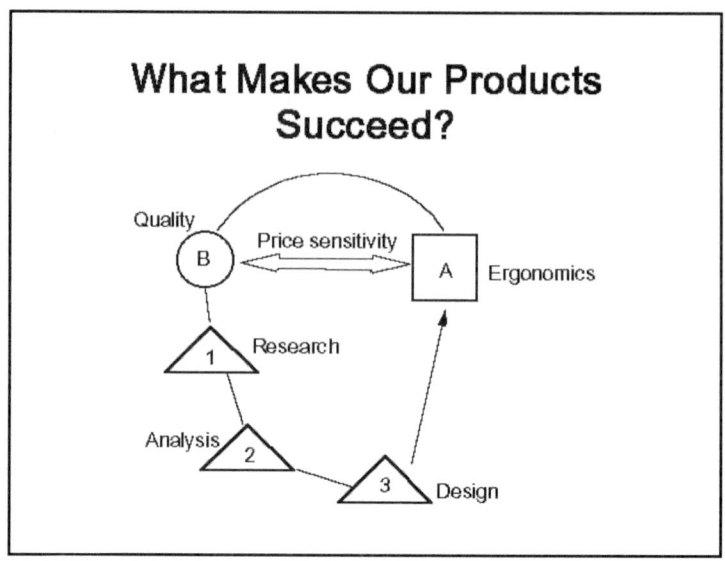

FIGURE 15.9. A hard-to-understand conceptual diagram.

Maps

When you need to depict the dip in sales in the Eastern region, the states where you plan to add new franchises, or your company's plans to market your products internationally, maps can help you communicate better by reinforcing the geographic dimension of your data and by adding visual appeal to your presentation. You can incorporate maps into text charts, data-driven graphics, or diagrams.

Freelance Graphics contains the following libraries that contain maps:

- EUROPMAP.SYM contains a map of Europe, including individual countries.
- CANADMAP.SYM includes a map of Canada and individual provinces.
- USAMAP.SYM contains a United States map and individual states.
- WORLDMAP.SYM contains two world maps, one with country boundaries and one without, and an image of the globe. You can ungroup the world map to extract just that part of the world you want to illustrate.

Location, Location, Location

You can mark the location of your manufacturing plant, latest franchise, home office, or new sales territory on a map. You simply can use a bullet chart to state that you have recently opened new sales offices in various states, but it is more dramatic, interesting, and effective to show it with a map. See figures 15.10 through 15.12 for examples of effective uses of maps.

FIGURE 15.10. This map shows the location of new sales offices. The United States map comes from USAMAP.SYM. To display the map without a fill, double-click the map and choose None for Pattern.

Highlight Regions

Sales teams operate in assigned sales regions, and business reports usually make assessments about the comparative profitability of these regions. Figure 15.11 shows a map with a supporting pie chart.

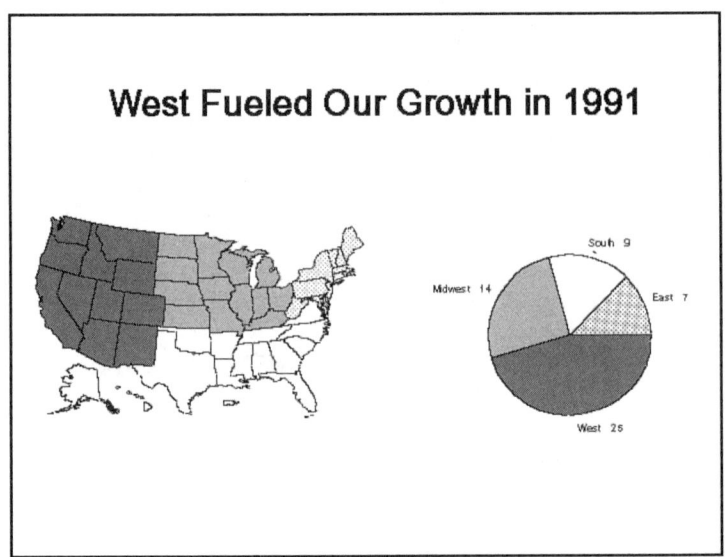

FIGURE 15.11. This combination map and pie chart shows sales results for U.S. sales regions. The dark Western region receives the most emphasis.

FIGURE 15.12. This map shows how you can divide a map of the United States (USAMAP.SYM) into sales regions. First you ungroup the map and then edit and move the areas of the map you want.

Choropleth Maps

Despite the difficult name, choropleth maps are not uncommon and are easy to understand. A *choropleth* map shows geographic areas ranked by ranges of values. Colors or shades of gray (make sure that the different fills are distinguishable when using black-and-white) indicate which region falls into a scale of values. Figure 15.13 illustrates this map type.

The choropleth map is often used to show political preferences or voting patterns.

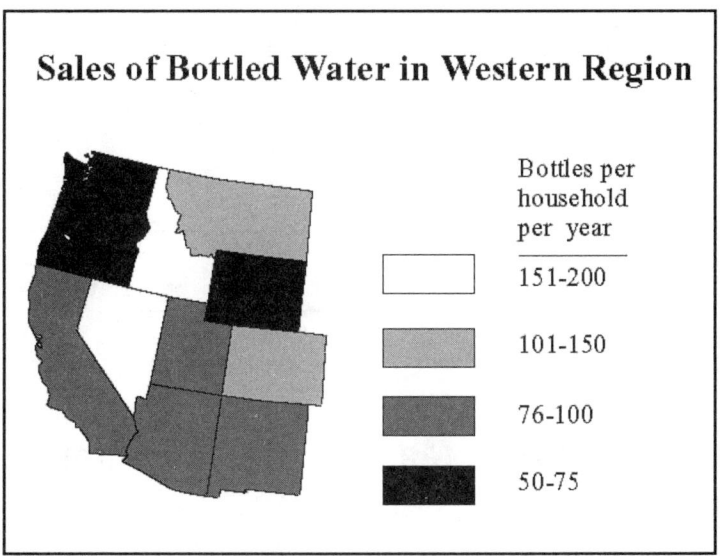

FIGURE 15.13. This choropleth map shows the sales of bottled water in the West.

Using a Map as a Background

A map can serve as a background to set the tone of a text chart or data chart, as in figure 15.14. Freelance Graphics embodies this technique in the SmartMaster set named WORLD1.MAS. To create your own version of this SmartMaster set, replace the world map on the Basic Layout page in SmartMaster Pages view with whatever map, or portions of a map, you want. For more information on how to create your own SmartMaster sets, read Chapter 26, "Creating Your Own SmartMaster Sets."

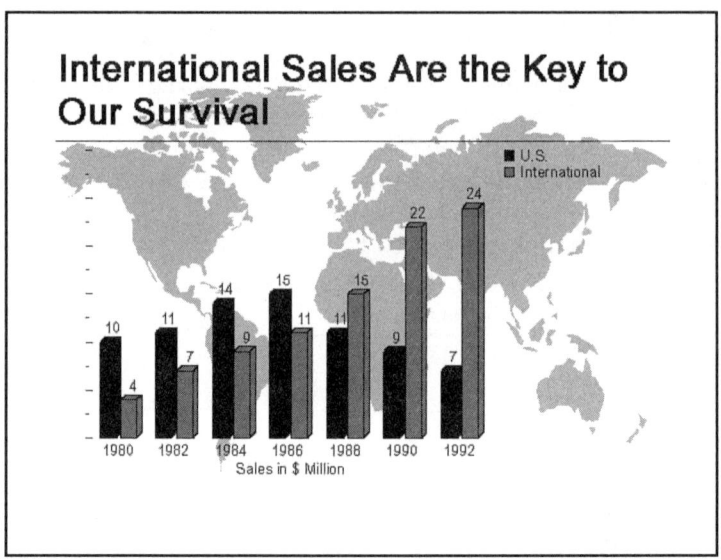

FIGURE 15.14. This bar chart uses the WORLD1.MAS set to reinforce the international theme of the chart.

Try It: Divide a U.S. Map into Sales Regions

Try dividing a U.S. map into sales regions by doing the following:

1. Click the light bulb icon in the Toolbox and open the USAMAP symbols library.
2. Double-click the U.S. map with state boundaries (the second one in the top row).
3. With the map selected, choose Arrange Ungroup twice (or click the Arrange Ungroup SmartIcon twice). Now each state is a separate symbol.
4. Select the states in one sales region by Shift-clicking each state (or simply drag a box around the states you want to select). To add or remove states from the selection, Shift-click the states. When you Shift-click, a selected state is deselected, and an unselected state is selected.
5. When you have selected all the states in a single sales region, choose Arrange Group.
6. Repeat steps 4 and 5 for each sales region.

Now you can select a sales region and move it slightly apart from the others, as in figure 15.12.

Routes

Routes are another way you can use maps in your presentation. This use may be for the cross-country delivery routes of a trucking company, the flight routes of transcontinental flights, or even the flow of raw goods from one region to another. You have been looking at maps like this since grammar school, when you viewed those maps of the routes of Magellan, Drake, or de Soto (remember those broad arrows swooping around Cape Horn?).

The Mechanics of Creating Diagrams

Freelance Graphics has a number of features that can help you create and fine-tune diagrams. The Arrange commands enable you to combine, manipulate, and change the shape of objects. The grid and the snap features help you draw and align objects precisely. And, SmartIcons can dramatically boost your efficiency. As you learn to put all these tools together, you should find yourself working faster and more efficiently. This section discusses the features and commands that boost your productivity as you create diagrams.

The Arrange Commands

The Arrange commands are among the most useful commands for creating diagrams. After you have added the basic shapes in your diagram, you can combine objects, align them, rotate and flip them, or even change their shapes. This set of commands is enormously useful for constructing diagrams. For a more comprehensive discussion of the Arrange commands, refer to Chapter 13, "Editing Objects."

Drawing with a Grid

A grid can provide a structure for laying out a diagram or illustration. Designers and technical illustrators use a grid to lay out the graphic elements that combine to make a finished piece of work. A grid can provide a useful structure for you as well.

To work with a grid, choose View Units and Grids and then complete the dialog box to set up the grid spacing. Chapter 12, "Drawing Objects," discusses how to draw with a grid and how to use the Units & Grids dialog box.

A grid is particularly useful for creating organization charts and flow diagrams, when the regular spacing of boxes or other graphic elements is essential to the success of the design.

It's a Snap

In the Units & Grid dialog box, you can toggle (turn on or off) the snap feature. You can perform many of the same tasks with a grid and the snap feature.

Use the snap feature to align objects automatically on a grid.

The snap feature works in conjunction with the grid. When snap is turned on, objects are aligned on the grid automatically as you add them, regardless of whether the grid is displayed.

If objects are already on a page, turning on the snap feature does not snap them to the grid. But as soon as you select and move an object, it snaps to the nearest grid dot.

In the course of creating a diagram, you may find yourself turning the snap feature on and off. For certain detail work, you may not want an object to snap to the grid. But for laying out the basic graphic elements, the snap feature is generally helpful. To turn the snap feature on and off quickly, you can press Shift+F7.

Using the Big Crosshair

The crosshair pointer is the shape you see when you are adding an object to the page. You can set the size of this crosshair to small or large. Your choice is partly a matter of personal preference and partly a matter of matching the configuration to the task at hand. Some people find the large crosshair somewhat cumbersome, but others prefer it. The large crosshair, because it fills the entire page horizontally and vertically, can be useful for aligning an object that you add to the page with another object already on the page.

To switch between the large and small crosshair quickly, press Shift+F4.

Working Swiftly with SmartIcons

As you work on diagrams, learn to click the SmartIcons for various editing operations. With a single click, you can accomplish what may take several choices from the menu. Especially useful are the Align, Replicate, Flip, Rotate, Group, and UnGroup SmartIcons.

Figure 15.15 shows a SmartIcon set useful for drawing. Use Tools SmartIcons Customize to add these icons to the SmartIcons palette and then save it as a set named Drawing. You can save this set and switch to it when you create diagrams. Read Chapter 23, "Using SmartIcons," for more information.

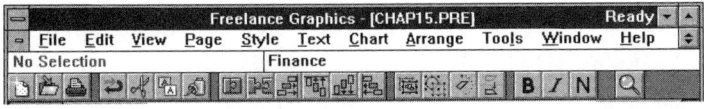

FIGURE 15.15. A collection of useful SmartIcons for speeding up the drawing process.

The Principles of Design

Even if you are not a trained graphic artist, you should know a few design principles if you plan to add diagrams to your presentations. You can use the principles in the following sections to make even the simplest diagram look professional.

Unity

This book repeatedly has stressed the value of consistency in presentations. This rule holds for the grammatical structure of bullet points and the structure of a single diagram. Just as a presentation must have a unified look to be effective, so must a single diagram. How can you give your diagrams a unified look? Here are some rules of thumb for ensuring unity in a diagram:

- Use consistent colors and fills for related elements.
- Use consistent line weights for boxes, lines, and circles.
- Use consistent typefaces for all text in a diagram. The title of the diagram may be in a different typeface, although it should not clash with the typeface chosen for the diagram.
- Use boxes and circles to group (or differentiate) graphic elements in a diagram.
- Use arrows and lines to connect graphic elements, to indicate movement, and generally to lead the eye where you want.

Emphasis

Every diagram needs a focus, a graphic element that grabs the viewer's attention. It is your job to provide this focus. Here are several ways to focus your viewers' attention:

- Use size to emphasize the most important graphic element, but don't forget to maintain a balance among the sizes of all elements in your diagram.
- Use text to call out the most important elements in a diagram. Add leader lines to point to these elements.
- Use a bold or bright color to draw the eye to the most important graphic element. In a black-and-white diagram, use a bold, contrasting black or white to emphasize a particular element.

Balance

A balanced illustration gives equal weight to the left and right halves of an illustration. The two types of balances usually discussed in design books are formal and informal. Figure 15.16 depicts the difference between formal and informal balance.

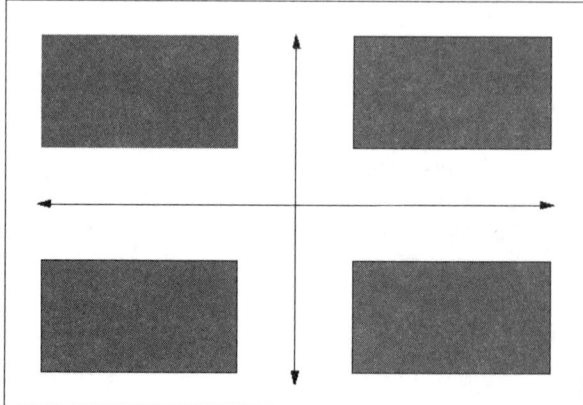

FIGURE 15.16. A diagram has formal balance if the halves match when you fold the diagram in half in the horizontal or vertical direction.

Proportion

The proportion of graphic elements in relation to each other and to the size of the page is quite important to the success of a diagram. Make sure that graphical elements on the page maintain proper proportions on a page. Using a grid to lay out the graphic elements of your diagram can help you achieve proportion in your work.

A sense of balance and proportion makes the sign in figure 15.17 work. The fish comes from the symbol library FOOD.SYM.

FIGURE 15.17. A sign with balanced proportions.

Movement

Movement makes graphics exciting. You can add movement to a diagram with several techniques. Arrows, for example, are explicit indicators of movement. Another technique to indicate movement is a repetitive sequence of shapes, each shape getting smaller or larger.

The arrows in the diagram in figure 15.18 create a sense of movement. The diagram consists solely of two symbols. The hub of arrows comes from DIAGRAM.SYM and the light bulb from COMMOBJT.SYM.

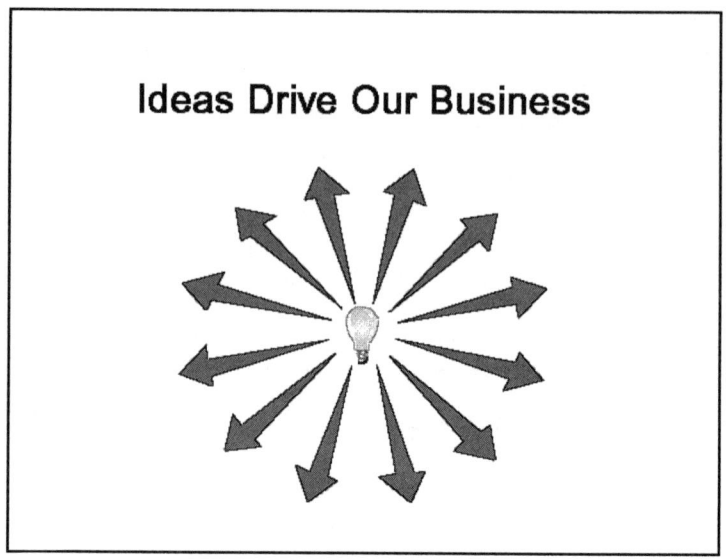

FIGURE 15.18. A diagram illustrating movement.

Simplicity

Even if you follow all the preceding rules, if your diagram lacks simplicity, you have failed. In presentations especially, remember that your audience is not going to have the time to examine a complex, overly sophisticated illustration. And, if you are giving a presentation using slides or overheads, you are somewhat limited as well in the complexity you can expect your audience to comprehend.

Wrapping Up

In this chapter, you learned how relatively easy it is to create simple business diagrams to enhance your presentations. By combining text, lines, and boxes, you can create an unlimited number of diagrams in short order. You should now be familiar with basic design principles that prevent you from making obvious design errors.

In the next chapter, you learn how to add instant, professionally drawn artwork to your presentation. The topic is clip art.

16

Adding Clip Art

Symbols, often referred to as *clip art*, are full-color, fully editable images created by professional artists that you can add to your presentation with a few clicks of the mouse.

Symbols add flair and professional polish to any presentation. But, as easy as they are to use, you must exercise some design skill to choose the right symbol and place it on the page properly. If you make the wrong aesthetic choices, you detract from, rather than enhance, your presentation. Whether you add symbols to a text chart, a graph, or an illustration, you must have a modicum of design sense to make it all work.

That's the aim of this chapter. You learn how to choose symbols and incorporate them into your presentation in an intelligent manner.

Freelance Graphics has more than 500 symbols in its libraries. You have available images of business equipment, cartoons, arrows, borders, frames, computers, people, buildings, maps, and flags. If that's not enough, you can purchase a variety of symbols from any number of third-party vendors. Lotus itself offers a clip art package named SmartPics, which offers a wide collection of high-quality images. No one ever had too many symbols.

The Freelance Graphics symbols (and SmartPics as well) are all full-color vector images, not bitmaps. Because bitmaps are formed from hundreds of tiny pixels, they don't look especially good when you try to resize or edit them. Vector images, however, are mathematical descriptions of objects that look good at any size and resolution. This difference means that you also can edit them as you do any Freelance object (see the section "Edit a Symbol" later in this chapter).

In this chapter, you learn how to:

- *Use the Freelance Graphics symbol browser*
- *Use clip art effectively in your text charts, graphs, and diagrams*
- *Create a pictorial graph*
- *Replace bullet markers with symbols*
- *Create diagrams based on symbols*
- *Use a symbol as the backdrop for a diagram*
- *Edit a symbol*
- *Create your own symbols and add them to a custom symbol library*

Adding Symbols to Your Presentation Page

One of the niftiest features of the Freelance symbol library is that you can view the more than 500 symbols right on your screen. This capability is often more convenient than flipping through the documentation. The symbols are arranged in thematic categories, such as Animals, Cartoons, Building, and Flags. After you choose the category you want, you can browse through the images in a window, in full color.

To add a symbol to a page, you first display the Add Symbol to Page dialog box (fig. 16.1). You can open this dialog box by clicking the Light Bulb icon in the Toolbox or by clicking the prompt text on the Bullet & Symbols or Title page that reads "Click here to add symbol." Both actions open the Add Symbol to Page dialog box.

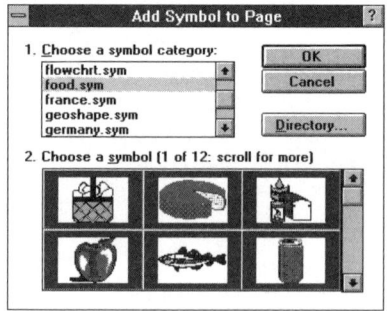

FIGURE 16.1. The Add Symbol to Page dialog box.

You see a list of symbol libraries in this dialog box, as well as the first six images in the highlighted symbol category. As you highlight the name of a category—such as FOOD.SYM—Freelance Graphics displays the images in that category in a scrollable window. Click the scroll arrow to display more names. Click the scroll area in the Symbol window to see more symbols in the currently selected category.

To add a symbol to the page, double-click it. This action adds the symbol to the page and closes the dialog box in a single step.

Putting Symbols To Work

Symbols can make your presentation more communicative and inviting in a number of ways. The following sections present some of the more useful techniques for putting symbols to work.

Reinforcing Content

If the subject of your diagram, graph, or bullet chart is automobile prices, you can add a symbol of a car to cue the viewer that this page is about automobiles. If the graph is about the telecommunications industry, a satellite dish may suffice. It sounds simple, but the trick to this technique is making the symbol an integral part of the illustration rather than a visual afterthought.

A symbol reinforces the content of a presentation page.

Freelance Graphics has a page layout designed specifically to enable you to add a symbol to support a bullet chart (Bullets & Symbol). The bulleted items are displayed on the left, and the supporting symbol appears on the right, as in figure 16.2. The symbol in this chart comes from the SmartPics collection of clip art.

FIGURE 16.2. Add a symbol to a bullet chart to reinforce the message in the text.

Adding Symbols to Graphs

A well-designed graph that presents numbers in a visually appealing form is inherently interesting and should hold the attention of your audience without extra adornment. Nevertheless, if your presentation has a lot of data-driven graphics, and particularly if you have used the same graph type over and over, your presentation can benefit from the addition of some well-chosen images. Symbols can put flesh on abstraction and change an otherwise mundane chart into a vivid representation of your message.

A well-placed symbol can add visual value to your graphs. But, before you begin merrily scattering symbols about your graphs like buckshot, recall that graphs contain data symbols—the bars, lines, areas, and pie slices that give shape to and interpret your numbers. By adding another visual ingredient to your graph, you run the risk of aesthetic overkill.

The following sections discuss several ways to make symbols work in graphs.

Incorporate a Graph into a Symbol

Sometimes you can place a graph inside a symbol to create a good effect. For example, you might place a pie graph about market shares in the computer industry within a computer screen.

Figure 16.3 shows the original symbol (from INDUSTRY.SYM), and figure 16.4 shows a single stacked bar that was neatly incorporated into the symbol. To create this diagram, replace the stack of boxes on the forklift with the stacked bar graph.

Direct the Viewer's Eye Where You Want with a Symbol

Graphics can lead the eye where you want, and that's a powerful design role for symbols. Arrows are the most obvious images to accomplish this task. Where the arrow points, the eye follows. But other symbols also can do the job, albeit more subtly. An airplane taking off, for example, directs the eye in the direction it's heading (see fig. 16.5).

Adding Clip Art 289

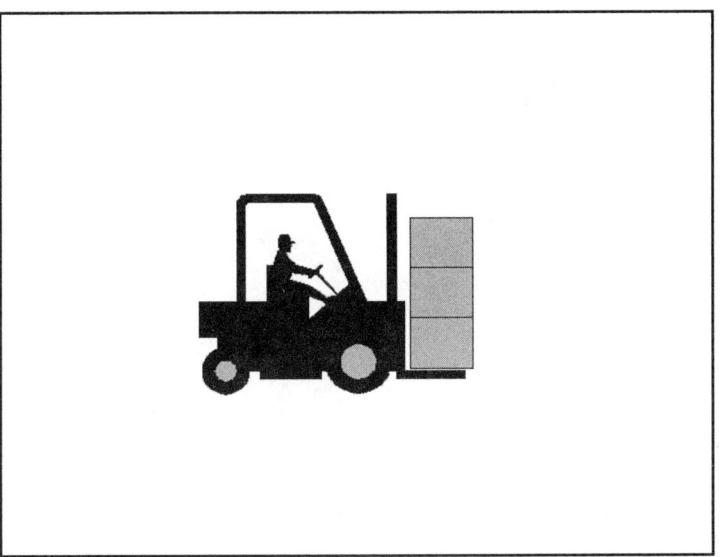

FIGURE 16.3. The original symbol (from INDUSTRY.SYM).

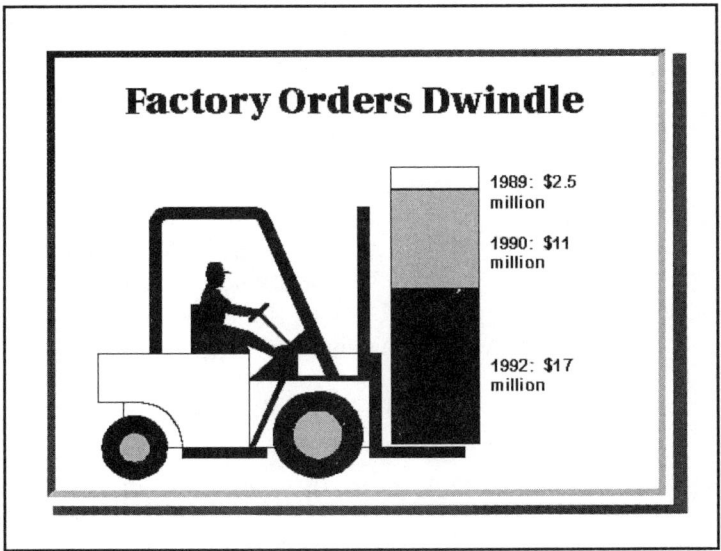

FIGURE 16.4. The graph added to the symbol.

FIGURE 16.5. In this figure, the nose of this airplane leads the eye directly to the bar representing the most profitable year.

Balance a Graph

Balance is an important design principle (as described in Chapter 15, "Creating Business Diagrams"). One of the dangers of graphs is that your data determines the balance (or lack thereof) in the graph, and you cannot control the data you have to work with. You can fill in white space, however, or correct an imbalanced graph, by adding a symbol (see fig. 16.6). But don't forget that white space also can be an important design element that can give your page an open, inviting look.

Replace the Bars in a Graph with Symbols

The pictorial graph is a clever (some would say overly cute) graphic style familiar to readers of publications like *USA Today* and *Time* magazine. Pictorial graphs use symbols to replace the data symbols in graphs (see figs. 16.7 through

16.10). This technique must be used sparingly. Once in a presentation is enough. It relies on visual trickery and, like many tricks, is amusing and interesting the first time only. In addition, it can be quite time-consuming to create such graphs.

Try It: Create a Pictorial Graph

To create the pictorial graph shown in figure 16.10, start with a horizontal bar graph (see fig. 16.7). Choose a symbol and add it to the page. Use Edit Replicate and Arrange Align to place the symbol over the bars (see fig. 16.8). In a zoomed-in view, create white rectangles (with a white edge color) the same width as the bars and use them to cover up the portions of the fish that extend beyond the length of the bar (see fig. 16.9).

1. First create the graph that you plan to use as the basis for your pictorial graph.
2. Choose a symbol for the repetitive pictorial element and add it to the page.
3. Size the symbol so that it fits within the bars and then use Edit Replicate (Ctrl+F3) to make multiple copies of the symbol.
4. Use Arrange Align to line up the symbols along the bars. Now comes the tricky part. You have to chop off part of the symbols to make them match the length of the bars. Resort to a little trickery here. Instead of chopping off the bars, take the simpler task of covering them up.
5. Create a rectangle of the same color and width of the bar you are planning to replace with the symbol. (This step is best done by zooming in on the end of the bar.) This technique only works if your output device supports drawing priority; for this reason, it does not work with plotters.
6. Move the rectangle until it just abuts the end of the bar (but leave the vertical line at the end of the bar visible).
7. Click one of the right center selection handles on the rectangle and size the rectangle until it covers the portion of the fish that extends to the right of the bar.
8. Select the graph and then choose Arrange Ungroup or click the Ungroup SmartIcon. You see a message reporting that you are now severing the link to your data. Your graph is now a collection of objects. Before you confirm this action, make sure that your data will not change. Keep a copy of the graph on a separate page in case you need the original graph.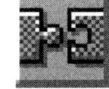
9. Now you can select the individual bars (which are now simply rectangles) and delete them.

That's it.

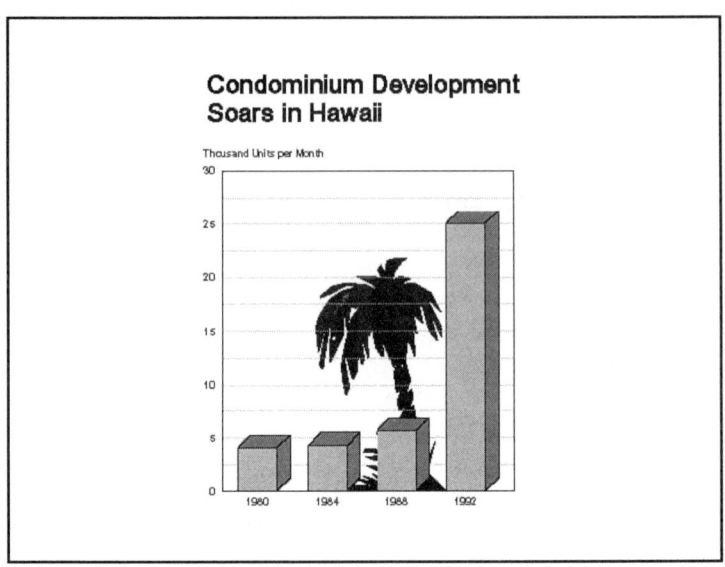

FIGURE 16.6. The symbol helped to fill white space while supporting the content. Note that the three-dimensional bars subtly suggest buildings.

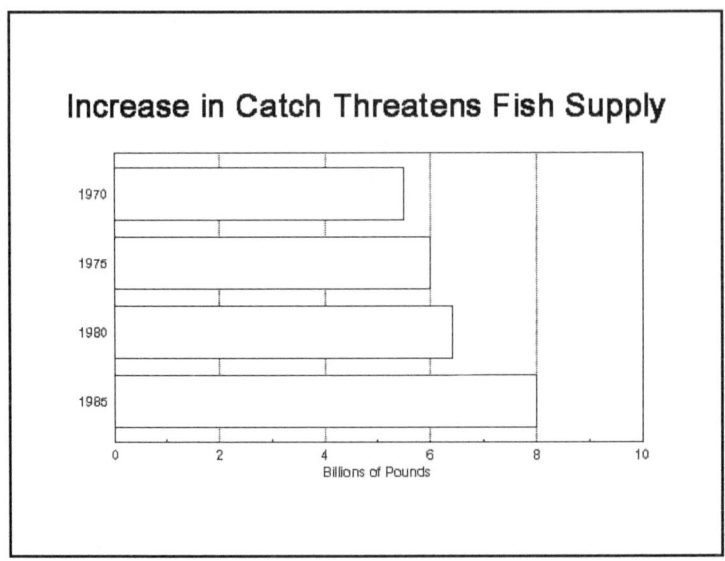

FIGURE 16.7. A horizontal bar graph (with empty bars).

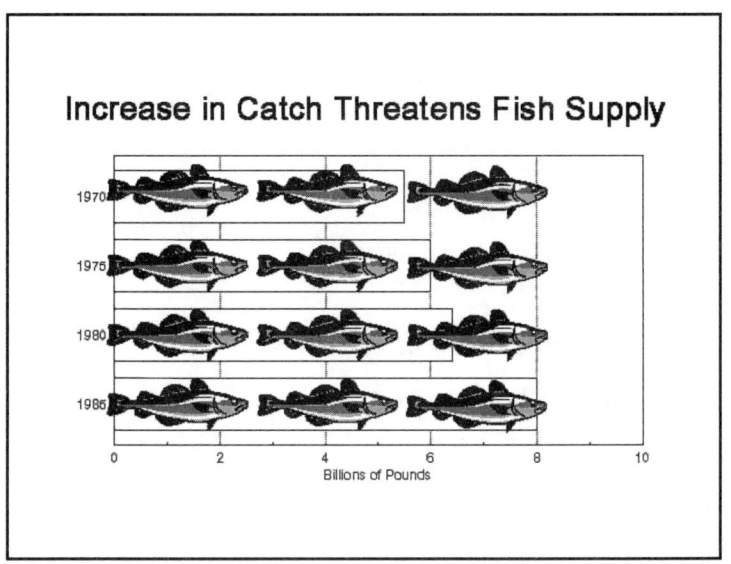

FIGURE 16.8. Place the symbols over the bars.

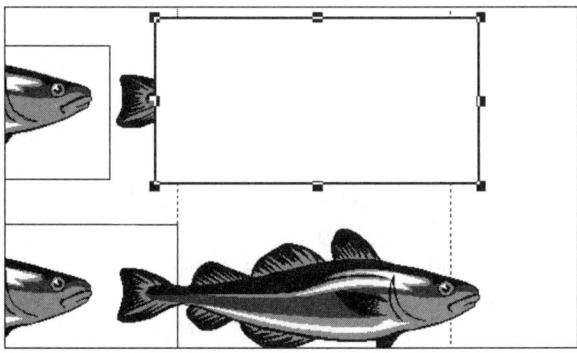

FIGURE 16.9. A zoomed-in view.

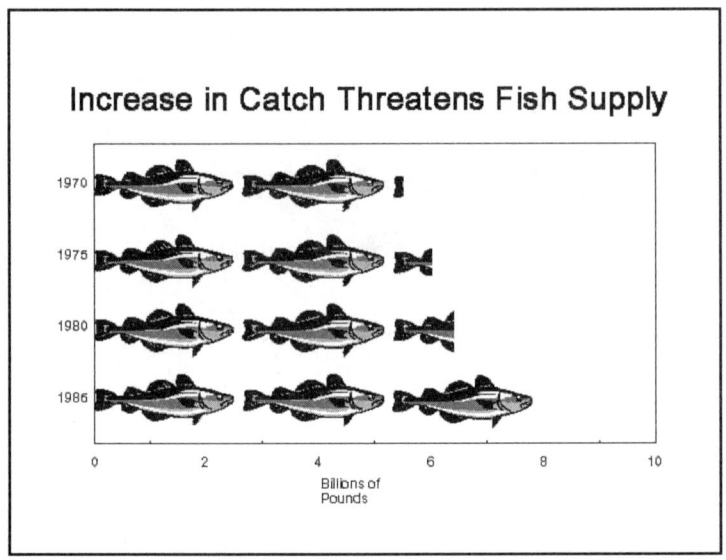

FIGURE 16.10. The final pictogram.

Adding Symbols to Text Charts

Add a symbol to spice up a text chart.

You already have read the remarkable statistic that more than 70 percent of most presentations consist solely of text charts. But even the most artistically formatted series of text charts can be monotonous if there are too many of them. You can relieve text chart-induced tedium by adding a symbol here and there, just to break up the visual monotony (see fig. 16.11).

As always, when adding special graphic touches, subtlety is the key. In other words, don't use too many symbols, and use them modestly. One symbol per page is almost without exception sufficient. If you pile a bunch of symbols on a single page, the result is graphic clutter. So don't do it.

Replacing Bullet Markers with a Symbol

Another common technique that can galvanize an ordinary word chart is to replace the bullet markers with symbols. In figure 16.12, for example, apples replace the conventional bullet markers.

Green Hills Orchard Thrives

- 5,000 tons harvested in 1991
- Widest variety of apples in region
- Most cider and juice produced on site
- Highest return on investment

FIGURE 16.11. The apple added to this text chart reinforces the subject without being obtrusive.

Green Hills Orchard Thrives

🍎 5,000 tons harvested in 1991

🍎 Widest variety of apples in region

🍎 Most cider and juice produced on site

🍎 Highest return on investment

FIGURE 16.12. Replacing bullet markers with an appropriate symbol can give an everyday bullet chart a visual boost. But don't overdo this technique.

Freelance Graphics enables you to use symbols as bullet markers and does the replacement for you automatically. To replace bullet markers with symbols, first double-click the text block for the bulleted list to which you want to add the symbols. In the Paragraph Styles dialog box, choose the paragraph level (1, 2, or 3) for which you want to add the symbol as a bullet marker. Then click the Bullet list box. Click Symbol at the bottom of the list. This action opens the Choose Symbol for Bullet dialog box, which is the same as the Add Symbol to Page dialog box. Locate the symbol you want to use as a bullet marker and double-click it. You see it in the Bullet box (see fig. 16.13). Click Preview to see how it looks on the page. If you want to make it smaller or larger, click the Bullet Size list box and choose a larger or a smaller size.

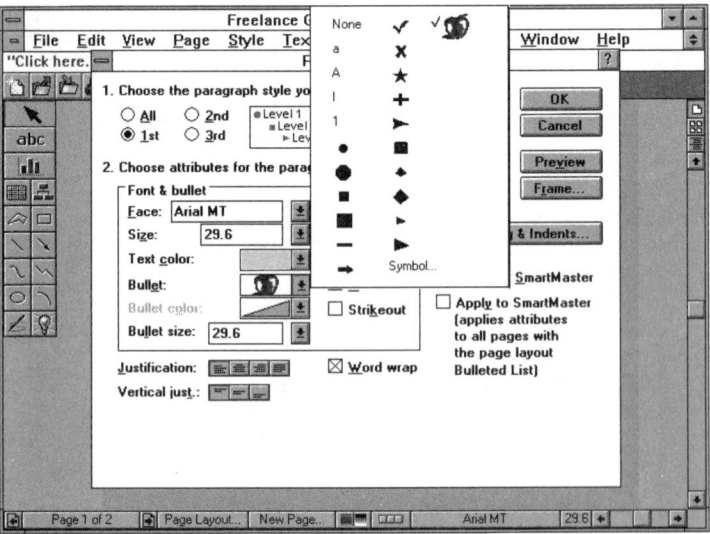

FIGURE 16.13. The Bullet box.

Adding Symbols to Diagrams

A symbol can spruce up simple business diagrams as well. You can enhance the visual power of organization charts, conceptual charts, and other simple diagrams by adding clip art. But make sure that the symbols you choose are germane to the illustration and not just something tacked on as an afterthought.

You can even build a diagram based almost entirely on clip art, as in figure 16.14. Each symbol was sized and placed in a rectangle to give the diagram balance and symmetry. The text was aligned at the bottom left of each rectangle.

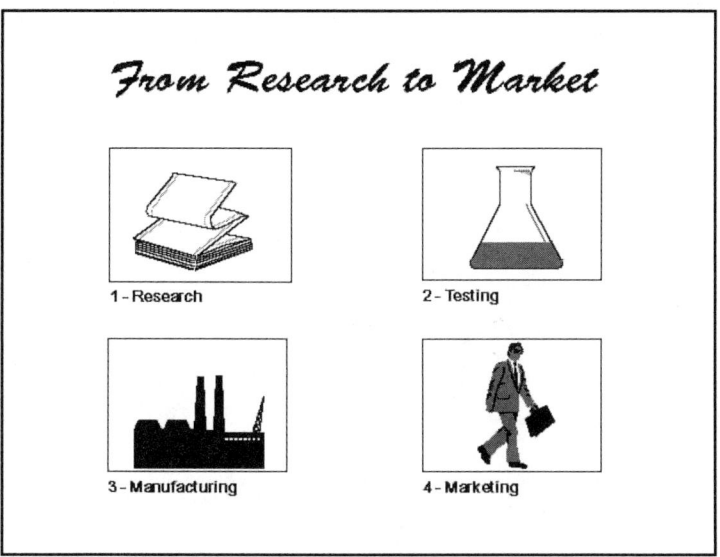

FIGURE 16.14. This diagram is built almost entirely with symbols.

Using a Symbol as a Backdrop

If you blow up a symbol to almost full-page size, you can use it as a backdrop for a graph. The rule here is to make the symbol a subdued counterpoint to your primary visual, which is the graph. This means displaying it in a muted color or gray scale. Freelance Graphics employs this technique in the SmartMaster set named 1993.MAS. This SmartMaster set contains a backdrop formed by a repetitive display of the word "1993" across the page, as shown in figure 16.15. Maps are often a good backdrop for this purpose (see Chapter 15, "Creating Business Diagrams," for a more complete treatment of maps).

Use a blown-up, subdued symbol as a presentation backdrop.

FIGURE 16.15. The SmartMaster 1993.MAS illustrates how a symbol can be used, in this case repetitively, as a backdrop. The small map of Europe at the bottom reinforces the point further.

Editing a Symbol

Most symbols in the Freelance Graphics symbol libraries are composed of simple objects grouped to form complex objects. A symbol may contain dozens of smaller objects grouped into one. You can move or size any symbol that you add to the page, or even change its color or edge style, without ungrouping it. But if you want to edit the individual objects within a symbol—suppose that you want to change the color of a man's hair—you first must use Arrange Ungroup.

Because many symbols consist of several grouped objects, you may have to repeat the Arrange Ungroup command several times before you get to the individual object you want to change.

Creating a Customized Symbol Library

If you have created an object such as a logo, you may want to reuse it in another presentation or give it to a co-worker to use. You can add just about any object you create in Freelance Graphics to a symbol file with Tools Add to Symbol Library. You can add an object to an existing symbol category or to the category named CUSTOM.SYM, which is an empty symbol category reserved for your use.

You may find yourself using the same symbols over and over. Perhaps you frequently use a particular arrow in the Arrows category, a house in the Building category, and the picture of the handshake in the Hands category. You can add these to the Custom symbol library so that they all reside in a single symbol category, where they are at your fingertips whenever you want to use them. You can even rename the symbol category (although you have to do this outside of Freelance).

To create a customized symbol library, first select the object you want to add. If you have created a complex object, first use Arrange Group to turn it into a single object before you add it to a symbol category.

Next, choose Tools Add to Symbol Library. If you have several objects selected and choose this command, each object is added to the selected category as a separate symbol.

Another way to create a custom symbol category is to save an entire presentation as a symbol file. First, create all the images you want to be in the new symbol category file and put them into a single presentation. Then choose File Save and select Symbol library (.SYM) as the file type. Make sure that you save this file in the MASTERS directory so that the new symbol category appears in the list of category names you see in the Add Symbol to Page dialog box. Every object in the file you save becomes an object in the symbol category. Even if you have placed several objects on a single page, each object receives its own panel in the Add Symbol to Page dialog box. For this reason, make sure that you group any images you want to add to the category.

You also can read in a symbol as a presentation with File Open and then edit it as you please. Choose File Open and then select the Masters subdirectory, which contains the Freelance symbol files. These files have a file name extension of .SYM. Double-click the name of the symbol file you want to edit. Freelance displays the symbol library file as a presentation. Each symbol occupies a separate page. You can edit the images as you like or add new images.

Unless you have a very good reason, however, you should not try to edit the symbol libraries of Freelance Graphics. These libraries have been carefully designed and fine-tuned by professional artists. If you do want to customize a Freelance symbol library, first copy it outside of Freelance to another name. Using this copy preserves the original symbol library.

Wrapping Up

In this chapter, you learned how to work with clip art (symbols, in Freelance Graphics parlance). You now should feel comfortable adding symbols to your presentations in a variety of ways. You learned how to add symbols to a page, how to create pictorial graphs, and how to use a symbol as a bullet marker. You also learned how to edit a symbol and how to add your own symbols to a custom symbol file.

In the next chapter, you learn about two other ways of transferring graphic objects to and from your presentation: importing and exporting.

17

Importing and Exporting Graphics

In the world of economics, imports and exports are the lifeblood of free trade and prosperity. In the world of software, importing and exporting graphics files can help ensure the balance of trade among your software applications.

Being able to import a variety of file formats enables you to preserve files created in older versions of Freelance, Freelance Plus, Freelance Graphics for DOS, and other software packages. Being able to export files enables you to share graphics files with colleagues or friends who create graphics using different software or who want to use your Freelance files in, say, a desktop publishing package.

Importing Files

With File Import, you can import a variety of file formats directly into the current page. You can import 26 different file formats into Freelance Graphics.

Freelance Graphics can import the following file types (listed alphabetically by file name extension):

- .AI (Adobe Illustrator). Files created in Adobe Illustrator Release 4.0.
- .BMP (Windows/PM Bitmap). Bitmap files created in Windows (Versions 3.0 and 3.1) and OS/2 (Version 1.3 and 2.0) applications. Freelance Graphics imports black-and-white, gray-scale, and color versions of bitmaps.

In this chapter, you learn:

- *The types of graphics and text files you can import and how to import them*
- *How to import ASCII text files to the current page, into the Outliner view, and into an open text block*
- *How to import a portion of a file with the Import Data window*
- *How to export files*
- *How to copy text and graphics by using the Clipboard*

- .CGM (Computer Graphics Metafile). Metafiles created by Freelance Plus Release 2.0 and later, Graphwriter II, 1-2-3 Release 3.0, and other sources supported by Freelance Plus Release 3.1 and higher.
- .CH3 (Harvard Graphics 3.0 Chart). Chart or drawing files created by Harvard Graphics DOS Version 3.0.
- .CHT (Harvard Graphics 2.3 Chart). Chart or drawing files created by Harvard Graphics DOS Version 2.3.
- .DRW (Freelance). Drawing files created by Freelance 1.0, Freelance Plus 2.0 and later, and Freelance Graphics for DOS.
- .DRW (Micrografx Designer 3.0). Picture files created by Micrografx Designer Version 3.0.
- .DXF (AutoCAD Drawing Interchange). Images created by AutoCAD Release 10.
- .EPS (Encapsulated PostScript). Encapsulated PostScript files created by Adobe Illustrator Release 4.0 and other programs that can create EPS files.
- .GAL (Hewlett-Packard Graphics Gallery). Files created by Hewlett-Packard Gallery.
- .GEM (Digital Research). Digital Research GEM Desktop graphics files created by programs such as Digital Research Artline, GEM Draw, GEM Presentation Team, and GEM Programmers' Toolkit 3.1.
- .GIF (Graphics Interchange). Bitmap graphics files created by GIF Version 89A.
- .HGL (Hewlett-Packard Graphics Language). Picture files created by various applications, including Hewlett-Packard GL/2.
- .PCT (Macintosh PICT). Monochrome and color QuickDraw files created by Apple Macintosh Versions 1 and 2.
- .PCX (Zsoft PC Paintbrush Bitmap). Bitmap files created by Microsoft Paintbrush (Version 3.0 and 3.1) and Zsoft Publishers Paintbrush (Revision 5 format). Freelance imports black-and-white, gray-scale, and color versions of bitmaps.
- .PFL (Freelance Portfolio). Portfolio files created by Freelance Plus 3.0 and later and Freelance Graphics for DOS.
- .PIC (1-2-3 PIC). Files created by 1-2-3 and Symphony.
- .PRN (ASCII). 8-bit ASCII files created by many applications. You can change the file name extension to import ASCII files with different extensions.
- .RND (AutoShade Rendering). Files created by AutoDesk AutoShade Release 2.0.

- .SY3 (Harvard Graphics 3.0 Symbol). Graphics image files created by Harvard Graphics DOS Version 3.0 (symbols only).
- .SYM (Harvard Graphics 2.3 Symbol). Graphics image files created by Harvard Graphics DOS Version 2.3 (symbols only).
- .TGA (Targa Bitmap). Bitmap files created by Targa Version 2.0.
- .TIF (Tag Image). Tagged image format files created by Freelance Plus 3.0 and later, Freelance Graphics for DOS, and Aldus/Microsoft/Hewlett-Packard TIFF Version 5.0. Freelance imports black-and-white, gray-scale, and color versions of bitmaps.
- .WMF (Windows Metafile). Graphics metafiles created by various Windows applications (3.0 and 3.1).
- .WPG (WordPerfect Graphic). Picture files created by WordPerfect for Windows Version 5.1 and DrawPerfect Version 1.1.

Try It: Import a Freelance Graphics .DRW File into a Presentation Page

Now try importing a Freelance Graphics for a DOS (.DRW) graphics file by following these steps:

1. Choose File Import. You see the Import File dialog box (see fig. 17.1).

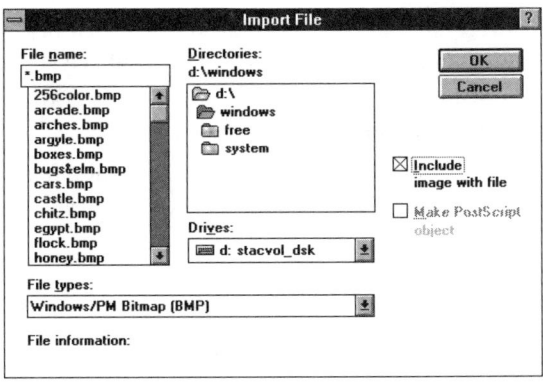

FIGURE 17.1. The Import File dialog box.

2. Click the arrow on the File Types list box and highlight Freelance (DRW).

3. To change to a different drive, click the Drives list box.
4. To change to a different directory, click a file folder icon in the Directories box.
5. Highlight the name of the .DRW file you want to import. The File information box displays the file size, date, and time of the selected file.
6. Click OK to import the selected file. You can double-click the name of a file to combine steps 5 and 6 into a single step.

If you are importing a bitmap file (for example, a .BMP or a .TIF file), you may want to select the check box labeled Include Image With File. If you don't select this option, when you save the .PRE file that contains the bitmap, Freelance does not save the actual image, but rather a reference to the image. If you subsequently save the .PRE file to a floppy disk and read the file on another computer, Freelance cannot find the bitmap file. If you select the check box, Freelance embeds the image itself in the file.

If you are importing an Adobe Illustrator (.AI) file or an Encapsulated PostScript (.EPS) file, select the check box Make This a PostScript Object.

Importing ASCII Files into the Current Page

ASCII text is the lingua franca of the computer universe. It's easy to come by because most applications enable you to export it. You can import an ASCII text file in the following two ways:

- In text edit mode—that is, within an open text block—the text is inserted at the insertion point. The text wraps to the width of the text block and receives the formatting specified by the current paragraph style.
- In Current page view, the ASCII file you import becomes a text block and is assigned the default text attributes.

You also can paste text you cut or copied from another Windows application. See "Copy Text and Graphics Using the Clipboard" later in this chapter for more information.

Importing an ASCII File into the Outliner

If you want to create bullet charts automatically from ASCII text, you can import directly into the Outliner view. Freelance Graphics interprets the ASCII text you import according to the number of leading spaces or tabs in the text. Here's how it works:

- Unindented text starts a new page and becomes the page title.
- Text preceded by a single space (or tab) becomes a level 1 bulleted item.
- Text preceded by two spaces (or tabs) becomes a level 2 bulleted item.
- Text preceded by three spaces (or tabs) becomes a level 3 bulleted item.

Importing Bitmaps

Freelance Graphics can import color, gray-scale, and black-and-white .BMP, .TIF, and .PCX bitmap files. Color bitmaps are displayed in color and, if you are printing to a color device other than a plotter, color bitmaps also are printed in color. If you print a color bitmap to a black-and-white device, the colors automatically are mapped to gray scales during printing.

You can edit a bitmap's attributes either by double-clicking the bitmap or by selecting the bitmap and choosing Style Attributes.

Importing Data Selectively with the Import Data Window

Suppose that you want to import a portion of a text file or a worksheet file into a Freelance Graphics text block, but don't have the source application on your system. (If the source application is a Windows program, it is generally easiest to copy the text via the Clipboard.) An example of this situation is when you want to copy the first six lines from a worksheet file to use in a text chart.

File Import copies the contents of an entire file to your page. But there is another method of importing data selectively, using the Import Data Window. This method displays the contents of the file you are importing and selects the range of data you want to import.

Press F6 to open the Import Data window.

You can use this method to import data from 1-2-3 or Symphony worksheet files, dBASE (.DBF) files, or ASCII numbers or text files. For more information on these file types, consult the Help system of Freelance Graphics.

You can import text or numbers into the Chart Data & Titles window, directly onto the current page, into an open text block, or into Outliner view. Chapter 9, "Creating Charts from 1-2-3 Worksheets," discusses how to import chart data selectively.

Try It: Import ASCII Text into a Text Block

Import a range of text from an ASCII text file into an open text block by doing the following:

1. In text edit mode, press F6. You see the Import Data File dialog box (see fig. 17.2).

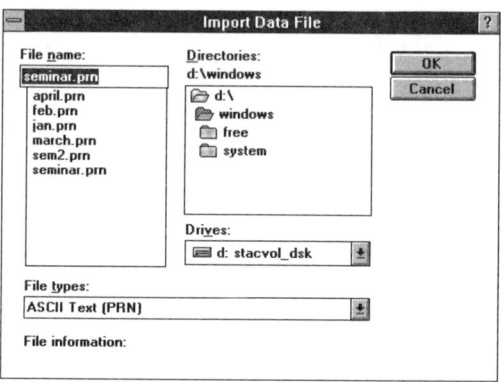

FIGURE 17.2. The Import Data File dialog box.

2. Select the ASCII Text (.PRN) file type from the File Types list box.
3. Highlight the name of the file you want to view in the Import Data Window and then click OK. Because ASCII text files can have any extension, you can type a different extension in the File Name box. For example, you can type *.*TXT* in the File Name box. Freelance displays all the files in the current directory with the extension .TXT. Highlight the file you want and then click OK. In this case, you don't have to make a choice from the File Types list box.
4. Drag the mouse to paint the range you want to import and then click OK (see fig. 17.3). You see a dialog box informing you that the selected range has been copied to the Clipboard (see fig. 17.4). Click OK to continue.

5. Choose Edit Paste to copy the imported text into the open text block or click the Edit Paste SmartIcon (see fig. 17.5).
6. Edit the text if necessary and click outside the text block.

Importing and Exporting Graphics   **307**

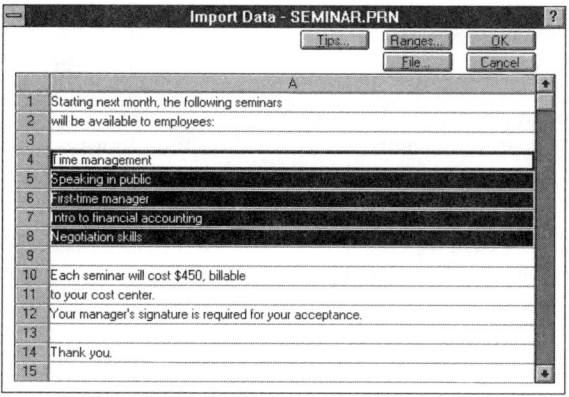

FIGURE 17.3. Highlight the range you want to import.

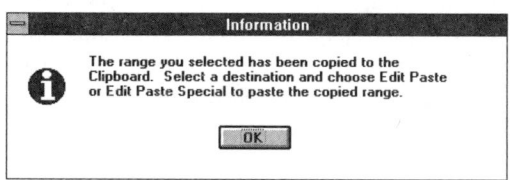

FIGURE 17.4. A message box informs you that the data has been copied to the Clipboard.

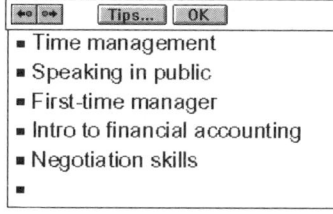

FIGURE 17.5. Make edits in the text block.

Import a Metafile

Freelance can import Windows metafiles (.WMF) or ANSI metafiles (.CGM). You can move or size metafiles like any object in Freelance but, to edit them, first use Arrange Ungroup to break them into individual objects or click the Ungroup SmartIcon.

If you want to use an object in another Windows application that you have on your system, it is probably easier to copy the object to Freelance via the Clipboard. (See Chapter 13, "Editing Objects," for more information on using the Clipboard.)

Exporting Files

You can create graphs, diagrams, or text charts in Freelance Graphics and export them to a number of file types so that you can give them to other people to use in other graphics packages, such as desktop publishing software.

To export a file, choose File Export and then complete the Export File dialog box (see fig. 17.6). Type a directory and file name in the File Name box. Click the arrow in the File types list box to choose the export file type.

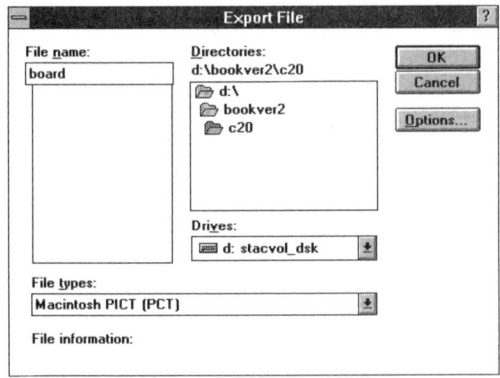

FIGURE 17.6. The Export File dialog box.

Depending on the export format you select, Freelance Graphics exports either a single page or the entire presentation. If you export a Portfolio file or a screen show, the entire presentation is exported. For every other file format, Freelance Graphics exports the current page only.

Freelance can export to the following 12 different file formats:

- ANSI metafile (.CGM). This export format creates a metafile that can be read by Freelance Plus Release 3.0 and later, Freelance Graphics for DOS, and many other DOS applications.
- .AI (Adobe Illustrator). Adobe Illustrator Release 4.0.
- .BMP (Windows Bitmap). Bitmap file for Windows (3.0 and 3.1) and OS/2 (Version 1.3).
- .CGM (Computer Graphics Metafile). Metafile for Freelance Plus Release 2.0 and later, Freelance Graphics for DOS, Graphwriter II, 1-2-3 Release 3.0, and other applications supporting this format, such as Harvard Graphics Release 2.3.
- .GIF (Graphics Interchange). Bitmap file usable by GIF Version 89A.
- .PCX (Zsoft PC Paintbrush Bitmap). Bitmap file for Microsoft Paintbrush (Version 3.0 and 3.1) and Zsoft Publishers Paintbrush (Revision 5 format).
- .PCT (Macintosh PICT). Monochrome or color QuickDraw file for Apple Macintosh Versions 1 and 2.
- .TIF (Tag Image). Tagged image format file for Freelance Plus 3.0 and later, Freelance Graphics for DOS, and Aldus/Microsoft/Hewlett-Packard TIFF Version 5.0.
- .TGA (Targa Bitmap). Image file for Targa Version 2.0.
- .WPG (WordPerfect Graphic). Picture file for WordPerfect for Windows (Version 5.1) and DrawPerfect (Version 1.1).
- .WMF (Windows Metafile). Graphics metafile for Windows applications (3.0 or 3.1).
- .DRW (Freelance). Drawing file for Freelance Plus Release 2.0 and later, Freelance Graphics for DOS, and Graphwriter II.
- .PFL (Freelance Portfolio). Portfolio file and its .DRW (drawing files) that can be read by Freelance Plus Release 3.0 and later and Freelance Graphics for DOS.

For all formats except .DRW, .PFL, and .WMF, you can click the Options button in the Export File dialog box to display a dialog box in which you can choose various output options. As an example, figure 17.7 shows the options for exporting to a Macintosh PICT file. You can save the settings you select as a profile that you can specify whenever you export to this file format. Click the New button and enter a profile name.

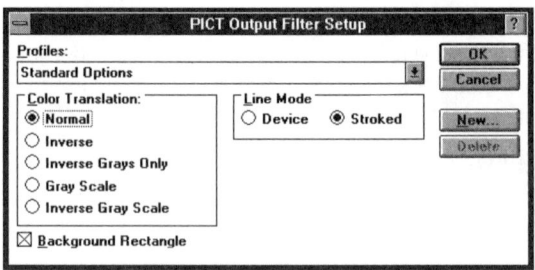

FIGURE 17.7. The options for exporting to a Macintosh PICT file.

Copying Text and Graphics via the Clipboard

The Clipboard is an area of memory in Windows that facilitates the transfer of data from one program to another. Like many Windows programs, Freelance Graphics has an Edit Cut, Edit Copy, and Edit Paste command. When you use the Edit Cut or Edit Copy command, the selected object is copied to the Windows Clipboard. Each time you use Edit Cut or Edit Copy, the contents of the Clipboard are replaced by the new operation. Note, though, that using Edit Paste does not clear the Clipboard, which means that you can paste multiple copies of the Clipboard contents onto different presentation pages. Data copied to the Clipboard may be in various formats, including text, a bitmap, or a metafile.

Because you can have several programs running in Windows at the same time, you can use the Clipboard as a means of transferring information among applications.

See Chapter 13, "Editing Objects," for more information about using the Clipboard to copy and paste objects.

Wrapping Up

In this chapter, you learned how to import graphics files from and export them to Freelance Graphics. Importing and exporting can save considerable time by letting you and others share existing graphics files across applications. You also learned how to copy text and graphics and objects into and out of Freelance via the Windows Clipboard.

In the next chapter, you learn how to work effectively with color in Freelance Graphics.

18

Working with Color

Everyone understands and appreciates the value of color in presentations. More and more, audiences have come to expect it. In fact, it can be difficult to capture the attention of an audience with monochrome images. People are so accustomed to color by their exposure to glossy magazines, television, rock videos, and movies that the absence of color is noticeable.

Until recently, it was expensive and difficult to create a presentation in color. But, in the last few years, color monitors have become the standard in personal computing, and more recently, the entry price point for color printers has dropped dramatically. Moreover, slide services that take your presentation files and create color slides for you overnight at reasonable prices abound. Freelance comes with a built-in slide service connection. For more information, read Chapter 21, "Creating 35mm Slides."

This chapter explores the various ways you can enrich your presentation with color and explains the system of color palettes that Freelance Graphics uses to make choosing colors easier for you.

The Role of Color in Your Presentation

Besides adding aesthetic appeal and visual excitement to your presentation, color can play more practical roles. You can use color for the following purposes:

- To emphasize. A bold or vivid color jumps out at the viewer. You can highlight a graphic object in a diagram or graph by assigning a bold color to it.

In this chapter, you learn how to:

- *Use color effectively in your presentations*
- *Switch between a color and black-and-white presentation instantly*
- *Create graduated fill patterns*
- *Understand the structure of the color palettes and the color library*
- *Edit and save a palette*
- *Change the RGB values of a library color*

- To differentiate. In graphs, the data symbols for each data set receive different colors automatically. In diagrams, though, this task is up to you.
- To group. You can make an association between objects in a diagram by displaying them in the same color. Use palette colors, but assign colors to groups of objects that are thematically or structurally related. In an organization chart, for example, you might place all personnel at the same level of the hierarchy in a box with the same background color.
- To suggest a mood. Color psychology is tricky, but there is no doubt that color influences mood. See the "The Psychology of Color" section later in this chapter for more details.

Try It: Change the Color of an Object

You can change the color of just about any object on the screen in Freelance, including objects in diagrams, text, bars in data charts, and boxes in organization charts. Try changing the color of a rectangle on the screen by doing the following:

1. Click the Rectangle icon in the Toolbox and draw a rectangle on the screen.
2. Double-click the rectangle.
3. In the Style Attributes Rectangle dialog box, click the 1st Color list box. This action displays the 40 colors in the current palette (see fig. 18.1). Note that, although a palette has 64 colors, you only see 40 when you are assigning colors to objects.
4. Click the new color you want to use. Because you are changing the color of a foreground object, use one of the suggested foreground colors.
5. If you want to examine the color change before committing to it, click and hold the Preview button to see how the new color looks on the presentation page. Release the mouse button to return to the dialog box and then click OK to accept the change.

Switching between Color and Black and White

Almost everyone has a color monitor these days, but few have color printers. To address this problem, every Freelance SmartMaster set has both a color and a black-and-white palette. You can switch from one to the other instantly by clicking the Color/B&W button on the status bar at the bottom of the Freelance window. This quick switch means that you can create color or black-and-white output from the same presentation without worrying about how the colors are translated to black-and-white output. Freelance's system of dual palettes takes care of these design details for you automatically.

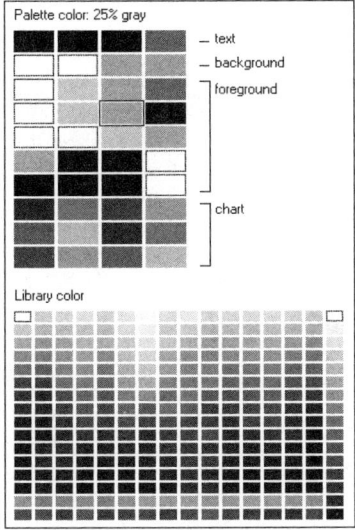

FIGURE 18.1. The palette and the color library that you see when you choose a new color for an object.

Color Design Tips

If you don't feel comfortable making color choices, Freelance Graphics can make appropriate color choices for you automatically. The entire system of SmartMaster sets and palettes was designed to free you from the necessity of making color choices. Nevertheless, you still have to make decisions about colors from time to time, especially when you are customizing a data chart or creating a diagram. The guidelines in the following sections can help you make those decisions.

Background Colors

The background of a page sets the overall mood for the entire slide: A white background is clean and crisp; a dark blue background projects a deep, serious image. Some colors, such as red or green, are usually not appropriate for background colors. A relatively deep shade of blue makes the best background color, which is why many of the Freelance SmartMaster sets have blue backgrounds.

Text Colors

Every Freelance Graphics palette recommends four text colors in the top row of the Palette. You see a preponderance of white, yellow, and black for suggested text colors in the SmartMaster sets. For a crisp and readable text in a slide or screen show, white and yellow text on a blue background is the classic combination.

Foreground Colors

Most colors, with the exception of very light colors, look fine on a white background. On a blue background, any of the foreground palette colors are acceptable. Following are some tips for using foreground colors:

- Avoid colors that clash. If you use colors from a palette, this usually should not be a problem.
- Avoid colors that blend too closely, making it difficult to distinguish objects. For example, don't display light blue text on a dark blue background.
- Don't include red and green on the same slide (a fair percentage of the male population is red-green color blind and perceive these colors as a muddy brown).

The Psychology of Color

There is a psychology of color, but it is a complex and subjective business. Obviously, you cannot persuade someone to buy your product and accept your point of view simply because you displayed your message in flag blue or crimson. Nevertheless, color is a real determinant of mood, and you should be aware of the connotations of various colors. Red, for example, has been shown in experiments to actually increase the metabolism of subjects!

Color psychology varies among cultures and individuals, among men and women, and among social classes. Following are some connotations of single colors as well as groups of colors that prevail in Western culture:

- Black suggests boldness and (in business) profit. Black is often used in consumer goods to suggest professionalism (think of certain tools or cameras).
- Green connotes nature and growth (grass, trees), money, and, in some cases, jealousy and envy.

- Red means STOP! and can suggest fear, danger, error, or even sensuality.
- Yellow connotes cheerfulness, warmth (the sun), happiness, and morning. This is a great color for making text or objects stand out. Yellow text on a blue background is especially readable.
- Blues and greens (the cool colors) can suggest calm, serenity, and a trusting attitude; but they also can evoke a cold and forbidding mood.
- The primary colors (red, yellow, and blue) evoke the nursery and the early years of childhood. Children's clothes and toys often use these colors.
- Bright colors (the brighter shades of red, blue, yellow, orange, green) suggest youth and vitality.
- Dark colors are natural, earthy colors.
- Warm colors (orange, brown, yellow) are the colors of sunsets, autumn, and fire.

One final note about color. You can break almost all the rules about color if you know what you are doing. Designers constantly are experimenting with new color schemes in the endless search for originality and attention-getting designs. Of course, if you don't know what you're doing, follow the rules and stick with palette colors.

Nothing stands out more than an ill-chosen color scheme. Even people with little knowledge of graphic design can often sense poor color harmony when they see it. So be careful when you experiment with colors.

Change the Background Color

For a consistent look, every page in a presentation should have the same background color. When you choose a SmartMaster set, every page has the same background color by default, regardless of what page layout you choose. If you like a SmartMaster set and the color palette it uses but want to change the background color only, you can do it with the Page Background command.

You can change the background color for a single page or for an entire presentation by using the Page Background command. If a page uses a page layout from a SmartMaster set, you can change the background color for the entire presentation only. You can change the background selectively only for those pages that use no page layouts.

For best results, use one of the suggested background colors in the palette for the new background color.

Limit the Number of Colors

Desktop computers, color monitors, and new color output devices—to say nothing of slide services—have brought unprecedented flexibility and power to your desktop. Just as you are free to choose from dozens of typefaces, you are free to choose from literally thousands of colors. And, it might be added, free to make a complete aesthetic shambles of your presentation in the process.

Use restraint and caution as you work with colors in your presentation. True mastery of color is a craft that takes years of experience and discipline. Nevertheless, you can experiment a little and be creative if you follow a few rules and avoid the most obvious aesthetic blunders.

Limit the number of colors to three or four.

Perhaps the number one rule is this: Limit the number of colors in a presentation to three or four.

For color bitmaps, symbols, and graphs with several data sets (in which you need a separate color for each data set), this rule does not apply. Otherwise, try to observe this limitation.

When To Use Graduated Fill Patterns

Graduated fills are special effects that consist of a gradual blending of two colors from one to the other. Although you can use graduated fills for any graphic object, they work best as backgrounds. Several SmartMaster sets (including BLOCKS.MAS, CORPORAT.MAS, ELEGANCE.MAS, GRADATE1.MAS, and GRADATE2.MAS) use backgrounds with graduated fills.

Graduated fills work best with slides.

Graduated fills work best with 35mm slides and with certain high-resolution color output devices. They do not reproduce well on black-and-white laser printers (and take forever to print).

Try It: Create a Graduated Fill Background

A graduated pattern creates a pattern based on two colors and a pattern you select. Freelance Graphics blends the first and second colors gradually, using the pattern you select as the backdrop. The best way to understand graduated fills is to create a rectangle, double-click it to change its attributes, and then experiment with different first and second colors and different patterns. Click the Preview button to see the result. Generally, a graduated fill works best if you use two shades of the same hue (from midnight to blue, for example).

1. Double-click an object such as a rectangle.
2. In the Style Attributes dialog box (fig. 18.2), choose a color for 1st Color. This color is used by the black areas in the Pattern list box (see fig. 18.3).

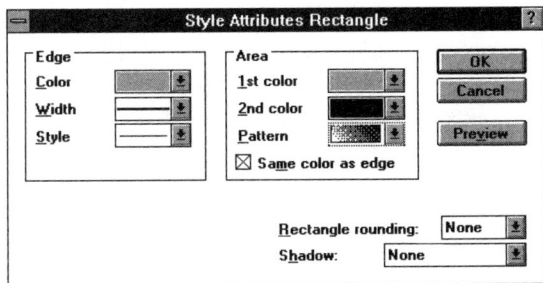

FIGURE 18.2. The Style Attributes Rectangle dialog box.

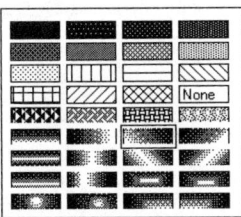

Figure 18.3. The graduated fill patterns available when you click the Pattern list box.

3. Choose a color for 2nd Color. This color is used by the white areas in the Pattern list box.
4. Choose a pattern for the area of the object or background.

Note that, if you choose None for pattern, you get no background color, regardless of the choices for 1st and 2nd Color. If you choose the solid black pattern, the fill uses only the first color, so you get a solid background color.

Black-and-White Design Tips

Even as color is becoming more available on desktop computers, it is ironic that some designers are now turning to black and white for both display advertisements and television commercials (not to mention rock videos).

Black and white offers unique design possibilities.

Perhaps color has been so overused that black and white now seems like a novelty and, thus, is an attention-getter.

In any event, black-and-white offers a rich source of possibilities for graphics. This has always been the case. In fine arts circles, for example, black-and-white photography is often considered superior to color. Think of the work of Ansel Adams. Of course, the term black and white overlooks "gray," and it is the combination of blacks, whites, and grays that enables you to create effective, interesting designs in monochrome. If you have a laser printer, you are all set.

Black-and-white presentations are especially effective as printed reports or handouts, but less so as slide presentations. As overheads, however, black and white works fine (and is much more economical than generating color output).

The graph in figure 18.4, which uses the SmartMaster set STACK.MAS, makes excellent use of gray scales.

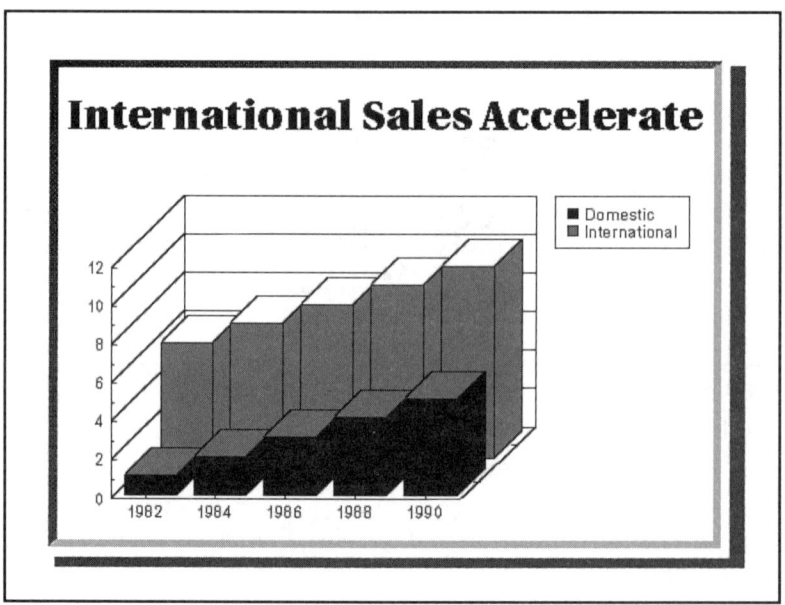

FIGURE 18.4. A graph that uses gray scales well.

Understanding Palettes and the Color Library

Every Freelance SmartMaster set has two palettes: one color and one black and white. This section examines the structure of a Freelance palette. Every palette in Freelance Graphics contains 64 colors, as shown in figure 18.5.

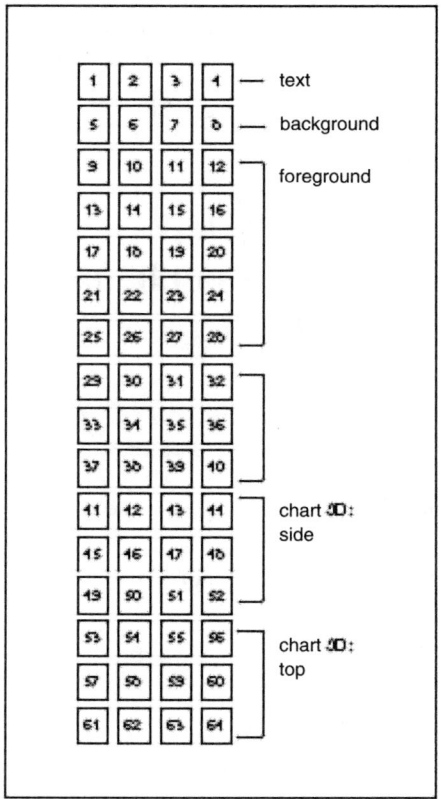

FIGURE 18.5. The structure of the Freelance Graphics palette.

The 64 palette colors are drawn from a color library that contains 256 colors. Both the palette and the color library are saved with your presentation.

When you change the color of objects, you have the choice of using palette colors or library colors. As a rule, you should use palette colors for the elements of charts and diagrams. Freelance Graphics always uses palette colors for bulleted lists and charts and for objects you draw with the Toolbox.

Use library colors to preserve colors even when you switch palettes.

Why use palette colors? Because, if you switch to a new SmartMaster set, you want the colors to look good. If you use a library color, when you switch to a new palette, the object drawn with the library color does not change (because every palette uses the same color library).

You can use this information to good advantage. Sometimes you want a color to remain the same no matter which palette you choose. Suppose that you have added the symbol of an apple, or perhaps a flag, to a page. When you choose a new palette, you want the apple and the flag to retain their original colors. Freelance Graphics uses library colors for symbols whose colors normally do not change, like the flag and the apple. When you assign a library color to an object and then choose a new color palette, the color remains the same because each palette uses the same color library.

What Happens When You Choose a New SmartMaster Set?

It is helpful to understand the structure of the palettes so that you know what happens when you switch to a new SmartMaster set (and thus a new palette).

When you switch to a new SmartMaster set, Freelance Graphics assigns the new colors to your text and graphics based on their position in the palette. For example, if the color assigned to a rectangle is the second color in the first row in the current palette, when you choose a new palette, Freelance Graphics replaces this color with the second color in the first row in the new palette. The same rule applies for every color in your presentation.

Creating Your Own Palettes

The system of palettes in Freelance Graphics eliminates much of the difficulty of choosing proper color combinations. Each palette contains a set of colors that look good together. Within each palette of 64 colors, however, Freelance Graphics groups colors according to suggested use. The first row of colors is recommended for text. The second row of colors makes the best background colors, and so on.

Of course, you are not obligated to follow the suggested uses and are free to assign any color to any object. But, if you feel unsure of your mastery of color, the suggested uses for colors are an excellent guide. When you create a text chart or graph, Freelance Graphics assigns colors to text or graphs automatically, based on these guidelines.

You are not restricted to using the palettes provided with the Freelance SmartMaster sets. You can create a new palette for any of a variety of reasons. Often, for example, a company uses certain colors as part of its corporate identity. You may want to incorporate some of these colors into a palette.

When you create a new palette, you can choose 64 colors out of the 256 in the color library. If you don't find the color you want among these, you can change the RGB value of any library color to get precisely the color you want (see the "Change the RGB Value of a Library Color" section for more information).

To create your own palette based on the 256 library colors, follow the procedure in the "Try It: Edit and Save a Palette" section.

How Freelance Uses Palette Colors

As shown in figure 18.5, the 64 colors in each palette are categorized according to their suggested uses. The first 4 colors are suggested for text, the 4 colors in the second row are good for backgrounds, the next 20 colors are foreground colors, and so on.

Figure 18.5 shows an abstract representation of the 64 colors in every palette. Note that each slot is numbered. Freelance uses the colors in certain slot numbers for graphic elements when it creates bulleted lists, data charts, organization charts, and tables. Incidentally, this information is invaluable if you decide to create your own SmartMaster sets (and palettes). Read Chapter 26, "Creating Your Own SmartMaster Sets," for more information.

The following sections explain how Freelance uses the palette colors. Refer to figure 18.4 as you read the text.

Text Colors (1-4)

The text colors are used for various text assignments, although they vary somewhat among SmartMaster sets. The color in position 1, for example, is used for different text items, depending on the SmartMaster set. The color of the title block, for example, may be position 1 in some SmartMaster sets, position 2 in others. Most SmartMaster sets use the following conventions:

Slot	Use
1	Page titles
2	Subtitle on Title page; text in bulleted items; text added with the Text tool.

Slot	Use
3	Text in data charts (title, axis titles, labels and values, legends, notes, table text); text in placement blocks and frame edges; frame edges of text blocks; text in organization charts; headers and footers; speaker notes; text used for drawing on-screen in screen shows.
4	Text used for grayed text in automatic builds.

Background Colors (5-8)

Background colors vary among SmartMaster sets, but the page background always comes from slot 5, 6, 7, or 8.

Foreground Colors (9-28)

Foreground colors vary among SmartMaster sets, but the following palette slots are used in all SmartMaster sets.

Slot	Use
15	Objects created with the drawing tools. Also used for the area and edges of graphic objects.
16	Frame edge (for charts, legend frames, headings and notes, number grids) and background edge (for data charts and organization charts).
17	Text frame area; data chart text frame area (legend, headings, and notes); data chart background area; number grid area; organization chart background area; placement block frame area.
18	Organization chart box areas, table background, and cell background in tables.
19	Sides of 3D organization charts.
20	Bottoms of 3D organization charts.
21	Shadows for objects, data charts, tables, and organization charts.
22	Bullets; lines, polylines, arrows, curves, and arcs (created with the Toolbox).
23	Organization chart connecting lines.
24	3D data chart floors.
25	Data chart grids and grid lines in a number grid.

Slot **Use**

26 Edges for bar charts, pie charts, area charts, 3D area/line charts, and organization charts.

27 Borders for edge of tables and cells within tables.

28 3D data chart walls.

Charts (29-64)

Freelance also uses slots 29-40 for colors for data symbols (that is, lines, bars, pie slices, and so on). Suppose that you are creating a bar chart with three data sets (or series). The first set of bars uses the color in slot 29, the second set of bars the color in slot 30, and so on. For a pie chart, the first slice uses color 29, the second color 30, and so on.

If you have more than 12 data series in a chart (not a recommended graphic practice, by the way), this sequence of 12 colors repeats with the thirteenth data set.

Colors 41 through 52 are used for the sides of 3D charts. If there are more than 12 data sets, the sequence repeats.

Colors 53 through 64 are used for the tops of 3D charts. If there are more than 12 data sets, the sequence repeats.

Try It: Edit and Save a Palette

Freelance Graphics saves the current palette with your presentation. If you change the colors in the palette, they are used for the current presentation only. They are not replaced permanently in the palette unless you explicitly save the palette. Follow these steps to practice saving a palette:

1. Choose Style Edit Palette.
2. Click the palette color you want to change.
3. Click the Modify Color list box.
4. Click a color from the color library to replace the selected color in the palette. After you have edited a color palette, you can save the palette so that you can use it with another presentation or to create a new SmartMaster set.
5. Click the Save button and then type a new name for the palette in the File Name box. Freelance Graphics adds the proper extension (.PAL) automatically. Make sure to save the palette in the MASTERS subdirectory along with the rest of the palettes, so that the new palette appears in the list when you use the Style Choose Palette command.

Change the RGB Value of a Library Color

Every palette is drawn from the color library (which has 256 colors). All the color palettes in the Freelance Graphics library use the same original color library.

Every time you save a palette, the color library is saved along with it. If you change a color in the library, the palette is saved with a new library. For this reason, it is not a good idea to change the color library. And, if you do, make sure that you have a very good reason. Here are two valid reasons for changing the color library:

- You need a precise color for your corporate logo.
- You need a color that your output device can print, but cannot find an exact match in the color library to have true WYSIWYG color.

Note that when you change a library color, you change it for the current SmartMaster set only. Because every palette saves a separate copy of the color library, if you want to make the same change to every color library, you must edit the color library for every SmartMaster set.

To change a library color, choose Style Edit Palette and then click the button labeled Edit Library in the resulting dialog box (see fig. 18.6). Click the color you want to change. The name of the color appears at the top of the color library (see fig. 18.7).

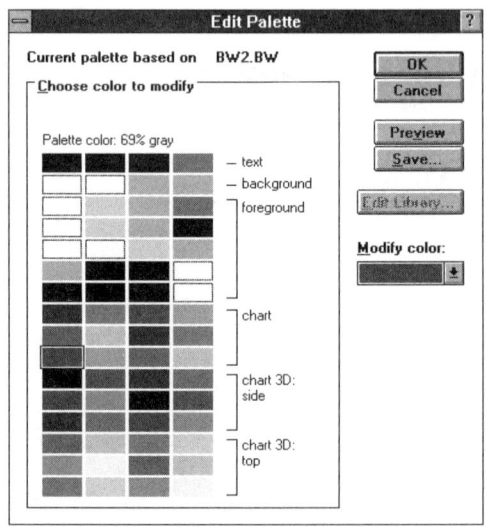

FIGURE 18.6. The Edit Palette dialog box.

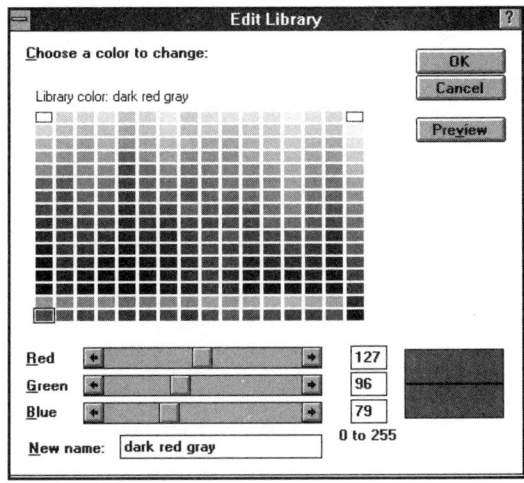

FIGURE 18.7. The Edit Library dialog box.

Note that each color has an RGB value. An RGB value specifies the precise mixture of red, green, and blue in a color. If you know the precise RGB value, you simply can type the numbers in the boxes provided. You also can click the Red, Green, and Blue scroll arrows to change the color interactively. Generally, if you want a precise color, it's best to find out the correct RGB value.

Wrapping Up

This chapter discussed the use (and abuse) of color in your presentation. You learned how colors can convey information and emotion. You know how to assign colors to objects and how to create a graduated fill. You learned how to change the colors in the palette and the color library and how to save new palettes that you can reuse. After reading this chapter, you should have a basic understanding of the structure of palettes in Freelance.

This chapter brings Part 5 to a close. In Part 6, you learn about printing, creating screen shows, and turning your presentation pages into 35mm slides.

Part 6
Printing, Screen Shows, and Slides

This part describes how to print your presentation in a variety of formats, including audience handouts and speaker notes. You learn how to create an attention-grabbing screen show with surprising transition effects, and how to create an interactive screen show, and even add multimedia effects. The last chapter of this section describes how you can turn your presentation into crisp, colorful 35mm slides using Freelance's built-in link to a slide service bureau.

This section includes:

Chapter 19. Printing a Presentation

Chapter 20. Screen Shows

Chapter 21. Creating 35mm Slides

19

Printing a Presentation

If you have ever had trouble printing with DOS applications, you should find printing in Windows applications to be somewhat simpler (if not altogether trouble free). In DOS, every application requires its own printer driver. Windows, however, supplies one set of drivers for all Windows applications, which simplifies matters considerably.

Consequently, printing in Freelance Graphics is a relatively clean operation. If you have printed from other Windows applications, you have found that Freelance Graphics follows standard printing conventions in Windows, with a few exceptions that are explained in this chapter.

Choose a Printer

Before you can print your presentation, the printer you plan to use must have been installed in Windows. (You cannot install a printer within Freelance Graphics.) To add a new printer, choose the Printers option in the Control Panel. Consult your Windows documentation for more information about this procedure.

In Windows, you can install as many printers as you like. Then within Freelance Graphics, you can choose any installed printer.

To select a printer, choose File Printer Setup, click the name of a printer from the list box, and click OK.

In this chapter, you learn how to:

- *Print an entire presentation, a single page, or a range of pages*
- *Print faster*
- *Print speaker notes, audience notes, handouts, and outlines*
- *Print headers and footers*
- *Choose page orientation*
- *Print from DOS or Windows without running Freelance Graphics*
- *Print a color presentation in black and white*
- *Optimize color printing*

Printing Options

To print all or part of a presentation, choose File Print to display the Print File dialog box (see fig. 19.1). Make your choices to set up the printing operation.

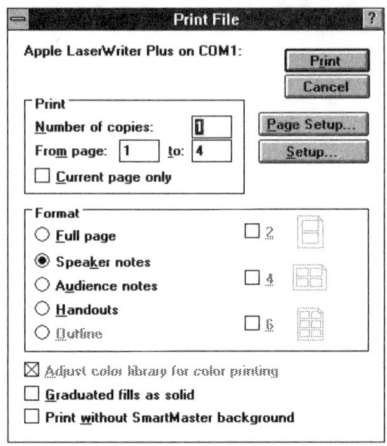

FIGURE 19.1. The Print File dialog box.

Choosing a Print Range

You can print your entire presentation, a range of pages, or a single page. Make your choices for the following options in the File Print dialog box:

- Number of Copies. Type a number to specify how many copies of your pages you want to print.
- A range of pages. Type the starting page number and the ending page number. The default values are 1 and 9999, respectively. These numbers print your entire presentation.
- Current Page Only. Often, it's useful to print the page you are working on to see how it looks in final form. Mark the Current Page Only check box. If you select this option, Freelance deselects it automatically after the page is printed.

> ## Tips for Printing Faster
>
> Printers haven't really kept pace with the increase in computer speed. On a reasonably fast computer, you can work with a graphically complex presentation with ease. But, when you try to print the presentation, you hit a brick wall. Printing to a PostScript laser printer can reduce printing times to a slow crawl. A single page may take half an hour to print. Two options in the Print File dialog box can ease this problem.
>
> If your presentation uses graduated fills, you can print these fills as solid colors by marking the Graduated Fills as Solid check box. Graduated fills generally look terrible in black and white, and some printers cannot print them at all. In addition, graduated fills can take a lifetime to print.
>
> Certain SmartMaster sets have complex designs that look great as color slides or even as laser output. But, the more complex the design, the longer these pages can take to print. Mark the check box labeled Print without SmartMaster Background to print your presentation without any of the SmartMaster design elements. This choice is a good one for printing drafts of your presentation as you are creating it.

Choosing a Print Format

Freelance Graphics enables you to print your presentation in a variety of special formats. You choose the format you want by marking the appropriate check box in the Print File dialog box.

Press Ctrl+P or click the Print SmartIcon to display the File Print dialog box.

Speaker Notes

Speaker Notes are an excellent tool for rehearsing your presentation (a highly recommended practice, by the way). To add speaker notes as you are working on your presentation, choose Page Speaker Notes and then type your notes in the Speaker Note dialog box (see fig. 19.2), which looks like a 3 x 5 index card. When you add a speaker note, the image of an index card appears in the margin to the left of your presentation page to remind you that this page has an attached speaker note. Read Chapter 22, "Managing Presentations," for more information on creating speaker notes.

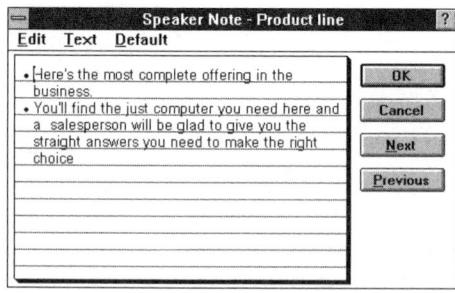

FIGURE 19.2. The Speaker Note dialog box. The title bar displays the name of the presentation page associated with this speaker note.

When you print speaker notes, Freelance prints the presentation page on the top half of the page and your notes on the bottom half.

These notes can be the script for your presentation. Use the speaker note feature to help memorize your speech, or at least key portions of it. If you feel comfortable speaking, or have given the same presentation many times, you can simply add brief facts, figures, or phrases to help jog your memory as you speak. If you need more help, or are giving a presentation for the first time, you can write more copious notes, or even the full text of your talk. Of course, you do want to avoid the appearance of reading your presentation, which makes you look unprepared and unsure of yourself.

Audience Notes

When you choose the Audience Notes format, Freelance prints a small version of your presentation page on the top half of the page and blank lines on the bottom half. The audience can use these pages to take notes as you speak.

Audience notes give your audience a place to take notes as you deliver your presentation and also serve as a walk-away summary of your presentation. With this ready reference source, people are more likely to remember your points.

On the negative side, if you distribute audience notes before or during the presentation, you run the risk of dividing the attention of the audience. They may read the presentation rather than listen to you. If they know they have a printed version of your talk, they may decide it's not necessary to listen and may let their attention wander.

On the other hand, distributing audience notes before a presentation involves the audience, which helps establish a relationship between you and your audience. If there is a question-and-answer session afterward, the audience has a reference to consult as a basis for asking questions.

If your presentation is highly technical, audience notes can help the audience write down the information necessary to jog their memory later. If you are giving a motivational speech, on the other hand, you probably want to forego audience notes. You want the audience to be riveted on you, not on the pages in their laps.

Handouts

Handouts are miniature versions of your presentation pages printed two, four, or six to a page (see fig. 19.3). You can distribute these handouts to your audience before or after your presentation. The same reservations expressed for audience notes also apply to handouts. You want to avoid distracting your audience or giving them an easy way to look ahead.

One solution is to keep the handouts until after the presentation. The handouts give your audience a printed record of your presentation and help them to remember your points.

To print audience handouts, click the Handouts button in the File Print dialog box. Then click 2, 4, or 6. The icons next to these numbers show the page layout for each of these choices.

If you have set up headers and footers, they appear only once for each handout page, at the top and bottom of the page, regardless of whether you have chosen the two-, four-, or six-page-per-handout format.

You also can use handouts to review the flow of your presentation paper, much as you do in the Page Sorter view. For this purpose, six presentation pages per handout page is a good choice. You also can give handouts to co-workers who are monitoring the creation of your presentation.

Outline

You can print an outline, but only if you are in Outline view. If you are not, the Outline radio button is dimmed. Freelance Graphics prints the outline as it appears in Outline view. If the outline is collapsed, only what is visible is printed. The icon that marks the start of each new page also is printed.

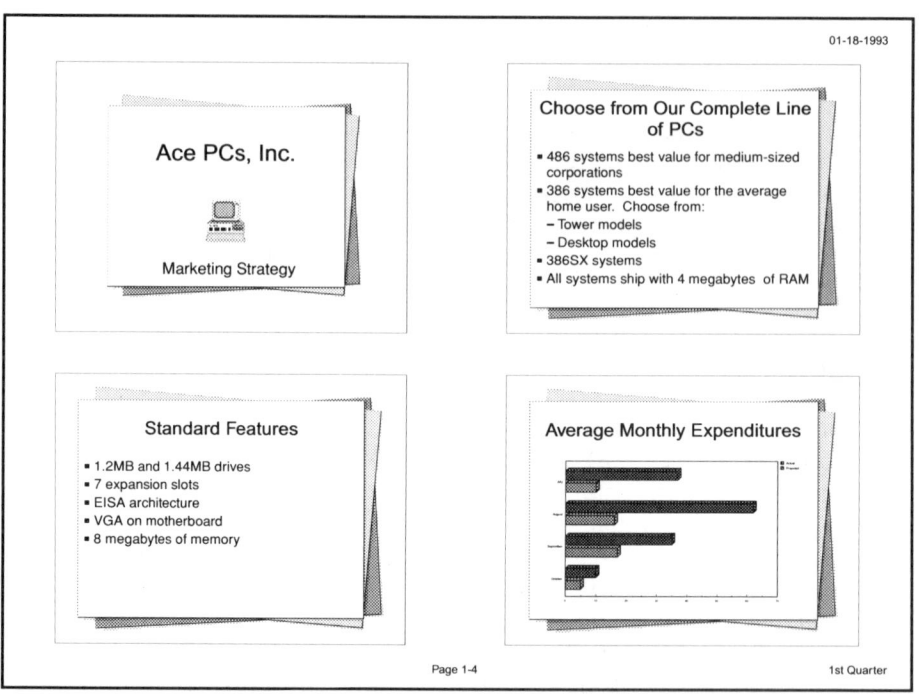

FIGURE 19.3. To create this handout page, choose File Print, click the Handouts button, and then choose the format for four presentation pages per handout page.

Adding Headers and Footers

You can add a header or footer to printed pages, choose the orientation (vertical or horizontal), and specify left, right, top, and bottom margins in the File Page Setup dialog box.

Because presentations often are viewed from a distance and projected on a screen, headers and footers are not often useful. Nevertheless, Freelance has the capability to add headers and footers to printed pages, albeit a bit awkwardly. To add headers and footers, choose File Page Setup and then type the header and footer in the entry boxes provided in the dialog box (see fig. 19.4).

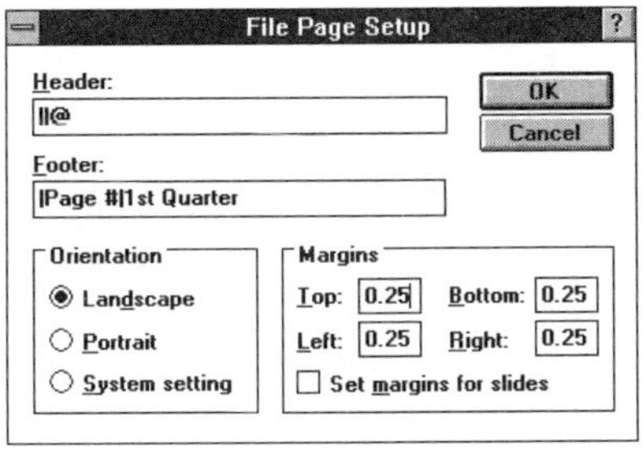

FIGURE 19.4. The File Page Setup dialog box.

You can add sequential page numbers, include the current date, and force a line break in the header or footer by typing special characters. Here's a rundown of these special characters:

- To print sequential page numbers (starting with 1), type the number sign (#) in the header or footer box. When you print the presentation, Freelance Graphics replaces each # with a sequential number. You can start the sequence at any number you want (see next bullet).
- To print sequential page numbers (starting with a specific number), type two number signs (##), followed by the starting page number. To start the page number sequencing at 10, for example, you type ##*10*.
- To print the current date, type the at sign (@) in the header or footer. Keep in mind that the current date in this context means the system date, or the date determined by the clock battery of your computer (which may be incorrect). Freelance uses the date format specified in Tools User Setup International.
- To add a header or footer of more than one line, separate each line with the tilde (~) character.
- To include one of the special characters in the header or footer, such as a vertical bar (|), tilde (~), number sign (#), or at sign (@), place a backslash (\) before each character.

The special characters in the Header and Footer boxes generate the header (01-18-1993) and footer (Page 3, 1st Quarter) in the presentation page shown in figure 19.5.

All in all, creating headers and footers isn't one of the stronger points of Freelance Graphics. In addition to the somewhat obscure syntax, Freelance uses a fixed font to print headers and footers (8-point Arial MT, if that font is on your system). You cannot specify a different font or change its size.

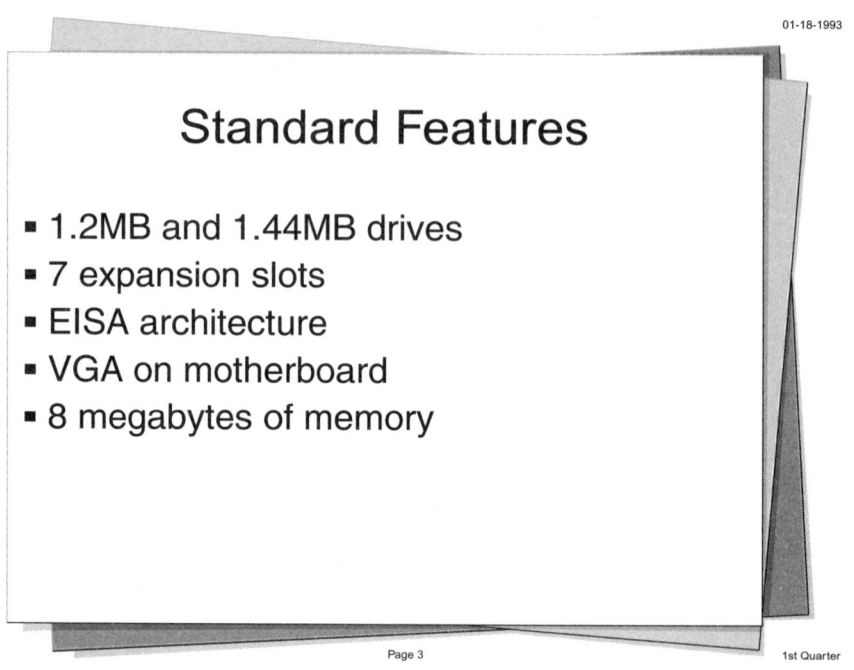

FIGURE 19.5. Presentation page using special headers and footers.

You may find it easier to type your header or footer on the Basic Layout SmartMaster page. This method gives you more control over the look of the header or footer. However, you do lose the capability to create sequential page numbers if you use this method. For more information about the Basic Layout SmartMaster page, refer to Chapter 25, "Understanding SmartMaster Sets."

Choosing the Page Orientation

You can print pages in Landscape mode (oriented horizontally) or Portrait mode (oriented vertically). Make your choice by clicking the appropriate button in the File Page Setup dialog box.

Most SmartMaster sets are designed for landscape (horizontal) orientation. For slide shows, landscape is the best orientation. For printed presentations, however, portrait (vertical) is generally the best orientation, because people are accustomed to this format from reading books and magazines.

When you choose a SmartMaster set, Freelance chooses the appropriate orientation automatically. But, if for some reason you want to print a page vertically, you can. Just click the Portrait button. If you click the System Setting button, Freelance uses whatever orientation is specified in the Printers options of the Windows Control Panel.

Try It: Print a Presentation Outside of Freelance Graphics

Suppose that a colleague requests a printed copy of your presentation or you simply need another copy yourself. You can print your presentation from Windows, or from the DOS command line, without running Freelance Graphics. You do need to have a copy of Freelance installed on your computer, however. Print a presentation named MARCH.PRE by doing the following:

1. From the DOS command line, type *win c:\flw\flw.exe /p march* and press Enter. Change the directory name and path if Freelance Graphics resides in a different drive and directory on your computer.
2. From Windows, choose File Run from the Program Manager. In the command line, type *c:\flw\flw.exe /p march* and then click OK or press Enter. Again, change the path and directory name as necessary.

Printing in Black and White

Even though your final presentation is in color, in the form of slides or color overheads, you may want to print in black and white for a variety of reasons. Black and white is perfect for speaker notes, audience notes, and handouts. Also, as you work on a presentation, you may want to print draft versions in black and white to economize (the costs of printing color pages can be high, even if you own your own color printer).

To make this task easier, every SmartMaster set in Freelance comes with both a color and a black-and-white palette. To print to a black-and-white printer, choose Style Use Black & White Palette or click the Color/B&W button on the bottom border. This action displays your presentation in a black-and-white palette designed specifically for the SmartMaster set you are using.

Optimizing Colors for Your Printer

Because Freelance Graphics is a what-you-see-is-what-you-get (WYSIWYG) software package, there is generally a close correspondence between what you seen on-screen and what you get with printed output. But the colors you see on your monitor may not be precisely the same color you get on a printed page. The printed colors may vary from the on-screen colors, depending on the color output device you are using.

Why this discrepancy? One reason is that color monitors and printers use different technologies to represent color. Another is that the manufacturers of monitors and color printers have not established standards that would enable screen colors to match printed colors precisely.

Freelance Graphics provides a partial solution to this problem. Before you print to a color device, choose File Print and then click the button labeled Adjust Color Library for Color Printing (this option is chosen by default). When you use this option, Freelance uses an alternate color library.

When you use the alternate color library, your device may yield colors that more closely match those you see on-screen. Your best bet is to experiment with your printer to see which setting works best.

In several cases, you may want to turn off this option. Here are three cases when you should probably not use the alternate color library:

- If you have changed the colors in the color library used by the current presentation (these changes are not reflected in the alternate color library)
- If the darkest colors in your printed output are too light
- If your color printer has a ribbon

Incidentally, you can edit the alternate color library. It is named CPRINTER.PAL, and you can find it in the \FLW directory. For safety, make a backup of CPRINTER.PAL before you change it. To edit it, choose Style Choose Palette, click the Directory button, and change the directory path to \FLW (or to the directory where you have installed Freelance Graphics). Double-click CPRINTER.PAL and then click OK in the Choose Palette dialog box. Now choose Style Edit Palette and change the colors as you like. Click the Save button to save the new version of CPRINTER.PAL. For more information on editing library colors, read Chapter 18, "Working with Color."

Wrapping Up

In this chapter, you learned how to print your presentation. You know how to print a range of pages or an entire presentation. You learned a few tips for printing faster. You know how to print speaker notes, audience notes, handouts, or an outline. You also learned how to add headers and footers to a printed presentation. You know how to print a presentation without starting Freelance Graphics. And, finally, you learned a few tips for printing in black and white and color.

In the next chapter, you learn all you need to know about screen shows.

20

Screen Shows

If you want to be in complete control of your presentation, are weary of lugging around the cumbersome equipment required to give a slide show, and want to add a touch of glitz to your presentation, screen shows could be your ticket to the big screen.

A *screen show* uses the computer screen itself as the delivery medium for your presentation, displaying each page of your presentation in sequence on your monitor.

Screen shows are ideal for showing finished presentations to small, informal groups or using as a self-running demonstration at a trade show. You even can save a screen show on a disk that you can distribute to anyone with a compatible computer. A special player module allows anyone to view the screen show, even if they don't have Freelance Graphics for Windows.

Because the development and presentation media are one and the same, it's no problem to make last-minute changes to a screen show. If you were giving a slide show, you would be limited by at least a 24-hour turn-around time to process the slides.

You also can use a screen show to check the flow of your presentation as you develop it. This latter capability is useful because, although Freelance Graphics is a WYSIWYG (what you see is what you get) application, the title bar, prompt text, menu bar, and the various icons on the screen can distract from a clear view of your presentation. Besides, the images in a screen show are bigger without this extra structure.

> *In this chapter, you learn how to:*
>
> - *Use screen shows to preview your presentation as you develop it*
> - *Set up a self-running screen show or control the pace yourself*
> - *Add special transition effects*
> - *Create build slides*
> - *Create a portable screen show that you can distribute to anyone with a computer, even if they don't have Freelance Graphics (or Windows)*

Viewing a No-Frills Screen Show

To run a screen show, first make sure that your presentation pages are in the right sequence—use the Page Sorter to do this most conveniently—and then choose the View Screen Show Run command, click the Screen Show SmartIcon, or press Alt+F10.

When you choose View Screen Show Run, you see a basic, no-frills screen show that displays your pages in order, with no transition effects. Click the mouse to advance to the next page or press the PgDn or Enter key.

Freelance Graphics offers a number of ways you can customize a screen show. You can add transition effects, choose manual or automatic mode, and even draw on the screen during a show.

If you are more ambitious, you can create *branching* screen shows, which means that the viewer can click words or objects on the screen during a screen show to jump to a specific page, end the screen show, launch another application, or play a sound or other multimedia object (with the proper hardware installed).

This chapter covers all these topics.

Adding Transition Effects

The perceptions and expectations of audiences have been raised considerably by television and movies. Hollywood routinely deluges audiences with stunning special effects. Audiences accustomed to such cinematic fireworks are not likely to be excited by a series of static images displayed on the screen, one after the other. You need to add some sizzle just to get their attention.

Freelance contains 33 special effects that can pique interest in your screen shows. These transition effects vary the way in which images replace one another on screen. You can apply these effects on a page-by-page basis or choose the same effect for the entire presentation.

To assign transition effects, choose View Screen Show Edit Effects. In the Edit Screen Show dialog box, choose a page to which you want to assign the effect and then highlight the effect from the list (see fig. 20.1). To use a single effect for all pages in the presentation, mark the Apply Effect to All Pages check box.

The effects have more or less self-descriptive names. Checkerboard, for example, displays the next page one small square at a time in a checkerboard pattern until the full page is revealed. Leftside displays the page from the left side of the screen to the right. Blinds emulates the effect of opening horizontal venetian blinds to reveal the page.

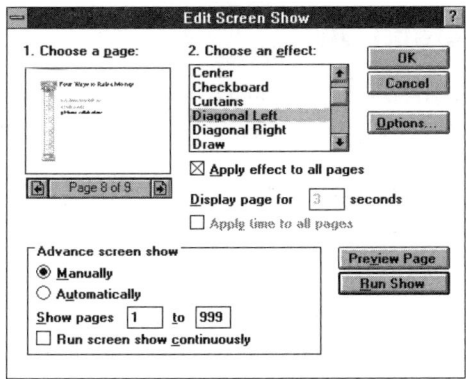

FIGURE 20.1. The Edit Screen Show dialog box.

Some of the effects are difficult to describe in words. But it's easy to test each effect. Highlight the effect you want and click the Preview Page button. Freelance displays the current page using the highlighted effect. Click once to return to the Edit Screen Show dialog box.

The following effects are worthy of special note:

- Curtains reveals the next page by opening a bright red, rialto-style curtain.
- Paint Brush displays a paint brush that strokes the image onto the page in several swipes.
- Shade reveals the page by closing and raising a blue curtain bedecked with an image of the moon and stars.
- Text Top, Text Bottom, Text Left, Text Right. These four effects add a bit of animation to your screen show. If you display a bulleted list with the Text Left effect, for example, the page moves into place from the left side of your screen: first the title, then the bulleted list. Movement on a slide helps keep an audience alert and attuned to your presentation.

The best way to get a feel for each effect is to create a simple presentation and test each effect. You soon find out which ones work best for you.

How many special effects should you use in a presentation? Use the same moderation in choosing transition effects as you do in choosing typefaces and colors. This moderation usually means choosing no more than a couple of effects for a single presentation. If you do choose several, try to use similar effects. If your presentation has several parts, you might choose Leftside for the first part, Rightside for the second part, switch back to Leftside for the third part, and so on. This pattern maintains a consistent look yet still adds variety to your screen show.

Controlling a Screen Show

Generally, you want to control the pace of a screen show yourself. As you talk, you can display the next image by clicking the mouse, pressing PgDn, or pressing Enter.

Choose View Screen Show Edit Effects and click the Manually radio button in the Advance Screen Show area of the Edit Screen Show dialog box. When you start the screen show, the first presentation page remains on screen until you press Enter or click the mouse.

At other times, you may want the images in your screen show to be displayed automatically, at fixed intervals, with each image remaining on the screen for the same amount of time. This type of automated display is ideal for an unattended computer. You can set up such a screen show at a trade show or in a retail store as a means of delivering information about your products or to drive home your marketing message.

To set up a self-running screen show, click the radio button labeled Automatically and type a value for the numbers of seconds each page is to remain on screen in the Display Page For box. When you run the screen show, Freelance displays your presentation pages one at a time at the specified time intervals.

If you want your screen show to be displayed repetitively, mark the Run Screen Show Continuously check box. When you play the screen show, Freelance runs it over and over until you press Esc. This method is the correct setup for a self-running demonstration.

A screen show is a flexible presentation medium. You can stop and start an automatic screen show, move forward or backward, or exit from a show altogether. Use the following keys:

- Press Spacebar to pause and resume a screen show.
- Click the left mouse button to move to the next page or press PgDn or Enter.
- Click the right mouse button or press PgUp or Backspace to go backward in a screen show.
- Press Esc to interrupt the display of a screen show and to display the List Pages dialog box.

You also can display a VCR-like control panel during a screen show that makes the control of a screen show even easier. This is really the easiest way to control a screen show. To set this up, click the Options button in the Edit Screen Show dialog box and mark the Display Screen Show Control Panel check box.

Drawing On-Screen

If you have ever scrawled on an overhead transparency during a presentation, you know that this spontaneous technique is a great way to draw the attention of the audience to the screen. You can circle a bar in a chart or emphasize an important word by underlining it.

Now you can do the same during a screen show (see fig. 20.2). Just hold down the left mouse button and drag the mouse on screen. You now can draw on the screen in freehand mode. If you want to erase what you have drawn, click the right mouse button to go back a page and then click the left mouse button to advance to the original page: Your marks are gone.

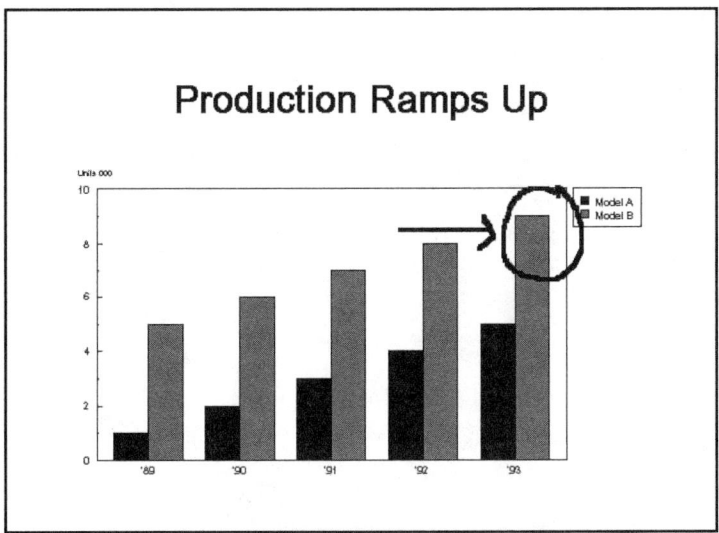

FIGURE 20.2. Drawing on-screen during a screen show brings an informal, interactive touch to your presentation.

You can change the color and width of the drawing line by clicking the Options button in the Edit Screen Show dialog box to display the Screen Show Options dialog box (fig. 20.3). Choose a new line color and width in the On Screen Drawing area.

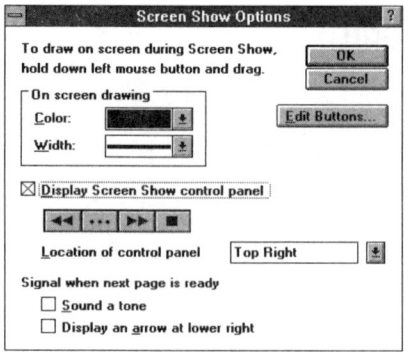

FIGURE 20.3. The Screen Show Options dialog box.

The Power of Screen Show Buttons

Freelance Graphics 2.0 introduces a new option that enables you to turn any object into a screen show button. Clicking a screen show button during a screen show can cause the screen show to:

- Jump to a designated page
- Play a multimedia object (sound or movie)
- Launch another application

The following sections examine each of these possibilities.

Creating an Interactive Screen Show

The capability to jump to another page during a screen show in response to a click on a designated object is a powerful feature that offers unlimited possibilities. You might use this capability, for example, to create an interactive screen show for a trade show or in a retail store.

By way of example, consider this scenario. You are the owner of a music store named Tom's MusicLand. To entice and inform walk-in customers, you devise a screen show to provide them with information about your products. This screen show is available on a computer in the front of your store. The following steps show you how to design the first couple of screens:

1. To get started, create a new presentation that uses the SmartMaster with Blank Background option.
2. Create the first screen, as shown in figure 20.4. Add the framed title and the list of product categories. Each product category (guitars, amplifiers, studio equipment, and keyboards) is a separate text block.

FIGURE 20.4. The first screen in the screen show.

3. Create the second screen, shown in figure 20.5. Choose Page New, type *Guitars* in the Page Name box, highlight the Blank Page layout, and click OK.
4. Add the text on the page as shown. Make each guitar name (Stratosphere, TrendSetter, and so on) a separate text block. The instructional sentences (Click a name to view product information) are set in light gray to set them off from the rest of the text on the screen.
5. Now you are ready to create the first jump. During the screen show, when a customer clicks Guitars, you want the screen show to display the screen that shows the list of guitars. Return to the first screen and click Guitars to select it.
6. Choose View Screen Show Create/Edit Button to display the dialog box shown in figure 20.6. Click the Jump to a Page radio button and then highlight Guitars in the list. The selected page appears in the box to the right, so you can see whether you selected the correct page.

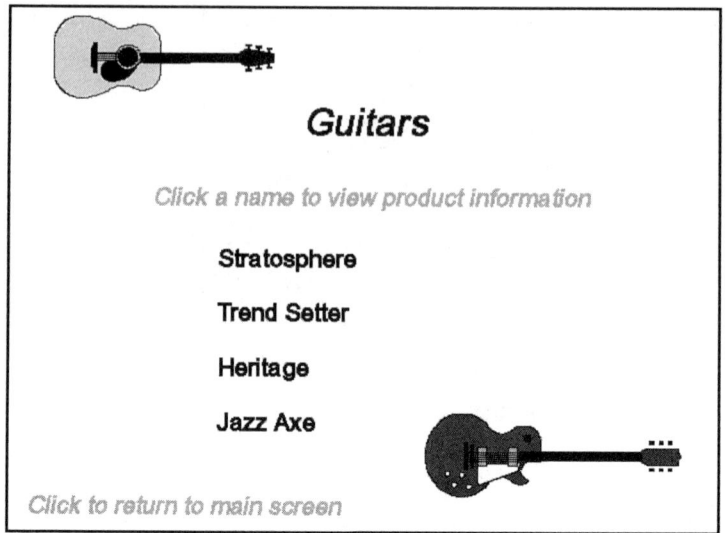

FIGURE 20.5. The second screen in the screen show.

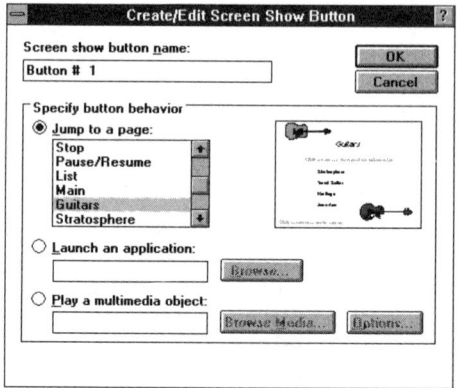

FIGURE 20.6. The main screen.

7. Click OK.
8. Return to the second page, select the text "Click to return to main screen," choose View Screen Show Create/Edit Button, click the Jump to a Page radio button, highlight Main in the list, and click OK.

9. Now test your work so far. Click the View Screen Show SmartIcon. When the first page appears, click Guitars. This selection should take you to the Guitars screen. Click Return to Main Screen to return to the entry screen.

To complete this screen show, use the same techniques to create whatever jumps you want. If you were creating a full-fledged, interactive screen show, you probably would set up a jump for each item in the Guitars list. During a screen show, for example, clicking Stratosphere jumps to a page containing information about that particular guitar, and so on for each guitar. You can use these basic techniques to create a screen show as complex as you want. Be sure that you add a button on each screen to enable a user to return to the main screen or to a previous screen.

To save time, you need only create a text button such as Click to return to the main screen once. You can copy this to any page in your presentation. The "jump to a page" information is copied with the text block.

Adding Multimedia Effects to a Screen Show

Computers have remained islands of silence in a sea of sounds. It's remarkable in a way that users have been content with the silence of computers for so long. This situation is changing fast, of course. Sound boards are readily available and relatively inexpensive. Multimedia is coming to your computer, ready or not.

Freelance Graphics offers a variety of multimedia capabilities. To tap Freelance's sound effects, you must have a sound board. You also must have installed the Multimedia Extensions to use sound and "movies." These are standard with Windows 3.1, but not Windows 3.0. If you have Windows 3.0, Freelance installs the necessary files for you during installation.

What multimedia capabilities do you get with Freelance?

- Two SmartMaster sets with Multimedia effects
- Lotus Sound
- Lotus Media Manager
- Lotus Annotator

Using the MultiMedia SmartMaster Sets

Freelance comes with two SmartMaster sets with built-in multimedia effects. These sets are MMGLOBE.MAS and MMLASER.MAS. Because these sets include sound effects, you need a sound board to use them effectively.

MMGLOBE.MAS features a three-dimensional spinning globe (a "movie") and an appropriately dramatic sound effect when you display the title page during a screen show. MMLASER.MAS features a scorching sound effect and a striking visual effect. Try these yourself for an introduction to multimedia screen show effects.

Creating a Screen Show Button

To play a sound or movie, you can create a screen show button and then associate a sound or movie file with the object. During a screen show, when you click the object, the sound or movie is played.

Try It: Add a Ringing Telephone to a Screen Show

Create a screen show that includes the symbol of a telephone. In these steps, you associate a sound file with the phone, so that when you click it during a screen show, the phone rings. This procedure requires a sound board. Follow these steps:

1. Start a blank presentation page and click the Symbol icon in the Toolbox.
2. Highlight the COMMUNIC.SYM category and then double-click the image of the telephone.
3. Select the telephone and choose View Screen Show Create/Edit Button.
4. Type *Telephone* in the Screen Show Button Name box.
5. Click the Play a Multimedia Object radio button.
6. Click the Browse Media button to open the Lotus Media Manager dialog box (see fig. 20.7).

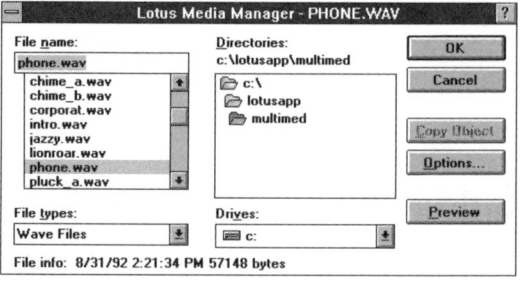

FIGURE 20.7. The Lotus Media Manager dialog box.

7. Click the File Types list box and choose Wave Files. This selection displays a list of sound files with the .WAV file name extension. You may have to change the Directory path to find any wave (sound) files. The wave files that come with Freelance are in C:\LOTUSAPP\MULTIMED directory (this directory may be in another drive on your computer).
8. Highlight PHONE.WAV.
9. Click the Preview button to test the sound. You see the PHONE.WAV dialog box, which has VCR-style controls. Double-click the ventilator (the thin white rectangle in the left corner) to close this dialog box. Click the question mark (?) in the right corner to view a help screen that explains these controls.
10. Click the Options button to open the Media Manager Options dialog box and then click the Play Once radio button. You also can choose to play the sound continuously or as many times as you specify when the object is clicked during a screen show.
11. Click OK as many times as necessary to return to the presentation page.
12. Click the Screen Show SmartIcon (the movie camera) to start the screen show. When you see the page with the telephone, click the telephone to make it ring. You can click it as often as you like.
13. Click away from the phone to advance to the next page or press Esc to exit the screen show.

Now, when you run the screen show, you can click the screen show button to play the sound file associated with it.

You can associate a sound with any object you can create or import: a chart, a table, a text block, a symbol, or any imported file such as a .PCX file.

Sound Effects: A Word of Caution

As desktop-publishing power came to the desktop, the business world witnessed an onslaught of unreadable documents created by overzealous users eager to cram as many typefaces into a document as possible. This "ransom-note" syndrome, as it came to be called, turned many a business report or newsletter into an amateurish hodge-podge of special type effects.

You can expect the same sort of excess as multimedia comes to the desktop. Soon you may hear the sound of train whistles, groans, tacky one-liners, flushing noises, and more wafting from the cubicles of corporate America.

When you add sound effects to a screen show, exercise some restraint. The first time you click the image of a ship on-screen and hear the blaring sound of a foghorn (SHIPHORN.WAV), your audience may be impressed. But, if you add too many clever sound effects to your screen show, your presentation loses some of its dignity and drifts into tackiness.

Adding Sound That Plays Automatically

You just learned the technique for creating a screen show button, which enables you to associate a sound to an object. As you learned, when you click the object during a screen show, the sound file (.WAV file) plays.

But this isn't the only way to create sound in a screen show. What if you want to insert a sound file that plays automatically during a screen show and not just in response to a mouse click?

This technique involves inserting an OLE object on a page. An OLE object—the acronym stands for Object Linking and Embedding—enables you to insert data created in another Windows program into Freelance Graphics. For example, you can insert a Lotus Sound object on a presentation page.

Try It: The Lion That Roared

This example explains how to set up a presentation page that plays a sound during a screen show automatically, not in response to a mouse click. This technique is good to use to add sound to an unattended screen show. Follow these steps:

1. Click the Symbol icon in the Toolbox, highlight the ANIMALS.SYM category, and double-click the image of the lion.
2. Choose Edit Insert Object.
3. Highlight Lotus Sound in the Edit Insert Object dialog box and then click OK (see fig. 20.8). This action opens the Lotus Sound control panel, which resembles the controls on a VCR.

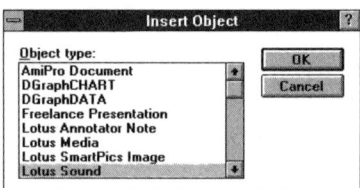

FIGURE 20.8. The Edit Insert Object dialog box.

4. To select a sound, choose File Read, change to the LOTUSAPP\MULTIMED directory, make sure that Wave File is the selected file type, and then highlight LIONROAR.WAV from the list of wave files.

Screen Shows **353**

5. Click OK.
6. To test the sound, click the Play button on the Control Panel.
7. Choose File Exit to return to the presentation page. Click the Yes button in response to the Save query.

    This response places the Lotus Sound Object on the page, in the form of an icon with a microphone. This icon is not visible during a screen show, unless you specify that it should be in the Play Options dialog box (see fig. 20.9).

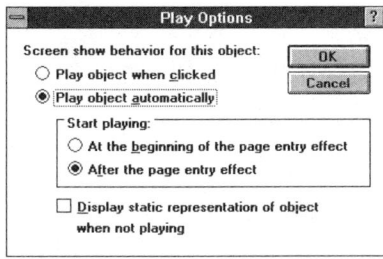

FIGURE 20.9. The Play Options dialog box.

8. Click the right mouse button over this icon and highlight Play Options.
9. Click the radio button Play Object Automatically and the button After the Page Entry Effect. Click OK.
10. Now click the Screen Show icon.

When the page with the lion is displayed, the lion roars. Note that you don't see the Microphone icon (although you can make this visible if you choose).

Launching Another Application from a Screen Show

You also can set up a screen show button to launch another application when you click it during a screen show. You can launch any application with .EXE, .COM, or .BAT file name extensions.

Suppose that you created a self-running demo for a technical trade show. The screen show presents highly technical information. To liven up the show, add the text "Play Solitaire" to a presentation page. Select this text block, choose View Screen Show Create/Edit Button, and then click the Launch an Application radio button. Click the Browse button, then, in the Find Application to Launch dialog box, change to the Windows directory, highlight SOL.EXE in the File Name list, and click OK (see fig. 20.10).

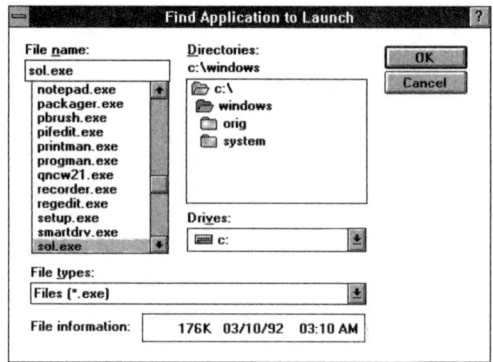

FIGURE 20.10. The Find Application to Launch dialog box.

Now run the screen show. When you see the text "Play Solitaire," click it. This click opens the Windows Solitaire game. Play it as long as you want. When you exit the game, you return to the screen show.

This capability opens up a number of interesting possibilites. Want to launch to 1-2-3 or Ami Pro during a screen show, work in those applications, and then return to the screen show? You can do it easily. Use your imagination to think up novel uses for this interesting capability.

Creating Build Slides

When your presentation consists of slides that are mostly bulleted lists, you are tempting the audience to tune you out and focus their attention on the bulleted list instead. In seconds, they can read the entire list and then let their attention wander.

You can get around this difficulty by creating build slides. *Build slides*, also known as *reveal slides*, present a sequence of points in a bullet chart one at a time, culminating in your complete message.

Besides adding a touch of suspense to your presentation, build slides focus your audience's attention on the topic at hand and prevent them from reading ahead.

Automatic Build Slides

Freelance Graphics can create a build slide sequence automatically. Here's how it works.

So you can see more clearly how this works, go to Page Sorter view. Select the page that contains the complete bulleted list and choose Page Create Build. Freelance displays a message informing you that the build sequence is complete. Click OK to see the pages it created. That's all there is to it. Figure 20.11 shows the last page in a build sequence.

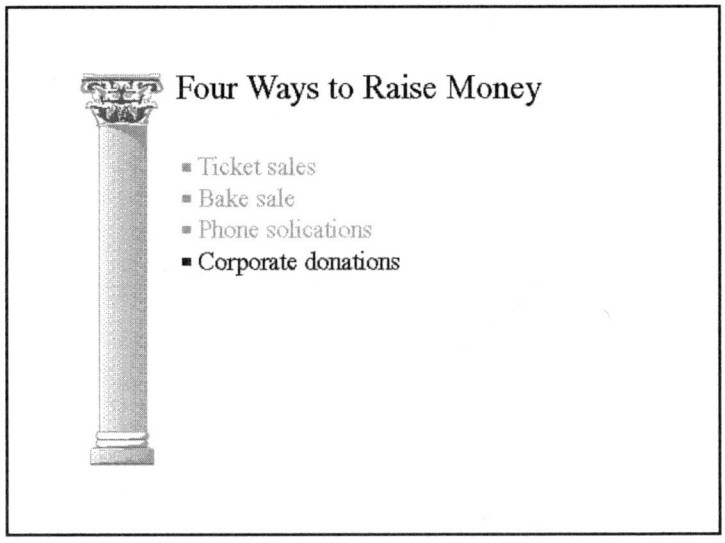

FIGURE 20.11. The last page in a build sequence.

If your original bulleted list contained four points, Freelance creates three additional pages. The second page contains the first two items, with the second point highlighted. The third page contains three items, with the third point highlighted. The other items in the list are dimmed.

When you play the screen show, Freelance displays each bulleted item one at a time, in sequence, building to the complete list.

Data Chart Build Slides

Build slides are not limited to bullet charts. You also can use this technique to make the display of data-driven graphs more interesting and focused. Suppose that you have a clustered bar chart that has three data sets, perhaps showing ticket sales for three plays for three years. Display the data for each play separately for a more dramatic effect (just the right touch for a theatrical company). This approach enables you to make points about each play separately. You can sum up your points by making general comments about sales for all three plays.

To create a build chart showing one data set at a time, first create the completed chart and then make two duplicate pages of it. In the first page, change the data values for the second and third data sets to 0; also delete the legend text (see fig. 20.12). For the second page, add the values and the legend for the second data set. Then, for the third page, add the values and the legend for the third data set. Use Chart Scale to set the Maximum value for the Y axis manually; otherwise, the chart is recomposed using a different scale each time. Make certain that you add actual zeros to the data sets you do not want to display rather than blanks. If you leave blanks, Freelance assumes you are working with one data set only and recomposes the chart accordingly.

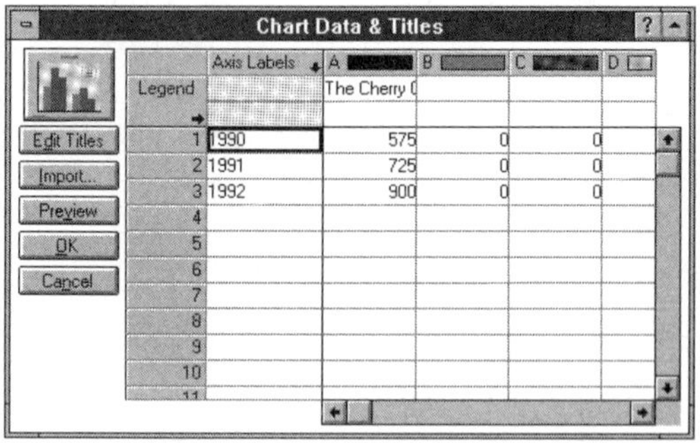

FIGURE 20.12. The Chart Data & Titles window showing the values for the first build chart.

Creating a Portable Screen Show

You can distribute a screen show on a single diskette.

You can export a screen show that you can run from the DOS command line by using a single command, even if the computer does not have Freelance Graphics or Windows. You also can use the screen shows you export in Freelance Graphics for DOS 3.0 and higher, as well as with Show Partner and Show Partner F/X from Brightbill-Roberts and Company Ltd.

The export feature also enables you to create a portable screen show that you can distribute on a single diskette to anyone who has a computer, regardless of whether they have Freelance Graphics. Consider the possibilities:

- Create a promotional screen show for your business that you can duplicate and distribute to clients or potential clients.
- Produce a training video that your employees can view at their leisure.
- Create a screen show of a presentation to distribute to people who missed your presentation.
- Give everyone in your audience a disk after your presentation so that they can review it at their leisure. (But handouts might be better for this purpose, as explained in Chapter 19, "Printing a Presentation.")

The possibilities abound. No doubt you can think of novel uses for your own portable screen show.

You can export a screen show that you can run from the DOS command line on your computer or on anybody's computer.

To create a portable, self-contained screen show on a single floppy, choose View Screen Show and then choose Prepare Standalone. You see the dialog box in figure 20.13. Choose Screen Show (SHW) from the File type list box. Unless you type a different name in the File Name box, the screen show receives the name of your presentation by default. Type the path and file name for your screen show (for example, *a:\chicago*) in the File Name box.

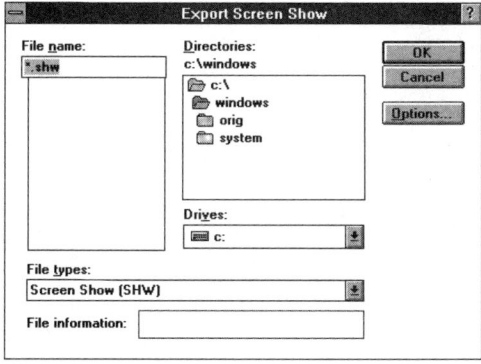

FIGURE 20.13. The Export Screen Show dialog box.

To set timing options or to specify a graphics adapter (VGA or EGA), click the Options button. You see the dialog box in figure 20.14. Choose the graphics adapter for the computer on which the screen show will be viewed. Note that you can display an EGA screen show on a VGA computer, but not the other way around.

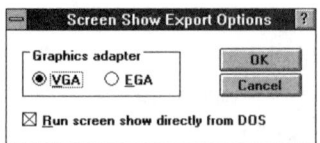

FIGURE 20.14. The Screen Show Export Options dialog box.

Finally, mark the check box Run Screen Show Directly from DOS. This choice copies the run-time file, SHOW.EXE, to the floppy to which you are saving the screen file.

When you click OK, Freelance Graphics creates a file with a .SHW extension, as well as a separate file for each presentation page, using the extension .GX2. The first part of the file name is based on the show file name. If you specify the name REPORT.SHW, the .GX2 files are named REPORT1.GX2, REPORT2.GX2, and so on.

After you export the .GX2 files to create your portable screen show, you run it from the DOS command line with the SHOW.EXE command. Just type *show filename* to run the show, where *filename* is the name of the .SHW file.

If your screen show has special effects, Freelance Graphics for Windows maps these effects to similar special effects available in Freelance Graphics for DOS.

Wrapping Up

In this chapter, you learned how to create basic screen shows, add sound to screen shows, create branching screen shows, and create build slides automatically.

In the next chapter, you learn how to go about turning your presentation pages into 35mm slides.

21

Creating 35mm Slides

Presenters who want the best in color contrast, saturation, and image clarity have always made 35mm slides their first choice. Although new technologies are beginning to challenge slides for image clarity, slides are still the staple of many a corporate presentation. For certain SmartMaster sets, especially those with graduated fills, 35mm slides are the ideal output medium. Many Freelance SmartMaster sets—particularly those with white or yellow text on deep blue backgrounds—were designed with 35mm slides in mind.

Freelance Graphics includes a printer driver and utility software that enable you to prepare and send presentation files directly to an Autographix service center via modem or disk for overnight delivery of 35mm slides. Autographix also can create transparencies, color prints, or laser output from your presentation files.

Although Freelance Graphics conveniently includes the Autographix driver, other slide services abound—both national and local—who are happy to give you their own file preparation and transmission software. You may prefer to shop around.

Freelance also comes with a driver for creating Stingray SCODL slide files, from which you can create high-quality slides on slide-making equipment such as a matrix camera or other film recorder. If you don't own your own slide-making equipment, many services accept SCODL files.

The Process

Preparing and sending your .PRE files to Autographix is a somewhat involved process, but after you have it down, it's automatic. The process, however, requires considerable preparation. Here are the major steps:

- Install and set up the Autographix slide driver.

In this chapter, you learn how to:

- *Install and set up the Autographix driver*
- *Prepare Freelance graphics for slide output*
- *Prepare and send the files to Autographix via modem or disk*

- Prepare your .PRE files for slide processing.
- Create the output files.
- Create an Autographix work order and transmit your files by modem or by disk.

Tips for Using a Slide Service

Whether you use Autographix or another slide service, it's wise to test a few slides before you send off a large presentation to be processed. Many slide services offer a free trial. You may find that some service bureaus accept .PRE files, but others accept other formats such as PostScript files. Prepare a small sample presentation to test for color quality. Freelance includes a presentation named 256COLOR.PRE that displays all 256 colors in the color library. You can find it in the MASTERS subdirectory. Create a slide file from this presentation for an excellent test of color fidelity. Results can vary widely from one vendor to another. It's also a good idea to test SmartMasters with graduated fills because these tend to be troublesome to render accurately.

Installing and Setting Up the Autographix Files

If you opted to install the slide service option when you installed Freelance Graphics, the correct files are already installed. If you skipped this option, you must install them now. Click the Freelance Install icon and use the Install with Options choice to install the Autographix Slide Service.

Adding Autographix as a Printer Choice

After the Autographix files are installed, you must add the Autographix driver as a printer choice. The following procedure is for Windows 3.1. If you are using Windows 3.0, the procedure and screens you see are somewhat different. First close Freelance Graphics and then complete the following steps:

1. Double-click the Control Panel icon and then double-click the Printers icon.
2. Click the Add>> button in the Printers dialog box.
3. Highlight Install Unlisted or Updated Printer under List of Printers. Then click the Install button.

4. Type your windows path (for example, C:\WINDOWS) in the Install Driver dialog box. Click OK.
5. Click Autographix 4.1 in the Add Unlisted or Updated Printer dialog box and then click OK.
6. If at this point the program displays the Install Driver dialog box, insert the requested Microsoft Windows 3.1 disk in the A drive, change the path to A:\, and click OK.

If you have a newer PostScript driver installed, Windows asks whether you want to overwrite it. Click No. You should now see Autographix 4.1 in the dialog box in the Installed Printers area (see fig. 21.1).

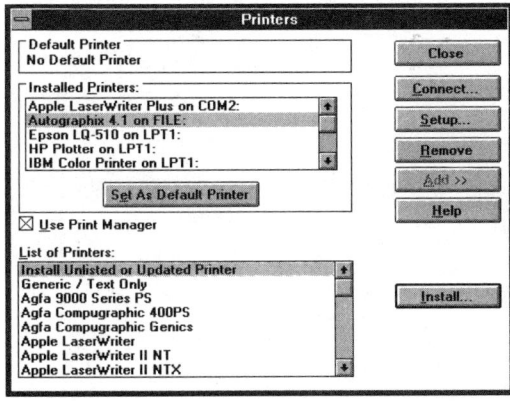

FIGURE 21.1. The Printers dialog box after you have installed the Autographix driver successfully.

Setting Up the Autographix Driver

The next procedure is to select the correct options for the Autographix driver. Follow these steps:

1. From the Printers dialog box (with Autographix highlighted), click Connect and highlight FILE: in the Ports list box. Then click OK.
2. Click the Setup button.
3. Complete the Autographix 4.1 on FILE dialog box (see fig. 21.2). Two choices are especially important. For Paper size, choose Note 8.5 x 11 In. For Orientation, choose Landscape.

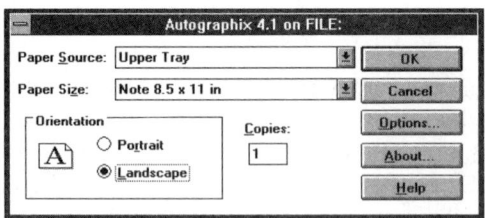

FIGURE 21.2. The Autographix 4.1 on FILE: dialog box.

4. Click the Options button and, in the resulting dialog box, click the Advanced button.
5. For Send to Printer As, choose Bitmap (Type 3).
6. Under Graphics, change Halftone Frequency to 60 and Halftone Angle to 45. Check your screen against figure 21.3.

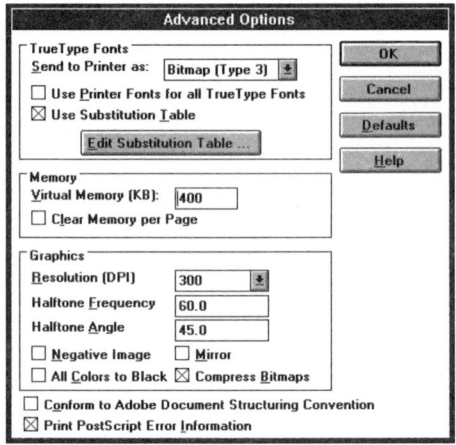

FIGURE 21.3. The Advanced Options dialog box showing the proper settings for slide output.

7. Click OK.
8. Click OK until you return to the Printers dialog box and then click Close.

If you plan to use True Type fonts, click the Edit Substitution Table button in the Advanced Options dialog box. In the resulting dialog box, shown in figure 21.4, highlight the name of a True Type font in the For True Type Font list and then highlight Download as Soft Font in the Use Printer Font list. Repeat this process for every True Type font you plan to use.

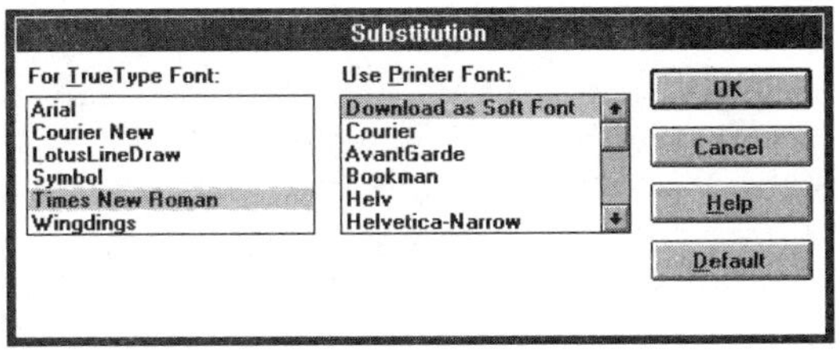

FIGURE 21.4. The Substitution dialog box.

Preparing Freelance for Slide Output

When you are preparing a Freelance presentation for slide output, you must make sure that the page has the proper dimensions. This precaution is necessary because a 35mm slide has a different aspect ratio (ratio of width to height) than an 8.5 x 11 page, the page size that most Freelance screens use. To match the 3:2 aspect ratio of slides, a Freelance page needs to be about 7.34 x 11 inches.

To automatically adjust your presentation pages for the dimensions of 35mm slides, open the presentation, choose File Printer Setup, and then mark the Set Margins for Slides check box. When you click OK and return to the presentation page, you see a dotted line that indicates the dimensions of a 35mm slide (regardless of the current output device). This line enables you to see the dimensions of a 35mm slide as you work.

You now should check all the pages of your presentation to make sure that everything fits within these margins, without overlapping graphic elements. To accommodate the new margins, Freelance actually changes the size of text and objects in your presentation. You may want to make a few adjustments too.

To remove the slide margins setting, choose File Printer Setup again, and click the Set Margins for Slides check box to remove the mark. Freelance restores your previous margins.

Creating Slide Files

After you have set up the Autographix printer options correctly, you are ready to turn your presentation (.PRE) file into PostScript print files. These files are the ones you send to an Autographix processing center to be processed as 35mm slides. Follow these steps:

1. Start Freelance Graphics and then choose File Printer Setup.
2. Click the check box labeled Set Margins for Slides. This option adjusts the aspect ratio and margins for 35mm slide frames. Note that you also can mark this check box with the File Page Setup command.
3. Choose one of the following drivers: PostScript Printer on FILE: (for Windows 3.0) or Autographix 4.1 on FILE: (for Windows 3.1). Then click OK.
4. Choose File Print to open the Print File dialog box.
5. Specify the range of pages you want to print (From Page n to n).
6. In the Format area, click the Full Page radio button.
7. Deselect the Adjust Color Library for Color Printing check box. Although the deselected setting generally is recommended, with some service bureaus you may discover that selecting this check box yields the best results. Test the same slides with this option on and off.
8. Click Print to display the Print to File dialog box.
9. Type the path and name of the file you want to create, making sure to add the extension .CPS.
10. Click OK.

You see a message indicating that your files are being printed. When the process is complete, the Windows Program Manager may be displayed. To return to Freelance Graphics, press Ctrl+Esc and double-click Freelance Graphics from the Task List.

Creating a Work Order

The next step is to use the ToAGX-Windows communications utility to create a work order so that you can send the files to an Autographix service center. The work order contains a variety of billing and shipping information as well as the PostScript print files.

Double-click the Autographix Slide Service icon in the Lotus Applications Program Group or double-click any PostScript print file in the Windows File Manager that you want to send to an Autographix center (these files have the extension .CPS). This action opens the ToAGX-Windows dialog box (see fig. 21.5).

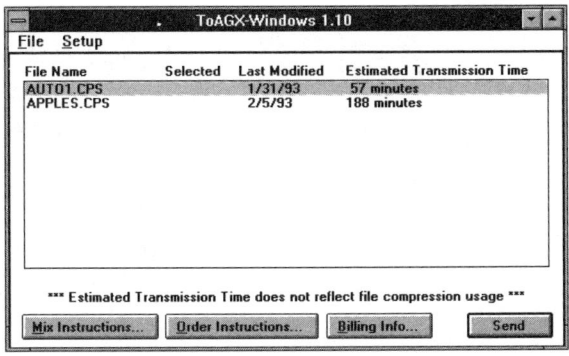

FIGURE 21.5. The ToAGX Windows 1.10 dialog box.

Check the defaults listed under the File menu and change them if necessary. You can change the default directory, change the file type (the default should be *.CPS), and specify whether file compression is to be used. If you are sending the files via modem, make sure to specify the Use Compression option. Compression makes the slide files smaller, which reduces the transmission time and saves you money.

Choose Setup Communications Setup to configure your modem and communication settings. After you have these set up properly, you do not have to change them again. If an entry for Autographix does not appear on the list, click the Add button. In the Add Entry dialog box, enter Autographix as the Destination and type the Autographix modem number in the Phone Number box. If you don't know this number, call the Autographix center nearest you. Click OK to return to the Communications Setup dialog box. Then click OK once more to return to the ToAGX-Windows dialog box.

Mix Instructions

If you have created the output file properly (as described in "Creating Slide Files"), you should see a file with the extension .CPS beneath the File Name heading.

The next step is to specify how many copies of each image you want and in what format (that is, slides, transparencies, prints, or laser printouts).

Click the Mix Instructions button and—in the resulting dialog box—specify how many slides, transparencies, prints, or lasers you want Autographix to create (see fig. 21.6). Click OK to accept your entries.

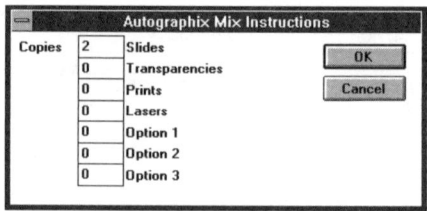

FIGURE 21.6. The Autographix Mix Instructions dialog box.

Order Instructions

The next step is to specify ordering instructions. Click the Order Instructions button. This action opens the Autographix Order Instructions dialog box, where you indicate how you are sending the slide files and how you want them returned (see fig. 21.7). You need to change these settings only once for each order.

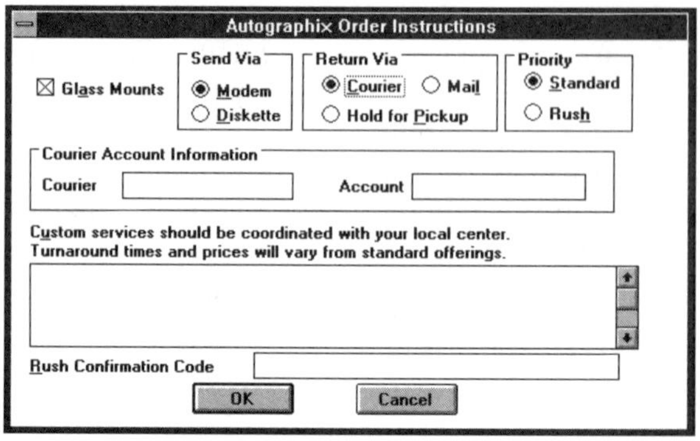

FIGURE 21.7. The Autographix Order Instructions dialog box.

Mark the Glass Mounts check box if you want the highest quality frame for your slides. If you are giving your presentation many times, glass mounts protect your slides from dirty fingers and from warping as well.

Billing Info

You also must fill out a screen of billing information. Click the Billing Information button and complete the Billing Information dialog box.

Sending the Files to Autographix

After you have completed all the dialog boxes, click the Send button. The program now compresses your files and, if you selected the modem option, transmits the files to Autographix. If you have a 9600-baud modem, check with your local bureau to see whether you can send your files at this baud rate; it reduces your long-distance costs considerably. To set up for 9600-baud transmission, click the Set Special button in the Communications Setup dialog box.

If you are in no rush, you also can copy the order file to a disk and send it to the Autographix Overnight Slide Center nearest you.

Wrapping Up

In this chapter, you learned how to turn your presentation pages into 35mm slides.

This chapter brings Part 6 to a close. In Part 7, you learn how to manage your presentations, how to use SmartIcons, and how to customize Freelance Graphics to suit your working style.

Part 7
Presentation Management Tools

Freelance Graphics offers a variety of tools geared to managing your entire presentation, from outline to printed output. In this part, you find out how to automate tasks with SmartIcons and even create customized SmartIcon palettes. This section also discusses how to customize Freelance to suit your working style.

This section includes:

Chapter 22. Managing Presentations

Chapter 23. Using SmartIcons

Chapter 24. Customizing Freelance Graphics

22

Managing Presentations

A presentation is not a disjointed collection of individual pages, but a unified entity that must work together as a whole. Some graphics packages force you to keep each page of your presentation in a separate file. When the time comes to assemble the entire presentation, locating and keeping track of the files you need can be a real nightmare.

Freelance Graphics solves this problem by keeping all the pages of your presentation in a single file. This feature means that you don't squander precious time saving individual pages or rummaging through your hard disk to find the pages of your presentation. You can display and edit any page in your presentation with a couple of mouse clicks.

As you build a presentation, sometimes you need to focus your attention on a single page. At other times, you want to make changes that apply to your entire presentation, such as changing the color scheme, choosing a new SmartMaster set, or adding a logo that you want to appear on every page.

In this chapter, you learn how to:

- *Use the three primary views of Freelance Graphics to create and organize your presentation*
- *Use the View menu*
- *Switch between Current Page view, Outliner view, and Page Sorter view*
- *Add speaker notes to your presentation*
- *Work with two or more presentations*

Views You Can Use

To accommodate these diverse needs, Freelance Graphics has three primary working views, each designed to serve a different purpose. These views are Current Page view, Outliner view, and Page Sorter view. Each of the three views of Freelance Graphics is appropriate for different situations. The view you choose to work in depends on the work you plan to do. Depending on the job to be done and your working style, you may switch frequently between these in the course of creating a single presentation.

The Three Primary Views

The second group of commands (Current Page, Page Sorter, and Outliner) in the View menu correspond to the three icons along the right side of the Freelance Graphics window (see fig. 22.1). Clicking one of these icons to switch to another view is faster than choosing a menu command. These commands are covered in individual sections of this chapter.

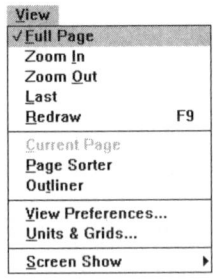

FIGURE 22.1. The View menu.

Changing the View of the Current Page

Several commands change the view of the current page, as follows:

- View Full Page is the normal working view of a single page in Freelance Graphics. This view displays the entire page you are working on. If you have zoomed in on a portion of a page, Full Page restores the view of the entire page.
- View Zoom In and View Zoom Out move in and out on the current page by fixed amounts. In general, it is easier to use the Zoom SmartIcon (the magnifying glass) to look at a section of a single page in greater detail. Chapter 12, "Drawing Objects," contains more detailed information about zooming.
- View Last returns you to the preceding view of the current page. This capability is useful when you are working on a diagram. You might zoom in

on a page to work on a detail of a diagram, for example, choose Full Page to see how the entire diagram looks, and then choose View Last to return to the enlarged view to continue working on the detail.

- View Redraw is useful when you want to clean up a page that contains complex graphics you have been editing. This command redraws the page, restores all objects completely, and removes any clutter that may remain from your editing activities. If you are editing a page that contains a lot of text and graphics, for example, you can press Esc to cause Freelance Graphics to stop redrawing the page. If you want to refresh the screen, choose View Redraw. This technique also can work well in the Page Sorter view, if your presentation has many pages. When you press Esc, Freelance Graphics stops drawing the content of pages but displays the page border and the page title.

Current Page View

Current Page View is the primary working view of Freelance Graphics (see fig. 22.2). When you want to craft an individual page, choose this view. Here, you roll up your sleeves and work on individual pages, creating the bullet charts, graphs, and diagrams that make up your presentation. Note that this is the only view that gives you access to the Toolbox, which you can use to create text charts, data-driven graphs, or free-form diagrams on a single page.

Click the Current Page icon on the right border to move to Current Page view.

Page Sorter View

When graphic artists work with color slides, they often lay out their work on a light table, which enables them not only to examine individual slides but to rearrange the slides as well.

Page Sorter view is Freelance Graphics's version of the artist's light table (see fig. 22.3). In this view, you get the big picture, so you can take it all in from a high level. You can change the order of pages in Page Sorter view as easily as the artist shuffles slides on a light table.

Although you don't have access to the Toolbox in Page Sorter view, you do have full use of the menu. You can add, move, copy, or delete selected pages, switch to a new SmartMaster set or palette, or choose new page layouts for selected pages. Click the scroll bar to view additional pages. For example, you can switch SmartMaster sets or palettes in Page Sorter view and see the effect on your entire presentation at the same time.

Click the Page Sorter icon to move to Page Sorter view.

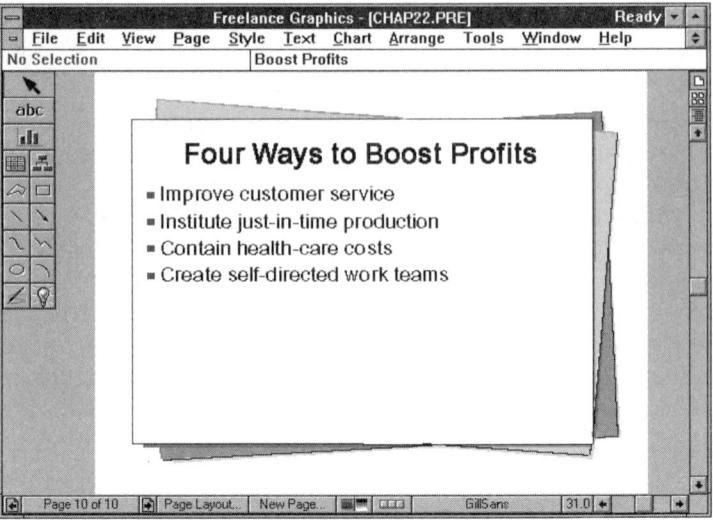

FIGURE 22.2. Current Page View is the primary working view of Freelance Graphics.

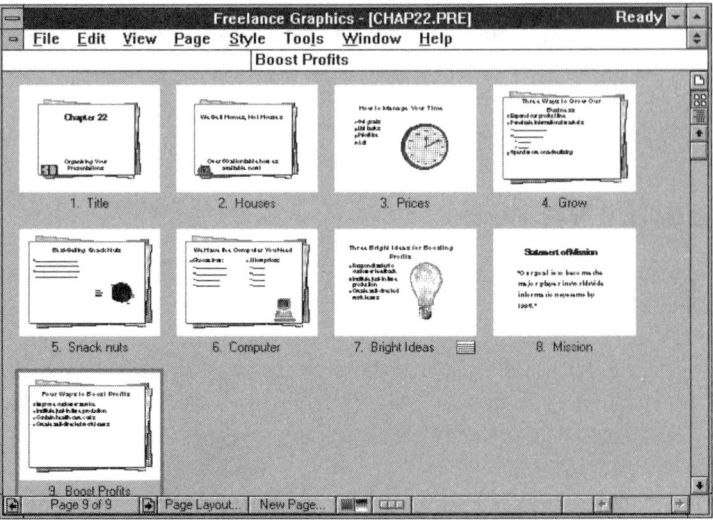

FIGURE 22.3. Page Sorter view.

But, generally, you should find the Page Sorter most useful for moving pages and for getting a quick glance of the structure of your presentation.

If you are working with more than one presentation, you can copy pages from one presentation to another in Page Sorter view. See the "Working with Several Presentations at the Same Time" section in this chapter for details.

Try It: Move a Page in Page Sorter View

Try moving a page in Page Sorter view by doing the following:

1. Click the page (or pages) you want to move. There are several ways to select multiple pages. Click the first page you want to select with the left mouse button and then press Shift as you click to select additional pages. You also can select multiple pages by clicking pages with the right mouse button. A third method is to drag a box around the pages you want to select. Click in the gray area (if you click on a page, you move it) and drag a selection box around the pages to be selected.
2. Drag the page (or pages) to a new location in the Page Sorter. A vertical bar shows you where the selection is going when you release the mouse button.
3. Release the left mouse button.

Outliner View

When you want a text-only view of your presentation, choose the Outliner view (click the yellow icon on the right border of the window). Here you can organize your thoughts, create bullet charts automatically, or change the order of pages. You also can collapse and expand the outline.

Click the Outliner icon to move to Outliner view.

Like Page Sorter view, Outliner view is also a high-level view of your presentation but with the emphasis on text (see fig. 22.4). This view shows you many pages of your presentation in a single view, but in a text-only format. You can use the Outliner to get a sense of the flow and continuity of your ideas, as reflected in your text. In Current Page view, you can read the text of a single bullet chart. But with the Outliner, you can read the text for several bullet charts at the same time and get more of a sense of context. Also, you easily can check the transitions from page to page, something you cannot do in Current Page view.

You can add or edit text in the Outliner. The text you add is reflected automatically on the actual presentation page. The reverse is true as well; that is, text you add in Current Page view is reflected in the Outliner view.

If you think in words more readily than in images, you may prefer to draft your presentation by using the Outliner. You can type your thoughts into the Outliner not only as a way of getting your ideas on the page, but as a way of generating perfectly formatted bullet charts in the process. Every point and subpoint you type in the Outliner view becomes part of a bullet chart (Freelance Graphics uses the 1-Column Bullets page layout automatically). Because most presentations contain more bullet charts than any other type of page, you may find that you can create most of your presentation in the Outliner view.

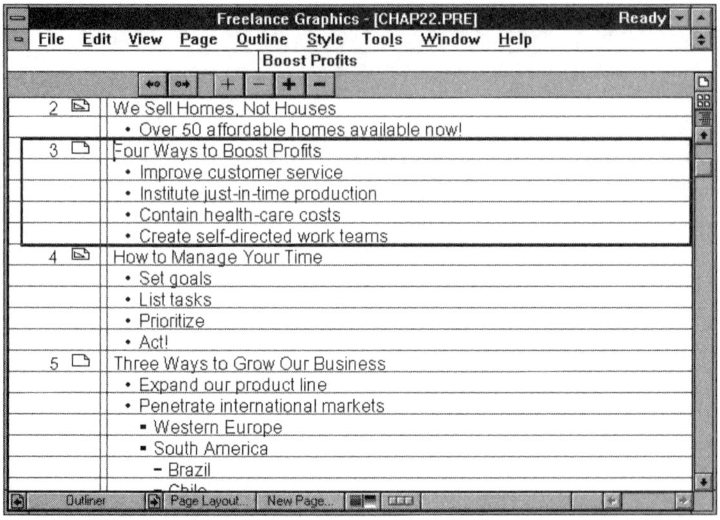

FIGURE 22.4. Outliner view.

When you need to add a page with a graph or an illustration, you can type the page title in the Outliner to serve as a placeholder page. If you want to see how an individual bullet chart looks in its final form, Current Page view is just a click away. If you add another bullet point in Current Page view, you see it when you return to Outliner view.

Refer to Chapter 4, "Using the Outliner," for a complete treatment of the Outliner.

View Preferences

View Preferences opens a dialog box in which you can specify options for changing the display of the screen, such as the size of the cursor and whether a drawing or text ruler is displayed, and for showing margins or printable area. Read Chapter 24, "Customizing Freelance Graphics," for more information.

Units & Grids

The Units & Grids command enables you to set up a grid for drawing diagrams and includes a setting that causes objects to snap into place on the grid. For more information on drawing with a grid, refer to Chapter 12, "Drawing Objects."

Screen Show View

The last command on the View Menu, Screen Show, displays an on-screen preview of all your presentation pages. You can use Screen Show to deliver a presentation or simply to check the flow of your presentation as you create it. For complete information on screen shows, read Chapter 20, "Screen Shows."

Moving from View to View

As you work in the various views of Freelance Graphics, you can work more efficiently if you can get quickly to the view you want.

As you have seen, the three icons along the right border of the window take you immediately to Current Page view, Page Sorter view, and Outliner view.

Changing the Look

As you know by now, Freelance Graphics uses a set of *templates*, called *SmartMaster sets*, to give your presentation a consistent, professional look. Each SmartMaster set contains detailed design information about typefaces, colors, and page layouts. In addition, each SmartMaster set has two palettes, one color and one black-and-white. You can change to a new SmartMaster set in any of the three views by using the command Style Choose SmartMaster Set.

The SmartMaster sets that come with Freelance Graphics have 11 page layouts, and each page layout has the same basic structure. Every Bulleted List page layout, for example, contains two text blocks: one for the page title and one for the list of bulleted items. Regardless of which SmartMaster set you choose, the structure for the Bulleted List page layout remains the same.

This consistent structure explains why you can choose an entirely new look for your presentation at the last minute, without worrying about losing content or, worse, having to spend a lot of time redesigning your page layouts. When you choose a new SmartMaster set, Freelance Graphics substitutes the new templates for the existing ones but does not alter the content of your presentation.

This feature enables you to experiment with the look of your presentation until you find the one you like best before, while, or after you create your presentation.

Adding Speaker Notes

As you create a presentation, you simultaneously can write your script. The speaker notes feature gives you an easy way to annotate each presentation page with your thoughts. Later, you can print your notes and take them with you to the podium.

To add a speaker note to a page, choose Page Speaker Notes or click the Speaker Notes SmartIcon. This action opens the Speaker Notes dialog box, which looks like a 3 x 5 index card (see fig. 22.5). Just type your notes here. As you type, words wrap automatically. To force a line break and display a new bullet, press Enter. To begin a new line without adding a new bullet, press Ctrl+Enter. Click the Next or Previous buttons (or press the PgDn and PgUp keys) to cycle through all the speaker notes in your presentation.

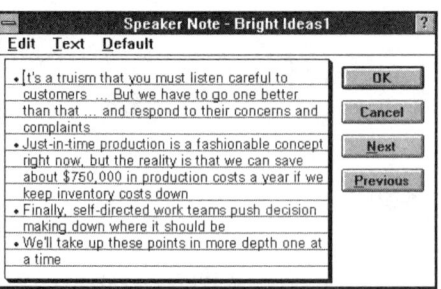

FIGURE 22.5. The Speaker Notes dialog box.

To change the typeface, bullet marker, or text size of your speaker notes, choose Text from the menu in the Speaker Notes dialog box. If you don't want bullets to appear in the card, for example, choose Text Bullet and then choose None. If you want to fit more text on a speaker note card, choose Text Size and choose a smaller point size. When you change the font, bullet, or size, you affect the current speaker note card only. To change the default Text settings for all the speaker notes in your presentation (except those that you have customized individually with the Text commands), choose Default Face, Default Bullet, or Default Size.

When you click OK in the Speaker Notes dialog box, Freelance adds an index-card icon to the left of your presentation page to indicate that this page has a speaker note attached. You'll see this icon in Current Page view and Page Sorter view (but not in Outliner view). Double-click the icon to open the Speaker Notes dialog box.

To print speaker notes, choose File Print and then click the Speaker notes button. Freelance prints the presentation page at the top of the page and your speaker notes at the bottom. You can use these pages as notes when you deliver your presentation.

Working with Several Presentations at the Same Time

You already have seen how valuable it is to have all the pages of your presentation in a single file; this feature enables you to work on your presentation as a whole. Just as valuable is the capability to have two or more presentations open at the same time on your desktop.

You can have as many open presentations as you want in Freelance Graphics. Realistically, though, two or three open at the same time is sufficient. More than that and you run the risk of confusion.

Probably the number one reason for having two or more presentations open at the same time is so that you can copy pages from one presentation to another. If you are starting work on a new presentation, you can copy pages from an earlier presentation (the next section shows you how). The capability to have several open presentations at the same time is also great for work groups—you easily can share presentations with your co-workers.

Try It: Copy Pages from One Presentation to Another

Try copying selected pages from one presentation to another by doing the following:

1. Open the presentation you are working on (call this the *target* presentation) and another from which you want to copy pages (the *source* presentation).
2. Display both presentations in Page Sorter view.
3. Select the pages you want to copy from the source presentation. After you select the first page, click the right mouse button to select additional pages.
4. Choose Edit Copy (or click the Edit Copy SmartIcon).

5. Move to the target presentation and select a page. The selected pages are copied after this page.
6. Choose Edit Paste.

Note that the new page assumes the attributes of the SmartMaster set in the target presentation. You have copied the content of the source presentation only; the SmartMaster page layouts of the target presentation supply the format.

Activating a Presentation

When you have more than one presentation open at the same time, you should be familiar with a few standard Windows techniques to manage your work.

No matter how many presentations you have open at a single time, only one presentation can be active. The title bar and borders of the active presentation are in color. You can activate a presentation in the following ways:

- Click anywhere within a visible presentation.
- Press Ctrl+F6 to activate the next open window. You can cycle through all open presentations with this keyboard shortcut.
- Click the name of a presentation in the Windows menu.

Rearranging Windows

You can change the size, position, and arrangement of windows in various ways to help you manage your desktop when you have several presentations open at the same time. Learning the simple techniques in the following sections will make you more productive and make you feel in control of your desktop.

Size a Window

Whether you have one or several windows open at the same time, you can size the presentation window or the Freelance Graphics window. The Freelance Graphics window contains the Freelance Graphics title bar, the menu, the border and its icons, and the SmartIcon palette. A presentation window falls within the Freelance Graphics window.

You can size any window by clicking the border or corner of the window and dragging. As you drag, the pointer turns into a double-arrow shape and the window changes its size and dimension horizontally or vertically, depending on how you drag. Release the mouse button when the window looks the way you want.

Move a Window

To move a window, just drag the title bar (or choose Move from the Control menu and then position the four-headed arrow over the title bar and drag—a slower method). Note that you cannot move a maximized window. Because a maximized window takes up the entire screen, you have no place to move it to.

Maximize a Window

Suppose that you have sized several open presentations on your desktop and now want to work on a single presentation in a size that occupies as much of your screen as possible. Click the Maximize button to fill a presentation window to its largest possible size. You also can maximize a window either by double-clicking its title bar or by choosing Maximize from the Control menu (see fig. 22.6).

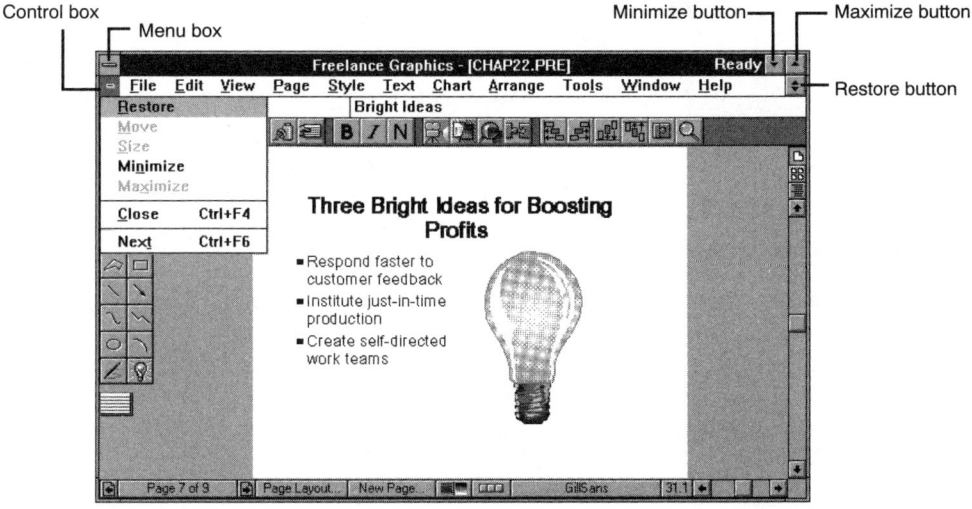

FIGURE 22.6. A title window with the Maximize, Minimize, and Restore buttons and the Control and Menu boxes labeled.

Restore a Window to Its Previous Size

Now suppose that you want to view a presentation just as it was before you maximized or minimized it. Click the Restore button or choose Restore from the

Control menu. If the window is currently maximized, double-click the Title bar. If the window is currently reduced to an icon, double-click the icon to restore it to it previous size.

Turn a Presentation Window into an Icon

You can turn a presentation into a small icon that is placed in the bottom left portion of the Freelance Graphics window. This technique is useful if you have several open presentations and want to clear the screen of clutter. To turn a presentation window into an icon, click the Minimize button in the top right corner of the window or choose Minimize from the Control menu. Double-click a presentation icon to restore it to its previous size.

Close a Window

To close a window, double-click the Control menu box (this does not work if the window is maximized), choose Close from the Control menu, or press Ctrl+F4. You are prompted to save the presentation if necessary.

Tile or Cascade?

The Windows menu offers two choices to automatically display several presentations at the same time: Windows Tile and Windows Cascade. These choices are useful if you want to display your open presentations in an orderly manner, with each presentation displayed at the same size.

Windows Tile fills the screen with all the open presentations in a tiled pattern (see fig. 22.7).

Windows Cascade overlaps and offsets each presentation from the succeeding one, much like a stack of cards spread out on a table (see fig. 22.8).

Managing Presentations

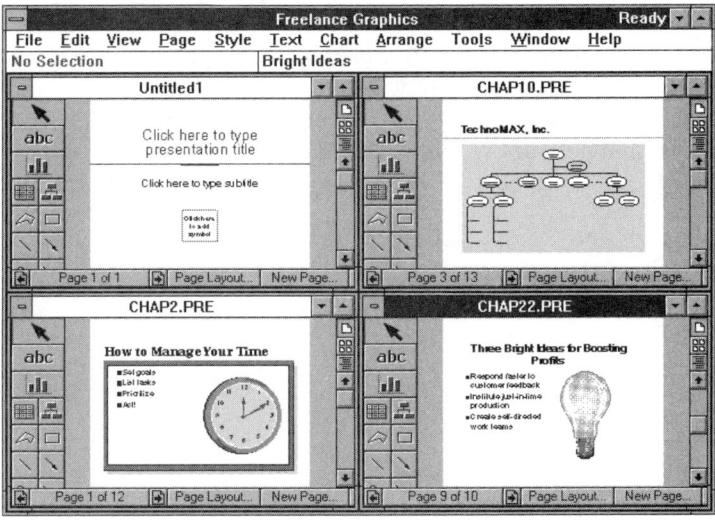

FIGURE 22.7. Open Presentations arranged with Windows Tile.

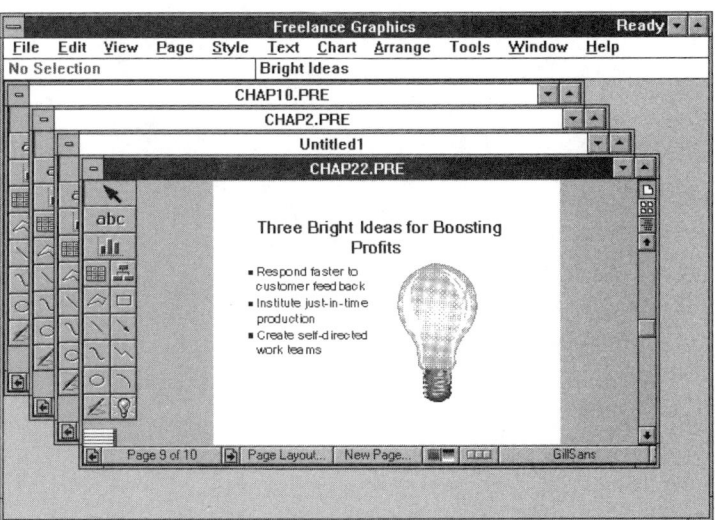

FIGURE 22.8. Open presentations arranged with Window Cascade.

Wrapping Up

In this chapter, you learned how to manage your presentations more effectively. You now should be familiar with the various views of Freelance Graphics, know how to add speaker notes to a presentation page, and feel comfortable working with several open presentations.

The next chapter focuses on SmartIcons, which are one of the greatest productivity enhancers in Freelance Graphics.

23

Using SmartIcons

SmartIcons—the ribbon of icons across the top of your screen—give you single-click access to more than 100 Freelance Graphics commands and functions.

After you click a SmartIcon and see a command instantly executed, you become hooked. Consider a few examples. Instead of choosing the lengthy command Arrange Flip Left to Right to flip an object horizontally, you can just click the corresponding SmartIcon. To delete an object from a page, instead of selecting an object and choosing Edit Cut, just select the object and click the Cut SmartIcon (the pair of scissors). To paste an object, click the Edit Paste SmartIcon (it resembles a paste pot).

If you are accustomed to selecting menu commands, you may have to retrain yourself to get in the habit of clicking SmartIcons to perform a task. But, when you discover how easily you can streamline your work with SmartIcons, you become an instant convert.

Because sometimes you must go three levels deep to find the command you want, the SmartIcons for the commands on the Arrange menu are especially useful. Arrange Priority Top is a good example of a real time-saver. In general, the SmartIcons for drawing are among the biggest time-savers of all, because when you are drawing you typically perform many repetitive tasks such as aligning objects, changing their priority, and grouping and ungrouping objects. And, because you already are using the mouse for drawing, it's easy to move the mouse up a bit and click a SmartIcon.

In this chapter, you learn how to:

- *Display the meaning of a SmartIcon*
- *Add, remove, and reposition icons to create a customized SmartIcon set*
- *Use the Spacer SmartIcon*
- *Display and Hide the SmartIcon set*
- *Change the size of SmartIcons*
- *Save customized SmartIcon sets*
- *Create your own SmartIcon*
- *Launch other Lotus applications by clicking SmartIcons*

Displaying the Meaning of a SmartIcon

The graphic artists who designed the SmartIcons went to great and clever lengths to make the SmartIcons as meaningful as possible. Even so, you may need help deciphering the meaning of some of the SmartIcons. Fortunately, help is just a click away.

To display a description of a SmartIcon in the current set, click the SmartIcon with the right mouse button. You see a description of the SmartIcon in the left part of the title bar. (Incidentally, you also can click Toolbox icons to see descriptions of their functions.)

Editing the Current SmartIcon Set

You can add or remove icons from the current set or reposition the icons on the screen. First choose Tools SmartIcons to open the SmartIcons dialog box (see fig. 23.1). Then do one of the following:

- To add a new icon to the palette, click an icon in the Available Icons list and drag it to the list on the right.
- To remove an icon from the current set, drag it out of the current list (you don't have to drag it back into the Available Icons palette).
- To rearrange icons in the current set, drag the icon to a new position in the list. You only can drag an icon to a position that is visible in the list (dragging an icon to the bottom of the visible list does not scroll the list). It's a good idea to drag the most frequently used SmartIcons to the front to ensure that they remain visible even if you change the size of the Freelance window.

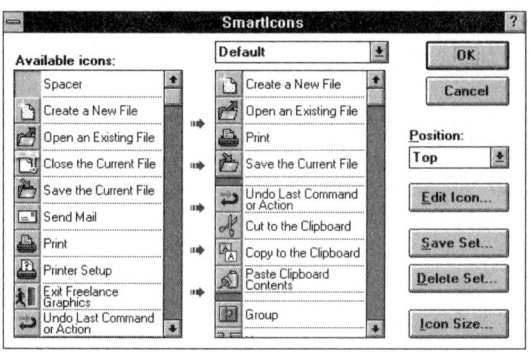

FIGURE 23.1. The SmartIcons dialog box.

> ## Use the Spacer Icon
>
> With Release 2.0, you can use a Spacer SmartIcon to create logical groups of SmartIcons within the current set. Use a Spacer SmartIcon, for example, to separate the file-handling SmartIcons from the Text SmartIcons. The Spacer icon—a solid gray square—appears at the top of the available icons list. Add it to the current set as you do any other SmartIcon: Just drag the icon from the Available Icons list to the current set. After you drag it to the current set, the Spacer icon assumes the shape of a gray dividing bar.

Repositioning the SmartIcon Set

To change the position of the current SmartIcon set, choose Tools SmartIcons and then click the arrow in the Position list box. The palette choices are Floating, Left, Top, Right, and Bottom. By default, Freelance Graphics displays the current set across the top of the window.

Use Floating if you have more SmartIcons in your set than can fit in any of the other views. You can display more SmartIcons across the top or bottom of the window than on the left or right. The number of visible SmartIcons depends on the size of the window.

Note that the size of the SmartIcons does not change when you size the Freelance Graphics window. If more SmartIcons are in the current palette than can fit across the top or down the sides of the screen, either maximize the size of the Freelance Graphics window or display them all by choosing the Floating option.

When you choose Floating, you can move the set anywhere on the screen or change its size and dimensions as you like. You can size it like any other window. When you click a corner or border, the pointer changes to a double-arrow shape. Now drag in any direction to size the palette. To move the floating set, just click it and drag it to a new location.

Hiding a SmartIcon Set

To turn off the display of the current SmartIcon set, click the SmartIcon box on the Status bar along the bottom border. Choose Hide to turn off the SmartIcon display. You also can choose a another set of SmartIcons by highlighting a name in this list.

Changing the Size of SmartIcons

You can change the size of the SmartIcons by clicking the Icon Size button in the SmartIcons dialog box. The three choices available are Small, Medium, and Large. These different sizes are intended for different screen resolutions. If you have a large screen set for 1024 x 768 resolution (8514 or XGA), you probably want to choose the large SmartIcons. When you install the program, Freelance automatically uses the correct set based on your screen resolution. If you just prefer larger or smaller SmartIcons, however, you can choose any size without regard to your screen resolution.

Saving a SmartIcon Set

As a new feature in Freelance Graphics 2.0, you can customize a SmartIcon set and then save it for future use. You can save as many SmartIcon sets as you like. It's a good idea to have several SmartIcon sets, each one for a different task. For example, you might have a SmartIcon set for creating tables, one for creating bullet charts, and one for creating diagrams. Figure 23.2 shows a SmartIcon set for drawing tasks.

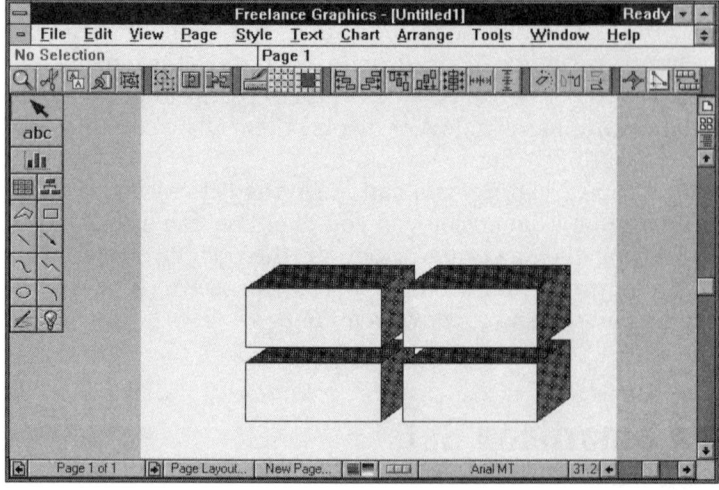

FIGURE 23.2. A SmartIcon set for drawing.

This set includes the icon for displaying the drawing ruler, the Alignment icons, and the Rotate and Flip icons, among others. It's a good idea to put the Next Icon Set SmartIcon as the last icon in a set. Click this icon to move quickly to the next saved set.

To save a SmartIcon set, first edit the current set to contain just those icons you want (see "Editing the Current SmartIcon Set") and then click the Save Set button in the SmartIcons dialog box. In the Save Set of SmartIcons dialog box, type the name of the set and the file name (these names are typically the same) and then click OK (see fig. 23.3). Note that you cannot change the directory here.

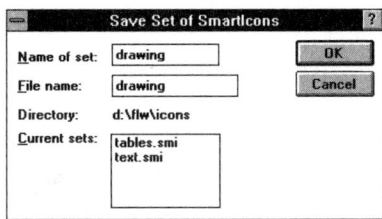

FIGURE 23.3. The Save Set of SmartIcons dialog box.

To delete a SmartIcon set, click the Delete Set button in the SmartIcons dialog box.

Creating Your Own SmartIcons

With Release 2.0, you can create your own SmartIcons. To create a new SmartIcon, click the Edit Icon button in the SmartIcons dialog box. In the Edit Icon dialog box, you can work in a matrix of pixels (see fig. 23.4). To create a good-looking icon, you must be something of a pixel artist (pixels are the individual bits that make up a bitmapped image). Starting with a blank gray icon, you can change the colors of individual pixels, using the colors in the list box below the icon. Click the color you want to use and then click a pixel in the icon to change it to the selected color. Click the Save As button to save the new icon. Note the small Preview area on the right, which shows how the icon appears on-screen.

After you create the icon, you can link it to an OLE object, a batch file, or a program. To launch 1-2-3 for Windows, for example, type the appropriate command in the Run Program or Insert Object box (for example, *c:\123w\123w.exe*).

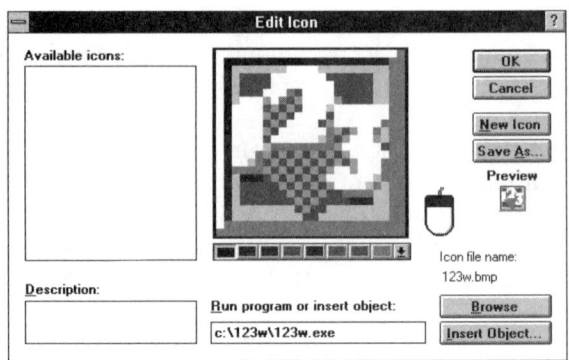

FIGURE 23.4. The Edit Icon dialog box.

To associate a SmartIcon with an OLE object, click the Browse button and make a choice from the list. For more information on OLE objects, see Chapter 20, "Screen Shows."

Launching Other Applications

The SmartIcons palette contains four icons that enable you automatically to launch 1-2-3 for Windows, Ami Pro, cc:Mail, or Lotus Notes. If you need to start one of these applications in a hurry, this is the fastest way to do it. If the program is already open, clicking the corresponding SmartIcon makes it the active window. If the program is not open, clicking the SmartIcon starts it. To use these icons, add them to the current SmartIcons palette.

If Freelance cannot find the program names by a launch SmartIcon (Ami Pro, for example), you may have to edit the FLW2.INI file in your Windows directory to correct the path name for Ami Pro. To make this change, retrieve FLW2.INI into an ASCII text editor such as the Windows Notepad and then locate the following lines:

```
123w=1-2-3 for Windows,C:\123W\123W.EXE
AmiPro=Ami Pro,C:\AMIPRO\AMIPRO.EXE
Notes=Lotus Notes,C:\NOTES\NOTES.EXE
ccMail=cc:Mail for Windows,C:\CCMAIL\WMAIL.EXE
```

If Ami Pro is actually in the D directory, make the appropriate correction and then resave the file. The next time you restart Freelance and click the Ami Pro SmartIcon, Ami Pro is launched.

Wrapping Up

In this chapter, you have learned how to tap into the power of SmartIcons, which give you one-click access to most Freelance commands. You have learned how to use SmartIcons, edit the current set, and save customized sets. If you ever have the need, you even know enough to create your own SmartIcons.

In the next chapter, you learn how to customize Freelance Graphics to make it fit smoothly into your working style.

24

Customizing Freelance Graphics

After you use a software product for a while, it becomes entrenched in your working habits. If you learn to do something one way and are successful at it, you tend to stick with it, even if there is a more efficient way of performing the same task. This scenario is true in work, sports, and just about any human endeavor.

As you work with Freelance Graphics, try to establish efficient working patterns. If you create mostly text charts, learn which tools, commands, and features of Freelance Graphics can best help you create text charts. If you create mostly graphs, learn to work with the features that ease the process of creating graphs.

This chapter describes the numerous ways you can customize Freelance Graphics to help you do your work most efficiently.

In this chapter, you learn how to:

- *Start Freelance in Current Page view, Page Sorter view, or Outliner view*
- *Change the way the Replicate command works*
- *Change the way File Save works and use the Autosave option*
- *Turn the Undo option on and off*
- *Change international options such as time and date formats*
- *Change default directories*
- *Change drawing options and set default attributes for objects you draw*
- *Display the function key panel, a text ruler, or a drawing ruler*
- *Set up a grid on the drawing page*
- *Display the page boundaries used by the current printer*
- *Change margins and page orientation (vertical or horizontal)*
- *Add headers and footers to printed presentations*
- *Set up a default chart*

About Settings

You can customize the working environment of Freelance Graphics in a number of ways. Default settings cover a wide range of default features and options.

User Setup Options

User setup options remain in effect from presentation to presentation until you change them again. To change your setup options, choose Tools User Setup and then complete the User Setup dialog box (see fig. 24.1). When you change them, these settings remain in effect automatically for all presentations.

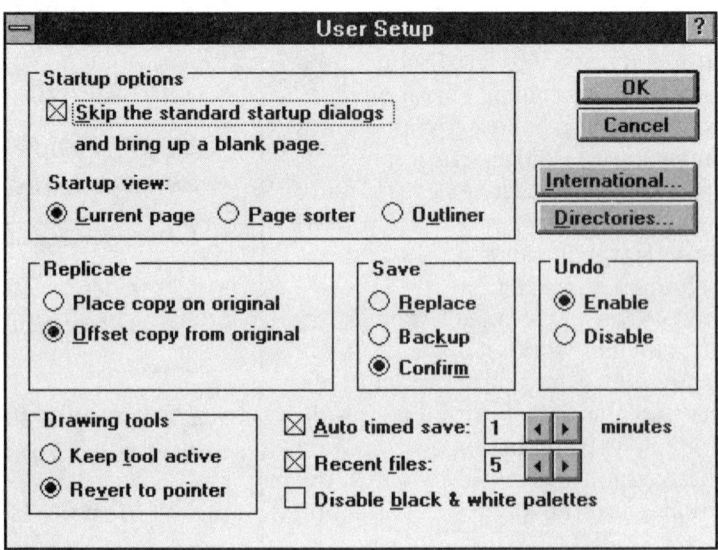

FIGURE 24.1. The User Setup dialog box.

Start-Up Options

You can choose the initial working view of Freelance Graphics (Current Page view, Outliner view, Page Sorter view). If it is your practice to work in Outliner view most of the time, you may want the program to start up in this view every time. To set up the default view, click the appropriate button for Start-up view.

Replicate, Replicate, Replicate

When you choose Edit Replicate (or press Ctrl+F3), Freelance Graphics makes a duplicate of the selected object. You can specify whether you want the copy to be placed on top of the original object or offset slightly from it by clicking a radio button in the Replicate area. Generally, the offset option is most convenient because the replicated object is easier to distinguish from the original. For more information about using this powerful command, refer to Chapter 13, "Editing Objects."

Keeping the Drawing Tools Active

When you click a Toolbox icon and draw an object such as a rectangle, you can specify whether the Rectangle icon remains active (so that you can draw another rectangle immediately) or whether you revert to the pointer. In the latter case, you must select the Rectangle icon again to draw another rectangle. If you generally draw several of the same object types at the same time, it is best to choose Keep Tool Active. Chapter 12, "Drawing Objects," discusses the pros and cons of this feature in more detail.

Save Options

When you save a file that already exists, you can set up Freelance Graphics to function in several ways:

- The Replace option automatically saves the file without asking for your confirmation (even if a file of the same name already exists). This option is a somewhat dangerous one to use and is not recommended. It's all too easy to click the File Save SmartIcon and write over the contents of an existing file when that was not your intent.

- The Backup option also saves the file without asking for your confirmation (even if a file of the same name already exists) but also places a copy of the file in the Backup directory. If you use this option, you may want to delete files from this directory every now and then to save space on your hard disk. Note that Freelance uses the same extension (.PRE) for backup files that it does for all presentation files.

- The Confirm option requests confirmation before saving a file (if a file of the same name already exists). Generally, Confirm is the safest and most logical choice.

Choosing the Autosave Option

You also can set up Freelance to save your file automatically at specified intervals. This feature can be useful if you are the type of person who tends to work on a complex presentation for an hour without saving the file. This habit can lead to disaster if, for example, the power suddenly fails. With the Autosave feature enabled, Freelance saves your file automatically at an interval you specify. Click the Auto Time Save check box and choose the interval in minutes when you want your file to be saved (choose from 1 to 99 minutes). If you are in the middle of a task, Freelance does not save your presentation until you have completed the task and started a new one.

Just Undo It

Undo the last ten actions with Edit Undo or click the Edit Undo SmartIcon.

You can turn the undo feature on or off. When Edit Undo is turned on (enabled), Freelance Graphics remembers the last 10 operations, and you can undo them one by one to reach a previous state. Note that you cannot undo an undo command.

Recent Files Display

When you choose File Open, Freelance displays a list of the last several files you worked on. You can change the number of files displayed. Mark the Recent Files check box and choose a value from 1 to 5. If you unmark this check box, no recent files are displayed (but this change doesn't take effect until you exit Freelance and start it again).

Disable Black & White Palettes

When you print to a black-and-white printer, colors are converted to gray scales. Normally, Freelance uses the black-and-white palette that comes with every SmartMaster set to determine the mapping of colors to gray scales. This method generally yields the best results. But, if you prefer, you can let Microsoft Windows perform the color to black-and-white mapping. Mark the Disable black & white palettes check box to specify this option.

International Options

Click the International button in the User Setup dialog box to bring up the International User Setup dialog box (see fig. 24.2). In this dialog box, you can set a variety of international options. You can change the time and date format (which are used in headers and footers), the currency format, the number format, and the file translation code page (which affects the way text files are imported).

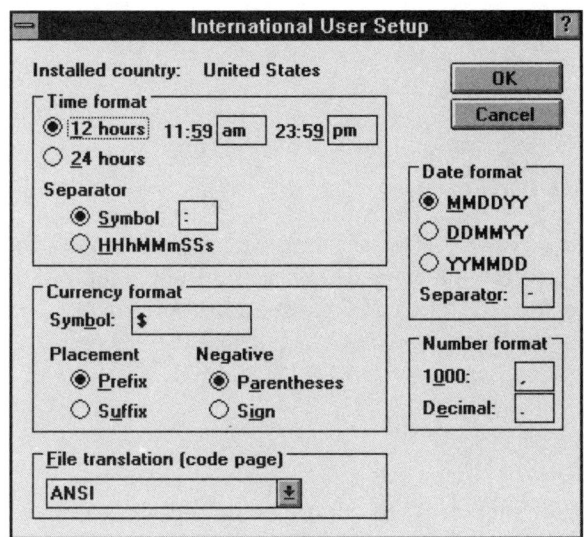

FIGURE 24.2. The International User Setup dialog box.

Default Directories

Freelance Graphics maintains a working directory (where your presentation files are saved by default), a masters directory (which contains palettes and symbol libraries), and the backup directory (which is used to keep backup copies of presentation files if the Save Backup option is selected). Click the Directories button to display a dialog box that enables you to change the defaults for these directories (see fig. 24.3).

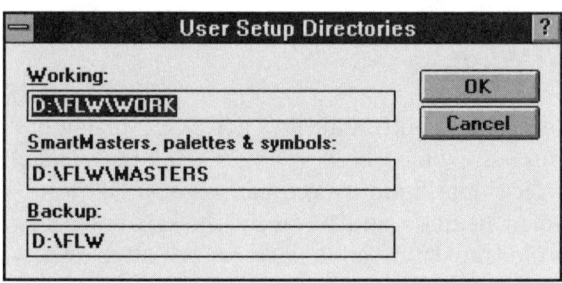

FIGURE 24.3. The User Setup Directories dialog box.

View Preferences

You can change a variety of on-screen options with the View View Preferences command. Choose View View Preferences and then complete the View Preferences dialog box (see fig. 24.4). Make selections here to change the cursor size, change display options, or display page borders.

Cursor Size

When you draw objects such as circles or rectangles, Freelance Graphics displays the crosshair pointer to indicate your location on the page. The crosshair pointer can be big or small. For the advantages of using the big crosshair, refer to Chapter 12, "Drawing Objects."

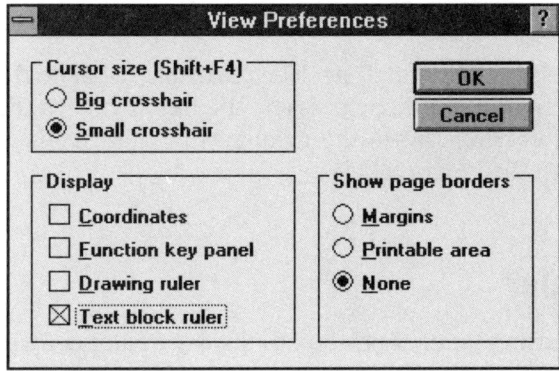

FIGURE 24.4. The View Preferences dialog box.

Page Borders

The Show Page Border options enable you to display a dashed line to indicate the margin of the presentation page or the printable area. Choose None to display neither of these. The options are as follows:

- Margins displays the margins that are set up in the File Page Setup dialog box. Note that margin settings are visual guides only. Objects outside the page margins are printed (provided they fall within the printable area).
- Printable Area shows the page area that the current printer uses. Anything that falls outside this area is not printed. Many printers cannot print all the way to the edge of the page. Instead, they leave a border of perhaps a quarter of an inch around the page. As you work, it's useful to know that you are not placing any text or graphics outside the printable area.
- None displays neither the margins nor the printable area.

Coordinates

Coordinates displays the X and Y coordinates of the objects you are drawing or sizing. These coordinates are the horizontal and vertical distances from the origin point. The origin point is located on the bottom left corner of the page. You cannot change the origin. You can use coordinates to help you draw objects to scale (in a floor plan, for example, where 0.5 inch represents 1 foot).

Function Key Panel

Mark the Function Key Panel check box to display a bar on the bottom border that lists the actions initiated by pressing the function keys (F1 through F10). Press Ctrl, Alt, or Shift to see the meanings of these keys when pressed in conjunction with the function keys.

Drawing Ruler

Mark the Drawing Ruler check box to display a ruler across the top and the left side of the screen. The units on the ruler are those specified with View Units & Grids.

Text Ruler

Mark the Text Block Ruler check box to display a text ruler (in addition to the Edit Panel). The units are as specified in View Units & Grids. For more information about the text ruler, refer to Chapter 3, "Creating, Editing, and Formatting Text."

Drawing Options

You can set up the drawing environment to suit your working style and your current drawing tasks. You can change the attributes of the objects you create with the drawing tools, for example. Or, if you are working on a diagram, you may find that displaying a grid eases the task.

Setting Default Attributes

When you create diagrams, you want the graphic elements that make up your work to be consistent. If you are creating a diagram, for example, you may want any text boxes to have the same edge color and width and the same fill color (if any). To give your diagrams a consistent look, the edge width of all the graphic objects you add generally should have the same edge width. As another example, perhaps you want all circles in a diagram to be green and all rectangles blue. If you are adding callouts to a diagram, you may want to use the same line width for the leader lines and the same typeface and size for the text throughout the diagram.

Customizing Freelance Graphics

You can set the default attributes for all the drawing tools. Chapter 12, "Drawing Objects," contains the procedure for setting these attributes.

In addition, the Replicate and Drawing Tools options in the User Setup dialog box affect the drawing environment. See the section "User Setup Options" earlier in this chapter for more information.

Setting Up a Drawing Grid

Drawing with a visible grid helps you to create diagrams that have balance and proportion. You also can turn on the snap-to-grid feature so that objects you add to the page automatically snap to grid points. To set up and display a grid, choose View Units & Grids. See Chapter 12, "Drawing Objects," for more information.

Page Settings

In addition to the page layout you choose to provide the formatting for a particular presentation page, you can choose settings that affect every page in a presentation, regardless of which page layout you choose. To change page settings, choose File Page Setup. The dialog box shown in figure 24.5 enables you to set up a header and footer, choose the page orientation, and set up page margins.

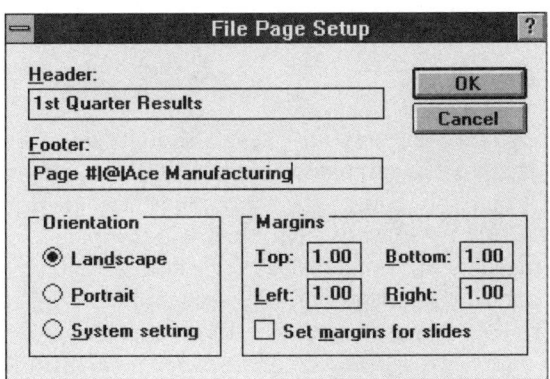

FIGURE 24.5. The File Page Setup dialog box.

Headers and Footers

Headers and footers are rarely used in presentation pages. For one thing, they are difficult to see on a slide or an overhead. If you are using Freelance Graphics to create printed reports, you may want to add headers or footers. You can type a header and footer in the File Page Setup dialog box and even add sequential page numbers and the current date. For more information about how to add these headers and footers, refer to Chapter 19, "Printing a Presentation."

Page Orientation

You can choose a landscape or a portrait orientation for your page (see fig. 24.6). The orientation is determined by the SmartMaster set you are using, but there may be times when you want to change it. You can choose Landscape or Portrait or use the orientation specified in your System settings. Landscape is the default for most SmartMaster sets. Keep in mind the following facts:

- Landscape is a horizontal page layout. Most SmartMaster sets use this page layout.
- Portrait is a vertical page layout.
- System Setting uses the orientation specified for the default printer in the Windows printer options. To change this printer, choose the Printers icon in the Windows Control Panel.

Margins

You can set up margins for your page, although these margins are visual guidelines only; that is, you can place objects outside the margins and they can still be printed. When you change the margin settings (with File Page Setup), Freelance asks whether you want the objects on the page to be rescaled to fit within the new margins. If you click Yes, Freelance changes the size of all the objects on the page so that they maintain the same relative size to the margins as they did before you changed margin settings. If you make the margins larger (leaving a smaller area for objects), for example, Freelance makes the objects on the page smaller so that they fit within the new margins.

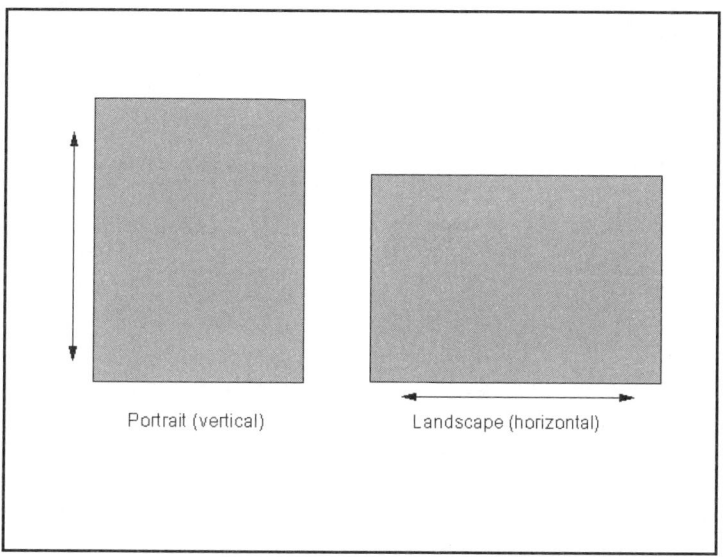

FIGURE 24.6. Portrait and Landscape page layouts.

Printer Options

In the Printer Setup dialog box, you can choose whether the default output device is a printer or a screen show (see fig. 24.7). If you choose Optimize for Screen Show, Freelance Graphics adjusts the presentation pages to display the proper aspect ratio and orientation for your screen rather than the current output device. Also, when you choose File Print, you see the View Screen Show dialog box.

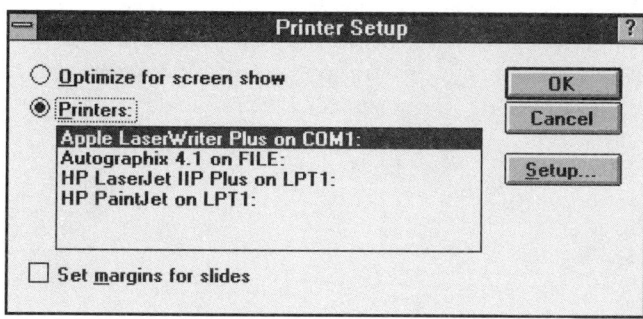

FIGURE 24.7. The Printer Setup dialog box.

Setting Up a Default Chart

If you create many graphs, and especially if you typically use the same chart customization options (such as the legend in a certain position, the size of grid lines, or the frame style), you can save these settings and use them for new graphs in the current presentation.

In the Chart Gallery is a button labeled Use Default Chart. Clicking this button displays the Chart Data & Titles window with settings for the default chart. You can change this default by selecting another chart type, changing any settings you want, and then issuing the command Chart Replace Defaults.

When you choose Chart Replace Defaults, the selected chart becomes the default for all new graphs in the current presentation only. If you include data in the selected chart, the data also becomes part of the default chart. You can use this feature to good advantage. Suppose that you create a quarterly presentation that includes the same bar chart every quarter. You can save this chart as the default chart, leaving the axis labels and axis titles in place. Then when it's time to create the next quarterly presentation, choose the default chart and add the new data.

Note that choosing Chart Replace Defaults does not change the default chart for existing presentations.

You also can save chart settings as part of the default presentation without saving the actual chart as well. First create a chart of the type you want and with all the settings you want (for example, a pie chart with an exploded slice). Next, delete all the data from the Chart Data & Titles window (or choose settings without entering any data in the first place). Next, choose Chart Replace Defaults.

Wrapping Up

In this chapter, you learned how to customize Freelance Graphics to make it work most effectively for you. You learned how to change the start-up view, specify drawing options, and set printer options. You know how to set up default directories and change international settings. You learned various ways to change the appearance of the screen, such as displaying a grid, text ruler, or drawing ruler.

Part 8
SmartMasters

SmartMasters are at the heart of Freelance Graphics, and the final part of this book explains SmartMasters from the inside out. You learn how to customize existing Smartmaster and create new SmartMaster sets from scratch.

This section includes:

Chapter 25. Understanding SmartMaster Sets

Chapter 26. Creating Your Own SmartMaster Sets

25

Understanding SmartMaster Sets

SmartMaster sets are at the heart of Freelance Graphics. They automatically give your presentations a consistent, professional look and take away the drudgery and detail work traditionally involved with creating presentations.

Each SmartMaster set has a unique look. Freelance Graphics offers a whole suite of styles, ranging from the staid to the showy. Perhaps best of all, you are never locked into one presentation style. After you choose a SmartMaster set, you can choose another without worrying about losing content or disturbing the structure of your presentation. After you create a bullet chart, for example, that bullet chart retains its basic format of a title and a list of bulleted items no matter which SmartMaster set you use. SmartMaster sets are designed to be interchangeable, so you can change looks in midstream, if need be.

One nice thing about SmartMaster sets is that you don't really have to understand them to use them successfully, any more than you need a degree in automotive mechanics to drive a car. Nevertheless, at some point you need to understand what they are all about. This chapter is the place to start.

In this chapter, you learn:

- *About the structure of SmartMaster sets*
- *How page layouts work*
- *How to edit page layouts*
- *How to make global edits by changing a page layout*
- *How to customize an existing SmartMaster set*
- *How to create a new page layout*
- *How to create "Click here..." text blocks and "Click here..." placement blocks*

The Structure of SmartMaster Sets

You can create presentations without knowing much at all about SmartMaster sets except how to choose one and how to choose page layouts for your presentation pages. But, if you want to customize an existing SmartMaster set or create new page layouts, you must have a basic knowledge of how SmartMaster sets work.

Freelance Graphics has 65 SmartMaster sets.

A SmartMaster set is a collection of page templates that gives your presentation a consistent, professional style. Each time you create a new presentation, you choose the design you want by choosing a SmartMaster set. Freelance comes with 65 SmartMaster sets. Every SmartMaster set has 11 page layouts for the most common types of page formats, such as title pages, bulleted lists, data charts, organization charts, tables, and various combinations of these. When you add a new page to your presentation with the Page New command, you choose a page layout that suits the type of page you are creating. (This procedure is described in Chapter 1, "Creating Your First Presentation.") To create a bullet chart, for example, choose the Bulleted List page layout or the 2-Column Bullets page layout. To create a chart on a single page, choose the 1 Chart page layout, and so on.

Every SmartMaster set has 11 page layouts.

Here's an important point. Every SmartMaster set has 11 page layouts. This fact is significant because some users are familiar with the master page concept used by other presentation packages, in which one master page governs the look of all your presentation pages. Freelance Graphics, with 11 page layouts for every SmartMaster set, has a more complex structure, which is correspondingly more powerful. Because page layouts are the key to understanding how SmartMaster sets work, this chapter looks at them in some detail.

How Page Layouts Work

To help you follow along with this discussion better, start a new presentation and choose the BLOCKS.MAS SmartMaster set. In the Choose Page Layout dialog box, highlight Title and click OK. You now should have a presentation with one page that uses the Title page layout (see fig. 25.1).

This page layout has a unique look, from the blue background to the three colorful blocks in the left corner of the page. As you soon see, all these design elements—such as the blocks in the left, the placement blocks, and the prompt text—originate on the Basic Layout page in the SmartMaster set. In general, a page layout in a SmartMaster set can contain any or all of the following components:

- SmartMaster text blocks, which determine the position, typeface, color, attributes, line spacing, and alignment of your text automatically.

- Placement blocks, which size and position charts, graphic objects, or symbols. If you add a chart or graphics to a placement block, SmartMasters size and position the graphics for you automatically.
- Prompt text (such as "Click here to type presentation title" or "Click here to add symbol"). Both SmartMaster text blocks and placement blocks contain prompt text.
- Fixed design elements. These are the design elements such as the three-dimensional blocks in the BLOCKS SmartMaster set.

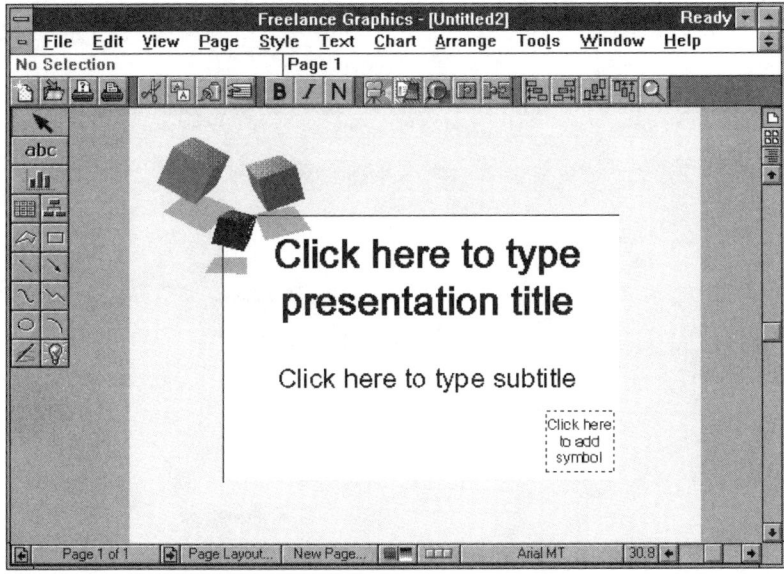

FIGURE 25.1. A presentation page from the SmartMaster set BLOCKS.MAS, shown here with the Title page layout.

See the "Placeholders and Prompt Text" section later in this chapter for more details about SmartMaster text blocks, placement blocks, and prompt text.

What is the relationship between the presentation page and the page layout it uses? One useful way to think of a page layout is as a second, underlying layer beneath your presentation page. Picture your presentation page as a transparent sheet of paper lying on top of a SmartMaster page layout. You can see the design elements of the page layout layer through your presentation page, but you cannot change a page layout from the presentation page. You can add text or graphics to the presentation page, but you can't make changes to the page layout without first peeling off the presentation page, as it were. To do this, you must edit the page layouts (choose Edit Page Layouts). This command peels off the presentation page layer, as it were, and enables you to change the page layouts that determine the look of your presentation.

Right now, you should have a blank title page on your screen that uses the Title page layout. If you click on the prompt text "Click here to type presentation title," you are placed in text edit mode and you can type the title of your presentation. Go ahead and type *Bellamy Box & Crate*. Then click the prompt in the subtitle block and type *Quarterly Sales Meeting*.

For good measure, click the placement block that reads "Click here to add symbol" and then add the box symbol from COMMOBJT.SYM. (Chapter 1, "Creating Your First Presentation," tells you how to add a symbol to the page.) The box serves as a logo. You now have a complete title page (see fig. 25.2).

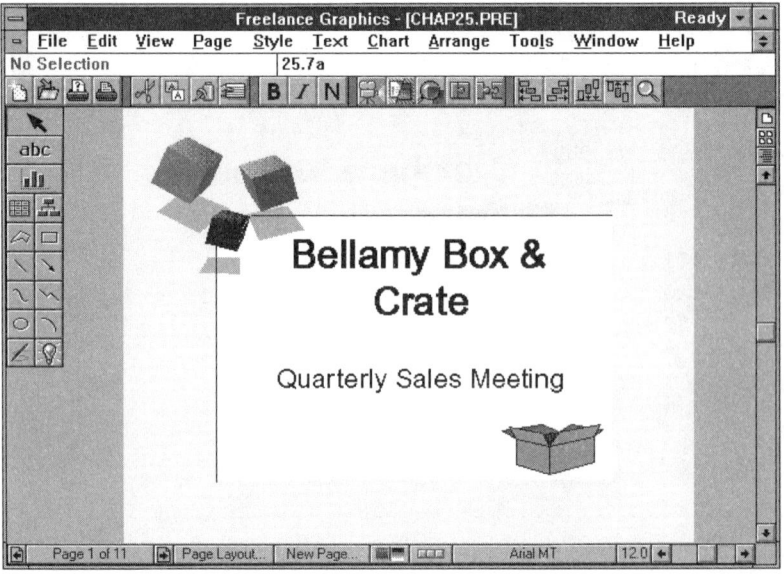

FIGURE 25.2. Title page with the placement blocks filled in with text and graphics.

Now click on one of the colored blocks at the top left corner of the page. Nothing happens. You cannot select the object. The message to the left in the Title line reads "No Selection." The reason you cannot select these blocks is that they originate on the layer beneath the presentation page, on a SmartMaster page layout.

You have two ways to change an underlying page layout. You can make changes to a SmartMaster text block on the presentation page. On the Title page you just created, for example, double-click the main title block. In the Paragraph Styles dialog box, make any attribute changes you want. If you want to apply the changes to the current page only, click OK. But, if you want to apply the changes to all pages in your presentation that use the Title page layout, first click the check box labeled Apply to SmartMaster. This action makes the change on the underlying page layout.

To make other changes to page layouts, however, you must be in a special view. To get there, use the command Edit Edit Page Layouts, press Shift+F9, or click the Edit Page Layouts SmartIcon. Notice the following several changes to the appearance of the screen (see fig. 25.3):

- Your titles vanish and are replaced by the prompt text ("Click-here..." text) on the SmartMaster page layout. The presentation page layer has been peeled off, as it were. Instead of the page title you entered, for example, you see "Click here to type presentation title."

- The dark gray background outside the borders of the presentation page is replaced by rather garish diagonal lines, to alert you that you are editing page layouts.

- The message at the left of the title bar reads "SmartMaster" to remind you that you are editing SmartMaster page layouts.

- Two buttons now appear just below the Toolbox. The Return button takes you back to your presentation pages. The Explain button displays an informational screen about editing page layouts.

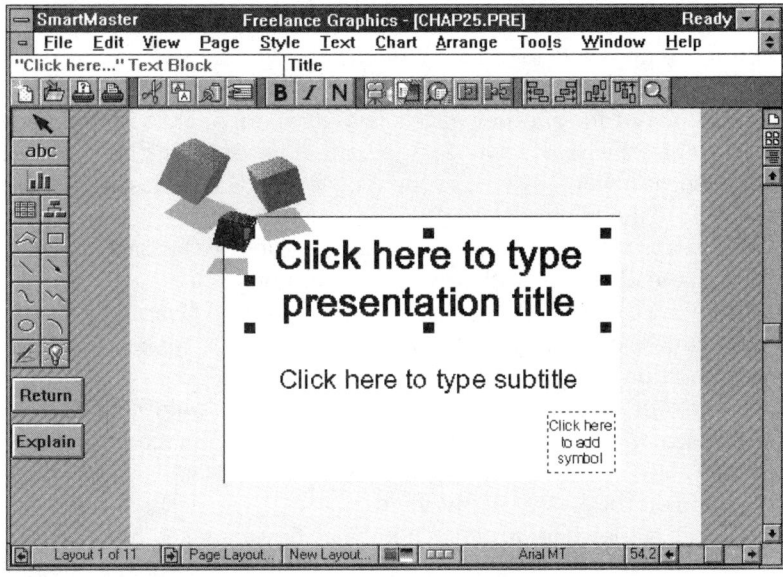

FIGURE 25.3. The Title page layout in page layouts view.

Now click one of the decorative blocks at the top of the page again. This time, you can select it. The message in the edit line reads "Group." (This message means that this object is composed of several objects that were grouped with the Arrange Group command.) Choose Arrange Ungroup (or click the Ungroup SmartIcon). Now click somewhere off the edge of the page to deselect all objects. Click the blocks again and then drag to move them to the right side of the page. Finally, click the Return button to go back to your presentation pages. You see that the group of blocks has moved to the right of the title page. If you create a new page and choose the Title Page layout, the blocks also are on the right side of the page, because you have changed the underlying page layout. Note, though, that these changes affect the current presentation only. If you start a new presentation and choose the same SmartMaster set (BLOCKS.MAS), the position of the blocks is again on the left side of the page. To make the change to the page layouts permanent, you must save the SmartMaster set. That subject is discussed later in this chapter.

How Basic Layout Works

Figure 25.4 illustrates the relationship between page layouts and presentation pages. As you can see, the Basic Layout and Title Page layouts are different from the nine page layouts in the gray area. Each of these nine page layouts is linked to the Basic Layout page; that is, everything on the Basic Layout page also appears on these nine pages.

Objects you place on the Basic Layout page layout appear on every presentation page (except title pages).

Just as you can choose a page layout for a presentation page, you also can choose a page layout for another page's layout when you are in Page Layouts view. For example, the Basic Layout page contains a text block for the page title that is inherited, as it were, by every other page in the SmartMaster set, with the exception of the Title page.

What this means is that any text or object you place on the Basic Layout page appears automatically on the Bulleted List, 2-Column Bullets, 1 Chart, 2 Charts, 4 Charts, Bullets & Chart, Bullets & Symbol, Organization Chart, and Table page layouts. Changing the Basic Layout page is a great way to make global changes to your presentation.

The Basic Layout page contains a title block and the graphic elements that you see on every page in the body of your presentation (again, excepting the Title page). As you have seen, in the BLOCKS.MAS SmartMaster set, the colored blocks originate on the Basic Layout page.

Although this somewhat subtle structure at first may seem confusing, it is quite a powerful feature. When you change the Basic Layout page, you make global changes to your entire presentation. If you add a logo to this page, for example, you get the logo on every page in the body of your presentation (with the exception of the title page). Likewise, if you change the text color for the title block on Basic Layout, you change the color of every title in the body of your presentation. Look again at figure 25.4 to verify that this is the case.

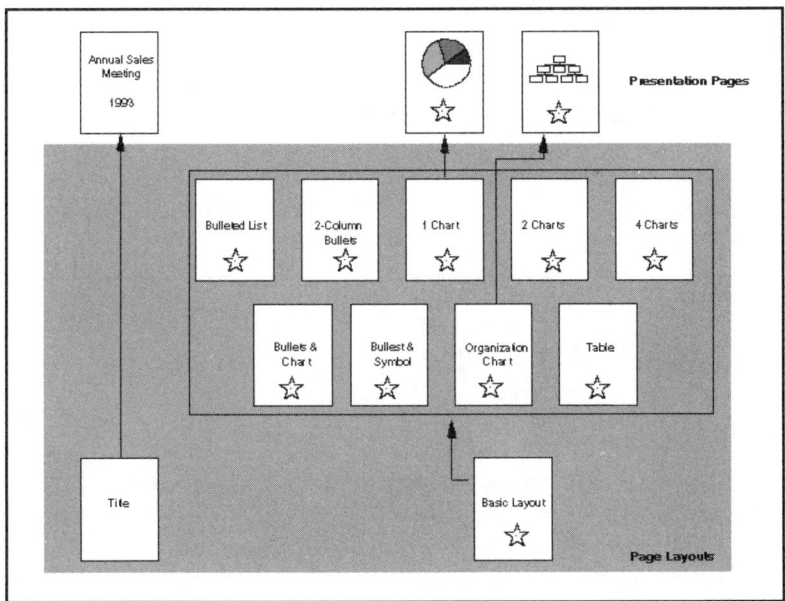

FIGURE 25.4. A representation of the page layouts in every SmartMaster set and their relationship to presentation pages.

How do you go about adding a logo to every page in your presentation? First, you add the logo to the Basic Layout page. This action causes the logo to appear on every page except those presentation pages that use the Title page layout. If you want the logo to appear on this page as well, you can place it either directly on the Title page in Presentation Pages view or in the Title page layout in SmartMaster Pages view.

Placeholders and Prompt Text

Page layouts contain placeholders for text and graphics, as you already have seen if you have created bulleted lists or data charts. The Bulleted List page layout, for example, contains two placeholders for text: one for the title and one for the list of bulleted items. Placeholders for text are known as SmartMaster text blocks.

> ## Why Title Page Layouts Are Different
>
> You may wonder why every page layout in a SmartMaster set but the Title page layout inherits elements from the Basic Layout page. The designers of Freelance Graphics decided to make the Title page layout completely independent of the other page layouts to give greater visual impact to the title page of your presentation, which is generally the first page your audience sees. In some SmartMaster sets, this difference can be subtle (BLOCKS.MAS, for example), but in others, you clearly notice the different look of the Title page layout. The title page of NOTEBOOK.MAS, for example, has a dramatically different look from the other page layouts in the same SmartMaster set.

SmartMaster Text Blocks

You can use SmartMaster text blocks without really understanding how they work. Every time you create a bulleted list by using the Bulleted List page layout, for example, you are using SmartMaster text blocks.

In Page Layouts view (press Shift+F9 to get there), with the Title page layout the current page, click the text "Click here to type presentation title." Note that instead of being placed in edit mode, as you were in Presentation Pages view, you have selected just the text block. The message in the edit line now reads "Click here... Text Block."

You can double-click this text block to change its attributes. Do so now. Double-clicking displays the Paragraph Styles dialog box. Note that the check box labeled Make This a "Click here..." Text Block is marked. If you unmark this box, the SmartMaster text block becomes an ordinary text block and the prompt text (in the Prompt Text box) is dimmed and reverts to the generic prompt "Click here to add text." If you now click OK, press F2, and type anything in the text block, this text now appears as a fixed text element on every presentation page that uses this page layout, and not as prompt text. You can use this feature to place a line of text on every page in your presentation, such as the date at the bottom of the page or perhaps your company name.

SmartMaster Placement Blocks

Now double-click the placement block that contains the text "Click here to add symbol." Note that the check box labeled Make This a "Click here..." Block is marked and that the Symbol radio button is selected. SmartMaster placement blocks—which can originate only on page layouts—are placeholders for graphics, which can include symbols, charts, tables, organization charts, imported graphic files, or whatever objects you create in Freelance Graphics.

SmartMaster placement blocks serve two purposes:

- They precisely position and size graphics on a presentation page.
- They cue the user about what is to go into the placement block and help start the appropriate process to put it there.

All types of placement blocks—no matter what prompt text they contain—share one feature. Whether you drag a chart, a symbol, or any other graphic object into a placement block, the placement block automatically sizes the object. The prompt text and the dotted border of the placement block disappear. If the object is a chart, the placement block sizes it to the precise dimensions of the placement block, regardless of the original dimensions of the chart. For any other graphic object, Freelance maintains the object's original proportions but makes it as large as possible within the placement block.

But placement blocks have another attribute that gives them additional power. When you click on an empty placement block on a presentation page, Freelance Graphics initiates an action based on the text in the placement block. Here's how it works:

- If a placement block contains the word *chart* or *graph*, when you click the placement block, Freelance opens the New Chart Gallery.
- If a placement block contains the word *symbol*, when you click the placement block, Freelance opens the Add Symbol to Page dialog box.
- If a placement block contains the words *organization chart*, when you click the placement block, Freelance opens the Organization Chart Gallery.
- If a placement block contains the word *table*, when you click the placement block, Freelance opens the Table Gallery.
- If a placement block does not contain either of these keywords, nothing special happens if you click the placement block. However, you still can drag a symbol, chart, or illustration into the placement block, where it is placed and sized automatically.

If you are creating your own placement blocks for charts, be sure to include the word *chart* in the prompt text. For a placement block that holds a symbol, include the word *symbol*. Do the same for the other keywords.

This special feature of placement blocks can help new users immensely. Not only does the prompt text tell them what goes into a placement block, but when they click the text, Freelance helps them along by displaying the appropriate dialog box. Even for experienced users, this feature is a great time-saver.

Note that even if a placement block contains the word *symbol*, this does not prevent you from adding a chart to it. You can drag any graphic object into any empty placement block. To drag a symbol into a placement block that contains the word *chart*, just drag the symbol into it. As long as you don't click the prompt text, Freelance Graphics does not display the Chart Gallery dialog box. The page layouts Bullets & Chart and Bullets & Symbol, for example, are structurally identical. The only difference is that the placement block on the right of each page layout contains different prompt text ("Click here to create chart" for Bullets & Chart and "Click here to add symbol" for Bullets & Symbol).

What Happens When You Switch to a New SmartMaster Set?

Every SmartMaster set has a standard set of 11 page layouts. This feature most easily is seen when you are editing page layouts and are also in Page Sorter view.

If you are not already editing page layouts, press Shift+F9 to get there. Now click the Page Sorter icon. You see 11 miniature page layouts. Note that each page layout has a title beneath it. Now choose a new SmartMaster set with the Style Choose SmartMaster Set command. The design changes as you read in the new SmartMaster set, but the names of the page layouts remain the same. (If you have edited the current SmartMaster set, you get a warning that the changes you have made are lost if you switch to a new SmartMaster set. Click Yes to continue.)

As you can see, every SmartMaster Set contains 11 page layouts, all with the same names: Title, Bulleted List, 2-Column Bullets, 1 Chart, 2 Charts, 4 Charts, Bullets & Chart, Bullets & Symbol, Organization Chart, Table, and Basic Layout.

These names are quite important. When you switch to a different SmartMaster set, Freelance uses these names to match the new page layouts with the existing page layouts.

Suppose that you have a bullet chart that uses the Bulleted List page layout. When you switch to a new SmartMaster set, Freelance matches the new Bulleted List page layout with all the presentation pages that use the existing Bulleted List page layout. Every bullet chart now receives the design imparted by the new SmartMaster set.

This feature is why you can change SmartMaster sets without affecting your content. The new Bulleted List page layout determines the look of all the bullet charts in your presentation that use the Bulleted List page layout.

This feature is one of the most powerful in Freelance Graphics, so you should think twice before changing the name of a SmartMaster page layout, particularly if you want to retain the capability to switch SmartMaster sets without penalty.

But suppose, for whatever reason, you do happen to change the name of the Bulleted List page layout to, say, Bullets1, and then switch to a different SmartMaster set. What happens? Because Freelance cannot find a page layout named Bullets1 in the new SmartMaster set, it leaves the presentation page that uses Bullets1 without a page layout. You do not lose the content of the page, but you have lost the benefit of interchangeable SmartMasters. You now have to use the Page Choose Page Layout command to assign the Bulleted List page layout to the page that was left without a page layout.

Customizing SmartMaster Sets

You may never need to edit a SmartMaster set. After all, SmartMasters help you turn out good-looking presentations automatically and take care of all the worrisome design details for you, such as choosing the right fonts, providing a set of colors that look good together, and even adding basic design elements to give your pages a professional touch.

Why, then, would you want to change a page layout? There are a variety of reasons. The number one reason is probably to add your company logo to all the pages of your presentation. Or, you may want to adjust the line spacing in a bullet chart, alter the color of a bullet marker without changing the color of the text next to it, or change some other design element on a page layout. If you need to make such minor adjustments, it's easiest to edit an existing SmartMaster set rather than create a new one from scratch. (You always can save it under a different name so that you preserve the original SmartMaster set.)

If you are satisfied with one of the 65 SmartMaster sets that come with Freelance Graphics but want to make just a few design tweaks, your task is a relatively simple one. The following sections explain how to make some simple but useful changes to SmartMaster sets.

How To Find Out What Page Layout a Page Uses

If you are not sure which page layout a presentation or SmartMaster page uses, you can find out easily. For example, in Page Layouts view, display the Bulleted List page layout. Then click the Page Layout button at the bottom of the window. Basic Layout is highlighted. This means that Bulleted List uses the Basic Layout page layout (as you already have discovered). Now display the Title page layout and, again, click the Page Layout button. This time [None] is highlighted. This means that the title page stands alone and uses no other SmartMaster page layout.

Changing Text Attributes

Why edit a SmartMaster text block? Here are some common reasons:

- You want to change the typeface.
- You want to change the line spacing between bullets. This is a common problem when your bullet charts have only a few items and you aren't using subpoints. The three lines are bunched up in the top half of the page, leaving too much space at the bottom.
- You want to change the text attributes in a title block or in the bullet points block. An example is when you want to italicize all page titles in your presentation.
- You want to change the color of a bullet (without changing the corresponding text). This is a nice, easy way to enliven a bullet chart.
- You want to change bullet markers or the indentation of levels 2 or 3. You can choose from a variety of bullet markers in Freelance Graphics.

Try It: Change the Colors of Page Titles Globally

After you understand how SmartMasters work, you can make global changes to a presentation by changing a simple page layout. Change the color of all the page titles in your presentation by doing the following:

1. Create a bullet chart in Presentation Pages view.
2. Double-click the title block to open the Paragraph Styles dialog box (see fig. 25.5). In this dialog box, you can change the font, size, color, and bullet markers for each level of text in a text block. You also can change indentation and line spacing, specify justification, or turn word wrap on or off. You can click the Frame button to add a border or fill to the text block. (See Chapter 3, "Creating, Editing, and Formatting Text," for more details.)
3. Click the Text Color list box and choose a new color for the text (it's best to use one of the suggested text colors).
4. Click the check box labeled Apply to SmartMaster and then click OK.

Now all presentation pages that use the Bulleted List page layout have titles of the color you used.

There is one drawback to changing a page layout. If you attempt to choose a new SmartMaster set after you have changed a page layout, you get a message saying that the page layouts have been changed and that switching to a new

SmartMaster set causes those edits to be lost. For example, if you have changed the spacing between bulleted items on the Bulleted List page layout, when you switch to another SmartMaster set, the line spacing is determined by the spacing of the Bulleted List page layout in the new SmartMaster set.

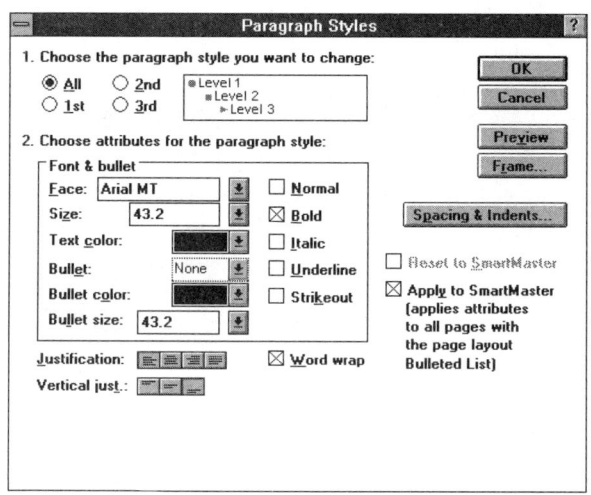

FIGURE 25.5. The Paragraph Styles dialog box.

If you want to make sure that your changes to the current SmartMaster set are preserved, either save the existing SmartMaster set or save it under a new name. It is probably preferable to save the SmartMaster set under a new name so that you do not change the original SmartMaster set. See Chapter 26, "Creating Your Own SmartMaster Sets," for more information about saving and retrieving SmartMaster sets.

Changing Bullet Color

Make Bulleted List the current page and then double-click the text block for the bullet points. In the Paragraph Styles dialog box, click the pop-up for Bullet color and then click a new color from the color palette or color library for each bullet for each text level (or change the color for all text levels at the same time with the All option). Mark the Apply to SmartMaster check box and click OK.

Changing the Spacing in Bulleted Lists

You can change both the paragraph spacing and the line spacing in a bullet chart. Double-click the text block and then click the Spacing & Indents button in the Paragraph Styles dialog box. This choice opens the Spacing & Indents dialog box (see fig. 25.6). You can make the choices for each text level or for all text levels at the same time.

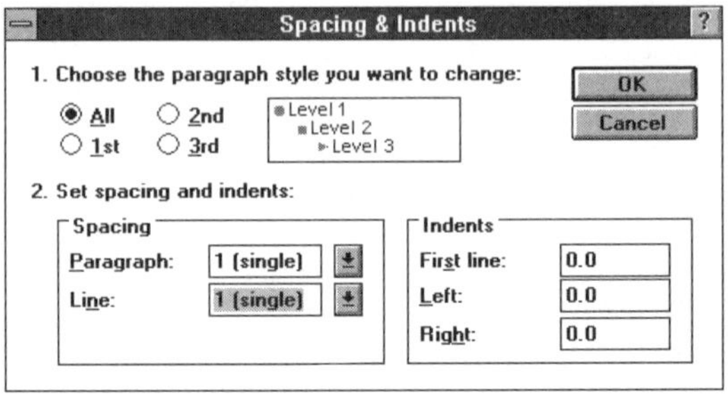

FIGURE 25.6. The Spacing & Indents dialog box.

Line spacing refers to the spacing between lines in a single paragraph or within a single bulleted item. Paragraph spacing refers to the spacing between paragraphs (or between bulleted items).

To add more space between bulleted items in a bullet chart, change the paragraph spacing. To change the spacing between the lines in one bulleted item (assuming the item is long enough to wrap to another line), change the line spacing.

You can change line or paragraph spacing only in fixed increments. You can choose from 1 (single), 1.5, 2 (double), 2.5, or 3.

Here is a confusing point. Paragraph spacing is a multiplier of line spacing. Suppose that you choose 2 for line spacing. Freelance Graphics places two line spaces between the lines in a single bulleted item (assuming the text wraps). So far, so good. But, if the paragraph spacing is set to 2, Freelance automatically places four line spaces between paragraphs (2 multiplied by 2). In other words, the setting for line spacing applies automatically to the setting for paragraph spacing. In general, it's best just to change the paragraph spacing and leave the line spacing alone.

Here's a quick way to add more space between bullet points without changing the SmartMaster page layout. After you type a bulleted item in Presentation Pages view, press Ctrl+Enter. This action inserts a blank line without adding a new bullet marker.

To apply these changes to the page layouts, mark the check box labeled Apply to SmartMaster.

Adding a Logo to Every Page in a Presentation

Adding an appropriate symbol or company logo to every presentation page can enhance your message and reinforce the visual power of your presentation. You either can take an appropriate symbol from the libraries of clip art shipped with Freelance Graphics or you can create your own. In the case of a company logo, it may be worthwhile to hire an artist to create one for you, which would be a one-time cost. After you have the logo in a graphics format that Freelance Graphics can use (see Chapter 17, "Importing and Exporting Graphics"), you can use it again and again.

If you want to add text or graphics to every page in your presentation, add it to Basic Layout. Doing so adds the object to every page layout except the Title page. If you want to add it to the Title page as well, put it in the placement block on the Title page.

To add the logo, first press Shift+F9 to edit page layouts. Then display the Basic Layout page and put the logo in an appropriate position: someplace where it does not obscure any text blocks on finished presentation pages (see fig. 25.7).

Of course, to add a logo, you must have the logo in some graphic format that Freelance Graphics can use. This format can be an .EPS file, a Freelance Plus .DRW file, a Windows metafile, a Windows bitmap (.BMP), a TIF bitmap (.TIF), a Paint bitmap (.PCX), or an image pasted from the Windows Clipboard. For a complete rundown and description of the types of graphics you can import, refer to Chapter 17, "Importing and Exporting Graphics."

Creating a New Page Layout

You can create your own SmartMaster text blocks and placement blocks when you are creating a customized SmartMaster set. Suppose that you want to create a page layout to use for displaying a weekly sales chart with accompanying text.

Use File New to start a new presentation, choose the FRAME.MAS SmartMaster set, and then click OK in the Choose Page Layout dialog box. (For now, it doesn't matter which page layout you choose.)

First, press Shift+F9 to edit page layouts. Then click the New Layout button on the bottom border. Because you want the new page layout to have the look of other pages in the SmartMaster set, highlight Basic Layout and click OK. Note that in the Edit line, Freelance has given this page the name Page Layout 1. Highlight this name, type *Weekly Report*, and press Enter. This is the name of the page layout.

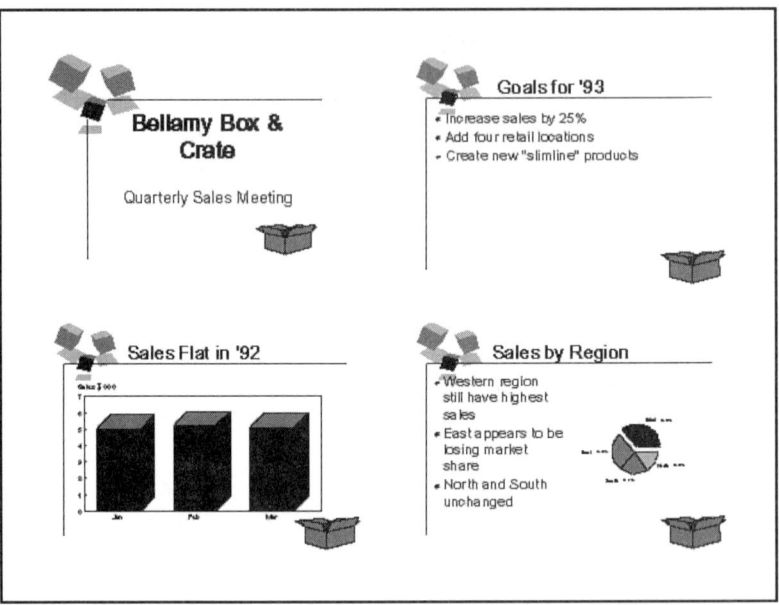

FIGURE 25.7. When you add a logo to the Basic Layout SmartMaster, every page in the body of your presentation displays it. To include it on the Title page, put the logo in the placement block.

Creating a "Click here..." Text Block

Click the Text tool and drag a rectangle on the left half of the page, below the existing title block. This action places you in edit mode. Now choose Text Paragraph Styles from the menu. In the Paragraph Styles dialog box, click the check box labeled Make This a "Click here..." Text Block. Doing so activates the Prompt text box at the bottom of the page. Highlight the prompt text in this box and type the text you want, such as *Click here to type sales summary*. If you want to change text color or bullet styles, do so now. When you have made all the style changes you want, click OK to return to the text block. Click OK again to close the text block. Figure 25.8 shows the results.

Creating a "Click here..." Chart Block

To create a "Click here..." chart block for the weekly sales chart, click the Rectangle icon in the Toolbox and drag a rectangle on the right half of the page. Double-click the rectangle and select the check box labeled Make This a "Click here..." Block. Now click the radio button for Chart. Highlight the existing text in the Prompt text box and type *Click here to add weekly sales chart*. Click OK.

Using the New Page Layout

Click the Return button to go back to your presentation pages. Choose Page New and note that "Weekly Report" now appears in the list of page layouts. Highlight this name and click OK. You see the prompt text you added, as shown in figure 25.8. The new page layout uses the Basic Layout page, so it will have the same title block and design elements as the rest of the page layouts in the SmartMaster set.

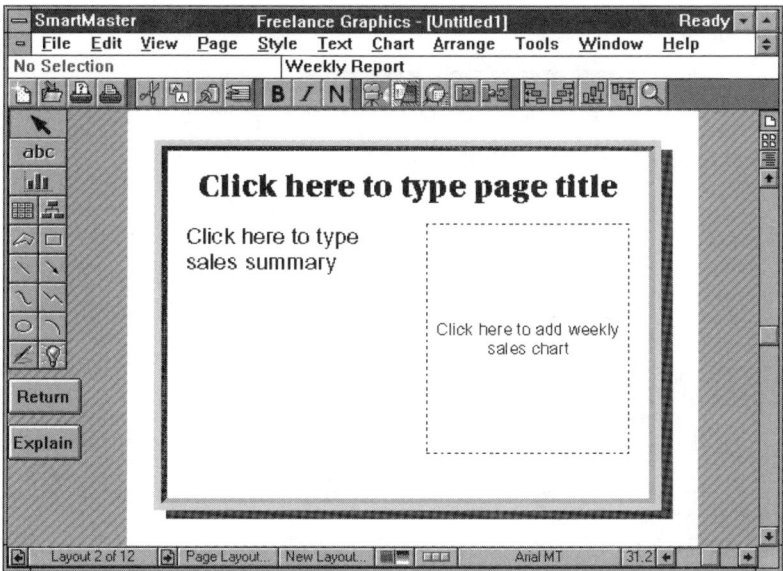

FIGURE 25.8. The new Weekly Sales page layout, with new text block and chart placement block.

Copying the New Page Layout to Other SmartMaster Sets

After you create a customized page, such as Weekly Report, you may want to copy it to other SmartMaster sets as well so that it is available in them.

To do this, you must be in Page Layouts view and Page Sorter view for both the source presentation that contains the new page layout and the target presentation. In the Page Sorter view in the source presentation, click to select the Weekly Report page layout. Then choose Edit Copy. Now move to the window that contains the target SmartMaster set. Make sure that you are in Page Layouts view and Page Sorter view.

Choose Edit Paste to copy the Weekly Report page layout to the target SmartMaster set. Next, you have to reassign the Basic Layout page to the new page layout. With Weekly Report selected, click the Page Layout button on the bottom border, highlight Basic Layout, and then click OK.

Finally, use File Save As to save the SmartMaster set with the new page layout. You can save just a SmartMaster set with the options as shown in figure 25.9. You have to repeat this procedure for every SmartMaster set that you want to contain the new page layout.

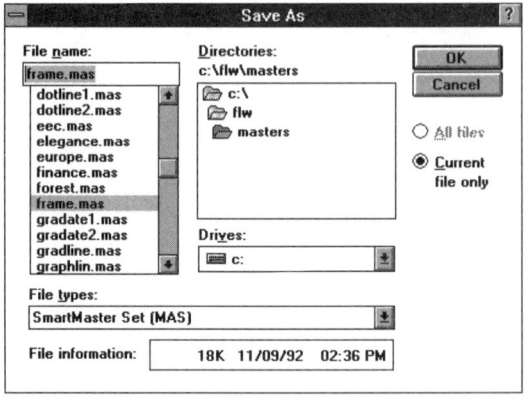

FIGURE 25.9. The Save As dialog box.

See Chapter 26, "Creating Your Own SmartMaster Sets," for more information about saving and retrieving SmartMaster sets.

Wrapping Up

This chapter covered the basics of editing SmartMaster page layouts. You now have the foundations required to change existing SmartMaster sets to better suit your needs. You know how to create your own "Click here..." blocks and how to create a new page layout. After you have mastered these basics, you may feel adventurous enough to create your own SmartMaster set. To find out how, read Chapter 26, "Creating Your Own SmartMaster Sets."

26

Creating Your Own SmartMaster Sets

Although Freelance Graphics comes with 65 SmartMaster sets, you still may not find the precise look you want among them. Maybe you want to create a SmartMaster set designed especially for your own company or for a group within your company. Or perhaps you need special page formats that are not included in the 11 page layouts of each SmartMaster set. Or maybe you just want to experiment. For whatever reason, the process of creating a new SmartMaster set is straightforward after you understand a few basics about the structure of SmartMaster sets.

If you have learned how to customize existing SmartMaster sets, as described in Chapter 25, "Understanding SmartMaster Sets," you already have most of the knowledge required to create your own SmartMaster sets. This chapter fills in a few more details and explains how to undertake this task in the most efficient manner.

The Scenario

Suppose that the sales and marketing departments of your company, EnviroTech, Inc. (which markets office supplies made from recyclable materials), gives numerous sales presentations to prospective clients. Everyone is already using Freelance Graphics, but different groups are using different SmartMaster sets for their presentations. The head of marketing, Stacey Greengrow, has

In this chapter, you learn how to:
- *Create your own SmartMaster set that everyone in your work group can use for consistent presentations*
- *Open just a SmartMaster set*
- *Add design elements to the Basic Layout and the Title page*

decided that to present a united front to customers and prospects, everyone should be using the same SmartMaster set. It is your job to create this new SmartMaster set.

You begin by looking through the SmartMaster sets that come with Freelance Graphics. After perusing the 65 SmartMaster sets in Freelance Graphics, you conclude that none quite projects the right image for your company.

You then decide to tackle the job of creating a SmartMaster set yourself. The rest of this chapter describes the process of creating this customized SmartMaster set.

Start with an Existing SmartMaster Set

Before you create a customized SmartMaster set, ask yourself this question: Do I want to create a SmartMaster set that is interchangeable with the 65 SmartMaster sets provided with Freelance Graphics? If the answer is yes, your best bet is to customize one of the SmartMaster sets that comes with Freelance. This foundation ensures that the new SmartMaster set has the appropriate name and number of page layouts.

As explained in Chapter 25, "Understanding SmartMaster Sets," Freelance Graphics uses the names of each SmartMaster page layout to map to the pages of the new SmartMaster set you choose. When you switch SmartMaster sets, every page that uses the Bulleted List page layout, for example, is matched with the Bulleted List page layout from the new SmartMaster set. That's why each of the 65 SmartMaster sets has precisely 11 page layouts, each with the same name.

If you create a SmartMaster set with an entirely new set of names for page layouts and then choose another SmartMaster set, none of the page layouts matches up with the custom SmartMaster set. If you do switch to another SmartMaster set, your presentation pages lose all page layout assignments. You don't lose any of your content, of course, and you can choose page layouts again for these pages. But this is an inefficient way to work.

On the other hand, if you plan to use the same SmartMaster set in all your presentations and you don't foresee switching SmartMaster sets, feel free to create your own SmartMaster set and use whatever names you want for page layouts. Just be aware of the consequences.

Try It: Open Just a SmartMaster Set

When you want to create a new SmartMaster set based on an existing one, it is best to open just the SmartMaster set, without any accompanying presentation pages. You are changing page layouts, not creating presentation pages. You can open a SmartMaster set with the File Open command.

Now, open a SmartMaster set only, so that you can edit it. Freelance Graphics comes with a SmartMaster set named CUSTOM.MAS. This SmartMaster set contains the standard 11 page layouts shared by all the SmartMaster sets. Each page layout contains the standard SmartMaster text blocks and placement blocks, so you don't have to start from scratch. What makes this SmartMaster set unique is a complete absence of design elements. Think of it as a blank canvas that you can use to create your own SmartMaster set. Follow these steps:

Use CUSTOM.MAS as the basis of your new SmartMaster set.

1. Choose File Open or click the File Open SmartIcon. You see the Open File dialog box (see fig. 26.1).

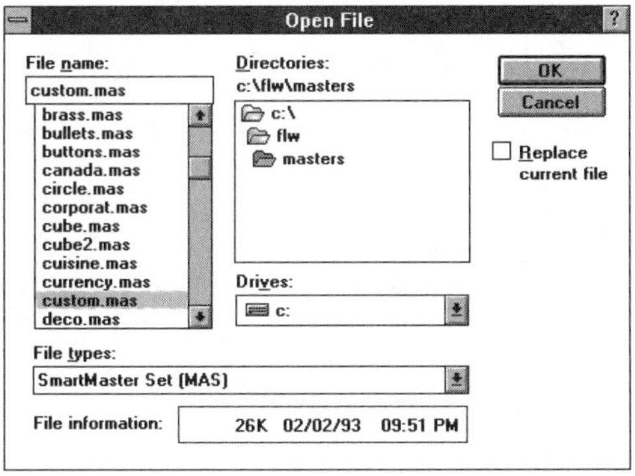

FIGURE 26.1. The Open File dialog box.

2. Choose SmartMaster Set (MAS) from the File Types list box.
3. In the Directories box, change to the FLW\MASTERS directory.
4. Double-click CUSTOM.MAS.

Freelance displays the SmartMaster set in Page Sorter view (see fig. 26.2). Notice the diagonal lines in the background and the message "SmartMaster" to the left in the Title bar. These clues indicate that you are in Page Layout view. Now you can customize these pages as you like or create additional pages.

Create the Design

As you learned in Chapter 25, "Understanding SmartMaster Sets," the basic design elements that give a SmartMaster set its unique look are found on the Basic Layout page. If you are creating your own SmartMaster set, this page is where you should add the design elements that give your custom SmartMaster set its unique look.

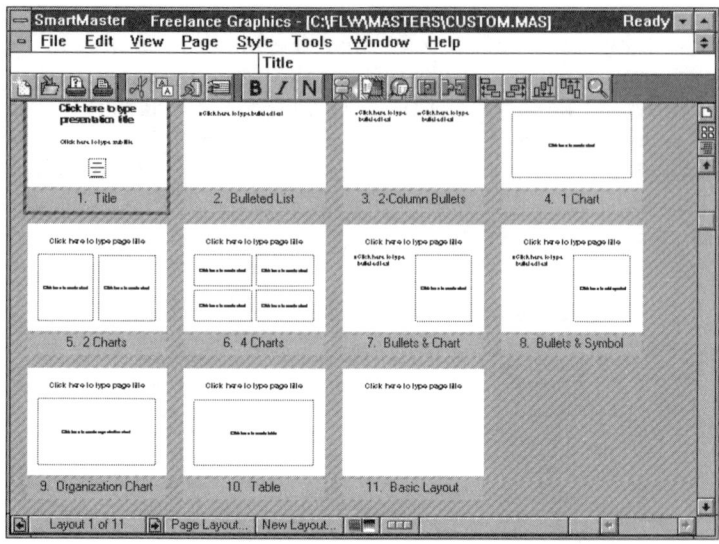

FIGURE 26.2. When you open a SmartMaster set, Freelance Graphics displays it in Page Sorter view, which contains the 11 page layouts common to every SmartMaster set.

To get started, make Basic Layout page the current page in SmartMaster Pages view (double-click it). Then use the drawing tools, add clip art (symbols), or import graphics to create the design for this page.

As you can see, the Basic Layout page in CUSTOM.MAS contains nothing but the SmartMaster text block for a page title. You can add whatever design elements you want to the rest of the page. Keep in mind that you really have only the area around the center of the page in which to work because the center space is used up by SmartMaster text blocks for bullet charts, placement blocks for graphs, and so on.

As you work on your design, you must be careful that nothing you add falls outside the margins of the page. Choose View View Preferences and click the Printable Area radio button under the Show Page Borders option. This option gives you a visual guideline of the printable area for your current output device and prevents you from adding any design elements outside this boundary. Incidentally, because Freelance adjusts the printable area depending on the current output device, use File Printer Setup to select the output device that you use to produce your presentation pages. (If you want your SmartMaster set to look good on a variety of output devices, the Apple LaserWriter Plus is a good all-around choice.) You can choose this printer driver even if you don't have the printer itself. (If this printer does not appear in the list of available printers, you can install it with the Printers option in the Windows Control Panel.)

If you are designing a SmartMaster set exclusively for slides, choose File Printer Setup and mark the check box Set Margins for Slides. When you click OK, notice that the margins change.

Use a Palette from an Existing SmartMaster

The next step is to choose a palette for your SmartMaster set. One method is to use the Style Choose Palette command to choose one of the six palettes included with Freelance (PAL1.MAS through PAL6.MAS).

Another method is to use the palette from an existing SmartMaster set. This method has the advantage of enabling you to see how the palette looks with an existing SmartMaster set. Suppose that you decide to use the palette used by the SmartMaster set CUISINE.MAS. Without closing the existing presentation, start a new presentation and choose CUISINE.MAS. Choose any page layout and then choose Style Edit Palette. This selection displays the palette for this SmartMaster set. Click the Save button, type a name for the palette (*ENVIRO*) in the File Name box, and click OK. Freelance adds the .PAL extension automatically.

Close this presentation and return to the new SmartMaster set you are creating. Choose Style Choose Palette. Highlight ENVIRO.PAL and click OK. (If this name does not appear in the list, make sure that you saved it in the FLW\MASTERS directory.)

Change the Background Color

To choose a new background for the presentation, choose Page Background. In the resulting dialog box, click the 1st Color list box. Choose Midnight as the background color (use the second color in the second row), click the Entire Presentation radio button, and click OK. This procedure gives a background color of Midnight (dark blue) to your entire presentation.

Add a Decorative Rule

Rules, or lines of varying widths, are at the same time the most common and effective of all design elements. Not only do they help set off text and graphics from the rest of the page, but they also give the page a cohesive, structured look.

Add a horizontal rule below the title block. Use the Rectangle tool to make the rule so that you can add a graduated fill pattern.

Click the Rectangle icon in the Toolbox and drag a long, thin rectangle below the title block (see fig. 26.5). This rectangle can extend off the edge of the page. (When you create presentation pages, it appears to stop at the edge of the page.) Extending it off the edge of the page ensures that the rule *bleeds* to the edge of the page no matter what output device you use.

To make the rectangle more interesting, add a drop shadow. Double-click the rectangle and, in the Style Attributes Rectangle dialog box, select Bottom Right from the Shadow list box (see fig. 26.3). Click the 1st Color list box and choose manganese blue for the rectangle's color (the second color in the third row of the palette). Click OK to close the dialog box.

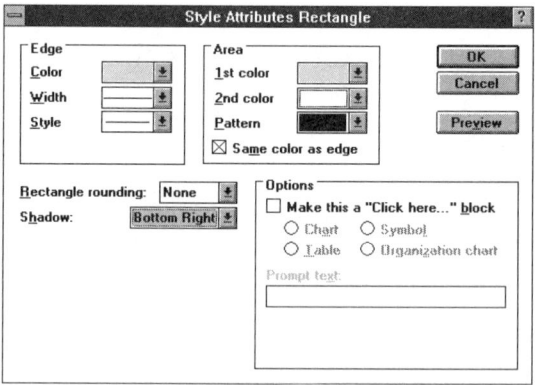

FIGURE 26.3. Use the Style Attributes Rectangle dialog box to add a drop shadow by choosing Bottom Right from the Shadow list box.

Add a Logo

After looking through the symbol library, you decide to use the international recycling symbol (from the symbol library ENVIRONM.SYM) as the basic design element of your SmartMaster set (see fig. 26.4).

Double-click the recycling symbol to add it to the page. To size the symbol, press Shift as you drag a corner selection to make it smaller. (For more information on sizing objects, see Chapter 13, "Editing Objects.") Then drag the symbol to the upper right corner, as shown in figure 26.5.

Creating Your Own SmartMaster Sets 433

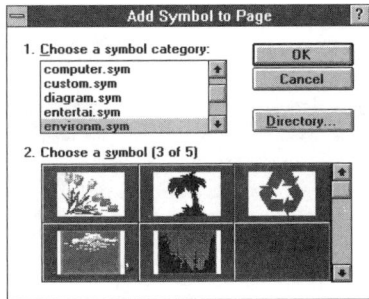

FIGURE 26.4. The Add Symbol to Page dialog box.

To frame the symbol and add another interesting design element, you can place a box with a drop shadow behind the symbol. To create the box, click the Rectangle icon and drag a box on the page (press Shift as you drag to constrain the shape to a square). Now double-click the square and make sure that the Same Color as Edge check box is marked. Click the arrow in the 1st Color list box and click the second color in the third row (manganese blue). Finally, click the arrow in the Shadow list box and choose Bottom Right. Click OK.

Now select the environmental symbol and drag it on top of the shadowed box. If the symbol vanishes, choose Arrange Priority Top to bring it to the top. You also may have to adjust the size of the symbol so that it fits nicely in the box. Next, hold down the left mouse button, drag a selection box around the box and the symbol, and choose Arrange Group (or click the Group SmartIcon). Finally, move the completed motif just above the rule, sizing it if necessary. Compare your results to figure 26.5.

Adjust the Title Block

The title text block is already in place. Double-click it. This text block just requires a couple of minor adjustments. This dialog box has two icons that adjust horizontal and vertical justification of the text block. Take a look at these icons. To left justify the title, click the first icon in the row of icons to the right of Justification.

The second justification choice, Vertical Justification, determines the direction (up or down) in which wrapping text expands. The first icon specifies that the text moves down on the page as the text grows. The second icon centers the text. The third choice specifies that the text expands up as more lines are added. The third choice is what you want here. This choice means a one-line text title sits just above the rule. A two-line title expands upward from the rule, just as you want. Make these changes and click OK. You may have to reposition the title block so it fits just above the rule.

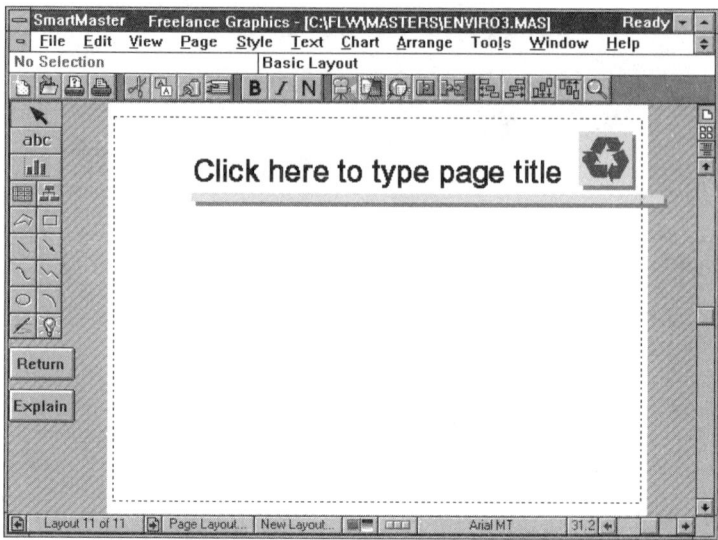

FIGURE 26.5. Adding the recycling symbol and placing a box with a drop shadow behind the symbol adds visual interest.

Chapter 3, "Creating, Editing, and Formatting Text," explains other options in the Paragraph Styles dialog box.

Because, as you learned in Chapter 25, "Understanding SmartMaster Sets," all the page layouts except Title inherit the design elements from Basic Layout, you have now completed the major design work for your SmartMaster set. To see the effect of your work, click the Page Sorter icon and note that all the pages (except the Title page) have inherited the contents of the Basic Layout page.

Create the Title Page Layout

The final step is to create the Title page. Double-click this page in the Page Sorter to move to Current Page view. The SmartMaster text block for the page title is already in place. Leave the typeface and text color as they are.

But because the Title page does not inherit design elements from the Basic Layout page, you must add design elements to this page separately. The Title page of CUSTOM.MAS contains place holders for a title and subtitle and a placement block for a symbol. You can use all of these, but you have to move them around a bit, change the typeface for the text blocks, and add a rule like the one you added to Basic Layout. Select the rule on the Basic Layout page and use Edit Copy and Edit Paste to move it to the Title page. Then use Edit Replicate to make a copy of the rule. Size and place the rules as shown in figure 26.6.

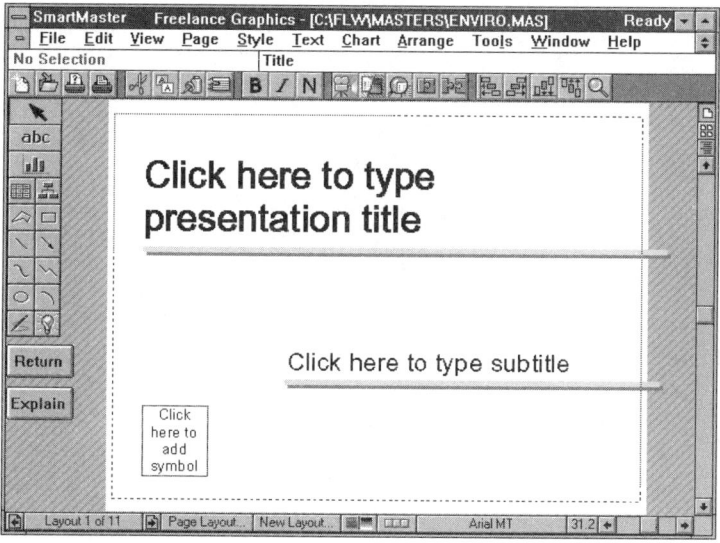

FIGURE 26.6. The completed Title page layout.

Select the title and the subtitle block and choose Text Paragraph Styles. Click the first icon in the Justification row and the third icon in the Vertical Just. row. Then click OK.

Use figure 26.7 as a guide to make any remaining necessary changes. Make sure, for example, that the main title block, the rule, and the "Click here..." symbol block are left-aligned. (Select all three objects and click the Align Left SmartIcon.)

Adjust the Remaining Page Layouts

You can keep the remaining page layouts pretty much as they are. Because they inherit most of their design elements from Basic Layout, you don't have to make many changes to them.

You may have to change the size of a few placement blocks, however, to make sure that they fit within the design. Some of the placement blocks for graphs or bullet charts may bump into the title block, for example. Just browse through all the page layouts (or click the Page Sorter icon) to verify that no SmartMaster text blocks or placement blocks overlap the rule beneath the title and logo. If they do, return to the Basic Layout page and adjust the size and position of the rule and the symbol to make sure that there are no collisions.

FIGURE 26.7. A Title page for EnviroTech, using the Title page layout from the new SmartMaster set.

Finally, you can save the SmartMaster set. Choose File Save, select SmartMaster set as the file type, type *ENVIRO* in the File Name box, and click OK. Make sure that you save the new SmartMaster in the FLW\MASTERS directory so that it appears in the list of SmartMasters when you create a new presentation or choose a new SmartMaster set.

To make sure that the new SmartMaster set is designed properly, create a new presentation and choose ENVIRO.MAS as the SmartMaster set. Add a title page, a bulleted list, a chart, and so on, testing each of the page layouts. You may notice minor details that you want to change. If you do, return to Page Layouts view and make the necessary changes. Remember to save your changes.

Figure 26.8 shows a complete presentation page that uses the Bullets & Symbol page layout. The image of the envelope was taken from the OFFOBJCT.SYM symbol library (with an added drop shadow).

Paper Products

- File folders
- Laser printer paper
- Envelopes
- Labels
- Notepads
- Clasp envelopes

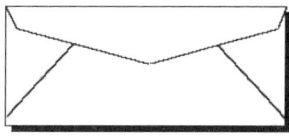

FIGURE 26.8. A completed presentation page.

What About Black and White?

If you plan to create both color and black-and-white presentations, you also should test the presentation in black and white. Because you chose a palette from an existing SmartMaster set, your presentation should look fine in black and white. Recall that every SmartMaster comes with both a color and a black-and-white palette. To test the black-and-white version, just click the Color/B&W button on the bottom border. In this case, everything looks fine. Sometimes, though, you may have to make changes to the black-and-white palette. For example, the background color may not be white. If necessary, choose Style Edit Palette and make any necessary changes.

Wrapping Up

In this chapter, you learned how to create a new SmartMaster set by using CUSTOM.MAS as a basic template. You learned how to use a palette from an existing SmartMaster set to save a good deal of work. You discovered that by incorporating a symbol and a couple of simple graphic elements into a simple design, you can create a high-quality SmartMaster set that is interchangeable with the 65 SmartMaster sets Lotus provides.

This chapter completes this book. The tools, tips, and techniques you learned in these pages should make the task of creating your next presentation easier and more pleasurable. Good luck!

Index

Symbols

1-2-3 for Windows, 390
2-Column Bullets page layout, 31, 34-35, 74-76
35mm slides
　creating, 359-367
　files
　　creating, 363-364
　　sending to Autographix service center, 364-367
　glass mounts, 366
　preparing presentations, 363
　work orders, creating, 364-367
3D
　area charts, 102
　bar charts, 99, 126-127
　pie charts, 105-106
　XYZ charts, 128
9600-baud modem, 367

A

accelerator keys, 54
accessing Toolbox, 373
activating
　presentations, 380
　Toolbox icons, 395
active voice verbs, 42
Add Column SmartIcon, 202
Add Entry dialog box, 365
Add Row SmartIcon, 202
Add Symbol to Page dialog box, 7
Add Unlisted or Updated Printer dialog box, 361
Adjust Color Library for Color Printing check box, 364
Advanced Options dialog box, 362
AI files, 301, 309
aligning objects, 240
Alignment icon, 389
All Chart Text dialog box, 149-150
Ami Pro, launching, 390
Annotate dialog box, 25
annotating pages, 161-162, 378-379
applications, launching, 353-354, 390
Arc tool, 219
arcs, drawing, 219
Area Chart Attributes dialog box, 131
area charts, 93-94, 101-103, 130-131
Arrange Align command, 240
Arrange commands, 279
Arrange Connect Lines command, 261
Arrange Convert to Polygon command, 254
Arrange Flip command, 240-241
Arrange Flip Left to Right command, 385
Arrange Group command, 239
Arrange menu SmartIcons, 385
Arrange Points Mode, 253-255
Arrange Rotate command, 242
arrows
　adding, 161
　drawing, 217-218

ASCII
    files, importing, 304-305
    text
        copying/pasting, 246
        importing, 81
assembling presentations, 371
attributes
    axis labels, 146-149
    chart, 145
    object, changing, 233-237
    organization charts, changing, 196
    text, default, 61-62
audience notes, 332-333
Auto Time Save check box, 396
Autographix 4.1 on FILE dialog box, 361
Autographix driver
    installing, 360-361
    options, selecting, 361-363
Autographix Order Instructions dialog box, 366
Autographix Slide Service, installing, 360
Autographix Slide Service icon, 364
Autosave command, 396
axis labels
    copying, 171-172
    customizing, 146-149
axis titles
    adding, 14-15
    charts, 122-123
    hiding, 149

B

Back button, 22
background, customizing, 159-160
background color palette, 322
Backup command, 395
Bar Chart Attributes dialog box, 118, 145-146

bar charts, 93-94
    3D (XYZ), 128
    clustered, 98
    horizontal, 16
    horizontal and vertical, 94-95
    labeling bars with values, 126
    stacked, 95-98
    step chart, 128-129
    three-dimensional, 99, 126-127
Bar-Line Chart Attributes dialog box, 130-131
bar-line charts, 109, 130
Basic Layout, 412-413
Bezier curves, editing, 257-259
Billing Information dialog box, 367
bitmaps
    copying, 247
    files, importing, 305
black and white
    design, 317-318
    palettes, displaying, 397
    printing, 337
bleeding rules, 432
blocks of text, *see* text blocks
BMP files, 301, 309
Bold (Ctrl+B) accelerator key, 54
Bold SmartIcon, 53
Bookmark Define command, 24
Bookmark Define dialog box, 24
bookmarks, 24
borders, page, 399-400
branching screen shows, 342
breaking objects, 262-263
Browse buttons, 22
build slides, 354-356
bullet charts, 30-31
    creating, 31-32
    guidelines, 38-42
    Outliner view, 73-76
    typpograhpy, 42-45
bullet page layouts, 31
Bulleted List page layout, 31-34, 74, 377-378
bulleted lists, creating, 9-11

bullets
   creating/editing, 378
   replacing with clip art, 294-296
   symbols, 68
Bullets & Chart page layout, 31, 35
Bullets & Symbol page layout, 31, 35-37

C

capital letters, 39
cascading windows, 382-383
categories of charts, 92
cc:Mail, launching, 390
CGM files, 302, 309
CH3 files, 302
character attributes, 53-54
Chart All Chart Text command, 149
Chart Attributes command, 126-131
Chart Axis Labels dialog box, 146-149
Chart Axis Titles dialog box, 146-149
Chart Background dialog box, 159
chart color palette, 323
Chart Data & Titles window, 13-16, 115-125, 404
Chart Edit command, 14, 123
Chart Frame command, 128
Chart Gallery, 12-13, 16, 114, 124
Chart Headings & Notes dialog box, 157
Chart icon, 123
Chart Legend command, 119
Chart Legend dialog box, 119
Chart menu, 144-145
Chart Number Grid command, 138
Chart Number Grid Under Chart command, 97, 126
Chart Options Date Fill command, 120, 132
Chart Options Date Fill dialog box, 120
Chart Replace Defaults command, 404
Chart Scale command, 150
Chart Scale dialog box, 150-151
Chart Type command, 124
Chart Value Labels command, 126

Chart Value Labels dialog box, 126
charts
   area, *see* area charts
   axis titles, 122-123
   bar, *see* bar charts
   bar-line, 109, 130
   build slides, 355-356
   bullet, *see* bullet charts
   copying, 179-181
   creating, *see* creating, charts
   customizing, *see* customizing charts
   data, *see* data charts
   data-driven, 111
   enlarging, 145
   flow, creating, 266
   headings, 121-122
   high-low-close-open, 131-141
   high-low-open-close, 105-106
   legends, 119
      hiding, 156
      positioning, 145, 156
   line, 93-94, 99-100, 129-130
   named, importing, 178-179
   notes, 122
   organization, *see* organization charts
   pages, 138-140
   paragraph, 37
   pie, *see* pie charts
   previewing, 121
   radar, 107-108
   SmartMaster page layouts, 113
   table, 108, 134
      creating, 134-136
      frames, 136-137
      grid style, 138
      sum of columns, 137
      width of columns, 138
   terminology, 111-112
   text, *see* text charts
   types, 92-94, 114-115, 124-125
   xy scatter, 107
Charts page layout, 140

check boxes
    Adjust Color Library for Color Printing, 364
    Auto Time Save, 396
    Drawing Ruler, 400
    Function Key Panel, 400
    Set Margins for Slides, 363
    Text Block Ruler, 400
Choose a Look for Your Presentation dialog box, 5
Choose Page Layout dialog box, 6
Choose SmartMaster Set dialog box, 17
choropleth maps, 277
CHT files, 302
circles, drawing, 218
clip art, 7, 285
    as background, 297-298
    customized libraries, 298-299
    diagrams, 296-297
    directing attention with, 288-290
    editing, 298
    graphs, 288-291
    presentation pages, 286
    reinforcing content with, 287
    replacing bullet markers, 294-296
    text charts, 294
Clipboard, 52, 243-244
    copying objects, 244-245
    copying text and graphics, 310
    keystrokes, 244
    pasting objects, 244
Close a File SmartIcon, 26
Close command, 382
closing
    files, 26
    windows, 382
clustered bar charts, 98
Collapse All icon, 81
collapsing outlines, 80-81
color
    design, 235-236, 313-316
    libraries, 319-320, 324-325
    objects, 312-313
    optimizing for printing, 338
    presentations, 311-313
color palettes, 319-320
    background, 322
    chart, 323
    creating, 320-321
    foreground, 322-323
    text, 321-322
columns, table chart
    deleting, 202
    equal width, 138
    inserting, 202-203
    moving, 204-205
    selecting, 202
    sizing, 203-204
    sum of, 137
commands
    Arrange Align, 240
    Arrange Connect Lines, 261
    Arrange Convert to Polygon, 254
    Arrange Flip, 240-241
    Arrange Flip Left to Right, 385
    Arrange Group, 239
    Arrange Rotate, 242
    Autosave, 396
    Backup, 395
    Bookmark Define, 24
    Chart All Chart Text, 149
    Chart Attributes, 126-131
    Chart Edit, 14, 123
    Chart Frame, 128
    Chart Legend, 119
    Chart Number Grid, 138
    Chart Number Grid Under Chart, 97, 126
    Chart Options Date Fill, 120, 132
    Chart Replace Defaults, 404
    Chart Scale, 150
    Chart Type, 124
    Chart Value Labels, 126
    Close, 382
    Confirm, 396
    Coordinates, 399
    Current Page, 372

Default Bullet, 378
Default Face, 378
Default Size, 378
Edit Automate, 25
Edit Clear, 52, 191, 248
Edit Copy, 52, 191, 244-245, 379
Edit Copy Whole Chart, 191
Edit Cut, 52, 191, 248
Edit Demote, 192
Edit Links, 182
Edit Page Layouts, 409
Edit Paste, 52, 81, 180, 191, 244-245, 379
Edit Paste Special, 180
Edit Promote, 192
Edit Replicate, 245-248, 395
Edit Select Cycle, 233
Edit Select Like, 232
Edit Undo, 228, 396
File Close, 26
File Exit, 26
File Import, 81
File Page Setup, 364
File Print, 21, 379
File Print Topic, 25
File Run, 4
File Save, 25
File Save As, 424
Floating, 387
Help Bookmark, 24
Install Unlisted or Updated Printer, 360
Install with Options, 360
Keep Tool Active, 395
Maximize, 381
Minimize, 382
Move, 381
Optimize for Screen Show, 403
Outline Collapse All, 81
Outline Make Second Column, 74
Outliner, 372
Page New, 8
Page Remove, 249
Page Sorter, 372
Page Speaker Notes, 331, 378
Replace, 395
Restore, 381
Screen Show, 377
Style Choose SmartMaster Set, 17, 377
Text Bold, 53
Text Bullet, 378
Text Paragraph Styles, 60
Text Reset To Style, 54
Text Size, 378
Tools Spell, 83
Tools User Setup, 25, 223-224
Units & Grids, 377
Use Compression, 365
view, 372
View Current Page, 79
View Full Page, 372
View Last, 372-373
View Outliner, 71
View Page Sorter, 18
View Preferences, 376
View Redraw, 373
View Screen Show Edit Effects, 342
View Screen Show Run, 20, 342
View Units & Grid, 219
View Units & Grids, 401
View View Preferences, 398
View Zoom In, 372
View Zoom Out, 372
Windows Cascade, 382
Windows Tile, 382
Communications Setup dialog box, 365-367
conceptual diagrams, 273
Confirm command, 396
connecting objects, 261-262
Contents button, 22
Control menu, 381
converting objects, 259-261
Coordinates command, 399
copying
    ASCII text, 246
    axis labels, 171-172
    bitmaps, 247
    charts, 179-181

customized SmartMaster sets, 424
data sets, 173-175
graphics, 310
metafiles, 247
objects, 243-249
organization chart entries, 191
pages, 379-380
text, 52, 310
creating
   bulleted lists, 9-11
   charts, 112-125, 165-166
      automatic updates, 182-184
      bullet, 31-32
      copying data, 176-178
      data, 11-16
      importing data, 166-175
      purpose, 92
      table, 134-136
      without leaving Freelance Graphics, 182-184
   color palettes, 320-321
   custom dictionary, 87
   diagrams, 213-215, 279-281
   flow charts, 266
   organization charts, 188-190
   SmartMaster sets, 427-428
   tables, 200-201
   title pages, 6-8
cross-references, 24
crosshair pointers, 280, 398
Ctrl+C (Copy) key combination, 54, 244
Ctrl+F3 (replicate) key combination, 395
Ctrl+F4 (windows, closing) key combination, 382
Ctrl+F6 (windows, activating) key combination, 380
Ctrl+V (Paste) key combination, 244
Ctrl+X (Cut) key combination, 244
cumulative area chart, 103
Current Page command, 372
Current Page icon, 79
Current Page view, 71, 79-80, 371-373
   duplicating objects, 247-248
cursors, sizing, 398
Curve tool, 217-218
curved text, 65-68
Curved Text dialog box, 66-67
curves, Bezier, 257-259
custom dictionary, creating, 87
CUSTOM.MAS SmartMaster set, 429
customizing
   charts, 143-144
      annotations, 161-162
      axis labels, 146-149
      background, 159-160
      Chart menu, 145
      data sets, hiding, 157-158
      double-clicking component, 145-146
      frame, adding, 155
      globally, 149-150
      grid lines, 153-154
      headings, 156-157
      legends, 155-156
      notes, 156-157
      number grid, adding, 158-159
      scale, 150-153
      settings, 404
      tick marks, 153-154
      titles, 146-149
   drawing options, 400-401
   drawing tools, 221-224
   SmartMaster sets, 417
      bullet color, 419
      bulleted list spacing, 420-421
      "Click here..." chart block, 423
      "Click here..." text block, 422
      copying customized pages, 424-425
      logos, 421
      page layout, 421-422
      text attributes, 418-419
Cut SmartIcon, 385
Cycle Selection dialog box, 233

D

data, 112
    importing for charts, 166-175
    presenting, 92
    reporting, 92
    time-series, 112, 119-120
data charts
    axis titles, 14-15
    checking spelling, 85-86
    creating, 11-16
    entering, 115-118
    page layout, 11-12
    previewing, 15
    text and numbers, 13
    types, 12-13
    windows, 14
data pairs, 112
data sets, 112
    copying, 173-175
    hiding, 157-158
data symbols, 112
data values, 112
data view, 14
data-driven charts, 111
DDE (Dynamic Data Exchange) links, 170
Default Bullet command, 378
Default Face command, 378
Default Paragraph Styles dialog box, 266-267
Default Size command, 378
default text attributes, 61-62
Default Text Frame dialog box, 267
definitions, help, 24
Delete Column SmartIcon, 202
Delete Row SmartIcon, 202
deleting
    icons, 386-388
    links, 184
    objects, 248-249
    organization chart entries, 191
    points, 254-257
    SmartIcon sets, 389
    table rows/columns, 202
    text, 52

dependent variable, 112
descriptions, displaying, 386
deselecting objects, 231
design
    black-and-white, 317-318
    color, 313-316
    principles, 281-284
diagrams, 265
    clip art, 296-297
    conceptual, 273
    consistency, 400-401
    creating, 279-281
    procedure, 272-273
    word, 270-271
dialog boxes
    Add Entry, 365
    Add Symbol to Page, 7
    Add Unlisted or Updated Printer, 361
    Advanced Options, 362
    All Chart Text, 149-150
    Annotate, 25
    Area Chart Attributes, 131
    Autographix 4.1 on FILE, 361
    Autographix Order Instructions, 366
    Bar Chart Attributes, 118, 145-146
    Bar-Line Chart Attributes, 130-131
    Billing Information, 367
    Bookmark Define, 24
    Chart Axis Labels, 146-149
    Chart Axis Titles, 146-149
    Chart Background, 159
    Chart Headings & Notes, 157
    Chart Legend, 119
    Chart Options Date Fill, 120
    Chart Scale, 150-151
    Chart Value Labels, 126
    Choose a Look for Your Presentation, 5
    Choose Page Layout, 6
    Choose SmartMaster Set, 17
    Communications Setup, 365-367
    Curved Text, 66-67
    Cycle Selection, 233
    Default Paragraph Styles, 266-267

Default Text Frame, 267
Edit Icon, 389-390
Edit Insert Object, 352
Edit Library, 325
Edit Links, 183
Edit Palette, 324
Edit Paste Special, 176
Edit Screen Show, 342-343
Export File, 308
Export Screen Show, 357
File Page Setup, 399-401
Find Application to Launch, 354
HLCO Chart Attributes, 132
Import Data, 168, 172
Import Data File, 167, 306
Import Named Chart, 179
Insert Column/Row, 202
Install Driver, 361
International User Setup, 397
Links, 183
Lotus Media Manager, 350
Mix Instructions, 365
Move Column/Row, 204-205
New Chart Gallery, 114
New Page, 8
Number Grid Chart, 136
Number Grid Chart Attributes, 136
Number Grid Frame, 137
Number Grid Style, 138
Number Grid Under Chart, 158-159
Organization Chart Attributes, 196
Organization Chart Gallery, 189
Organization Chart Staff, 193-194
Paragraph Styles, 48, 60-64, 419
Paste Special, 180
Play Options, 353
Print File, 21, 330, 364
Printer Setup, 403
Printers, 360-361
Save As, 424
Screen Show Export Options, 358
Screen Show Options, 346
Search, 23

Select Like Objects, 232
Size Column/Row, 203-204
SmartIcons, 386-389
Spacing & Indents, 62-63, 420
Speaker Note, 332
Speaker Notes, 378-379
Spell Check, 85
Style Attributes Polygon & Shape, 234
Style Attributes Rectangle, 215
Style Default Attributes Mixed, 222-223
Symbol for Bullet, 68
Table Attributes, 205
Text Color, 54
Text Frame, 64
ToAGX-Windows, 364
Units & Grids, 225, 280
User Setup, 394, 397
View Preferences, 376, 398
View Screen Show, 403
Welcome to Freelance Graphics, 4-5
directories, default, 398
drag-selecting, 51
drawing
  arcs, 219
  arrows, 217-218
  circles, 218
  during screen shows, 345-346
  ellipses, 218
  lines, 217-218
  options, customizing, 400-401
  polygons, 219-220
  priority, 249
  rectangles, 212-213
  rounded rectangles, 215-216
  saving time with SmartIcons, 224
  squares, 212-213
  undoing actions, 228
  with grids, 225-226
  zooming drawing area, 226-228
Drawing Ruler check box, 400

Index **447**

drawing tools
   Arc, 219
   Curve, 217-218
   customizing, 221-224
   default attributes, setting, 400-401
   Freehand, 220-221
   keeping active, 223-224
   Polygon, 219-220
   Zoom, 226-228
drivers, Autographix, 360-363
drop shadows, 68, 269
DRW files, 302, 309
duplicating objects, 247-248
DXF files, 302
Dynamic Data Exchange, see DDE, 170

E

Edit Automate command, 25
Edit Chart Data SmartIcon, 123
Edit Clear command, 52, 191, 248
Edit Clear SmartIcon, 52
Edit Copy command, 52, 191, 244-245, 379
Edit Copy SmartIcon, 52
Edit Copy Whole Chart command, 191
Edit Cut command, 52, 191, 248
Edit Cut SmartIcon, 52
Edit Demote command, 192
Edit Icon dialog box, 389-390
Edit Insert Object dialog box, 352
Edit Library dialog box, 325
Edit Links command, 182
Edit Links dialog box, 183
Edit Page Layouts command, 409
Edit Palette dialog box, 324
Edit Paste command, 52, 81, 180, 191, 244-245, 379
Edit Paste SmartIcon, 52, 81, 385
Edit Paste Special command, 180
Edit Paste Special dialog box, 176
Edit Points SmartIcon, 253
Edit Promote command, 192

Edit Replicate command, 245-248, 395
Edit Screen Show dialog box, 342-343
Edit Select Cycle command, 233
Edit Select Like command, 232
Edit Undo command, 228, 396
editing
   axis label attributes, 146-149
   Bezier curves, 257-259
   bullets, 378
   clip art, 298
   color library, 324-325
   FLW2.INI file, 390
   links, 182
   organization charts, 190-194
   points, 253-257
   quick, 55
   SmartIcon Set, 386-388
   table entries, 201
   text
      curved, 66-67
      in charts, 123-124
   text blocks, 50-55
   titles, 146-149
effects, transition, 342-343
ellipses, drawing, 218
EPS files, 302
Esc key, 373
Exit Freelance Graphics SmartIcon, 26
expanding outlines, 80-81
Export File dialog box, 308
Export Screen Show dialog box, 357
exporting files, 308-310

F

File Close command, 26
File Exit command, 26
File Import command, 81
file links, 170
File Page Setup command, 364
File Page Setup dialog box, 399-401
File Print command, 21, 379

File Print Topic command, 25
File Run command, 4
File Save As command, 424
File Save command, 25
File Save SmartIcon, 25
files
   AI, 301, 309
   ASCII, importing, 304-305
   Autographix, installing, 360
   bitmap, importing, 305
   closing, 26
   displaying recent, 396
   exporting, 308-310
   extensions, 301-303, 309
   FLW2.INI, 390
   importing, 301-305
   metafiles, importing, 308
   PRE, 359-360
   saving, 395-396
   slide
      creating, 363-364
      sending, 364-367
   Stingray SCODL slide, 359
fill patterns
   changing, 235
   graduated, 316
Find Application to Launch dialog box, 354
Flip Left to Right SmartIcon, 241
Flip Top to Bottom SmartIcon, 241
flipping objects, 240-241
Floating command, 387
flow charts, creating, 266
FLW2.INI file, 390
fonts, 43-44
   True Type, 362
footers, 334-336, 402
foreground color palette, 322-323
FRAME.MAS SmartMaster set, 421
frames
   adding, 155
   table charts, 136-137
   for text charts, 38
Freelance Graphics window, 372

Freehand tool, 220-221
Freelance Graphics
   installing, 4-6
   printing outlines, 82
   quick editing with right mouse button, 55
   starting, 4-6
Freelance Graphics window, 380
Function Key Panel check box, 400
function keys, 400

G

GAL files, 302
GEM files, 302
GIF files, 302, 309
glass mounts (slides), 366
globally customizing charts, 149-150
graduated fill patterns, 236, 316
graph type table, 92-94
graphics, copying, 310
graphics placeholder, 9
graphs
   clip art, 288-291
   copying, 245
grid lines, 153-154
grid style table charts, 138
grids, 279-280, 377
   customizing appearance, 145
   drawing with, 225-226
   setting up/displaying, 401
Group SmartIcon, 239
grouping objects, 239, 251-252

H

handouts, 333
headers, 334-336, 402
headings
   charts, 121-122
   frames, adding, 157
help, on-line, 22-25

Help (Alt+H) shortcut key, 22
Help Bookmark command, 24
help icon bar, 22-24
HGL files, 302
hiding
   axis labels, 149
   data sets, 157-158
   legends, 156
   SmartIcon sets, 387
   titles, 149
high-level views, 373-375
high-low-close-open charts, 131-141
high-low-open-close charts, 105-106
highlighting
   regions on maps, 275-276
   table rows, 205-206
History button, 22
HLCO Chart Attributes dialog box, 132
horizontal bar charts, 16, 94-95
horizontal page layout, 402

I

icon bars, help, 22-24
icons
   adding/removing, 386-388
   Alignment, 389
   Autographix Slide Service, 364
   Chart, 123
   Collapse All, 81
   creating, 389-390
   Current Page, 79
   Index-Card, 378-379
   Line, 217
   Move Page, 78
   Next Icon Set SmartIcon, 389
   Outliner, 71
   Page, 73
   Polyline, 217
   Promote, 78
   rearranging, 386
   Rectangle, 212
   sizes, modifying, 388
   Text, 48, 61
   Zoom, 145, 372
Import Data dialog box, 168, 172
Import Data File dialog box, 167, 306
Import Data Window, 305
Import Named Chart dialog box, 179
importing
   ASCII text into Outliner, 81
   data for charts, 166-175
   files, 301-308
   named charts, 178-179
indents, 62-63
Index-Card icon, 378-379
Insert Column/Row dialog box, 202
Install Driver dialog box, 361
Install Unlisted or Updated Printer command, 360
Install with Options command, 360
installing
   Autographix driver, 360-361
   Autographix files, 360
   Autographix Slide Service, 360
   Freelance Graphics, 4-6
interactive screen shows, 346-349
international options, modifying, 397
International User Setup dialog box, 397
Italic (Ctrl+I) accelerator key, 54

J-K

Keep Tool Active command, 395
key combinations, 51
   Alt+F10 (View Screen Show Run), 20
   Alt+H (Help), 22
   Ctrl+C (Copy), 244
   Ctrl+F3 (replicate), 395
   Ctrl+F4 (windows, closing), 382
   Ctrl+F6 (windows, activating), 380
   Ctrl+V (Paste), 244
   Ctrl+X (Cut), 244

keyboards
    moving objects, 243
    navigating in Outliner view, 79
    sizing objects, 238
    tables, 207-208
    text blocks, sizing, 57
keys
    arrow, moving points, 256-257
    Esc, 373
    function, 400

L

labels
    axis, copying, 171-172
    hiding, 149
    pie charts, 105
    skip factor, 148
Landscape orientation mode, 336, 402
launching applications, 353-354, 390
legends
    charts, 105, 119
    hiding, 156
    positioning, 145, 156
libraries
    clip art, 68, 298-299
    color, 319-320, 324-325
line charts, 93-94, 99-100, 129-130
Line icon, 217
line spacing, 62
linear axes, 107
lines
    drawing, 217-218
    selecting, 77
    starting without bullets, 59
links
    DDE, 170
    deleting, 184
    editing, 182
    file, 170
    one-time, 181

Links dialog box, 183
lists
    bulleted, creating, 9-11
    numbered, 62-63
logarithmic axes, 107
Lotus Media Manager dialog box, 350
Lotus Notes, 390
lowercase style, 44-45

M

magnifying glass (Zoom Smarticon), 372
major tick marks, 154
maps, 274
    as background, 277-278
    choropleth, 277
    highlighting regions, 275-276
    marking locations, 275
    routes, 279
margins, 62-63
    modifying, 402-403
    sizing, 399
markers, replacing with clip art, 294-296
marking locations on maps, 275
Maximize command, 381
maximizing windows, 381
menus
    Arrange, 385
    Chart, 144-145
    Control, 381
    Windows, 382
metafiles
    copying, 247
    importing, 308
Minimize command, 382
minimizing windows, 382
minor tick marks, 154
Mix Instructions dialog box, 365
MMGLOBE.MAS SmartMaster set, 349-350
MMLASER.MAS SmartMaster set, 349-350
modems, 9600-baud, 367

modes
   Arrange Points, 253-255
   Landscape, 336
   Portrait, 336
   text edit, 6, 85
mouse
   drag-selecting, 51
   moving objects, 242
   quick editing, 55
   table columns/rows, sizing, 204
   text blocks, sizing, 56
Move Column/Row dialog box, 204-205
Move command, 381
Move Page icon, 78
moving
   between views, 79-80, 377
   objects, 242-243
   pages, 375
   points, 255-257
   table rows/columns, 204-205
   windows, 381
multimedia screen shows, 349-350
multiple
   pages, selecting, 375
   pie charts, 105
   presentations, 379-383
   text blocks, editing, 55

N

named charts, importing, 178-179
New Chart Gallery dialog box, 114
New Page dialog box, 8
Next Icon Set SmartIcon icon, 389
Normal (Ctrl+N) accelerator key, 54
notes, 122
   audience, 332-333
   sizing, 157
   speaker, 331-332, 378-379
novelty text charts, 38
Number Grid Chart Attributes
  dialog box, 136

Number Grid Chart dialog box, 136
Number Grid Frame dialog box, 137
Number Grid Style dialog box, 138
Number Grid Under Chart
  dialog box, 158-159
number grids
   adding, 158-159
   displaying, 158
   see also tables
numbered lists, 62-63
numbers, data charts, 13

O

objects
   aligning, 240
   attributes, changing, 233-237
   breaking, 262-263
   color, 312-313
   connecting, 261-262
   converting, 259-261
   copying, 243-249
   deleting, 248-249
   deselecting, 231
   duplicating, 247-248
   fill pattern, changing, 235-236
   flipping, 240-241
   grouping, 239, 252
   mirror images, creating, 241
   moving, 242-243
   overlapping, 249
   pasting, 243-249
   replicating, 395
   rotating, 242
   selecting, 229-233
   sizing, 237-238
   ungrouping, 251-263
OLE (Object Linking and Embedding),
  associating SmartIcons, 390
on-line help, 22-25
one-time links, 181
opening SmartMaster sets, 428-429

Optimize for Screen Show command, 403
options, start-up, 394-395
Organization Chart Attributes
   dialog box, 196
Organization Chart Gallery dialog box, 189
Organization Chart Staff dialog box, 193-194
organization charts, 187-188
   attributes, changing, 196
   checking spelling, 85-86
   collapsing entry list, 193
   connection lines, adding, 197
   creating, 188-190
   demoting entries, 192
   editing, 190-194
   presentation page, 191-192
   promoting entries, 192
   staff position, adding, 193-194
   styles, changing, 194-197
   text size, controlling, 197
origin point, 399
Outline Collapse All command, 81
Outline Make Second Column command, 74
Outliner command, 372
Outliner icon, 71
Outliner view, 19-20, 71-72, 371-376
   bullet charts, 73-76
   checking spelling, 85
   display, 73
   importing ASCII files, 304-305
   moving to other views, 79-80
   outlines
      expanding/collapsing, 80-81
      printing, 82
   pages
      adding, 78
      deleting, 78
      moving, 78
      navigating, 79-81
      selecting, 77
   text
      importing ASCII, 81
      pasting, 81-82, 246

outlines, 333
   expanding/collapsing, 80-81
   printing, 82
overlapping objects, 249

P

Page icon, 73
page layouts, 8-9
   2-Column Bullets, 34-35, 74-76
   Bulleted List, 33-34, 74, 377-378
   Bullets & Charts, 35
   Bullets & Symbol, 35-37
   Charts, 140
   data charts, 11-12
   SmartMaster, 31, 49, 61-62, 113, 139
Page New command, 8
Page Remove command, 249
Page Sorter command, 372
Page Sorter view, 18-19, 71, 371-375
   checking spelling, 85
   pages, moving, 375
   screens, refreshing, 373
Page Speaker Notes command, 331, 378
pages
   adding, 8-9, 78
   annotating, 378-379
   borders, 399-400
   charts, 138-140
   copying, 379-380
   deleting, 78
   moving, 78
   multiple, selecting, 375
   orienting, 402
   placeholder, 376
   presentation, clip art, 286
   selecting, 77
   settings, 401
   sorting, 373-375
palettes
   black-and-white, displaying, 397
   color, 319-323

Index

paragraph charts, 37
paragraph styles, 57-58
    borders, 64
    lines without bullets, 59
    Outliner view, 76
    settings, 59-61
Paragraph Styles dialog box, 48, 60-64, 419
parallel sentence structure, 41
Paste Special dialog box, 180
pasting
    ASCII text, 246
    objects, 243-249
    organization chart entries, 191
    text, 52, 81-82, 246
patterns, fill, *see* fill patterns
PCT files, 302, 309
PCX files, 302, 309
PFL files, 302, 309
PIC files, 302
picas, 44
pie charts, 16-18, 103-104, 133
    legends versus labels, 105
    multiple, 105
    three-dimensional, 105-106
pixels, 389-390
placeholders, 9, 376
Play Options dialog box, 353
points, 44
    adding, 254-257
    deleting, 254-257
    editing, 253-257
    moving, 256-257
    origin, 399
Polygon tool, 219-220
polygons, drawing, 219-220
Polyline icon, 217
portable screen shows, 356-358
Portrait mode, 336
Portrait orientation, 402
positioning
    legends, 145, 156
    SmartIcon set, 387
.PRE files, 359-360

presentation pages
    annotating, 378-379
    clip art, 286
    copying text into, 246
presentations
    activating, 380
    assembling, 371
    charts
        bullet, 30-32
        text, 29-42
    color, 311-313
    copying pages, 379-380
    drafting, 375-376
    management, 371-384
    multiple, 379-383
    preparing for slide output, 363
    printing, *see* printing, presentations
    saving, 25
    screen shows, 20
    SmartMaster sets, 17-18
    source, 379-380
    target, 379-380
    views, 18-20
previewing charts, 15, 121
Print File dialog box, 21, 330, 364
Print SmartIcon, 21
Printer Setup dialog box, 403
printers
    choosing, 329
    options, 403
Printers dialog box, 360-361
printing
    black-and-white, 337
    help topics, 25
    outlines, 82
    presentations, 20-21
        audience notes, 332-333
        footers, 334-336
        handouts, 333
        headers, 334-336
        optimizing colors, 338
        outlines, 333
        page orientation, 336-337

    printers, choosing, 329
    range, 330
    speaker notes, 331-332
  speaker notes, 379
PRN files, 302
procedure diagrams, 272-273
programs, associating SmartIcons, 390
Promote icon, 78

Q-R

quick editing with right mouse button, 55

radar charts, 107-108
rearranging
  icons, 386
  windows, 380-382
Rectangle icon, 212
rectangles, drawing, 212-213
refreshing screens, 373
Replace command, 395
replicating objects, 395
reporting data, 92
resolution, sizing icons, 388
Restore command, 381
restoring windows, 381-382
reveal slides, 354
RGB values, 325
right mouse button, quick editing, 55
RND files, 302
Rotate SmartIcon, 242
rotated text, 65
rotating objects, 242
rounded rectangles, drawing, 215-216
routes, 279
rows, table chart
  deleting, 202
  highlighting, 205-206
  inserting, 202-203
  moving, 204-205
  selecting, 202
  sizing, 203-204

rule of sevens, 40-41
ruler, 400
rules, 431-432

S

sans serif typefaces, 44
Save As dialog box, 424
saving
  files, 395-396
  presentations, 25
  SmartIcon sets, 388-389
scale, 150-153
SCODL files, 359
Screen Show command, 377
Screen Show Export Options dialog box, 358
Screen Show Options dialog box, 346
Screen Show SmartIcon., 20
screen shows, 20, 341
  automatic sound, 352-353
  branching, 342
  build slides, 354-356
  controlling, 344
  interactive, 346-349
  launching applications, 353-354
  multimedia, 349-350
  on-screen drawing, 345-346
  portables, 356-358
  transition effects, 342-343
  viewing, 342
screens
  display, modifying, 376
  refreshing, 373
  resolution, sizing icons, 388
Search button, 22
Search dialog box, 23
Select All SmartIcon, 230
Select Like Objects dialog box, 232
selecting
  objects, 229-233
  pages, multiple, 375
  table columns/rows, 202

selection handles, 231
sequential page numbers, 335
serif typefaces, 44
Set Margins for Slides check box, 363
settings, page, 401
shortcut keys, *see* key combinations
Size Column/Row dialog box, 203-204
sizing
    charts, 145
    cursors, 398
    headings, 157
    margins, 399
    notes, 157
    objects, 237-238
    SmartIcons, 388
    table rows/columns, 203-204
    text blocks, 56-57
    windows, 380
skip factor, 148
slides, 35mm
    creating, 359-367
    files
        creating, 363-364
        sending to Autographix service center, 364-367
    glass mounts, 366
    preparing presentations, 363
    work orders, creating, 364-367
SmartIcon sets
    deleting, 389
    editing, 386-388
    hiding, 387
    positioning, 387
    saving, 388-389
SmartIcons
    Add Column, 202
    Add Row, 202
    applications, launching, 390
    associating with OLE objects, 390
    Bold, 53
    Close a File, 26
    creating, 389-390
    Delete Column, 202
    Delete Row, 202
    descriptions, displaying, 386
    diagrams, creating, 280
    drawing time, saving, 224
    Edit Chart Data, 123
    Edit Clear, 52
    Edit Copy, 52
    Edit Cut, 52
    Edit Paste, 52, 81
    Edit Points, 253
    Exit Freelance Graphics, 26
    File Save, 25
    Flip Left to Right, 241
    Flip Top to Bottom, 241
    Group, 239
    Print, 21
    Rotate, 242
    Screen Show, 20
    Select All, 230
    size, modifying, 388
    Spell Check, 83
    utilizing, 385
    Zoom, 226-228
SmartIcons dialog box, 386-388
SmartMaster page layouts, 49, 61-62, 113, 139
SmartMaster sets, 5-11, 17-18, 38, 377-378, 407
    Basic Layout, 412-413
    creating, 427-428, 434-437
    CUSTOM.MAS, 429
    customizing, 417
        bullet color, 419
        bulleted list spacing, 420-421
        "Click here..." chart block, 423
        "Click here..." text block, 422
        copying customized pages, 424
        logos, 421
        page layout, 421-422
        text attributes, 418-419
    designing, 429-434
    FRAME.MAS, 421
    MMGLOBE.MAS, 349-350

MMLASER.MAS, 349-350
opening, 428-429
page layouts, 31-33
placement blocks, 409, 414-416
prompt text, 409
structure, 408-412
switching, 320, 416-417
text blocks, 408, 414
Title page layout, 408
snap feature, 280
snap-to-grid feature, 401
sorting pages, 373-375
source presentation, 379-380
Spacing & Indents dialog box, 62-63, 420
Speaker Note dialog box, 332
speaker notes, 331-332
   adding, 378-379
   checking spelling, 85
Speaker Notes dialog box, 378-379
Spell Check dialog box, 85
Spell Check SmartIcon, 83
spell checking, 83-87
squares, drawing, 212-213
stacked area charts, 103
stacked bar charts, 95-98
start-up options, 394-395
starting Freelance Graphics, 4-6
step charts, 128-129
Stingray SCODL slide files, 359
Strikeout (Ctrl+S) accelerator key, 54
Style Attributes Polygon & Shape
  dialog box, 234
Style Attributes Rectangle dialog box, 215
Style Choose SmartMaster Set command, 17,
  377
Style Default Attributes Mixed
  dialog box, 222-223
SY3 files, 303
SYM files, 303
Symbol for Bullet dialog box, 68
symbol library, 38, 68

symbols, 7
   as bullets, 68
   data, 112
   see also clip art

T

Table Attributes dialog box, 205
table charts, 108
   columns, equal width, 138
   creating, 134-136
   frames, 136-137
   grid style, 138
   sum of columns, 137
Table tool, 108, 200-201
tables, 199-200
   columns
      deleting, 202
      inserting, 202-203
      moving, 204-205
      seleting, 202
      sizing, 203-204
   creating, 200-201
   editing entries, 201
   global changes, 206
   graph type, 92-94
   keyboard, 207-208
   mouse, 206-207
   rows
      deleting, 202
      highlighting, 205-206
      inserting, 202-203
      moving, 204-205
      selecting, 202
      sizing, 203-204
   see also number grids
target presentation, 379-380
templates, *see* SmartMaster sets
text
   active voice verbs, 42
   ASCII, 81, 246
   color, 314

conciseness, 39-40
copying, 52, 310
data charts, 13
deleting, 52
editing, 123-124, 149-150
legibility in charts, 39
parallel structure, 41
pasting, 52, 81-82
rule of sevens, 40-41
rulers, 400
selecting, 50-52
special effects, 64-68
spell checking, 83-86
symbols as bullets, 68
titles in charts, 42
text attributes, default, 61-62
Text Block Ruler check box, 400
text blocks, 48
character attributes, 53-54
copying, 52
creating, 48
deleting, 52
editing, 50-55
paragraph styles, 57-64
pasting, 52
sizing, 56-57
text panel, 49
text ruler, 49
Text Bold command, 53
text boxes, adding, 161-162
Text Bullet command, 378
text charts, 29, 32
active voice verbs, 42
bullet guidelines, 38-42
bullet charts, 30-32
capital letters, 39
clip art, 294
conciseness, 39-40
emphatic titles, 42
novelty, 38
page layouts, 34-37
paragraph, 37
parallel structure, 41
rule of sevens, 40-41

text legibility, 39
title pages, 33
typography, 42-45
Text Color dialog box, 54
text color palette, 321
text edit mode, 6, 85
Text Frame dialog box, 64
Text icon, 48, 61
text panel, 49
Text Paragraph Styles command, 60
text placeholder, 9
Text Reset To Style command, 54
text ruler, 49
Text Size command, 378
text-only view, 375
TGA files, 303, 309
three-dimensional, *see* 3D
tick marks, 153-154
TIF files, 303, 309
tiling windows, 382-383
time-series data, 112, 119-120
title pages
creating, 6-8
layouts, 33
text charts, 33
titles
customizing, 146-149
text charts, 42
titles view, 14-15
ToAGX-Windows communications
utility, 364-367
ToAGX-Windows dialog box, 364
Toolbox, 48
accessing, 373
icons, activating, 395
tools, drawing, *see* drawing tools
Tools Spell command, 83
Tools User Setup command, 25, 223-224, 394
transition effects, 342-343
True Type fonts, 362
type size measurements, 44
typefaces, 43-44
typography, 42-45

U

Underline (Ctrl+U) accelerator key, 54
ungrouping objects, 251-263
Units & Grids command, 377
Units & Grids dialog box, 225, 280
up-and-down style, 44-45
Use Compression command, 365
User Setup dialog box, 394, 397
user setup options, modifying, 394

V

values
    labeling bar charts, 126
    RGB, 325
vertical
    bar charts, 94-95
    page layout, 402
view commands, 372
View Current Page command, 79
View Full Page command, 372
View Last command, 372-373
View Outliner command, 71
View Page Sorter command, 18
View Preferences command, 376
View Preferences dialog box, 376, 398
View Redraw command, 373
View Screen Show dialog box, 403
View Screen Show Edit Effects command, 342
View Screen Show Run command, 20, 342
View Units & Grids command, 219, 401
View View Preferences command, 398
View Zoom In command, 372
View Zoom Out command, 372
views
    Current Page, *see* Current Page view
    data, 14
    high-level, 373-375
    moving between, 377

Outliner, *see* Outliner view
Page Sorter, *see* Page Sorter view
start-up, 394-395
text-only, 375-376
titles, 14-15

W

Welcome to Freelance Graphics
    dialog box, 4-5
windows
    activating, 380
    cascading, 382-383
    Chart Data & Titles, 13-16, 115-125, 404
    closing, 382
    Freelance Graphics, 372, 380
    Import Data, 305
    maximizing, 381
    minimizing, 382
    moving, 381
    rearranging, 380-382
    restoring, 381-382
    sizing, 380
    tiling, 382-383
Windows Cascade command, 382
Windows menu, 382
Windows Tile command, 382
WMF files, 303, 309
word diagrams, 270-271
word wrapping, 63-64
WPG files, 303, 309

X-Z

X and Y coordinates, 399
xy scatter charts, 107

Zoom SmartIcon, 145, 226-228, 372
Zoom tool, 226-228
zooming drawing area, 226-228